Finding Jerusalem

Finding Jerusalem

Archaeology between Science and Ideology

Katharina Galor

UNIVERSITY OF CALIFORNIA PRESS

University of California Press
Oakland, California

Suggested citation: Galor, Katharina. *Finding Jerusalem: Archaeology between Science and Ideology*. Oakland: University of California Press, 2017. doi: https://doi.org/10.1525/luminos.29

Library of Congress Cataloging-in-Publication Data
Names: Galor, Katharina, author.
Title: Finding Jerusalem : archaeology between science and ideology / Katharina Galor.
Description: Oakland, California : University of California Press, [2017] | Includes bibliographical references and index. | "Archaeological discoveries in Jerusalem capture worldwide attention in various media outlets. The continuing quest to discover the city's physical remains is not simply an attempt to define Israel's past or determine its historical legacy. In the context of the ongoing Israeli-Palestinian conflict, it is also an attempt to legitimate—or undercut—national claims to sovereignty. Bridging the ever-widening gap between popular coverage and specialized literature, *Finding Jerusalem* provides a comprehensive tour of the politics of archaeology in the city. Through a wide-ranging discussion of the material evidence, Katharina Galor illuminates the complex legal contexts and ethical precepts that underlie archaeological activity and the discourse of 'cultural heritage' in Jerusalem. This book addresses the pressing need to disentangle historical documentation from the religious aspirations, social ambitions, and political commitments that shape its interpretation"— Provided by publisher. | Description based on print version record and CIP data provided by publisher; resource not viewed.
Identifiers: LCCN 2016056688 (print) | LCCN 2016058728 (ebook) | ISBN 9780520968073 (ebook) | ISBN 9780520295254 (pbk. : alk. paper) Subjects: LCSH: Archaeology—Political aspects—Jerusalem. | Jerusalem— Antiquities.
Classification: LCC DS109.15 (print) | LCC DS109.15 .G36 2017 (ebook) | DDC 933/.442—dc23
LC record available at https://lccn.loc.gov/2016058728

26 25 24 23 22 21 20 19 18 17
10 9 8 7 6 5 4 3 2 1

For Michael

CONTENTS

PREFACE

My longstanding interest in Jerusalem goes back to 1983, when I first found myself in the trenches of an excavation near the Ottoman city wall. The desire to understand the complexities of my own roots—religious, cultural, and national—led me to pursue a career dedicated to exploring ancient civilizations from an angle at once completely academic, abstract, and removed, while at the same time involved, hands-on, and concrete. Jerusalem's past and present have played a central and consistent role in shaping this dual perspective.

The physical and visual dimensions of the fields of archaeology, architecture, and art history have allowed me to deeply penetrate the tangible truths of vanished cultures and, at the same time, to maintain a certain distance and ambiguity with regard to the real. Jerusalem's antiquities are concrete and tangible; they can be seen and touched. Yet our knowledge regarding the sites, monuments, and artifacts is based on incomplete data and perceived ideas. Some of those ideas and related beliefs have given birth to centuries- and millennia-old traditions, producing valuable religious and artistic creations. Others, however, have brought forth conflict and violence. It is this interaction and duality I have tried to examine.

I began teaching the archaeology of Jerusalem in 1996, in two different academic institutions, the École biblique et archéologique française de Jérusalem (EBAF, the French Biblical and Archaeological School of Jerusalem), founded in 1890 by a Dominican priest, which specializes in archaeology and biblical exegesis, and at the Rothberg School of Overseas Studies at the Hebrew University, the first Jewish university in the city, established in 1918. This unique opportunity brought me in contact with students from various national and religious backgrounds, including Israelis, Palestinians, Jews, Christians, and Muslims. This diversity has led me to approach a highly controversial subject in a manner that scrutinizes carefully all facts and data, using an array of traditional and innovative methods of investigation and presenting a variety of complementary, diverging, and opposing interpretations. My goal—and perhaps fear—was to remain objective without offending anyone's religious and/or political outlook. This teaching model also shaped the nature of my coauthored (with Hanswulf Bloedhorn) book *The Archaeology of Jerusalem: From the Origins to the Ottomans* (Yale University Press, 2013). Over the years, the difficult task of negotiating facts and fiction, data and interpretation, and objectivity and bias has taught me how significant the impact of Jerusalem's religious, social, and political context has been and still is on archaeological activity and interpretation, and that science and ideology are two entities that are surprisingly interdependent. The experience of living, working, and teaching in both areas of Jerusalem (East and West) and of maintaining sustained dialogue with the city's Israeli, Palestinian, and international archaeological communities has allowed me to experience, explore, and analyze the situation firsthand. Rather than relegating religiously and politically explosive and controversial matters—the primary aim of my coauthored book on the archaeology of Jerusalem—to a safe distance, *Finding Jerusalem: Archaeology between Science and Ideology* is an attempt to examine these topics head on, to present the different views, and to bring them into dialogue. Yet, despite my sustained effort and desire to remain objective and fair in my presentation and analysis, I am aware that, first, objectivity in the case of Jerusalem is highly debatable, and second, objectivity is not the same as neutrality. Jerusalem's antiquities present a highly charged and multifaceted entanglement of facts and values.

My immersion in Zionist ideology during my childhood, youth, and young adulthood in Germany and France and my early conviction that Jews owned the land of Israel were quickly shattered when I made *aliyah* (immigration to Israel) at the age of twenty-two. I came to learn that Christian and Muslim Palestinians, who were only modestly present in the narrative I had been exposed to, had very similar historical and religious attachments to the region. I also came to realize the injustice of being prioritized simply on grounds of my religion, and that being Jewish, regardless of family history (which I can trace down to the sixteenth century in Eastern Europe), gave me prerogatives that were denied to Palestinians, who had lived in the land for multiple generations. Thus, despite my sincere efforts to study Jerusalem's past in an informed and objective manner, the result of this monograph reflects my own personal journey of inquiry about the significance of tradition, myth, religion, historical records, archaeological data, and political partisanship, for all those nations who claim alliance and ownership of the land of Israel/Palestine.

One area that reflects the contested nature of the current Israeli-Palestinian conflict is the ambiguity and inflected nature of certain terms, often indicative of one or another ideological or political opinion. Without going into the debates about terminology, here is a brief account of words and idioms I use in this manuscript:

1. Palestine refers to the geographical entity of the larger region in which Jerusalem is located. From the time the name is first recorded, in an ancient document written by Herodotus in the fifth century B.C.E., through its revival as an official place name at the onset of the British Mandate period, the exact boundaries changed frequently.

2. Israel is the name of the kingdom mentioned in the Bible. It also refers to the modern state, which was established in 1948. The borders of the State of Israel have changed repeatedly since its establishment and are highly contested.

3. The Israelites were a Semitic people who lived, according to the biblical narrative, in parts of Canaan from the Exodus (ca. twelfth century B.C.E.) onward. Israelis are citizens or nationals of the modern State of Israel.

4. In the more recent and contemporary context of this manuscript, I reserve the term Palestinian for the people who lived in this region before the establishment of the State of Israel, to those who were expelled in 1948 and 1967, to Christians and Muslims who continued to live within the current boundaries of Israel, and, finally, to those who live in the Palestinian territories (Gaza Strip and the West Bank, including East Jerusalem).

5. I use the term Judeo-Christian to identify common origins of Jews and Christians in antiquity, as formed specifically between the first and fourth centuries C.E., before more distinct forms of rituals and beliefs were formulated. I will also use it, and so indicate my usage, in the contemporary context of its deployment by American Evangelicals to supply a values-based foundation for their interest in Judaism and their political sympathy with the State of Israel. Though their interest in the Christian legacy of the city clearly overlaps with that of Palestinian Christians, the different political alignments of these two groups impacts their heritage outlook and thus their heritage politics.

6. Jews, Christians, and Muslims, also known as the three Abrahamic faiths—thus indicating their common origins and overlapping monotheistic beliefs—define the religious identities of the main protagonists of this study. Though frequently used in the context of an exclusive narrative (Jewish, Christian, or Muslim) or as an indicator of a unified heritage, no one category represents a homogenous group or a monolithic interest.

7. Though the religious and ideological struggles in Jerusalem over the last century have often opposed Arabs and Jews, other populations of Jerusalem have also been affected by or involved in theses conflicts, such as, for

example, the Armenian, Greek, and Ethiopian communities. I will thus specify the particular ethnic and religious groups under discussion.

8. I define the struggle between Israelis and Palestinians as the "Israeli-Palestinian conflict" and refer to the region as Israel/Palestine.

9. The term *normalization,* as understood by the great majority of Palestinian civil society since November 2007, reflects Israel's intention to present occupation as a "normal" state.

10. I use the term West Jerusalem for the section of the city that remained under Israeli control after the 1948 Arab-Israeli War, whose ceasefire lines delimited the boundary with East Jerusalem, the rest of the city. East Jerusalem between 1948 and 1967 was under Jordanian jurisdiction. Its occupation by Israel in the post-1967 era has spurred significant development and expansion of the city (64 km² / 25 sq. mi.).

11. In 1980, the Knesset (the Israeli parliament) passed the Jerusalem Law, which declared Jerusalem as the "complete and united" capital of Israel. United Nationals Security Council Resolution 478 declared this action to be "null and void," and international law defines East Jerusalem as part of the West Bank and as occupied territory. My use of the term "occupied East Jerusalem" reflects the international view.

12. The term "First Temple period" is frequently used by archaeologists working in Israel to define the material culture of Iron Age II (ca. tenth century to 586 B.C.E.) and the "Second Temple period" to refer to the material culture of the Hellenistic and early Roman periods (ca. 332 B.C.E. to 70 C.E.). As these terms are based on written sources that do not reflect the larger geographical region associated with characteristic developments and changes in material culture, most European scholars and a growing number of American scholars eschew the use of this terminology. I use the terms "First Temple period" and "Second Temple period" only in places where they represent the nomenclature chosen by the archaeologist, scholar, or curator associated with the interpretation of the artifact or site in question.

The literature that deals with the politics of Jerusalem and the Israeli-Palestinian conflict is too vast to reference here. More relevant to the present study is the rapidly expanding interest among scholars of various backgrounds in the politics of the archaeology, history, and cultural heritage of the city. Among the numerous articles and books I have consulted, I would like to highlight a few particularly useful sources that have influenced and guided me. Neil Asher Silberman's *Digging for God and Country: Exploration, Archaeology and the Secret Struggle for the Holy Land, 1799–1917* looks at archaeological discoveries in the region from a critical cultural and sociopolitical point of view, focusing on the late Ottoman period. Nadia Abu El-Haj's anthropological investigation of recent archaeological work in the region, *Facts on the Ground: Archaeological Practice and Territorial Self-Fashioning in Israeli Society,* applies methodological and theoretical insights from the philosophical and social scientific literature. One of Abu El-Haj's chapters is dedicated specifically to archaeological activity in Jerusalem, with a focus on the immediate post-1967 period leading up to 1982. In *Just Past? The Making of Israeli Archaeology,* Raz Kletter studies documents from the State of Israel Archive pertaining to the administrative setting of archaeological activity in Israel and the West Bank. He analyzes how fieldwork and interpretation were shaped by social, political, and economic factors, in particular during the first three decades after the creation of the State of Israel in 1948. Other important publications touching upon the roles that archaeology and cultural heritage play in the regional conflict of Israel/Palestine include historian Meron Benvenisti's *City of Stone: The Hidden History of Jerusalem* and political scientist Michael Dumper's *Politics of Sacred Space: The Old City of Jerusalem in the Middle East Conflict. The Struggle for Jerusalem's Holy Places,* by Wendy Pullan, Maximillian Sternberg, Lefkos Kyriacou, Craig Larkin, and Michael Dumper, successfully investigates the role of architecture and urban identity in relation to the political economy of the city seen through the lens of the holy places. Shmuel Berkovitz, in *The Wars of the Holy Places: The Struggle Over Jerusalem and the Holy Sites in Israel, Judea, Samaria and the Gaza District,* examines the most significant religious sites and monuments and the related reli-giopolitical conflict from the viewpoint of the Israeli legal system.

The numerous publications by Raphael Greenberg and Yonathan Mizrachi on the role of archaeology in Israeli society and in the Israeli-Palestinian conflict have been particularly helpful to my understanding of many of the issues at the core of this book. Written by archaeologists, rather than most other studies dealing with the political aspects of archeological fieldwork, interpretation, and presentation (produced mostly by historians, anthropologists, architects, urban planners, social and political scientists), Greenberg and Mizrachi's work has supplied me, as well as numerous other scholars working on related issues, with valuable data and reflections. Their scholarly work and activism are the result of numerous years of dedication to the subject.

. . .

This study would not have been possible without the help and assistance of many colleagues to whom I am deeply indebted. The diversity of their views does not compromise a shared commitment to the preservation and safeguarding of Jerusalem as an essential site of cultural heritage. Special gratitude goes to Yonathan Mizrachi, Jean-Baptiste Humbert, and the late Yoram Tsafrir for having taken the time to discuss with me the missions and views of their contributions to archaeology, as well as to Michael Dumper, Ross Holloway, Dieter Vieweger, and the anonymous reviewers who have commented on some or all of my manuscript.

Hanswulf Bloedhorn's encyclopedic knowledge of Jerusalem and his sharp eye for detail and accuracy have been tremendous in the proofreading stages. Daniel Herwitz's remarks in light of his own work on cultural heritage and politics in South Africa have been most insightful. Special thanks goes to Franziska Lehmann, for both her patience and diligence while working with me on the line drawings for this study. The careful reading and the most thoughtful and constructive comments and suggestions made by Sa'ed Atshan have allowed me to correct many facts as well as to reshape some of my arguments. I would also like to acknowledge the numerous colleagues and professionals I have interviewed. Their expertise and data sharing contributed to countless aspects dealt with in this study. Among them, in alphabetical order, are[1]: Ibrahim Abu Aemar (director, Institute of Islamic Archaeology, Al-Quds University), Amro Arafat (archaeologist, Islamic Museum, Waqf Administration), Michal Atias (Department of Education and Guided Tours, Tower of David Museum), Gideon Avni (head of the archaeological division, Israel Antiquities Authority), Tali Gavish (head of the Ruth Youth Wing for Art Education, Israel Museum), Seymour Gitin (former director, W. F. Albright Institute of Archaeological Research), Raphael Greenberg (professor, Sonia and Marco Nadler Institute of Archaeology, Tel Aviv University), Michael Grünzweig (former academic consultant and curriculum developer, State of Israel, Ministry of Education), Nir Hasson (columnist, *Ha'aretz*), Mahmoud Hawari (director, The Palestinian Museum, and research associate, The Khalili Research Centre for the Art and Material Culture of the Middle East, University of Oxford), Ahron Horovitz (director, Megalim-City of David Institute for Jerusalem Studies), Nazmi Jubeh (professor, Department of History and Archaeology, Birzeit University), Yehuda Kaplan (education director, Bible Lands Museum), David Mevorah (curator, Israel Museum), the late Jerome Murphy O'Connor (lecturer and professor, École biblique et archéologique française), Yusuf Natsheh (director of archaeology and tourism, al-Aqsa Mosque, Waqf Administration), Hagit Neugeborn (director, Jerusalem Center of Archaeology, Israel Antiquities Authority), Hani Nur el-Din (director, Jerusalem Archaeological Studies Unit, Al-Quds University), Nour Rajabi (tour guide, Tower of David Museum), Jon Seligman (director of excavations, Surveys and Research Department, Israel Antiquities Authority), Renée Sivan (curator, Tower of David Museum), Ahmad Taha (director, Islamic Museum Waqf Administration), Hamdan Taha (director, Palestinian Department of Antiquities and Cultural Heritage), Jean-Michel de Tarragon (director, photothèque, and professor, École biblique et archéologique française), Mandy Turner (director, Kenyon Institute, Council for British Research in the Levant), Michael Turner (former chairman of UNESCO's Israel World Heritage Committee), Zeev Weiss (former director, Institute of Archaeology, Hebrew University), Omar Yousef (head of the graduate program of Jerusalem Studies, Center for Jerusalem Studies, Al-Quds University), and Yossi Zadok (inspector, State of Israel, Ministry of Education).

I am especially grateful to University of California Press editor Eric Schmidt, for his unfailing patience and support throughout the review and publication process, and to Jennifer Eastman, for her careful copyediting and the numerous perceptive comments throughout. Thank you also to Maeve Cornell-Taylor from the acquisitions department of University of California Press. Lastly and mostly, I would like to thank my husband, Michael Steinberg, for inspiring and encouraging me to undertake this project, for discussing the challenges, the risks, and the benefits of venturing into a new direction of inquiry, for debating many of the ideas, arguments, and viewpoints at the core of this investigation, and most of all, for providing me with the sustained courage, support, and love to see the project through. The book's content is my responsibility alone.

AAI	Association of Archaeologists in Israel
AL	Antiquities Law
AO	Antiquities Ordinance
ARCH	Alliance to Restore Cultural Heritage in Jerusalem
ASOR	American Schools of Oriental Research
BSAJ	British School of Archaeology in Jerusalem
CBRL	Council for British Research in the Levant
CDC	Centre for Development Consultancy
CISS	International Cooperation South South
DAI	Deutsches Archäologisches Institut
DAP	Department of Antiquities of Mandatory Palestine
EBAF	École biblique et archéologique française de Jérusalem
Elad	Hebrew acronym for "To the City of David"
IAA	Israel Antiquities Authority
ICAHM	International Committee on Archaeological Heritage Management
ICCROM	International Centre for the Study of the Preservation and Restoration of Cultural Property
ICOM	International Council of Museums
ICOMOS	International Council on Monuments and Sites
IDAM	Israel Department of Antiquities and Museums
IDF	Israel Defense Forces
IES	Israel Exploration Society
INPA	Israel Nature and Parks Authority
IPAWG	Israeli Palestinian Archaeology Working Group

JPES	Jewish Palestine Exploration Society
JQDC	Jewish Quarter Development Company
LWHD	List of World Heritage in Danger
NGO	Non-governmental organization
OCJRP	Old City of Jerusalem Revitalization Program
PAM	Palestine Archaeological Museum
PAMI	East Jerusalem Development Company
PDA	Palestine Department of Antiquities
PEF	Palestine Exploration Fund
PLO	Palestine Liberation Organization
POS	Palestine Oriental Society
SBF	Studium Biblicum Franciscanum
SMC	Supreme Muslim Council
UN	United Nations
UNESCO	United Nations Educational, Scientific and Cultural Organization
UNIDROIT	International Institute for the Unification of Private Law
WBEJAD	West Bank and East Jerusalem Archaeological Database
WHC	World Heritage Committee
WHL	World Heritage List
WHP	World Heritage Properties
WHS	World Heritage Site

Bronze Age: 3300–1200 BCE
Iron Age: 1200–586 BCE
Babylonian and Persian periods: 586–539 BCE
Hellenistic period: 332 BCE–70 CE
Roman period: 70–324
Byzantine period: 324–638
Early Islamic period: 638–1099
Crusader and Ayyubid periods: 1099–1250
Mamluk period: 1250–1516
Ottoman period: 1516–1917
British Mandate period: 1917–1947
Partition between Israel and Jordan: 1947–1967
Arab-Israeli War: 1948 (in Hebrew known as Milhemet Ha'atzmaut, or the War of Independence, and in Arabic as al-Nakba, or the Catastrophe)
Battle for Jerusalem: 1948
Armistice Agreements: 1949
Arab-Israeli War: 1967 (in Hebrew known as Milhemet Sheshet Ha Yamim, or the Six-Day War, and in Arabic as an-Naksa, or the Setback)
The Jerusalem Law: 1980 (enacted by Israel but not recognized by international law)
First Intifada: 1987–1991
Oslo I Accord: 1993
Oslo II Accord: 1995
Camp David Summit: 2000
Second Intifada: 2000–2005 (also known as al-Aqsa Intifada)
Construction of Barrier Wall: 2000–

Introduction

The Archaeology of Archaeology

Finding Jerusalem is not about bringing back to life ancient stones and walls hidden underground. It is not an adventurer's quest for long-lost treasures and monuments of a city venerated by the three Abrahamic traditions. And least of all, it is not an attempt to uncover the biblical truth. *Finding Jerusalem: Archaeology between Science and Ideology* is concerned with archaeologists, professionals, scholars, institutions, and governmental agencies, who and which are engaged in excavating and interpreting Jerusalem's past; it deals with those who support, control, and promote endeavors of cultural heritage; it examines the implications for individuals, communities, and nations affected by the processes of archaeological activity; and, finally, it aspires to differentiate between the real, concrete, and material on the one hand and the created, imagined, and perceived on the other.

In more concrete terms, this book surveys the history of archaeological exploration, discovery, and interpretation in Jerusalem in the contexts of social, political, and religious debates from the mid-nineteenth century to the present, with an emphasis on the post-1967 period. It examines the legal settings and ethical precepts of archaeological activity, the developing discourse of cultural heritage, as well as archaeology's place in the various educational systems and institutions in the city. It analyzes the ongoing struggle to discover and define the city's past, to expose its physical and historical legacy, and to advance claims of scientific validity and objectivity against the challenges of religious zeal and political partisanship—the latter two intimately related to each other in ways not necessarily limited to the ongoing Israeli-Palestinian conflict.

Jerusalem's Historic (or Holy) Basin (which includes the Old City and surrounding area), the primary focus of this study, is one of the most intensely excavated

FIGURE 1. Aerial view of Jerusalem's Old City, looking northeast. Photo by Hanan Isachar.

and thoroughly researched places in the world and one of the most historically and culturally complex areas (see figure 1).[1] Over the last 150 years, leading archaeologists under the auspices of major academic institutions have conducted numerous excavations there, by and large following standard professional procedures of fieldwork and research, as well as conventions of public education and presentation. At the same time, however, religious and national conflicts have increasingly blurred the lines between past and present and between fact and fiction. The claims that modern Israeli citizens are descendants of the Israelites or Hasmoneans and that the early Christians and first Muslims of the region were the ancestors of today's Palestinian Christians and Muslims, respectively, are only rarely challenged. The numerous exiles, emigrations, immigrations, conquests, destructions, and annihilations, as well as the countless intermarriages, interculturations, and conversions, render these assumptions clearly a product of tradition and religious beliefs rather than one based on historical probability. Instead of making claims of direct lineage, more interest should be placed on cultural and religious similarities and continuities, which are often more significant across different religious groups within the same geographical and chronological context, and less so within the realm of a single faith or religious tradition over centuries or millennia.

Finding Jerusalem is an attempt to create clarity within an increasingly confusing maze of archaeological initiatives used and manipulated to form public opinion, locally and internationally. By laying out the factual record, it invites us to participate in a multifaceted voyage through time, spatially defined by numerous boundaries and layers, vertically and horizontally intertwined, and to explore a space interspersed with monuments and artifacts, fashioned and colored by a multitude of cultures and nations.

Excavation, survey, and research in the city between the mid-nineteenth century and the early twentieth century were shaped by Western imperial interests in the region, which combined scientific curiosity with the desire to establish the physical reality of the Hebrew Bible and the New Testament narratives. This model of biblical archaeology, initiated by Jerusalem's first Catholic and Protestant explorers, influenced early Zionist endeavors aspiring to establish a tangible link between Judaism's local roots and the growing Jewish presence in the city and region. From the beginning, and increasingly during the twentieth century, the pursuit of archaeological investigations has had an impact not only on professional and academic circles but also on society at large, both regionally and internationally. This impact came to fullest fruition after the creation of the State of Israel in 1948, and in particular after Israel's capture of East Jerusalem in 1967. The new political reality of occupation has had various practical, administrative, legal, and political consequences for the field of archaeology. Since 1967, the Israeli state has held almost exclusive monopoly over the excavation of antiquities sites in Jerusalem. As a governmental agency, the Israel Antiquities Authority (IAA, known before 1990 as the Israel Department of Antiquities and Museums, or IDAM) has managed fieldwork in East Jerusalem according to the same legal precepts as in West Jerusalem.[2] According to international law, however, East Jerusalem is occupied territory, and therefore, these initiatives have been condemned and declared illegal by UNESCO (United Nations Educational, Scientific and Cultural Organization).

Given this political framework, Palestinians have desisted from excavating in the city, thus indicating their objection to occupation and imposed Israeli sovereignty, archaeological administration, and control. For these reasons, Palestinian cultural heritage initiatives have almost entirely been dedicated to standing monuments, mainly Mamluk (1250–1516) and Ottoman (1516–1917) buildings, which to this day dominate the Old City's urban landscape. In contrast to several large-scale excavations conducted in East Jerusalem during the immediate aftermath of the 1967 war, which highlighted the Jewish heritage and which some scholars have classified as nationalistic and colonial state-building efforts, Israeli archaeological activity since the mid-1990s has evolved significantly, following higher professional standards.[3] Recent excavations are characterized by a much more even treatment of different periods and cultures, also exposing and documenting features of significance to the Palestinian cultural heritage, encompassing finds relevant to both Christians and Muslims.[4] The scholarly results of these field projects, however, remain mostly accessible to a small circle of professional archaeologists. The more broadly projected narrative of archaeological findings, in particular as offered in public presentations, displays, and outreach efforts, still aligns with the early Zionist ambition of providing a direct link between the city's Israelite and Jewish past and Israel's present. Palestinian efforts to engage archaeology as a means of claiming sovereignty over the city of Jerusalem have been relatively modest in comparison. The lack of an official Palestinian-controlled municipality, the poorly coordinated and competing efforts of the Palestinian Authority, the local and the Jordanian Waqfs (religious foundations)[5], as well as the emerging Islamic Movement in Israel—also known as the Islamic Movement in 48 Palestine—have limited the success of fostering appreciation of a distinct Palestinian material and cultural legacy.[6] Palestinian archaeological activity in Jerusalem is thus almost exclusively limited to the survey, study, and conservation of architectural structures preserved above ground, rather than on the excavation of underground sites.

. . .

Instead of examining the archaeological remains of Jerusalem chronologically, structuring the city's history of occupation sequentially, horizontally according to area or site, vertically according to layers or strata—as most archaeologists would proceed—I decided to present and analyze the archaeology of the city in terms of its history of exploration. My study places the emphasis on the archaeologists who have explored the city's material culture: their schools, their training, and their personal, cultural, religious, professional, institutional, and national contexts. Rather than assuming that the exposed objects, structures, and more generally material culture have an intrinsic, indisputable, and static nature, which can be presented and understood in a monolithic way, I argue that it is the archaeologists' unique and permanently changing sociocultural and political contexts that shape the archaeological finds and sites and give meaning and significance to them. Thus, instead of telling the story of Jerusalem's archaeological exploration in a progressive manner, producing a narrative in which knowledge and professionalism grow exponentially, I present the history of excavation in cumulative levels, periods, and paradigms, in which the latest achievements build upon earlier ones, depend on them, and, indeed, never quite liberate themselves from the inseparable components of science and ideology.

The inherent motivation of the archaeologist to expose physical and tangible data, with the goal of producing a scientific analysis of the finds and an unbiased presentation of data and results, has proven elusive. Archaeological evidence per se is always partial and contaminated, and our knowledge, regardless of how meticulous and comprehensive our investigation, relies primarily on extrapolation, interpretation, and imagination.[7] In the case of Jerusalem, moreover, the ambition to enhance our knowledge of the city's cultural development has been linked consistently with aspirations to settle and own the land: to own—legally and intellectually—not only the visible and palpable ground but also, and perhaps even more importantly, the foundations and roots hidden below the ground, both metaphorically and physically. Scientific progress, scholarly curiosity, and knowledge, have continuously been linked with the desire to exert power and authority: social, religious, and political. In Jerusalem, as in many other places, archaeological excavation and interpretation have consistently relied on the practice of exclusionary science and practices. This interdependence of science, power, and ideology—which has determined the shaping of a field and its interrelation with various religious, political, and national entities—has persevered, rather than regressing over time, and in fact, it has reached new heights in the escalating conflict between Israelis and Palestinians.

The categories of science and ideology remain famously difficult to control, all the more so when—as is the case here—their mutual imbrication is asserted. Without rehearsing the voluminous literature on this topic, let me characterize my use of the term *science* to describe a practice or discourse that evinces the search for objectivity by subjecting itself to review, correction, and verifiability or falsifiability. The claims of science understand their own ephemerality, as Max Weber famously argued in "Science as a Vocation."[8] Ideology, on the other hand, seeks credibility by posing as science, but its truth claims are based on strategies of interest rather than on objective analysis, a gap that can be intentional or not, conscious or unconscious.

. . .

My inquiry is framed chronologically by four stages, beginning with *Colonialist Archaeology,* between 1850–51 and 1948, and leading to a phase of *Nationalist (Neo-Colonial) Archaeology,* from 1948 to 1967. The decades between 1967 and 1996 I understand according to the duality of *Archaeology and Occupation,* followed by the age of the *Archaeology of Occupation,* from 1996 to the present.

The historical framework of *Colonialist Archaeology* begins with the first excavation conducted in the city of Jerusalem by French numismatist Félix de Saulcy in 1850–51 and ends with the establishment of the State of Israel in 1948. This period of archaeological exploration is characterized by Palestine's colonial rule, transitioning from the last few decades of Ottoman governance through the full duration of the British Mandate (the British civil administration in Palestine between 1920 and 1948). Throughout this period, most of the city's archaeological explorations were conducted by educated and privileged Westerners and proceeded without much participation and support of the indigenous population. This is the era that gave birth to the field of biblical archaeology and the image of the explorer holding a "spade in one hand, and the Bible in the other." The relationship between religious belief and political ambition in the realm of late Ottoman explorations was aptly described by Neil Asher Silberman as "digging for God and country," a combination that continued to shape archaeological work during the Mandate period, although characterized by a more regulated and sophisticated practice.

Between 1948 and 1967, the period defined by its *Nationalist (Neo-Colonial) Archaeology,* the city of Jerusalem was divided into West Jerusalem, governed by Israel, and East Jerusalem, under Jordanian rule.[9] Archaeological governance and procedure, despite the political and administrative transformation, changed little during these years. The Department of Archaeology in Jordan remained in the hands of a British archaeologist. The Israel Department of Archaeology and Museums (IDAM) was directed and staffed primarily by Jewish archaeologists. The field of biblical archaeology continued to be the main focus of exploration, with the original, almost exclusively Catholic and Protestant angle now officially joined on the Israeli side by Jewish perspectives and interests. Though both Israel and Jordan saw themselves as the rightful owners of the respective land slots and, indeed, as indigenous to the land, archaeological exploration continued to be shaped by Western institutional models and rules, and fieldwork and research continued to be carried out primarily by individuals educated overseas.

Archaeology and Occupation begins in 1967, when Israel captured East Jerusalem and extended Jerusalem's municipal boundaries to enclose areas and villages inhabited predominantly by Palestinians. The Israel Department of Archaeology and Museums, as of 1990 the Israel Antiquities Authority (IAA), have administered all and executed most archaeological excavations and surveys in the city since then. The majority of field projects have focused on the Old City and its immediate surroundings, located within the occupied sector of the city. Massive archaeological projects in East Jerusalem have gone hand in hand with Israel's occupation policies, which have instigated the creation of Jewish settlements, Palestinian house demolitions, and the establishments of national and archaeological parks. Nadia Abu El-Haj, in *Facts on the Ground,* has shown that by exposing layers and highlighting finds that are predominantly of relevance to the Jewish/Israeli narrative of the city, in particular in East Jerusalem, archaeologists produce finds that are often presented as tangible proof of Israel's entitlement to return to its ancestral homeland. Despite repeated efforts of the international community to promote peace negotiations in the region (the Oslo Accords of 1993 and 1995 and the Camp David Summit of 2000), during the period following Benjamin Netanyahu's election as Israel's prime minister in 1996, the Israeli-Palestinian conflict has reached new heights, fostering radical religious and national movements on both sides. The final status negotiations of Jerusalem have remained, for the most part, off the table, but continued and coordinated investment in Jewish settlements, Palestinian house demolitions, archaeological sites, and tourist development in East Jerusalem indicate Israel's commitment to render the occupation an irreversible reality.

The *Archaeology of Occupation,* from 1996 to the present, is defined by the Israel Nature and Parks Authority (INPA), the IAA, and Elad (also known as the City of David Foundation or Ir David Foundation), an Israeli settler NGO, which in strong coordination and collaboration, have determined the archaeological landscape of East Jerusalem. UNESCO's ability to counter Israel's monopoly of cultural heritage decisions in the context of the increasingly volatile political climate has been negligible. Palestinians, though implicated in matters of cultural heritage, have, for the most part, been passive onlookers. With the increasingly populated and built-up areas of the Old City and its immediate surroundings, limited zones have remained available for large-scale excavations. Rather than creating "facts on the ground," there has been a shift to producing "facts below the ground." The most controversial activities that have transformed Jerusalem's historic landscape are the extensive tunnel excavations conducted under the auspices of the IAA, as well as the underground Marwani Mosque construction initiated by the Islamic Movement in Israel (also known as the Islamic Movement in 48 Palestine). Though Israel maintains that all excavations carried out in East Jerusalem since 1967 are "salvage (or rescue) excavations"—suggesting that they are carried out merely to protect or save an endangered site that was or is threatened to be damaged as a result of development work—it has become increasingly obvious that virtually all excavation efforts in the Historic Basin are directly or indirectly linked with Israel's occupation policy. The political act of occupation and claimed ownership has taken on new dimensions, which go beyond the surface and the present reality of a densely populated and built-up city.

. . .

Against the background of this conceptual framework, I have organized the following nine chapters of *Finding Jerusalem,* in three parts, all of which are dedicated to untangling the enmeshed complexity of a world-contested city's ancestry and heritage—an encounter of archaeology, science, religion, and ideology.

Part 1 of this book lays out the physical and historical backdrop of the study. Chapter 1 provides a description of the physical landscape, summarizing the topographic and geographic features of the Historic Basin, delineating the frequently changing city boundaries, barriers, and walls from the Bronze Age to the present. Chapter 2 surveys the process of institutionalization of archaeological exploration in the city, highlighting several key excavations and surveys, some of the most legendary individuals, establishments, and governmental agencies who have administered the field. It demonstrates the persistent overlap of archaeology, science, and ideology.

Based on the background information provided in part 1, part 2 then delves into the timely interest in the multifaceted cultural heritage of Jerusalem, heightened among others by the recent international lawsuits questioning the ownership of antiquities worldwide. Awareness that archaeological activity can be harmful to the natural and urban landscape and the call for excavation and restoration procedures to comply with international standards of cultural, scientific, and ethnic principles began to emerge in North America and Europe as a result of massive destructions caused during World War I and II. Though Jerusalem's cultural legacy had been recognized as significant in the context of world heritage long before the beginning of archaeological exploration, it was not until 1981 that the Old City was added to the UNESCO World Heritage List (WHL). In spite of the international involvement in Jerusalem's cultural-heritage management, however, Israeli forces continue to operate with apparent autonomy. Destruction and preservation policies appear to reflect domestic political rivalries rather than global heritage legacies.

Chapter 3 investigates the roles that the IAA, the Waqf, and UNESCO—as well as several additional Israeli, Palestinian, and international organizations—have played in the forming of cultural-heritage perceptions and preservation programs. The chapter clarifies the complex administrative governance of the city's cultural legacies in the context of two differing approaches: the excavation and possibly intrusive intervention in the case of underground sites, and the largely restorative surface work involved in the built heritage, whether domestic or monumental.

Chapter 4 surveys the display of archaeological sites and artifacts as an effective means of disseminating professional and scientific work to the wider public. It examines how different modes of presentation reflect religious and ideological arguments. Archaeological sites and monuments—some within the Old City, others located in the designated national parks and West Jerusalem—are integrated into Jerusalem's urban landscape, thus forming a vital part of the contemporary city. Numerous artifacts with an explicit Jerusalem provenance can be viewed in the context of various permanent or rotating exhibits on display at, among others, the Islamic Museum of the Haram al-Sharif, the Palestine Archaeological Museum (PAM), the Israel Museum, the Bible Lands Museum, and the Tower of David Museum.

Chapter 5 examines how the recent history of the city and its geographic and cultural divides contribute to the complexity of educational systems engaged with the field of archaeology. The numerous foreign establishments in the city devoted to the study and research of archaeology include the École biblique et archéologique française (French Biblical and Archaeological School); the William Foxwell Albright Institute; the Deutsches Evangelisches Institut für Altertumswissenschaft des Heiligen Landes (German Protestant Institute of Archaeology of the Holy Land); the Kenyon Institute; and the Studium Biblicum Franciscanum (Franciscan Biblical School); all of which were established around the turn of the twentieth century and are still active centers of learning to this day. The first Jewish establishments in the city dedicated to the field of archaeology were the Hebrew Society for the Exploration of Eretz-Israel and Its Antiquities (since 1948, the Israel Exploration Society, IES) as well as the Institute of Archaeology at the Hebrew University, both of which have continuously remained involved in the fieldwork, research, and education of the field. Al-Quds University's Institute of Archaeology, the Center for Jerusalem Studies, and the Jerusalem Archaeological Studies Unit represent the leading Palestinian academic establishments dedicated to the learning and teaching of the field. The curricula of the Yad Izhak Ben-Zvi Institute; as well as the education departments of the IAA, the Israel Museum, the Bible Lands Museum, the Tower of David Museum, and Megalim (also known as City of David Institute for Jerusalem Studies) are primarily invested in the dissemination of knowledge among the wider Jewish and Israeli public. Since fieldwork and other related activities in Jerusalem as of 1967 have become the almost exclusive domain of Israeli archaeologists, the most significant contributions to archaeological education and public knowledge and opinion have been made by Israeli experts.

Chapter 6 focuses on archaeological ethics, scrutinizing the current methods and policies of excavation, documentation, and preservation; examining the laws and practice of trading antiquities and the associated fakes and forgeries market; and finally, analyzing the controversies of digging up ancient burials. Since the early 1980s, various associations and societies have established codes of ethics that formulate scientific and ethical standards of archaeological investigations. Several archaeological projects in Jerusalem have been criticized for not following those guidelines. Among these are the excavations in the City of David / Silwan, resumed in the early 1990s. This project has been criticized for its outdated methods, including tunnel excavation, as well as for the resulting destabilization of modern construction and the exclusion and even harassment of the Palestinian residents of the neighborhood. Ethical questions also pertain to commercial aspects of antiquities. According to a law implemented in 1978, the trading of antiquities in Israel is legal, a situation which, according to some, encourages the illegal excavation and looting of antiquities. This activity has also impacted the local market in fakes and forgeries, exemplified by the notorious "James, brother of Jesus" ossuary. The flourishing antiquities business, stimulated by sensational claims of Jewish and Christian discoveries and artifacts, not only boosts the tourist industry but also has significant ideological consequences. Finally, further initiatives raising ethical concerns are the excavation, potential desecration, and reburial of human remains in Jerusalem, which have led to heated debates, repeated protests, and occasional violence. Hostilities between archaeologists and ultra-Orthodox Jewish groups, instigated by the excavation of Jewish tombs from the Roman period in the modern Jerusalem neighborhood of French Hill, reached a peak in 1992. Following those clashes, the Israeli government issued new legal directives, severely restricting the scientific study of human bones. Meanwhile, the construction of the Museum of Tolerance by the Simon Wiesenthal Center over a historic Muslim cemetery in Mamilla was approved by Israeli authorities in 2011. This project has been broadly condemned for denying the religious, cultural, and historical impact of a site of significance to Muslims.

Building upon the discussions in part 2, part 3 then turns to a more detailed look at three highly contentious sites—the City of David / Silwan, the Church of the Holy Sepulchre, and the Temple Mount / Haram al-Sharif—exploring how religious beliefs and ideological discourses impact archaeological excavation and interpretation, notwithstanding claims of scientific neutrality. Chapter 7 reports on early, recent, and current excavations in the City of David / Silwan. Part of the discussion is based on the fieldwork results from a professional standpoint, evaluating the scholarly discourse on material culture as well as the related typological and chronological assessments. It examines how surveys and excavations conducted in the area over 150 years have contributed to our knowledge of Bronze and Iron Age Jerusalem, how perceptions have changed over time, and why the same physical evidence has led to diverse and sometimes even opposing interpretations. The major part of this chapter is devoted to an in-depth analysis on how archaeological methodologies have been compromised by religious and political agendas. The recent activities of Elad—their involvement in fieldwork, scholarship, site management, and education—are evaluated independently and also in light of recent criticism voiced by another Israeli NGO, Emek Shaveh (translated the "Valley of Equality," referencing Genesis 14:17). Finally, the relationship of both institutions with the Israeli and the Palestinian publics and their impact on local and international opinions and policies is scrutinized.

Chapter 8 lays out the major site transformations and archaeological investigations carried out in and near the Church of the Holy Sepulchre, exploring the impact of the Eastern and Western churches on the site's history from its inception under Constantine the Great in the Byzantine period (fourth century) to the present. A detailed study of the archaeological and architectural remains, preserved both below and above ground, establishes the major building sequences and sheds light on the related scholarly interpretations and controversies. These pertain to the question of authenticity of the church's location, traditionally marking the place of Christ's crucifixion and burial. The prevailing Catholic tradition of identifying the Church of the Holy Sepulchre as the site of Jesus's burial is compared to a more marginalized Protestant tradition, which locates it in the Garden Tomb. Attention is also given to the evolving role the different Christian communities have played in the Church of the Holy Sepulchre and in the city more generally. Recent and current tensions are largely based on the shared control of the church among the Greek Orthodox, the Latins (Roman Catholics), the Armenians, the Copts, the Syrian-Jacobites, and the Ethiopians. This division is enrooted in a longstanding agreement confirmed by an Ottoman *firman* (decree) in 1852, the Status Quo of the Christian Holy Places. Recurring incidents of verbal and physical confrontations involving members of the different religious orders have required police intervention and have resulted in local and international media coverage. Though the Christian communities in Jerusalem only represent a small minority of the city's population, their role has been defined as religiopolitically sensitive and thus significant in the context of global public opinion.

Chapter 9 reviews all major excavations and surveys carried out on, near, and under the Temple Mount / Haram al-Sharif platform, originally built by King Herod (first century B.C.E.) to support the Second Jewish Temple and transformed into one of Islam's most important sanctuaries during the Umayyad period (seventh century). The chapter evaluates both scholarly assumptions and political claims made in connection with this architectural complex and its associated monuments. The Haram, crowned by the Dome of the Rock and the al-Aqsa Mosque, has been venerated by Muslims since the mid-seventh century. From the mid-nineteenth century onward, explorers have been intrigued by its structural relation to the former Jewish Temple. Excavations and surveys of the site and its surroundings have led to turmoil, political tension, and physical violence. The opening of the Western Wall Tunnels in 1996 brought about armed confrontations between Palestinians and Israelis, resulting in more than one hundred casualties. Various other initiatives of the IAA, including excavation and restoration projects bordering the southwestern corner of the platform, have been perceived as an attempt to undermine the Muslim compound politically, religiously, and structurally. Local demonstrations, regional protests, and international condemnations, as well as UNESCO's attempts to halt those activities, have been largely ineffective, and archaeological investigations have proceeded without apparent delays.

Conducting an archaeological journey of the archaeology of Jerusalem in the framework of these chapters is thus a somewhat unconventional attempt to peal away and expose the different layers of exploration and motivation, rather than of its archaeological strata of cultural deposits. It is also a means of revealing the growing enmeshment of knowledge, science, professionalism, religion, ideology, and politics.

Cityscape and History

PART 1 OF THIS STUDY EXAMINES the contribution of archaeology to the evolving understanding of Jerusalem's history and its tangible as well as intangible components. Parts 2 and 3, with their more recent and contemporary focus, will build on this foundation. Respecting the basic concerns of the discipline, especially its juxtaposition of soil, stone, and text, "Cityscape and History" also finds the roots of the stubborn entanglement of material reality, factual events, and storied heritage. It highlights the persistent interplay between archaeological practice and ideology, an increasingly powerful combination in the context of the discipline's evolving institutionalization.

1

Boundaries, Barriers, Walls

Jerusalem's unique landscape generates a vibrant interplay between natural and built features where continuity and segmentation align with the complexity and volubility that have characterized most of the city's history. The softness of its hilly contours and the harmony of the gentle colors stand in contrast with its boundaries, which serve to define, separate, and segregate buildings, quarters, people, and nations. The Ottoman city walls (see figure 2) separate the old from the new; the Barrier Wall (see figure 3), Israelis from Palestinians.[1] The former serves as a visual reminder of the past, the latter as a concrete expression of the current political conflict. This chapter seeks to examine and better understand the physical realities of the present: how they reflect the past, and how the ancient material remains stimulate memory, conscious knowledge, and unconscious perception. The history of Jerusalem, as it unfolds in its physical forms and multiple temporalities, brings to the surface periods of flourish and decline, of creation and destruction.

TOPOGRAPHY AND GEOGRAPHY

The topographical features of Jerusalem's Old City have remained relatively constant since antiquity (see figure 4). Other than the Central Valley (from the time of the first-century historian Josephus also known as the Tyropoeon Valley), which has been largely leveled and developed, most of the city's elevations, protrusions, and declivities have maintained their approximate proportions from the time the city was first settled. In contrast, the urban fabric and its boundaries have shifted constantly, adjusting to ever-changing demographic, socioeconomic, and political conditions.[2]

FIGURE 2. Section of Ottoman city wall, south of the Citadel. Photo by Katharina Galor.

FIGURE 3. The Barrier Wall separating two Jerusalem neighborhoods, French Hill (with mostly Jewish residents) from Issawiya (with exclusively Palestinian residents). Visible here beyond the wall are buildings in Issawiya. Photo by Katharina Galor.

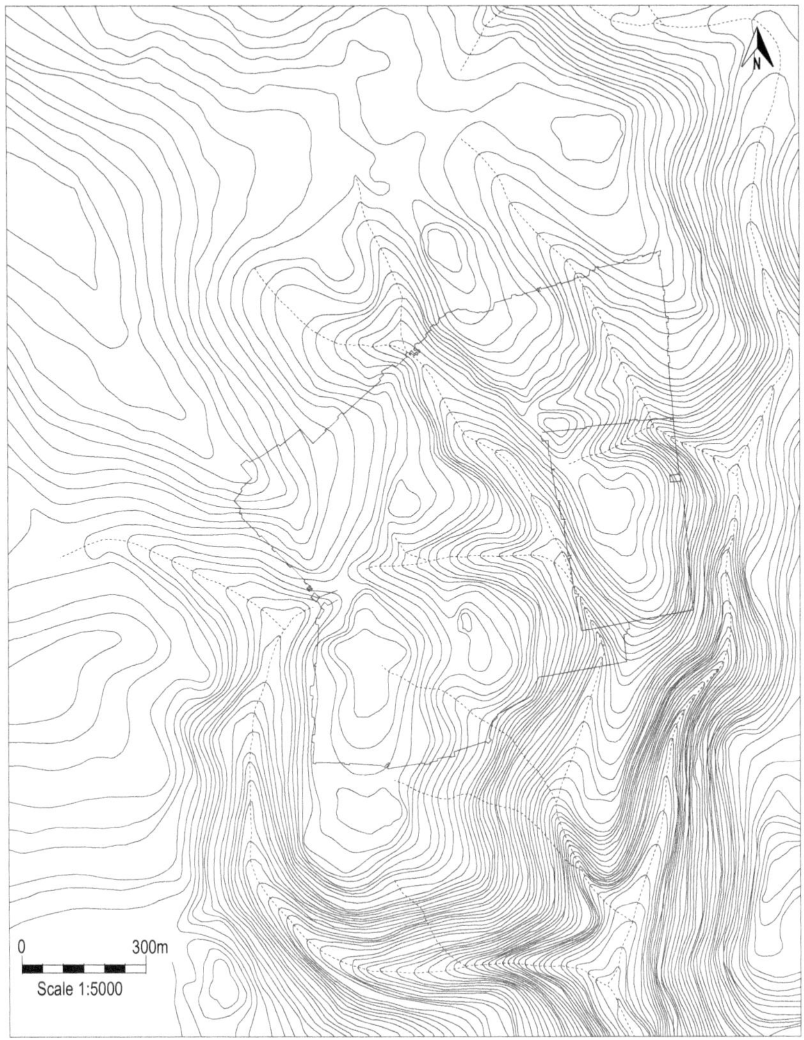

FIGURE 4. Topographical map of Jerusalem. Redrawn by Franziska Lehmann, after: Vincent and Steve, *Jérusalem,* I, plate 1.

Israel/Palestine lies on the narrow strip known as the Fertile Crescent, at the southern end of the Levantine coast. At its center, the Judean Hills mark the dividing line between the drainage basin of the Mediterranean Sea and that of the Jordan Valley.[3] Within this context, Jerusalem stands on a promontory, enclosed on either side by valleys that converge near its southernmost protrusion and continue onward to the Dead Sea. In antiquity, the settlement often functioned as the capital of the larger region.[4] Geographically, this is somewhat surprising, as it was not easily accessible, and there were no simple lines of communication between the coastal region, the hill country, and the place that would ultimately give birth to the city.

Ancient Jerusalem spread over several hills or spurs (see figure 4), surrounded by slightly more elevated mountains. From north to south, the Old City is divided by the Central Valley, which separates the so-called Western Hill, or Upper City (765 meters)—now occupied by the Armenian and Jewish Quarters and Mount Zion further south (770 meters)—from the Eastern Hill, or Lower City. The latter encompasses the area of the Temple Mount, or the Haram al-Sharif (745 meters), and south of it (the Southeast Hill), the modern village of Silwan (660 meters), popularly referred to as the City of David.[5] The shape of the Old City is determined on the east, south, and west by valleys and deep ravines. The eastern border is marked by the Kidron Valley, which separates it from the Mount of Olives ridge. Its western border is the Valley of Hinnom, which runs north to south, skirting Mount Zion, and then turns east along the southern border of the ancient city until its convergence with the Kidron Valley. Today, the city's northern border has no clear-cut topographical delineation. In the past, the only morphological feature that separated the city from the northern hills was the (now filled) Transversal Valley. From the late Hellenistic period onward, the city's boundaries spread beyond this natural feature.

During the early periods of the city's existence, the inhabitants relied exclusively on its only perennial spring, the Gihon, located on the lower eastern slopes of the Southeast Hill. It was only when greater efficiency was achieved in the utilization of rainwater and in the diversion of distant spring sources that Jerusalem was able to expand in other directions.

ANCIENT CITY LIMITS

The city's changing boundaries can be traced relatively accurately for most periods, as numerous sections of the ancient walls have been surveyed, excavated, and studied. Information on urban development and the city limits can also be determined by defining the location and extent of Jerusalem's necropoleis.[6] The plans in figure 5 reflect the most commonly accepted opinions on the extent of the city during the different periods of its history. Population estimates, based both on historical and archaeological evidence, range from approximately eight hundred people during the Bronze Age (3300–1200 B.C.E.) to approximately eighty thousand in the late Hellenistic period (mid-first century C.E.).[7]

The earliest permanent settlements, from the Bronze Age through the beginning of the Iron Age (3300–ca. 960 B.C.E.), were located outside Jerusalem's Old City walls on the Southeast Hill, in the area of present-day Silwan. The city's

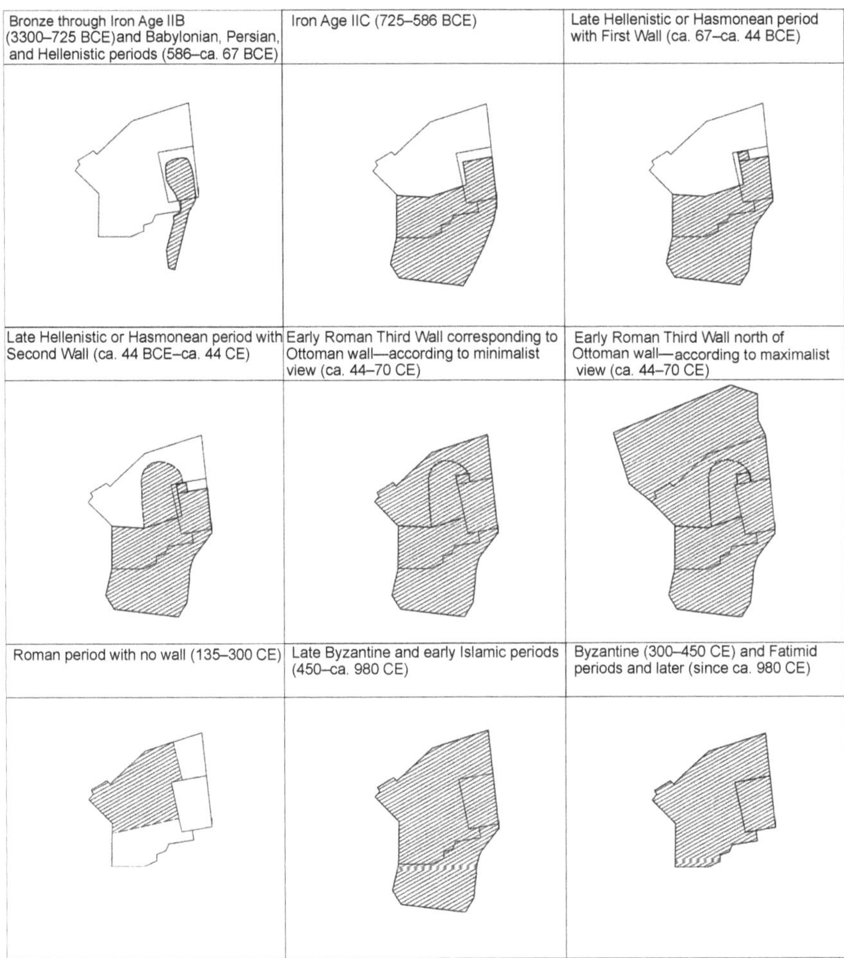

FIGURE 5. Maps indicating settled areas throughout the periods under discussion. Redrawn by Franziska Lehmann, after: Broshi, "The Expansion of Jerusalem," 12–15.

earliest fortifications, however, were not erected until around 1850 B.C.E.[8] It is commonly believed that only after the construction of King Solomon's Temple in the tenth century B.C.E. did the city spread northward to enclose Mount Moriah (the traditional site of the sacrifice of Isaac, as mentioned in Genesis).[9] Toward the end of the eighth century B.C.E., the settlement extended to the Western Hill, indicating a demographic shift, which is usually related to the destruction of numerous settlements in the Northern Kingdom of Israel by the Assyrians and the relocation of refugees in the Southern Kingdom of Judah, most of which settled in Jerusalem.[10] Throughout the Babylonian, Persian, and early Hellenistic periods the city remained relatively small, not extending beyond the eastern mountain ridge. Around the second century B.C.E., the settlement spread once again to the Western Hill, which thereafter remained continuously inhabited. The city experienced significant growth during the decades prior to the destruction of the Herodian Temple by the Romans in 70 C.E., though the extent of the expansion northward is debated. According to some, the line of the northern line of fortification was where the present Ottoman wall is located; according to others, it was located significantly further north.[11] From 70 C.E. onward, the area enclosed within the present-day Old City has constituted the heart of Jerusalem, with extensions toward the south (during the early Roman, Byzantine, and Islamic periods). Jerusalem's extent during the late Roman, Fatimid, Crusader, Ayyubid, and Mamluk periods corresponded roughly to the present-day Old City walls built during Ottoman rule in the sixteenth century.

RECENT AND CURRENT BOUNDARIES

The ethno-religious partition of the Old City as originally featured on nineteenth-century maps is rooted in the Crusader period, when Jerusalem absorbed heterogeneous populations from different European and Oriental countries, who settled in clusters determined by linguistic, cultural, and religious affiliations.[12] From then on, the Greek Orthodox and the Roman Catholics lived in the area surrounding the Church of the Holy Sepulchre in the northwest, and the Armenian community, near the Cathedral of St. James in the southwest. Population shifts occurred after the Ayyubid conquest in 1187, when the city was repopulated by Muslims, and once again under Mamluk rule, with growing numbers of pilgrims coming from all parts of the Islamic world.[13] Since the twelfth century, most Muslims aspired to settle in the areas abutting the northern and western walls of the Haram compound. Toward the mid-twelfth century, Jews had begun to settle in the southern section of the city, just to the west of a small area inhabited by a Muslim community of North-African origin.[14]

Only minor demographic changes occurred during the first centuries of Ottoman rule, which from the beginning established a new administrative system, the so-called *harat* (neighborhoods) network (see figure 6).[15] A late nineteenth-century guidebook for Christian pilgrims written in Arabic features a map of the harat division into quarters and streets, a configuration that reflects the spatial organization of the city familiar to the locals at the time.[16] The current division of the Old City into the four ethno-religious quarters is based on nineteenth-century survey maps of Jerusalem drawn by European travelers, army officers, and architects, and it is the version the majority of pilgrims and visitors have relied on since.[17]

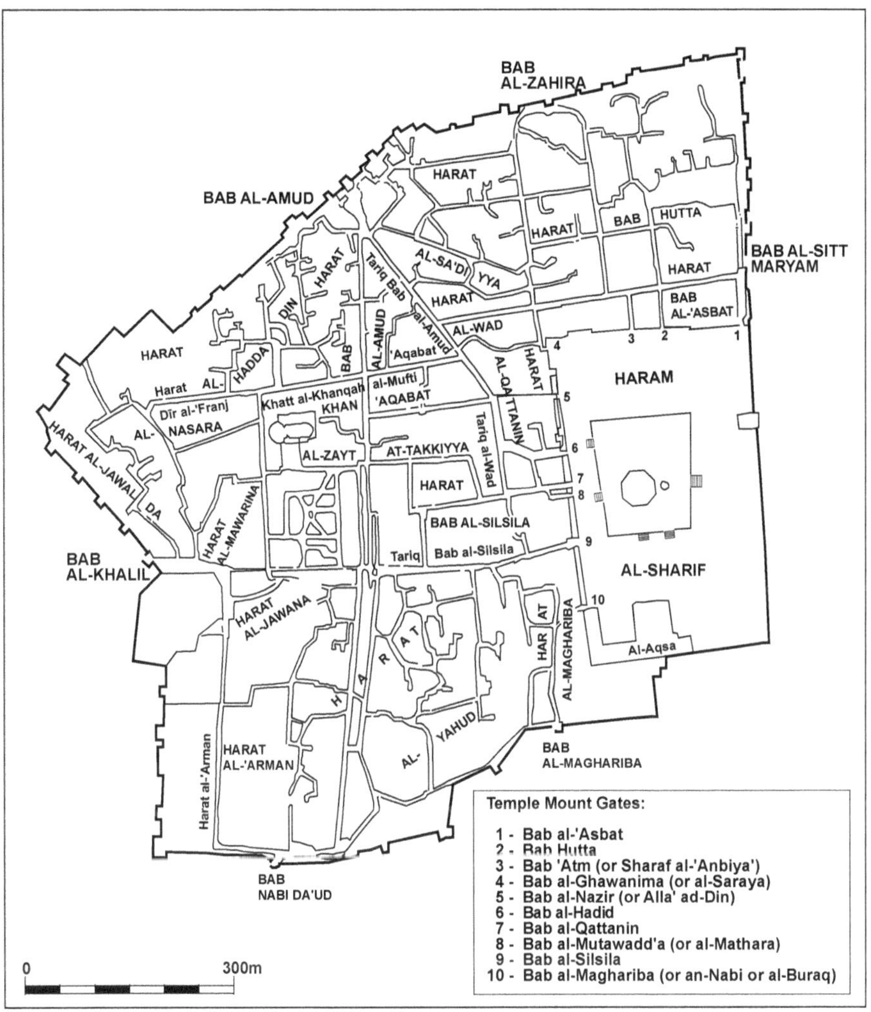

FIGURE 6. Old City divided into *harat* neighborhoods, nineteenth century. Redrawn by Franziska Lehmann, after: Arnon, "The Quarters of Jerusalem in the Ottoman Period," 14.

Three of the city's four quarters are named after the major religious communities who have lived in Jerusalem since antiquity—Muslim, Christian, and Jewish. The fourth, the Armenian Quarter, although Christian, is defined ethnically, by its language and culture (see figure 7).[18] Additional concentrations of ethnic or religious groups include the Syrian enclave close to the Armenian Quarter, the Mughrabi (Moroccan) neighborhood within the Muslim Quarter, and a separate Protestant area near the Jewish Quarter.[19]

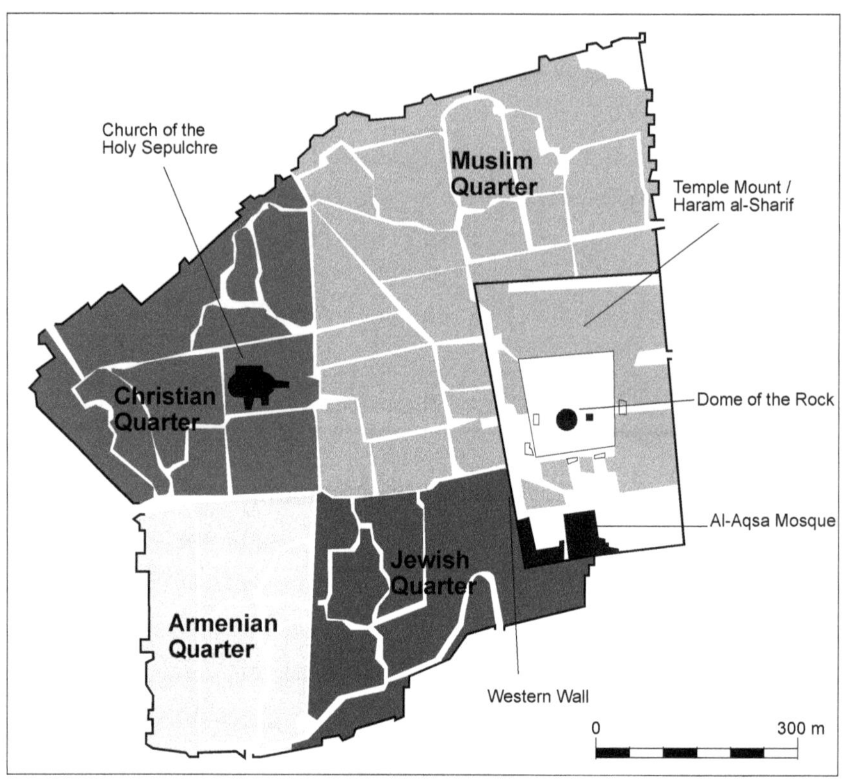

FIGURE 7. Plan of Old City featuring the four quarters. Drawn by Franziska Lehmann.

Population estimates for Jerusalem in the 1870s range between 14,000 and 22,000 people.[20] According to the Ottoman census of 1905, 32,400 Ottoman nationals lived in the city, including 13,400 Jews, 11,000 Muslims, and 8,000 Christians.[21] These statistics, however, do not include the numbers of residents living outside the Old City boundaries, and they do not reflect individuals with foreign nationality living in Jerusalem at the time, which, according to most scholars, would increase the percentage of Jewish and Christian residents.[22] Regardless of the exact numbers, it was clearly the heterogeneity of the population and the religious ethnic differences, along with the *millet* system (an Ottoman policy that granted autonomy to some of the non-Muslim communities), which resulted in the official creation of the city's religious and ethnic enclaves.[23] As such, the spatial organization of Jerusalem was not very different from that of many other cities in the Middle East, whose populations were most commonly defined by religion, culture, and society.[24]

The physical boundaries of Jerusalem's neighborhoods derived mainly from the street network, public buildings, or small plazas. The choice of where to settle within the context of the city was mostly determined by the location of holy sites and places of worship, religious affinity, cultural inclinations, availability of land, and political considerations. Unlike in some Middle Eastern cities, in Ottoman Jerusalem, each quarter and enclave had a similar mix of residents from different social and economic groups.[25]

The first suburbs of Jerusalem were established in the second half of the nineteenth century and the beginning of the twentieth century, when various religious and ethnic groups started to build institutes, estates, and private houses outside the Old City. Exact numbers are not available for this period, but it is known that by the beginning of the British Mandate, the populated area of the New City, as it came to be known, was four times greater than that of the Old City.[26] Among the first to settle beyond the walls were various Christian communities, which, mostly backed by European governments, competed in erecting large, impressive complexes, including monasteries, churches, hospitals, pilgrim hostels, and schools.[27]

The harat system of the Ottoman period was abandoned under Mandate rule, though the division of the Old City into the four principal quarters was maintained. None of these, however, was inhabited exclusively and homogenously by only one religious group, and for the most part, the boundaries were not clearly demarcated. In spite of the numerous historic landmarks and their significance to the different ethnic and religious communities, during the Mandate period, the Old City gradually emerged as little more than an impoverished older neighborhood.

On November 29, 1947, the UN General Assembly approved a plan that partitioned the British Mandate of Palestine into two entities: a Jewish state and an Arab state.[28] According to this plan, Jerusalem was to fall under international control. With the declaration of the establishment of the State of Israel on May 14, 1948, and following the conclusion of the Battle for Jerusalem (December 1947 to July 18, 1948), however, the UN proposal for Jerusalem was never instituted.

The 1949 Armistice Agreements left the Hashemite Kingdom of Transjordan (which soon after became the Hashemite Kingdom of Jordan) in control of East Jerusalem, including the Old City, and West Jerusalem was held by Israel and declared the capital of the state (see figure 8).[29] By the end of the year, all of West Jerusalem's Arab residents, who before 1948 numbered about twenty-eight thousand, were fully evacuated; most of their houses were settled by Israelis.[30] Some two thousand Jewish residents were expelled from the Old City and were no longer entitled to visit their holy sites, many of which were desecrated.[31] Access to Christian holy places, in contrast, remained unrestricted.[32] The Western Wall, where Muhammad is said to have tied his winged steed, al-Buraq, before ascending to heaven, was transformed into an exclusively Muslim site.[33]

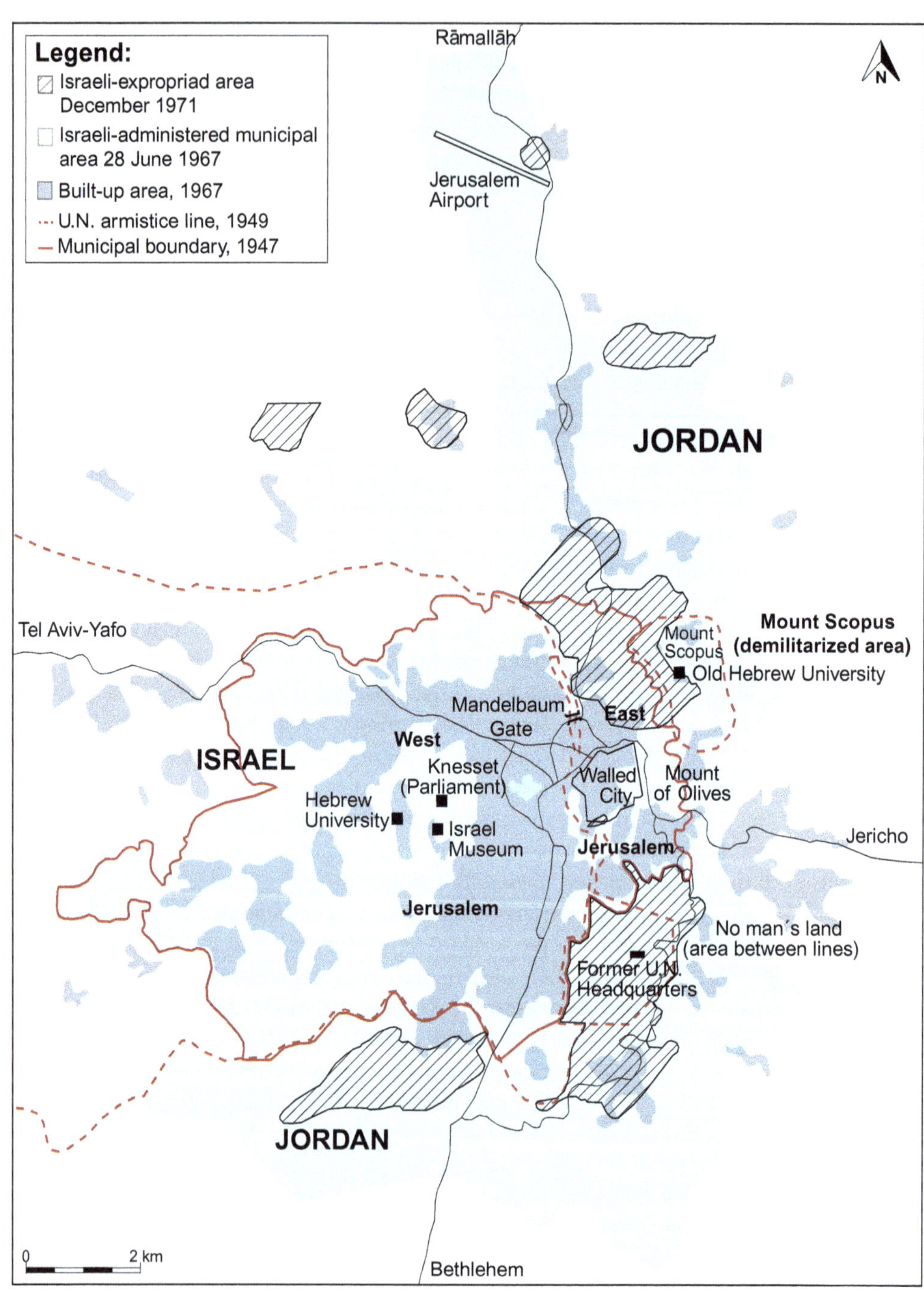

FIGURE 8. Divided Jerusalem, 1949–67. Drawn by Franziska Lehmann.

In June of 1967, the Israel Defense Forces (IDF) captured the Old City and extended its law and jurisdiction to East Jerusalem and the surrounding area, incorporating it into the Jerusalem Municipality.[34] Access to the Jewish and Christian holy sites within the Old City was restored, and though the Islamic Waqf retained its administrative authority over the Haram al-Sharif platform, most of its properties within the Old City and beyond were expropriated.[35] The Mughrabi Quarter (Harat al-Magharib), located near the Western Wall, was demolished to create an open plaza facing the wall, and Arab residents of both the Mughrabi and the Jewish Quarters were evicted.[36] Other major urban transformations and restoration initiatives were carried out in the Jewish Quarter, which completely transformed its religious, socioeconomic, and architectural makeup and turned it into an area apart from the rest of the Old City.[37] The less densely built territory stretching between the Old City and the eastern municipal boundary was turned into national parks.[38]

Over the course of the next decade, Palestinians from the West Bank began moving to Jerusalem, increasing the Arab population by more than 100 percent. As a countermeasure, seven Jewish districts, commonly referred to as the Ring Neighborhoods, were established around the city's eastern edges to prevent East Jerusalem from becoming part of an urban Palestinian bloc stretching from Bethlehem to Ramallah. Since then, the Israeli government has allocated additional areas within East Jerusalem for the construction of Jewish housing zones, and some Israeli Jews settled within Arab neighborhoods.[39]

Since 1967, when Israel captured East Jerusalem—along with the West Bank, the Sinai, and the Golan Heights—it has considered the entire city as the capital of the Jewish state. Only on July 30, 1980, however, did the Knesset (the unicameral parliament of Israel) pass an official bill formalizing the annexation of Arab East Jerusalem. This so-called Jerusalem Law, as an addition to its Basic Laws, declared Jerusalem the "complete and united" capital of Israel.[40] In response, the UN Security Council unanimously passed Resolution 478, stating that "enactment of the 'basic law' by Israel constitutes a violation of international law," and affirming that "all legislative and administrative measures and actions taken by Israel, the occupying Power, which have altered or purport to alter the character and status of the Holy City of Jerusalem, and in particular the recent 'basic law' on Jerusalem, are null and void and must be rescinded forthwith." The resolution furthermore asserted, "this action constitutes a serious obstruction to achieving a comprehensive, just and lasting peace in the Middle East."[41] In other words, according to international law, the occupation of East Jerusalem by Israel is illegal.[42]

Though officially unrelated to the political divide, the Old City of Jerusalem and its walls were inscribed on the World Heritage List (WHL) in 1981. In 1982, the Kingdom of Jordan requested that it be added to the List of World Heritage in Danger (LWHD).[43] In 2000, Israel proposed that the area recognized by UNESCO

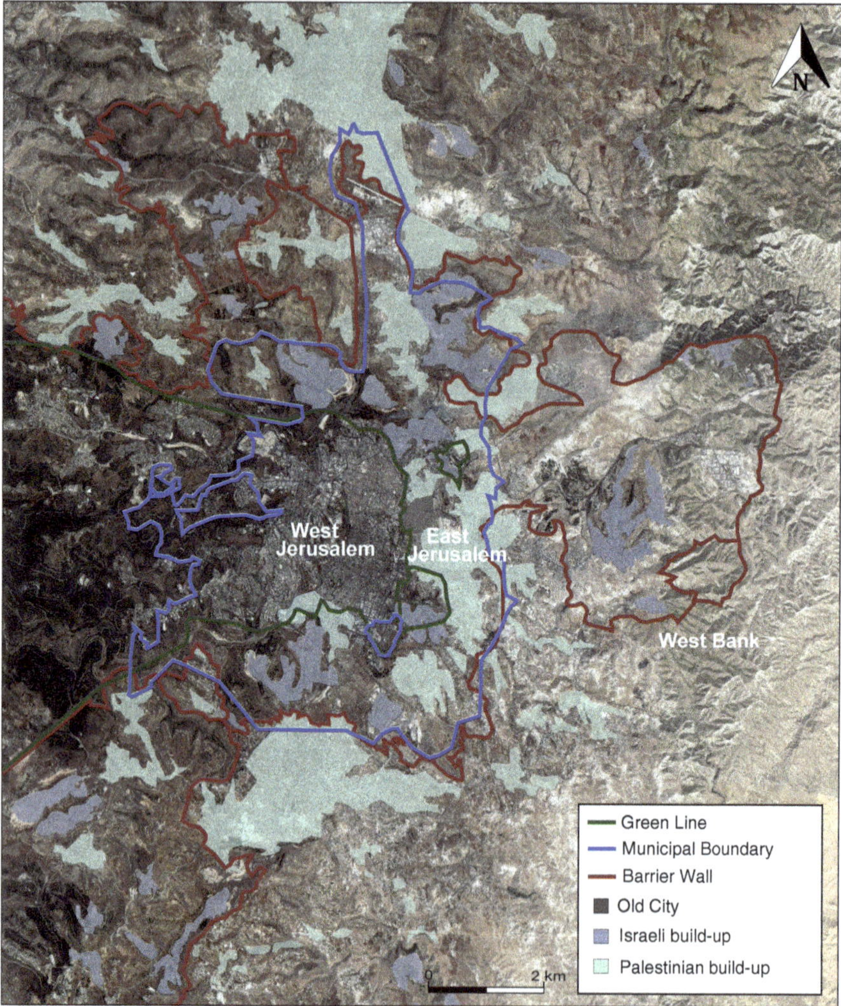

FIGURE 9. Map of Jerusalem with municipal boundaries, Green Line, Jewish and Palestinian build-ups, and Barrier Wall. Redrawn by Franziska Lehmann, after: *Ir Amim: Greater Jerusalem 2013.*

as protected heritage be expanded to include Mount Zion as well as those places and monuments that bear a unique testimony to the cultural traditions of Judaism, Christianity, and Islam, the area sometimes referred to as the Historic Basin.

The most recent initiative to segregate Jerusalem residents is the Barrier Wall (see figure 9), built in and around East Jerusalem. The Jerusalem section (202 kilometers long), is part of a much longer wall (upon completion, roughly

708 kilometers long) running through the West Bank. It is built alternately as a concrete wall and a chain-link fence, and its course is determined in relation to the municipal boundaries of Jerusalem as well as in relation to the settlements that surround the city.[44] Separating areas that are densely populated with exclusively Palestinian residents (housing some seventy thousand individuals) from predominantly Jewish neighborhoods, it reflects Israel's aspirations to both enlarge the territory of the Jerusalem Municipality but at the same time maintain a Jewish majority in the city. Beyond the frequently discussed psychological, socioeconomic, and political implications for the local populations, the construction of this wall restricts the access of Palestinians, both Christian and Muslim, to cultural heritage and holy sites.

Jerusalem's barriers and walls, its natural as well as its built features, have thus defined its spaces, buildings, and people, both physically and symbolically. On the positive side, they have contributed to enclose, unite, and protect; on the negative, they have fostered isolation, segregation, and confrontation. To the explorer, these boundaries serve as important markers of time and space, at once concrete and scientifically established, yet flexible and elusive, as they take on different roles in the many narratives that link the past to the present. In this study, they will assist in framing Jerusalem's history of archaeological investigation, as well as the city's populated, settled, claimed, and contested lands.

2

———

Institutionalization

Histories of explorations usually focus on the explorers or the director of the excavation, as well as the artifacts or sites they uncover. They rarely emphasize the institutional setting that quickly emerged as the necessary agent of most archaeological endeavors. At stake here are the interaction and interdependency of archaeologists, discoveries, and institutions—how these have evolved over time and, most significantly, how professionals in their administrative contexts have produced together what I argue represents the inseparable interplay of science, knowledge, and ideology.

The political climate in the Near East toward the end of the eighteenth century and the beginning of the nineteenth century was one of great rivalry and confrontation between various European states. In Palestine, much of this conflict was based and enacted on the grounds of traditional religious attachments. During this period, the Palestinian provinces of the Ottoman Empire were visited by an "unprecedented influx of western traders, explorers, missionaries, adventurers and military men."[1] Five foreign schools of archaeology operated in Jerusalem prior to World War I: French, American, German, British, and Italian. It was the British, however, who dominated the practice of the field in Palestine, and Jerusalem more specifically.[2] In 1865 the Palestine Exploration Fund (PEF) was founded in London, followed in 1870 by the American Palestine Exploration Society, the Deutscher Palästina-Verein (German Society for the Exploration of Palestine) in 1878, and the American Schools of Oriental Research (ASOR) in 1900.[3] The foreign presence and their archaeological activities were not always welcomed by the local population. In 1863 the Jewish community prevented the completion of the first excavation (begun in 1850–51) conducted in an ancient burial structure north of the Old City. Similar resistance to excavations on, around, and even near the Haram was voiced by the Muslim community. It would not be until the beginning of the twentieth century that some of the local inhabitants showed interest in participating in archaeological endeavors.[4]

The involvement of the Ottoman government was minimal. Initially, much of the archaeological activity depended on diplomatic relations among local governors, foreign diplomats, and religious authorities both in Jerusalem and Constantinople. It was only toward the end of the nineteenth century that the Ottoman government appointed an official commissioner to supervise excavations and decreed that all finds uncovered were to be regarded as state property.[5] Expeditions were required to obtain firmans from the sultan in Constantinople.[6] Those legal documents and precepts, however, were ill defined and had only limited authority. They were often ignored, and the local government officials could be easily manipulated with bribes.[7]

BETWEEN MISSIONARY AND SCHOLARLY ACTIVITIES

In 1837 Edward Robinson, one of the leading biblical authorities in America, was offered the first professorship of biblical literature at the new Union Theological Seminary in New York City.[8] His expertise has won him titles such as "father of biblical geography" or "founder of modern Palestinology."[9] In 1838 Robinson traveled to Palestine together with Reverend Eli Smith. Guided by his objective to differentiate between fact and fantasy and to separate the ancient from the modern, he studied Jerusalem's walls, gates, water supply, and topography. Regarding the Haram, he was forced to restrict his investigations to the exterior features of the complex. He was, however, able to make an important observation. He noticed the beginning of a protruding arch near the southern end of the western wall of the platform, still known today as Robinson's Arch. His familiarity with the writings of the first-century Jewish historian Flavius Josephus allowed him to associate the arch with the Temple Mount complex restored by King Herod the Great. This was, in fact, one of many observations that led to Robinson's conclusion that the enclosure wall of the Haram as a whole was originally built in the first century B.C.E. For his scholarly achievements, Robinson was the first American to be awarded the gold medal of the Royal Geographical Society in London in 1842. His accomplishments were hailed by scientists, geographers, biblical scholars, and clerics, and his work "had far transcended both missionary goals and the New England battle for the authenticity of the Bible." In his quest for the past, he established the foundations for an entire "new scholarly, religious, and political enterprise in the Holy Land." The field of biblical archaeology was born.[10]

JERUSALEM'S FIRST EXCAVATION

Félix de Saulcy was born into a noble Flemish family at Lille, France.[11] After a career in the army, he was appointed curator of the Musée d'artilleries in Paris. He was an Orientalist, numismatist, and archaeologist and had published numerous scholarly treatises. In 1850–51 he conducted the first archaeological dig in Jerusalem—in fact, in all of the Holy Land. He traveled twice to Jerusalem to excavate a structure that he mistakenly identified as the burial site of the Hebrew kings of Judah; it is still known today as the Tomb of the Kings. He initially discovered a sarcophagus he believed to have been of King David. During his second visit, in 1863, he recovered a sarcophagus with a Hebrew inscription including the word *queen,* which he identified as belonging to King Zedekiah's wife. The tomb has since been recognized as belonging to the Mesopotamian Queen Helena of Adiabene, a convert to Judaism who lived in the first century C.E.[12] De Saulcy was forced to suspend the dig and flee the country when the Jewish community of Jerusalem suspected him of desecrating Jewish burials. The sarcophagus and other artifacts were sent to France and displayed at the Louvre. Unlike his solid work as a numismatist, de Saulcy's excavations and associated documentation have never been much appreciated for their scientific value.

WATER RELIEF EFFORTS

The Ordnance Survey of Jerusalem was the first official expedition to Jerusalem. It was funded by Angela Georgina—later Baroness—Burdett-Coutts, who had the philanthropic goal of supplying the inhabitants of Jerusalem with a new water system. On the basis of her personal interest in the history of the city, a decision was made to undertake a complete and accurate survey of the Old City of Jerusalem. The task was carried out by Dean Stanley of Westminster, who presented a petition to Lord de Grey and Ripon, British Secretary of State for War. Thus, in an effort to solve the recurring problems of malaria, dysentery, and cholera, the Jerusalem Water Relief Society engaged the Royal Engineers to survey the city's topographical features and the existing water systems, using the most modern equipment and the most competent surveyors who could be hired.[13] In 1864 the Royal Engineers identified Captain Sir Charles William Wilson for the task.[14] Wilson was thus the first Western explorer in the Holy Land who did not come to satisfy his personal interest in the biblical past. Instead he came on a specifically outlined assignment representing his government. His detailed map of Jerusalem (scale 1:2,500) featured all the streets and important buildings. Benchmarks were cut at the corners of the city walls, its gates, and at various public buildings. A smaller map (scale 1:10,000) of the city environs included topographical features and buildings located outside the Old City (see figure 10). Wilson also produced plans of the Citadel complex and the Church of the Holy Sepulchre.

FIGURE 10. Detail from Wilson's Survey of Jerusalem, 1864–65, showing the Old City and surroundings, featuring existing water cisterns in blue (PEF-M-OSJ 1864–5 PLAN 1). Courtesy of Palestine Exploration Fund.

More significantly, he was the first to carefully investigate and document the hidden underground features of the Haram, including numerous cisterns, channels, and aqueducts. Above ground, on the western enclosure wall of the Haram, he discovered a well-preserved span of a monumental arch, similar in size to Robinson's Arch and parallel to it. Still today known as Wilson's Arch, this feature was identified as another entrance leading to the Herodian Temple Mount. Wilson joined the PEF in 1867 and served as chairman from 1901 until his death in 1905.[15] Ironically, although the Ordnance Survey and the Jerusalem Water Relief Society provided the Western world with the first accurate map of Jerusalem, including the plans of some of the city's most important historic monuments, it ultimately did not alleviate the problem of Jerusalem's water supply.[16]

EARLY INVESTIGATIONS

It was ultimately the success of the historically significant work conducted on behalf of the Ordnance Survey of Jerusalem that led to the founding of the PEF in 1865. The original *Prospectus* of the PEF stated that Jerusalem was a prime target for digging operations and that "what is above ground will be accurately known [only] when the present [Ordnance] survey is completed; but below the surface hardly anything has yet been discovered. . . . It is not too much to anticipate that every foot in depth of the 'sixty feet [ca. eighteen meters] of rubbish' on which the city stands, will yield interesting and important materials for the Archaeologist or the Numismatist."[17]

As the next representative of the Ordnance Survey, Lieutenant Charles Warren continued Wilson's work in Jerusalem between 1867 and 1870.[18] He was assisted by Sergeant Henry Birtles and several sappers from the Horse Guards, as well as the photographer Corporal Henry Phillips (see figure 11). His endeavors were supported by Dr. Thomas Chaplin, the Reverend Dr. Joseph Barclay, and the Consul of Jerusalem, Noel Moore.[19]

With the permission of the Ottoman general Izzet Pasha to excavate in the area surrounding the Haram's retaining walls, Warren initially inspected the area against the southern wall. This activity, however, disturbed the daily prayers in the al-Aqsa Mosque, and to put down the disturbance, the pasha was forced to suspend the work.

Warren then started to sink probes in the Christian Quarter, with the goal of determining whether the site of Church of the Holy Sepulchre lay inside or outside the city walls at the time of Jesus. Once again his work was interrupted, this time by soldiers of the Ottoman garrison.

Warren's work on the Southeast Hill, outside the Old City boundaries, aimed to establish the southern extent of Jerusalem in biblical times. Here he investigated an ancient subterranean aqueduct, associated with the shaft that was later named after him. For over a century, this vertical feature was identified as the path chosen by King David to conquer the city from the Jebusites.

As the first major expeditions of the PEF, in addition to the specific information it provided on Jerusalem, Wilson's and Warren's efforts also served to raise the public interest in and support for the work of the establishment more generally. As a result, the fund was able to initiate and finance a significantly more ambitious survey, the great Survey of Western Palestine.[20]

Only a few individuals associated with the early decades of archaeological exploration in Jerusalem were not of British nationality. These included Charles Clermont-Ganneau, Conrad Schick, and Hermann Guthe. While serving as a secretary at the French Consulate in Jerusalem between 1865 and 1872, Clermont-Ganneau conducted intensive archaeological investigations in Jerusalem and surroundings.[21] In 1873, he was on an official mission of the PEF. Although he could

FIGURE 11. Jerusalem survey team in 1867, featuring Lieutenant Charles Warren, R.E., the Reverend Dr. Joseph Barclay, and Corporal Henry Phillips (seated from left to right), Mr. Frederick W. Eaton (reclining), and Jerius, Dragoman to the British Consulate (standing). Photo by H. Phillips. Courtesy of Palestine Exploration Fund.

not obtain an excavation permit, he was able to carry out his work. His documentation was published nearly thirty years later.[22]

Schick, a Protestant missionary from Germany and an amateur architect and archaeologist, settled in Jerusalem in the mid-nineteenth century. A protégé of Charles Wilson, he conducted extensive studies on ancient Jerusalem and built numerous models of the city. During his residence in Jerusalem, until his death in 1901, Schick published more than one hundred reports within the pages of the *Palestine Exploration Fund's Quarterly Statement* as well as the *Zeitschrift des Deutschen Palästina-Vereins.*[23]

Around the same time, another German scholar, Guthe, was active in Jerusalem. He, however, excavated on behalf of the Deutscher Palästina-Verein (German Society for the Exploration of Palestine), established in 1877 according to the British model.[24]

The last official endeavors of the PEF under Ottoman rule in Jerusalem with an exclusively archaeological goal were conducted by Frederick Jones Bliss and

Archibald Campbell Dickie.[25] After training under Flinders Petrie in Egypt, Frederick Jones Bliss became involved with the PEF, leading an expedition in Jerusalem during the final years of the nineteenth century to investigate the area south of the Old City, including the traditional Mount Zion on the west and the City of David to the east. First alone and later with the assistance of architect Archibald Dickie, he exposed numerous segments of walls, towers, and gates. The results of their excavations were promptly published.[26]

LAST OTTOMAN VENTURES

The final years of Ottoman rule witnessed the unfortunate episode of a treasure hunt that was highly publicized and severely criticized in the local and international media. In 1909, after obtaining cooperation of the Ottoman authorities in Constantinople, Montague Brownslow Parker, the thirty-year-old son of the Earl of Morley who came from a military background, initiated the famous expedition of King Solomon's Temple treasures.[27] He was advised by Valter H. Juvelius, who sent telegraphs from Europe containing the telepathic instructions of an Irish clairvoyant. After Parker's failed attempt to uncover a secret passage on the Ophel slope, he returned the following year to excavate under the southeast corner of the Haram platform. The suspicion aroused among scholars of the American and European archaeological institutions in Jerusalem prompted Parker to invite Louis-Hugues Vincent from the École biblique et archéologique française to document the findings during the course of his expedition.[28] The protests of members of the city's Jewish community and ultimately the threats of its Muslim residents forced him to halt this highly questionable enterprise and to flee the country to escape serious reprimand.

Fortunately, the last excavation project under Ottoman rule was less scandalous. It was initiated and sponsored by Baron Edmond de Rothschild, motivated by his desire to uncover the Tomb of the Kings of Judah. On his behalf, Raymond Weill began digging on the Southeast Hill in 1913 (see figure 12).[29] Weill's most important discovery was the famous Theodotus inscription, indicating the presence of an early synagogue in use during the time of the Herodian Temple.[30]

BRITISH MANDATE INITIATIVES

Archaeological activity underwent a dramatic change after the British conquest of Palestine during World War I. Initially, to avoid damage to sacred places and monuments, the capture of Jerusalem was somewhat delayed.[31] This awareness of the city's physical legacy soon led to the establishment of the Pro-Jerusalem Society and its charter providing for "the protection and preservation, with the consent of the Government, of the antiquities of the district of Jerusalem."[32] Soon, in

FIGURE 12. Raymond Weill's expedition in Silwan, 1913–14. Courtesy of École biblique.

particular with the establishment of the Department of Antiquities of Mandatory Palestine (DAP), Jerusalem turned into one of the most dynamic centers of excavation and archaeological research in the world. It was during the British Mandatory period that the foundations for much of modern scientific archaeological investigations in the city were laid.

By following the model of similar establishments in other British colonies and the establishment of the Antiquities Law (AL) in 1928, the director of the newly founded DAP was able to impose professional standards and regulate archaeological activity through a much more rigorously controlled issuance of excavation licenses.[33]

Until 1930, the British School of Archaeology and the DAP occupied the same building, although as early as 1926 the directorates were separate. The director of the DAP and its advisory board were appointed by the high commissioner from the British, French, American, and Italian schools of archaeology in Jerusalem. In addition, two Palestinians and two Jews were appointed to represent the Muslim and Jewish communities.[34] The department had five subunits: the inspectors, a records office and library, a conservation laboratory, a photographic studio, and the Palestine Archaeological Museum (PAM). The latter, financed by a $2 million gift, was dedicated in 1938.[35] Its main purpose was to collect and display the antiquities of the country for the benefit of its citizens, a change from the earlier practice of removal of the region's most important artifacts to other states.[36]

John Garstang wore two hats during his stay in Jerusalem: one as the director of the DAP (1920–26) and the other as head of the British School of Archaeology (1919–26). He was pivotal in formulating the Antiquities Ordinance (AO), and though he himself did not excavate in Jerusalem, he urged the PEF to resume archaeological work in the city and to collaborate with scholars from other countries (see figure 13).[37]

The period between the two World Wars (1918–39) is often referred to as the golden age of archaeological exploration in the Holy Land.[38] A total of 140 excavations were carried out in Jerusalem alone, seventy-six of which were conducted by the staff of the DAP, including both British and local archaeologists.[39] Many of the excavations were salvage operations, conducted after the chance discoveries of antiquities during development.[40]

Between 1923 and 1925, the first official expeditions of the British Mandate period were carried out on the Southeast Hill by Robert Alexander Stuart Macalister and John Garrow Duncan on behalf of the PEF.[41] Several residential buildings as well as a massive support wall, later known as the Stepped Stone Structure were exposed. More generally, their excavation appeared to establish that this area corresponded to the biblical description of Zion and that it was surrounded by a wall. Two years later, in 1927, John W. Crowfoot and Gerald M. FitzGerald continued work in the same location and discovered a massive gate.[42]

The focus of the next major expedition shifted to the Citadel, near the modern Jaffa Gate. Beginning in 1934, it was directed by Cedric N. Johns under the auspices of the DAP. Though the project was planned as a salvage operation, the soundings revealed the northwest corner of an ancient system of fortifications (presumably associated with King Herod's palace), and work continued for another five years.[43]

Other notable excavations conducted under the aegis of the DAP were carried out by John Illife at the YMCA, by Dimitri Baramki near the so-called Third Wall, and by Robert Hamilton at the Damascus Gate and along the northern wall of the Old City.[44]

The DAP was also involved in the management of the city's holy sites. Close working relations with officials of the Islamic Waqf and the Christian communities were established. Inspectors had access to the Haram and were entitled to measure and document all its major monuments. Most notable were Ernest Tatham Richmond's survey of the Dome of the Rock and Robert Hamilton's architectural survey and excavation of the al-Aqsa Mosque.[45] Renovations were carried out in the Church of the Holy Sepulchre, most importantly the replacement of the dome of the Katholikon and the removal of the lintels of the Crusader entrance, and William Harvey conducted detailed architectural studies and structural reports of the entire complex.[46]

FIGURE 13. John Garstang, director of the British School of Archaeology in Jerusalem, shown photographing a recently excavated archaeological deposit (PEF-GAR-JER- PN21–2). Courtesy of Palestine Exploration Fund.

In 1914 a group of local Jewish intellectuals had established the independent Society for the Reclamation of Antiquities, renamed the Jewish Palestine Exploration Society (JPES) in 1920.[47] Its purpose was to advance historical, geographical, and archaeological research concerning the Land of Israel.[48] During the Mandate period, it was responsible for the first archaeological excavations ever conducted by a local Jewish organization, including the Tomb of Absalom and the Third Wall in Jerusalem. To support the professional training of Jewish archaeologists, in 1935 the Hebrew University of Jerusalem established a department of archaeology.[49] In order to provide a proper setting for the few Christian and Muslim scholars interested in the folklore and customs of the country, the Palestine Oriental Society (POS) was founded in 1920. Their interest, however, did not encompass archaeological fieldwork.[50]

TWO DEPARTMENTS OF ANTIQUITIES

Following the 1948 Arab-Israeli War, the official framework of archaeological activity adjusted to the new reality, with Israel ruling West Jerusalem and the Hashemite Kingdom of Transjordan East Jerusalem, including the Old City.

Until 1956 the Department of Antiquities of Jordan continued to be headed by a British archaeologist, Gerald Lankester Harding, who was based in Amman. In East Jerusalem (which came under Jordanian rule in 1948), his representative,

Yosef Sa'ad, was keeper of the PAM, also known as the Rockefeller Museum. Lankester Harding was replaced by Saeed al-Durrah, who administered the Jordanian Department of Antiquities between 1956 and 1959, to be followed by Awni al-Dajani between 1956 and 1968.[51] Until 1948 all documents pertaining to the archaeology of the region, including artifacts, files, maps, and plans were kept at the PAM in Jerusalem. According to UN decisions made prior to the 1948 war, the museum and its holdings were going to be managed by an international committee. This plan, however, proved difficult to be implemented and by 1966 the committee was officially disbanded with the museum collection nationalization by Jordan.[52] The working relationship between the Department of Antiquities of Jordan and the Islamic Waqf during this period was rather poor.[53]

The main archaeological project in the Old City during this eighteen-year period of Jordanian rule was directed by British archaeologist Dame Kathleen Kenyon. After completing her first excavations in Palestine at Jericho in 1957, Kenyon worked in Jerusalem between 1961 and 1967.[54] Trenches were opened in areas near the Old City that were not built-up, including the Southeast Hill and the area north of the Ottoman city wall, as well as within the Old City, in the Armenian Quarter and in the Muristan near the Church of the Holy Sepulchre. Kenyon's primary goal was to establish clear stratigraphic sequences; exposing specific architectural complexes was secondary.[55]

As part of the now officially recognized territory of the State of Israel, the antiquities of West Jerusalem were subject to some pro-forma changes. The new Israel Department of Antiquities and Museums (IDAM) was established on July 26, 1948. This relatively modest office was made part of the public works department under the Ministry of Labor and Construction. In August 1955, it was transferred to the Ministry of Education and Culture. The department's first director was Shmuel Yeivin, followed by Avraham Biran in 1961. All activities were based on the British Mandate Department of Antiquities Ordinances. The department maintained control of all antiquities and was in charge of the administration of small museums. Along with inspecting and registering antiquities sites and conducting excavations and surveys, it facilitated the storage and curation of the state collection of antiquities and maintained an archaeological library and research archive.

Archaeologists Emanuel Ben Dor and Benjamin Maisler (Mazar) were immediately appointed archaeological officers in charge of the Jerusalem District (naturally, not including East Jerusalem). In 1950 they were joined by a third officer, Shmuel Yeivin.[56] It was during this period that the concept of archaeological inspection developed, establishing a framework that efficiently controlled the scientific level and professionalism of archaeological fieldwork. Michael Avi-Yonah was the first to serve as Jerusalem's scientific secretary and antiquities inspector. In 1951 he was replaced by Ruth Amiran.[57]

Between 1949 and 1967, eighty-eight excavations, mostly of burial complexes, were conducted in West Jerusalem. The majority of them were salvage excavations connected to the massive urban development projects of road and housing construction. Given the budgetary constraints, however, very little was invested in conservation and preservation, and many antiquities had to be destroyed as construction projects continued.[58]

ISRAELI JURISDICTION

On August 30, 1967, after Israel had captured East Jerusalem, the Old City and its surrounding were declared protected antiquities sites according to the provision of the Antiquities Ordinance.[59] The IDAM extended its control of archaeological activity and supervision to the newly occupied areas. Although The Hague convention, to which Israel was a signatory, explicitly prohibited the removal of cultural property from militarily occupied areas, numerous excavations were initiated almost immediately.[60] In January 31, 1978, the Knesset passed the Law of Antiquities, officially superseding the Mandate ordinances.

Avraham Eitan, appointed director of IDAM in 1974, was replaced in 1988 by army general Amir Drori, who set in motion the conversion of IDAM into an independent government authority. The passage of a new law, the Antiquities Authority Law, was finalized on September 1, 1989, and the following April, the Israel Antiquities Authority (IAA) officially came into existence, with Amir Drori as its first director. Several significant changes in the administration and management of all archaeological excavation and research activities were initiated, affecting primarily the procedures of archaeological inspection, salvage excavation, and site and artifact conservation. Furthermore, the ultimate authority of archaeological governance was placed into the hands of an administrator with limited expertise in the field of archaeology. In 2000, Drori was replaced by another army general, Shouka Dorfman, who served as director until 2014.[61] Since then, former Shin Bet (Israel's internal security service) deputy director and Knesset member Israel Hasson has been directing the IAA, equally limited in his professional exposure to and immersion in the field of archaeology.[62] As head of excavations and surveys between 2000 and 2011, archaeologist Gideon Avni was given the task of overseeing the development of a new Jerusalem Department, including some twenty-eight staff members.[63] The efforts of this unit have been distributed regionally between West Jerusalem, East Jerusalem, the Old City, and the Judean Hills located within the Green Line (also referred to as the "pre-1967 borders").[64]

The significant urban growth and construction following the 1967 war, expanding into previously uninhabited areas, had an unavoidable impact on the archaeological landscape. To counter the impending destruction that would be caused by this development, the IAA carried out an extensive survey of the ancient city and its surroundings, documenting some nine hundred sites.[65] This non-intrusive initiative was supplemented by numerous modestly sized and several large-scale excavations. As originally many of these activities were in response to modern development and only a few linked to preservation or conservation projects of existing structures, most archaeological activities in the city were classified by the Israeli archaeological administration as salvage operations.

Excavations conducted promptly after the 1967 war, were carried out prior to urban development in the newly established neighborhoods of Givat HaMivtar, French Hill, Mount Scopus, Ramot, East Talpiyot, Har Nof, and Giloh, and slightly later in the neighborhoods of Emek Rephaim, Malha, and Pisgat Ze'ev. Sites located near the Old City include Akeldama, Gethsemane, Mamilla, and the Mandelbaum Gate. Among those located within and adjacent to the Old City, are the Citadel, the Armenian Garden, the Damascus Gate, Herod's Gate, Daraj el-Ain at Ohel Yitzhak, and the Church of the Holy Sepulchre. In terms of sheer size, the most ambitious projects were conducted in the Jewish Quarter, near the Temple Mount / Haram al-Sharif, and finally in the City of David / Silwan.[66]

Since 1967 only a limited number of excavations and surveys have been carried out under the auspices of foreign institutions. Notable among these are the recent salvage excavations of the École biblique at the Church of St. John and the work carried out within the Lutheran Church of the Redeemer by the Deutsches Evangelisches Institut für Altertumswissenschaft.[67] The current excavations on Mount Zion, conducted on behalf of University of North Carolina at Charlotte and the University of the Holy Land, represent the only archaeological project not motivated by a conservation or development project.[68]

Two significant surveys of Mamluk and Ottoman monuments—initiatives that were not intrusive and thus did not require (or chose not to request) approval or licenses from the Israeli authorities—were carried out under the auspices of the British School of Archaeology. British scholar Michael Hamilton Burgoyne directed the survey of Mamluk architecture in Jerusalem, beginning in 1968.[69] Two other surveys were conducted by Palestinian archaeologists in the Old City; Mahmoud Hawari led a study of all Ayyubid monuments, and Yusuf Natsheh, one of all Ottoman monuments.[70]

Before the dissolution of the IDAM and the establishment of the IAA in 1990, some 245 sites had been excavated and documented. Since then, an additional 210 excavations have been carried out.[71] This brings the total number of officially registered and documented excavations since the beginning of archaeological exploration in the mid-nineteenth century to roughly 1,200.[72] The number of illegal or undocumented excavations, carried out by amateurs or by looters supplying the antiquities market, is estimated to be around five hundred.[73]

. . .

As Jerusalem has moved through changing political realities, archaeological explorations have flourished. They have evolved from several individually motivated endeavors to countless institutionalized and governmental undertakings, at an ever-growing speed and scale. Significant accomplishments were achieved under colonial rule. The Ottoman authorities made the initial modest moves toward regulating fieldwork and discoveries. Most impressive and long lasting, however, were the contributions to the administrative and professional standards established under the British, who imposed an increasingly structured protocol and scientific framework on the growing number of expeditions. The noticeable progress and success of biblical archaeology under British rule may in no small part be due to the fact that the cultural and religious aspirations of the predominantly Western explorers and institutions and the ideological outlook of the government were merged for the first time.

With the new reality of the divided city between 1948 and 1967, Jordanian and Israeli rules shaped a period of different nationalist aspirations, though the structural and scientific framework of fieldwork continued to be governed by the British model of exploration. Methodological innovations were successfully implemented, professionalism increased, and the biblical interest persisted, largely from a Christian perspective on the Jordanian side and from a Jewish one on the Israeli side.[74]

By far, the most extensive and expansive field projects in Jerusalem have occurred since Israel's capture of East Jerusalem in 1967. Some of these have been linked to new development efforts, but most have been motivated by the desire to explore and better understand—as well as to display—the national and religious roots of the city's antiquities. By defining all excavations in the occupied sector of the city as salvage work, the Israeli government circumvents international law, according to which all excavation in East Jerusalem is illegal. For this reason, more so than in any other previous political context of colonialism, archaeological activity in the city under occupation is both conducted and governed—apart from a few exceptions—by one nation: the Jewish State of Israel, an escalation that in no minimal way reflects the radical constitutional framework, in which state and religion are merged. Apart from the legal implications, however, Israeli archaeology has been taking the field to new levels of mastery, management, and scientific excellence, building on the professional advances made in previous decades. One could thus argue that the story of the success of archaeological exploration in Jerusalem is one of increasing professionalism, at its best when the zeal of the explorers converges with the ideology of the state.

PART TWO

Cultural Heritage

Jerusalem's heritage is a cultural amalgam, recently absorbed into the discourse about who owns the past. Questioning the proprietorship of antiquities, determining the international standards of cultural, scientific, and ethnic principles, and examining how these have been applied and governed by various religious and political administrators form the core of this part of my study, in which science meets ideology. Relevant to this investigation is the understanding of how decisions are made as to where to expose, what to preserve, and how to showcase archaeological ruins capable of telling a story. This discussion of cultural heritage explores who produces knowledge and how the information is disseminated, presented, and consumed in educational settings and in public displays such as monuments, sites, parks, and museums. The heritage at stake is of relevance to Jews, Christians, and Muslims, as well as, more recently, Israelis and Palestinians, none of whom are homogenous groups or holders of monolithic interests.

3

From Destruction to Preservation

When Theodor Herzl, the founder of political Zionism, visited Jerusalem in 1898, he was repelled by "the musty deposits of two thousand years of inhumanity, intolerance and foulness" in the "reeking alleys" of the Old City. He vowed that the first thing the Zionists would do when they got control of Jerusalem would be to tear most of it down, building an "airy, comfortable, properly sewered, new city around the holy places."[1] Similarly, when East Jerusalem and the Old City were captured by Israel in 1967, David Ben-Gurion (the founder of the State of Israel and the first prime minister of the country), then a member of Knesset, called for the demolition of the walls of Jerusalem because they were not Jewish and thus threatened to disrupt the visual continuity of Israeli control.[2]

Though neither Herzl's nor Ben Gurion's vision or goal was realized, massive and deliberate destructions of material legacies occurred following the UN Partition Plan of 1947. During the period of Jordanian rule of the Old City and East Jerusalem between 1948 and 1967, numerous synagogues and other Jewish institutions, particularly in the Jewish Quarter, were abandoned, neglected, or demolished.[3] Then, in June 1967, immediately following the armistice that concluded the Arab-Israeli War, all inhabitants of the Mughrabi Quarter near the Western Wall were evacuated, and the historic district was razed to create room for a wide, open plaza that would be joined to the Jewish Quarter.[4] Additional destruction occurred throughout the Jewish Quarter. Here, instead of preserving the original character of the neighborhood, the municipality replaced medieval alleys and buildings with a completely new cityscape, creating a deliberate segregation—ethnic, religious, cultural, and architectural—between the refurbished area and the

45

other quarters in the Old City.[5] Since 1967, campaigns seeking the destruction of significant historic monuments have continued. For example, the Temple Mount Faithful as well as other radical groups have repeatedly militated for the destruction of the holy Muslim shrines and the return of the compound to Jewish control as the first step toward the rebuilding of the Temple on the site of the Dome of the Rock.[6]

Individual, public, and institutional attitudes toward the paradigms and problems of cultural heritage and its preservation have undergone significant changes and developments, both conceptually and practically, over the course of the last century. Despite the significant progress of the public and academic discourse on cultural heritage, in particular in Europe and the United States, the implementation of progressive policies in Israel, especially in Jerusalem's Historic Basin, have been limited or hindered as a result of political conflict.[7]

Indicative of both the progress and stagnation with regard to honoring Jerusalem's diverse building heritage is one of the IAA's most important current conservation projects, which once again turns our attention to the city walls. Exactly fifty years after Ben-Gurion suggested demolishing the walls of Jerusalem's Old City, the IAA identified the Ottoman fortifications as one of the city's "most important cultural heritage assets."[8] The Jerusalem City Wall Conservation Project was launched in 2007. But in addition to conserving and stabilizing the original sixteenth-century construction, the project also aims to use the Ottoman walls to highlight the modern history of the State of Israel. When the Hagana (the Jewish paramilitary organization active during the time of the British Mandate, which later became the core of the IDF) tried to break into the Jewish Quarter in May of 1948, they damaged the ashlars surrounding the Zion Gate (see figure 14). After the 1967 war, the bullet-scarred gate became one of the hallmarks of a "united Jerusalem," a symbol that the IAA decided to preserve as "the single most important event to have left its stamp on the gate's façade in its 468 year history."[9] In other words, the Ottoman city walls—whether perceived as a hurdle to the construction of a new Jewish city, an obstacle for a "united Jerusalem," or as a means of commemorating the Israeli narrative of the "conquest" of the Old City—have played a consistently important role in the ideological discourse on Jewish Jerusalem.

The notion that physical remnants of the past, whether intact, damaged, or even largely destroyed, should be valued as common human heritage and protected from exploitation by nation-states has taken an increasingly important place in academic as well as public discussions of cultural heritage.[10] The task of preserving the tangible and intangible legacies of nations or peoples without fostering religious zeal, supporting ideological discourse, or endorsing national agendas, however, is particularly complex and challenging for a contested city like Jerusalem.

FIGURE 14. The bullet-scarred Zion Gate. Photo by Katharina Galor.

INTERNATIONAL CONVENTIONS, GUIDELINES, AND CHARTERS

The concept of protecting cultural property from the effects of war was first defined in The Hague conventions of 1899 and 1907 and in the Washington Treaty of 1935.[11] The serious damage to cultural property that occurred during the Second World War dramatically increased the perceived need to establish more effective guidelines and laws to protect cultural heritage, especially in areas that had suffered significant wartime damage. In the preamble to The Hague convention of 1954, the concept of the common heritage of humanity as applied to cultural property finds expression for the first time.[12] That convention was followed by a UNESCO convention in 1970 titled "Prohibiting and Preventing the Illicit Import, Export and Transfer of Ownership of Cultural Property."[13]

In 1972, the World Heritage Convention Concerning the Protection of the World Cultural and Natural Heritage stipulated the obligation of states—or parties acting as states—to report regularly to the World Heritage Committee on the conservation of their World Heritage Properties. This convention was one of UNESCO's most successful endeavors, reflected by the fact that 167 states ratified it. It covered the protection of cultural heritage both in peace and wartime, it transcended national boundaries, and it set rules for both natural and cultural heritage. Its primary mission was to "define and conserve the world's heritage by drawing up a list of sites whose outstanding values should be preserved for all humanity and to ensure their protection through a closer cooperation among nations."[14]

The 1972 World Heritage Convention was followed in 1995 by the International Institute for the Unification of Private Law (UNIDROIT) Convention on Stolen and Illegally Exported Cultural Objects. Finally, the UNESCO Underwater Convention of 2001 established the protection of underwater cultural heritage. These initiatives shared the conviction that cultural heritage should not be regarded as a purely local, ethnic, or national endowment. Instead, it should be viewed and treated as the cultural property of humankind as a whole and should thus be preserved.

In 1990, the International Council on Monuments and Sites (ICOMOS), a nongovernmental organization, published its Charter for the Protection and Management of the Archaeological Heritage, providing guidelines for the management of cultural heritage in all its forms and diversity.[15] Although this document does not have the status of an international treaty, it represents a consensus reached by academics and professionals in the field of culture preservation. The charter explicitly states that "legislation should be based on the concept of the archaeological heritage as the heritage of all humanity and groups of peoples, and not restricted to any individual person or nation."[16] These international guidelines and conventions have certain implications for Jerusalem, though most of them affect the academic and public discourse rather than the reality of archaeological fieldwork and preservation.

CULTURAL HERITAGE IN JERUSALEM

Perceptions of what constitutes the cultural heritage of Jerusalem have evolved, changed, and embraced different and sometimes opposing views over time, reflecting the numerous cultural, ethnic, religious, and national groups claiming ownership of the city's past and present. A number of local and international administrative bodies—both NGOs and governmental institutions, representing various religious, secular, political, and apolitical groups—have been established to ensure the preservation of the city's heritage.

Though some of the most important monuments and sites in Jerusalem have sacred status, an attribute that tends to increase in significance over time, much of the city's cultural heritage can be categorized as secular.[17] In other words, Jerusalem's cultural heritage encompasses not only places of worship, holy sites, consecrated monuments, and sacred artifacts. It equally concerns buildings, objects, and traditions—both in the private and public realms of the city—that have no religious or spiritual attributes, including residences, industrial installations, tools, weapons, or various literary and artistic memorabilia, such as songs, poems, and photographs.

During the late nineteenth century, the growing appreciation of antiquities led the Ottoman authorities to formulate the first legal precepts designed to protect the region's cultural heritage. The Ottoman Law of 1884 established national patrimony over all artifacts in the empire and tried to regulate scientific access to antiquities and sites by introducing excavation permits. Movable artifacts could no longer leave the empire's territory and automatically became the property of the Imperial Museum in Constantinople (Müze-i Hümayun), indicative of the now more established and legal form of cultural imperialism.[18] In 1918 the British Mandate Antiquities Proclamation, which endorsed the importance of the region's cultural heritage, imposed a more rigid legal framework on excavation and the export of antiquities. Based on the Ottoman Law of Antiquities, the newly established Antiquities Ordinance vested the ownership of moveable and immoveable cultural heritage in the civil government of Palestine. For the first time, the protection and oversight of cultural heritage in the region were administered locally rather than from an imperial capital.[19]

Despite the fact that East Jerusalem had maintained its religious significance under Hashemite rule, it temporarily ceased to function as a capital.[20] Regardless of Jordan's investment in the image of Jerusalem as a magnet for Christian and Muslim pilgrims and tourists, by losing direct access to the coast, the city suffered economically and thus the restoration of ancient monuments of historic and religious significance—apart from the 1952–64 restoration of the cupola of the Dome of the Rock—was not of primary concern.[21] Following this period of relative inattention, considerable damage occurred during the military conflict of 1967, especially in the Old City's Jewish Quarter.

A dramatic shift in the history of archaeological exploration and conservation took place with the onset of Israeli rule, at which point the domain of cultural heritage turned into a battlefield between Jews and Arabs, between Israelis and Palestinians. Massive excavation and restoration projects have been carried out in Jerusalem ever since the creation of the State of Israel, first in West Jerusalem, beginning in 1948, and then in East Jerusalem, with an emphasis on the Historic Basin, starting in 1967. The administrative framework, as defined by Israeli law and enacted by the Israel Nature and Parks Authority (INPA) and the IAA (and before 1990 the IDAM), has treated archaeological activity and the preservation of cultural heritage in East and West Jerusalem as a unit, thus serving the political concept of the greater and united city. From an international point of view, however, which coincides with the Palestinian perspective, all archaeological work carried out in the occupied sector of the city after 1967 is illegal. Israel has countered international pressure and condemnation of massive excavation projects in the city's occupied sectors by framing these as salvage operations. Perhaps more deserving of the term *salvage operations* are the Hashemite restorations of various holy places on the Haram al-Sharif, including Salah al-Din's *minbar*, following the arson in the al-Aqsa Mosque in 1969, and additional restorations of the Dome of the Rock cupola between 1992 and 1994.

Structurally, up until 1978, the Antiquities Ordinance of 1928 remained in effect as the primary legal reference for cultural heritage—along with most of the general legislation enacted during the Mandate period—at which point it was replaced by the Israeli Antiquities Law.[22] Whereas many formalities that regulated fieldwork under British rule were adopted under Israeli governance, the new realities of rapid urban growth along with the massive excavation activity imposed an updated structure for the oversight of archaeological heritage. New rules regarding the discovery and the scientific and commercial handling of antiquities were formulated.

Though the continued surveys and excavations carried out by Israelis in West Jerusalem led to the discovery of innumerable archaeological remains, only some of them were preserved in their original locations or in nearby museums. The majority of them were sacrificed for the benefit of urban development.[23] Given the astonishingly rapid and expansive urban growth of the city, the difficulty of preserving all or most antiquities is hardly surprising or unusual. The cost of such preservation would have been exorbitant and unrealistic. In contrast, the preservation of archaeological remains in East Jerusalem, and specifically in the Historic Basin, has been dealt with differently, and the Israeli government has been exceedingly generous in allocating municipal and national funds to the display and preservation of archaeological sites and artifacts.[24] Numerous museums and parks, expanding above and below the ground, have been established.

ISRAELI ADMINISTRATION

Since Israel's capture of East Jerusalem, governmental policies as they pertain to matters of cultural heritage have been based on two legislative concepts: the 1967 Protection of Holy Places Law and the 1978 Antiquities Law. The first law, under article 1, guarantees that holy places are "protected from desecration and any other violation and anything likely to violate the freedom of access of the members of the different religions to the places sacred to them or their feelings with regard to those places." Israel has officially recognized the Ottoman Status Quo of the Christian Holy Places and has made only some minor adjustments to the Mandatory status quo arrangement with regard to the Temple Mount / Haram al-Sharif.[25] The Palestine Order in Council (Holy Places) 1924, as originally enacted by the British Mandate government, ruled that all cases concerning worshippers, members of religious communities, and holy sites should be excluded from the civil courts and can thus be overruled by the British high commissioner.[26] Under Israeli rule, the 1967 Protection of Holy Places Law was first administered by the Israeli minister of religious affairs, but after the disbanding of the Ministry of Religious Affairs in 2004, authority over decisions regarding designated holy places has resided with the prime minister.[27] Religious and potentially sensitive matters concerning cultural heritage have thus gradually moved away from legal frameworks and are increasingly handled by political authorities.

The 1978 Antiquities Law also plays a key role in defining and protecting cultural heritage in Israel. Based on the Mandatory ruling for the protection and preservation of indigenous antiquities—defined as "any object [that] was made by man before 1700 C.E., or any zoological or botanical remains from before the year 1300 C.E."—the Antiquities Law establishes state ownership of antiquity sites, monuments, and artifacts. Hence, it accords the IAA as a governmental institution the power to excavate, preserve, study, and publish archaeological finds. This responsibility includes major public-policy decisions regarding the development and urban planning around heritage sites.[28]

Among the more problematic aspects of this law is the fact that it does not provide legal protection to antiquities that postdate 1700 C.E., thereby leaving three centuries of heritage unprotected.[29] It is only recently that excavations have documented this more recent history. Several large-scale excavations conducted immediately after Israel's capture of East Jerusalem reserved their primary focus on remains from the so-called First and Second Temple periods, including those in Silwan (City of David excavations) and in the Jewish Quarter and around the southwest corner of the Haram al-Sharif (Southern Temple Mount excavations).[30] Excavations conducted since roughly the mid-1990s, on the other hand, have been far more meticulous in exposing and recording all construction and deposit layers evenly, thus doing justice to the official category of salvage work. Examples include the recent initiatives carried out in the Western Wall Tunnels and near the New Gate, which even show evidence of the destruction from the 1948 and 1967 wars.[31] Conservation, preservation, and display practices, however, do not reflect this professional development; they continue to highlight the material culture most relevant to the city's Jewish origin.

According to the IAA's mission statement, significant efforts are invested in the preservation and presentation of antiquities. Their conservation department *(minhal shimur)* aims to safeguard the cultural assets and built heritage in Israel "from a national point of view." "This heritage," according to the official definition, "is a mosaic of cultures that have existed in the region from the dawn of humanity until the present."[32] The ultimate authority to preserve or destroy sites lies in the hands of IAA's director-general and requires the approval of the Ministerial Committee for Holy Places.[33] In other words, the current administrative framework reserves the power to decide what aspects of the heritage should be highlighted to a governmental body, in which the professional archaeological voice plays only a marginal role.

To underline and formalize the governmental link to all archaeological activity in the country, the Knesset Lobby for Archaeology was established in 1996, assisting the IAA in accomplishing its tasks. The lobby's work is based on the view that archaeological sites and artifacts constitute the cultural heritage of Israel. In theory, it embraces tolerance toward members of all religious and cultural groups, but in practice, it reserves ultimate control and decisions regarding the protection and preservation of cultural heritage in the name and interest of the Jewish state, which openly and explicitly prioritizes its Jewish citizens and their religion, traditions, and cultural roots.

PALESTINIAN EFFORTS

Given the lack of an official Palestinian-controlled municipality in Jerusalem, various independent administrative bodies have adopted social, cultural, economic, and political, functions that attend to the needs and customs of the local non-Jewish population.[34] The efforts of the Waqf in service to the Islamic Palestinian community have included the preservation of cultural heritage. Since 1983, this work has been supplemented by the Palestinian Welfare Association, which is dedicated to the cultural heritage of both the Christian and Muslim populations. The significantly reduced authority of the city's Islamic leadership following the Israeli occupation in 1967 has led to a highly complicated situation regarding the administration of sites previously under Islamic ownership and, most significantly, the preservation of the city's monuments which hold a sacred significance to Muslims, locally, regionally, and internationally.[35] The unresolved power struggle among Jordan, Israel, and the Palestine Liberation Organization (PLO) has contributed to the recent growing presence and leading role of the Islamic Movement in Israel in the preservation of cultural heritage.[36]

The first Islamic Waqf foundations in Jerusalem were created as early as the mid-seventh century. It was not until the Ayyubid period that these foundations began to play an important role in the economic, political, and cultural life of the city of Jerusalem. Since 1967—at which point the Jerusalem Waqf was absorbed into the newly established Jordanian Ministry of Islamic Affairs and Awqaf—it is mostly known for controlling and managing the Islamic buildings on the Haram, but their property, encompasses about half of the Old City, and thus determines most of the urban landscape and architectural framework.[37] From the time of British rule, the Waqf administration *(idarat al-awqaf)* has been strongly identified with efforts to preserve the Arab and Islamic character of the city.

Numerous building projects were initiated under Ayyubid ruler Salah al-Din, with a further significant increase occurred during the Mamluk period.[38] The Abu Madyan foundations constituted one of the most important assets in the city. Encompassing most of the Mughrabi Quarter, it was founded in 1320 C.E. and destroyed during the construction of the Western Wall Plaza of 1967. Since Israel's occupation of East Jerusalem, the Jerusalem Waqf administration is accountable to the Ministry of Waqf in Amman. A director-general in Jerusalem oversees its multiple departments, which include Islamic archaeology, engineering and maintenance, the al-Aqsa Mosque Restoration Project, and pilgrimage affairs. Though the Israeli government does not legally recognize the Waqf administration—and the latter rejects Israeli jurisdiction—in 1967 Israel conceded the management and maintenance of the Haram platform and all associated buildings to the Waqf.[39] Before the outbreak of the Second Intifada in September of 2000, some informal contacts existed between individuals on both sides. Since the beginning, however, cooperation on matters touching upon the preservation of cultural property has been minimal.[40] Most of the restoration projects carried out under the auspices of the Jerusalem Waqf concern domestic structures, a program that in most places would be carried out by an antiquities department or housing ministry.[41] One major Waqf project is the al-Aqsa Mosque Restoration Project, which in 1986 was granted the Aga Khan Award for Islamic Architecture. This project concerns primarily the fourteenth-century painted decorations of the dome interior, using the *trateggio* technique, a method in which fine vertical lines are used to distinguish reconstructed areas from original ones.

In 1983 the Welfare Association was established to support Palestinian development throughout the region. It is a Palestinian NGO, based in Geneva, that finances and implements restoration projects in the Old City through its technical branch, known as the Center for Development Consultancy (CDC). In 1995, the Welfare Association, in cooperation with the Islamic Waqf and UNESCO, launched the ambitious Old City of Jerusalem Revitalization Program (OCJRP), dedicated to the preservation of historical monuments and to the creation of a better quality of life for residents. In addition to restoring ancient monuments, the project aims to provide training and education opportunities to the local population and to raise public awareness of the value of historic buildings. To date, the program has supported over 160 projects, including domestic structures—either single buildings of two or three floors housing one or two families or traditional residential complexes *(hosh)* that comprise several units built around a central courtyard, which are inhabited by up to ten families. Additional work is geared toward the restoration of public buildings, both secular and religious, including hostels, madrasas (religious schools), churches, and mosques. One exemplary public monument is the Dar al-Aytam al-Islamiya complex, also a recipient of the Aga Khan Award for Islamic Architecture, which was restored between 1999 and 2004. The structure consists of five buildings from the Mamluk and Ottoman periods, with the earliest dating to 1388. Another project concerns al-Imara al-Amira (Khassaki Sultan) and Dar al-Sitt Tunshuq, which in 1921–22 were combined and transformed into an orphanage. These along with several other buildings serve a variety of educational purposes.

The Palestinian contribution to the preservation of cultural heritage in Jerusalem is clearly a difficult task. Unlike the Israeli mission, which is government controlled and administered through an efficiently organized and unified network, Palestinian efforts are still relatively fragmented. The preservation of the Haram, the most significant historic and religious Islamic monument in the city, is hampered by competing administrative authorities (Jordan, Israel, the PLO, and, more recently, the Islamic Movement in Israel). No unified program exists for the preservation of East Jerusalem's cultural assets, despite significant progress in recent years. The existence of separate administrative powers for the city's Islamic and Christian heritages also accounts, at least partially, for the absence of a cohesive program and centralized management. Finally, public attention, both local and international, to cultural heritage has been overshadowed by sociopolitical, economic, and humanitarian problems and conditions, which tend to be considered higher priorities among most agencies that provide financial and logistical support.

UNESCO INITIATIVES

UNESCO's definition and appreciation of Jerusalem's cultural heritage covers a broad chronological and thematic spectrum of the city's legacy. Distinct from the IAA's main focus on the "excavated, archaeological and built heritage" of the city, UNESCO's principal concern is with the "tangible and intangible" attributes of the city's past and present cultures. It complements the activities of the IAA and, in fact, invests primarily in those areas that are a low priority to the Israeli governmental institutions.

As early as 1968, soon after Israel captured East Jerusalem, UNESCO issued its first condemnation of Israeli archaeological activity in the Old City, objecting to any attempt to alter its "features or its cultural and historical character, particularly with regard to Christian and Islamic religious sites."[42] It was not until UNESCO's World Heritage Convention of 1972, however, that a system enabling member states to nominate sites for inclusion on the World Heritage List (WHL) was established. This method was designed to protect and manage natural and cultural heritage sites considered of outstanding universal value. On the initiative of Jordan, Jerusalem's Old City was declared a World Heritage Site (WHS) in 1981, and the following year it was inscribed on the List of World Heritage in Danger (LWHD).[43] The significance of listing the Old City on both the WHL and the LWHD has been to endorse the principle that its heritage belongs to all and that it therefore requires protection by the international community.

In 1973 the first official UNESCO representative for Jerusalem was appointed, charged with reporting on the evolution of the urban fabric of the city. Until the mid-1990s, relations between UNESCO and Israel were relatively friendly, which chronologically—and to some extent ideologically—coincided with Professor Raymond Lemaire's tenure as director general of UNESCO's Special Representative on Jerusalem between 1971 and 1997.[44] Though mostly supportive of Israel's preservation activities, from the beginning UNESCO repeatedly criticized the excavations at the southwest corner of the Haram al-Sharif (Southern Temple Mount excavations), which, according to international opinion, were illegal.[45] UNESCO also questioned the tunnel project north of the Western Wall Plaza (Western Wall Tunnels excavations), both with regard to its ideological mission and the scientific methods used. The dire state of Jerusalem's Islamic heritage also became apparent early on.

In 1987, in response to an appeal, UNESCO created a Special Account for the Safeguarding of the Cultural Heritage, focusing in particular on the Islamic monuments of Jerusalem.[46] This effort led to a tripartite cooperation between UNESCO, the Islamic Waqf, and the Welfare Association, formalized in 1997. This partnership enabled various renovation and restoration programs with the primary goal of encouraging and increasing the permanent residence of Palestinian Muslims in the Old City. [47] These efforts included the surveying and mapping of historic buildings, restoration work of the Dome of the Rock and the al-Aqsa Mosque along with training programs in conservation methods, and finally various social-outreach programs to support the local community.

The heightened political tensions in the region during the Second Intifada and the almost daily clashes between Israeli and Palestinians in Jerusalem prompted UNESCO to send a special delegation to the city to once again reassess the state of conservation. The inspection resulted in the Action Plan for the Safeguarding of the Cultural Heritage of the Old City, along with the formal acknowledgment that the cultural heritage of Jerusalem encompasses not only the WHS, but also museum collections and archives, as well as the city's intangible heritage and spiritual values. The first phase of the plan, consisting of a unified database featuring all of Jerusalem's heritage resources, was initiated in January 2005 and has since been completed. In 2008 the second phase was launched, designed to support an apprenticeship program to train local craftsmen, targeting mostly Jerusalem residents.

Structurally, the Action Plan encompasses multiple projects for the conservation of ancient monuments, streets, and open spaces. Within this context, numerous residential and commercial buildings have been renovated, with the dual aim of preserving the city's unique urban landscape and improving the living quality of its inhabitants. Noteworthy examples include the rehabilitation of the al-Saha Compound facades, the conservation project of the St. John Prodromos Church, the establishment of a Centre for Restoration of Islamic Manuscripts located in the Madrassa al-Ashrafiyyah, and, finally, the safeguarding, refurbishment, and revitalization of the Islamic Museum of the Haram al-Sharif and its collection. Most of these efforts provide education and training opportunities for local residents. In spite of numerous collaborative efforts between UNESCO and Palestinian organizations over the years, it was not until October 2011 that Palestinians were granted full membership of UNESCO.[48] Significantly less effective than most of these proactive initiatives benefiting primarily Jerusalem's Palestinian communities were UNESCO's attempts to impact Israeli initiatives. For instance, efforts to halt the City of David and Mughrabi Gate excavations or the planned constructions of the Kedem Center in Silwan and the Beit Haliba Building opposite the Western Wall have mostly failed.

Contrary to UNESCO's claims to be a nonpolitical agency and to be operating on behalf of the cultural heritage of all humankind, their activities have often been perceived as partial, both locally and internationally. Symptomatic of their difficulty to maintain a neutral position is the recent Memorandum of Understanding on Cooperation between UNESCO and Israel, a document recognizing and acknowledging existing partnership and heritage commitments, signed in 2008. To Israelis, this agreement represents an official recognition of their role in Jerusalem; to Palestinians, however, it signals UNESCO's adherence to the political normalization process, legitimizing Israeli occupation of the city. Official and unofficial discussions and meetings between UNESCO representatives and Israeli officials regarding the possibility of extending the area inscribed on the WHL were initiated around the same time. Israelis proposed incorporating Mount Zion and other sites outside the city walls into the officially protected area.[49]

In spite of these isolated attempts to cooperate, however, in particular with regard to verbal or written efforts of communication, relations between Israel and UNESCO have deteriorated further over the course of the last two decades.[50] Indicative of the tense relationship is the difficulty UNESCO showed in selecting representatives acceptable to the Israeli authorities and the repeated short-term appointments.[51] Furthermore, UNESCO's harsh criticism of Israeli archaeological activity—along with their explicit support of Islamic and, to some extent, Christian monuments, and more generally, their support of Palestinian cultural heritage and the living Palestinian community—is viewed by the Israeli community as proof of a pro-Palestinian and anti-Israeli agenda.

There is no doubt that UNESCO's role as an independent mediator and global guardian of threatened world heritage has been compromised by the difficult social and political climate in Jerusalem.[52] To some, their impotence and inability to protect Jerusalem's cultural heritage is in fact more apparent than their efficacy in preserving its tangible and intangible legacies.[53]

OTHER AGENCIES

Additional local establishments dedicated to the city's cultural heritage include Elad and the Western Wall Heritage Foundation, both actively involved in the excavation and presentation of archaeological findings.[54] As their activities are almost exclusively focused on the Jewish narrative (excluding the Christian and Muslim heritage) of the ancient city, their initiatives are criticized internationally.

Locally, their activities are countered by Emek Shaveh, an organization of Israeli archaeologists and community activists focusing on "the role of archaeology in Israeli society and in the Israeli-Palestinian conflict." In their view, "the cultural wealth of the archaeological sites is an integral part of the cultural assets of this country and is the joint property of all the communities, peoples and religious groups living here."[55] Most of Emek Shaveh's initiatives are dedicated to the city of Jerusalem, including lectures, tours, and publications. An additional local organization, mentioned previously, is the Islamic Movement in Israel, which is dedicated to preserving the Islamic heritage of the city. Similar to the way cultural heritage, ideology, and politics are intertwined for many of the organizations discussed earlier, the cultural heritage program designed by Islamic Movement in Israel is also imprinted with a clear ideological and political agenda.[56]

An international organization involved in the cultural heritage of Jerusalem, the Alliance to Restore Cultural Heritage in Jerusalem (ARCH), was established in 2010 in Geneva, Switzerland. Their research activities focus both on the physical and nonphysical aspects of the city's cultural heritage, as stipulated by UN resolutions.[57] ARCH's interests encompass "archaeology, architecture, antiquities, holy sites, historical monuments, manuscripts and culturally significant landscapes," as well as intangible aspects of cultural heritage, such as "language and dialects, oral histories, traditional festive rituals and ceremonies, handicrafts, folklore, music, dance and other indigenous arts."[58]

HERITAGE BELOW AND ABOVE THE GROUND

Several communities, nations, and multiple organizations thus share the ambition to preserve the city's cultural heritage. Unlike Israel's imposed monopoly over excavations in Jerusalem, administered through the governmental agencies of the IAA (or the IDAM before 1990) and the INPA, other aspects of the city's cultural heritage are either partly or fully handled by other institutional bodies. The Waqf operates on behalf of the Muslim population and the Welfare Association in the interest of the Palestinian community in general. Representing the international community, UNESCO supplements the efforts and initiatives of those major local organizations. In spite of the common claim that these initiatives are not politically motivated, it has proved difficult and even impossible to maneuver without becoming entangled with the diverse political and ideological agendas of the different groups and institutions implicated in the construction of Jerusalem's origin narratives and the preservation of the city's cultural legacy.

The focus of Israeli activity contributing to the preservation of the city's cultural heritage consists of massive excavation, mostly (or consistently for projects in East Jerusalem) presented as salvage work, dedicated to the exposure of material remains that can be linked to the roughly six hundred years of disrupted Israelite and later Jewish sovereignty in the city. Given the increasingly limited open land above ground, over the last two decades, much of this activity is conducted underground, creating an intricate network of tunnels and spaces that serve not only as the working space of numerous archaeologists, staff, and laborers, but also as a rapidly growing destination for local visitors and international tourists. The goal to create a tangible link between the city's Jewish past and the Zionist return to the Holy Land has been stated often and explicitly. This physical and ideological connection has enabled a concrete justification of the appropriation of land, particularly relevant in the realm of Israeli's policy of a united Jerusalem, building restrictions for Palestinian residents, and development of archaeology, tourism, and Jewish building initiatives in East Jerusalem.[59]

Palestinian activity in support of the city's cultural heritage is dedicated to the preservation of the Haram platform and numerous standing monuments within the Christian and Muslim quarters of the Old City. The 1,300 years of almost uninterrupted Islamic rule constitute the chronological focus, encompassing the Umayyad Dome of the Rock as well as countless churches, mosques, and vernacular buildings from the Ayyubid, Mamluk, and Ottoman periods, which still largely determine the present character of the Old City. The main objective of this activity is to protect the living community, to raise awareness of Palestinian cultural heritage, to improve housing conditions, and to educate and train locals in preservation and conservation techniques.[60]

Israeli archaeological activity in East Jerusalem is mostly dedicated to uncovering hidden layers by excavating and creating underground levels. It can be viewed as a dubious attempt to compensate for and overshadow the exposed built heritage, which is often of monumental dimensions and mostly Christian and Islamic in character.

Given the absence of a political resolution and international consensus regarding the status of Jerusalem, as well as the lack of coordination and agreement among the various players in charge of or advocating for the city's cultural heritage, implementing a comprehensive plan for the protection of the city's cultural heritage has proved extremely difficult.

There is increased attention to matters of cultural heritage in Jerusalem, more carefully designed principles and legal concepts regulating excavation and preservation procedures, and a growing number of communities and institutions dedicated to these initiatives, but these factors are hindered by the principal players' opposing interests. Efforts to preserve the city's Palestinian heritage are regrettably scattered and, as a result, largely inefficient. Interventions to preserve and construct the Israeli legacy, in contrast, are increasingly coordinated, centralized, and powerful.

4

Display and Presentation

In late 1947, a group of senior Jewish archaeologists gathered to discuss the future of the Palestine Archaeological Museum (PAM). Their wish was to maintain this "unique centre of knowledge" so as not to disrupt the scientific completeness of the collection and compromise its cultural and public merit.

> Whatever the future of the land of Israel, there is no doubt that its past is one and united, and must be learned as one unit. This is possible archaeologically only in a central museum of the entire land. . . . Dividing the museum will be against Jewish interests, for the study of the past of the land is important in maintaining the living, organizing relations between the people and its land. This connection is one of the sure means to induce Zionist conscience in the hearts of the people. . . . We need to act in the best way possible to ease that study, and not to burden it. Furthermore, we must strive to maintain and develop our cultural positions in Jerusalem. . . . Dozens of thousands of tourists and immigrants will visit Jerusalem in the future. By keeping our interest in the museum, which thousands of foreign people will visit, we maintain a valuable means of propaganda and influence.[1]

Defining a museum as a "means of propaganda and influence" may appear radical. However, it is not unique to Jerusalem or the period in question. Napoleon's concept of a museum as an agent for nationalistic fervor, after all, had a profound and long-lasting influence throughout Europe and numerous art museums around the world. Even today's "encyclopedic collections," born of the Enlightenment, which claim to promote a greater understanding of humanity, are being examined for a lack of political neutrality and suspected for their implicit support of imperialisms, past and present.[2]

Any ancient artifact or monument that is taken out of its original context and displayed in a museum takes on an entirely new meaning. Curators may strive to represent the artifact in a specific cultural context, but it is often reduced to little more than an aesthetically pleasing object. Similar choices determine conservation policies of archaeological sites, where specific layers or structures are preserved to the detriment of others, as if they were representative of an entire region or culture—a claim that is difficult to sustain as ruins are, by definition, partial.

Contrary to the intentions expressed during the 1947 meeting of archaeologists regarding the PAM, the collection never gained much public attention, even after control of the buildings fell into Israeli hands in 1967. Officially renamed the Rockefeller Museum, it has housed the head offices of the IDAM (and, as of 1990, the IAA), and thus many major decisions regarding the management and execution of archaeological activity, as well as the policies of Jerusalem's cultural heritage, have been made within the confines of the complex. Very few visitors, however, and hardly any Israelis—as a result of its location in the city's Arab sector—have explored the displays of the museum's showcases, especially after the First and Second Intifadas (1987–91 and 2000–05). More importantly—and also in contrast to the intentions expressed in the 1947 meeting—the completeness of the collection was compromised by the removal of a number of significant artifacts to other museums that have been more readily accessible to Israeli and Jewish visitors.

Numerous other museums and open-air facilities, both in East and West Jerusalem, have enabled the presentation of local antiquities. Other than the PAM, two additional museums were established in the city prior to 1947: the Islamic Museum of the Haram al-Sharif and the Museum for Jewish Antiquities on Mount Scopus. During Jordanian rule, the Israel Museum was built in West Jerusalem to enable Jewish residents, not allowed to visit the Old City, to view some of the country's principal antiquities collections. Upon Israel's 1967 capture of East Jerusalem, numerous parks, monuments, and additional museums in and around the Old City as well as in West Jerusalem were established to present the city's historical and archaeological heritage to the public.

The display and presentation of archaeological finds in Jerusalem, including artifacts, monuments, and sites, have been the subject of both high praise and harsh criticism. Accomplishments and failures in this context can be best measured and appreciated in light of the recommendations made by the International Council on Monuments and Sites (ICOMOS), which were approved in 1990. Article 7 of the ICOMOS charter, which underlines the significance of presenting archaeological findings and disseminating information, states that "the presentation of the archaeological heritage to the general public is an essential method of promoting an understanding of the origins and development of modern societies. At the same time, it is the most important means of promoting an understanding of the need for its protection. Presentation and information should be conceived as a popular interpretation of the current state of knowledge, and it must therefore be revised frequently. It should take account of the multifaceted approaches to an understanding of the past."[3] Much effort, time, and funding has been invested to promote Israel's Jewish origins through the lens of its archaeological heritage. Artifacts, monuments, and sites in the Old City and beyond have been mobilized to inform the wider public: in the streets, in parks, in museums. And the approaches to display and interpret the city's antiquities are indeed multifaceted, but also surprisingly unified in the message they promote.

NATIONAL PARKS

Jerusalem is one of the region's fastest growing cities, and yet compared to many other urban centers, public green spaces and open areas are abundant. Numerous national parks (see figure 15) have been established by the Israeli government and enhance the impression of a sparsely built and carefully planned city. These parks provide a natural and particularly attractive setting for archaeological findings, both embracing and contrasting the city's architectural heritage. As a governmental agency, the INPA is charged with the protection of nature, landscape, and heritage, which includes Jerusalem's Old City as a World Heritage Site (WHS) and the city's national parks. Contrary to popular belief, however, the Old City itself is not a national park.[4] The city's national parks, established after Israel's capture of the Old City and East Jerusalem, form a nearly continuous and only sparsely built territory between the walled city and the eastern municipal boundary—with the exception of the densely populated Silwan neighborhood.[5] The natural and archaeological heritage, however, plays only a minor role in the decision to gradually expand the territory of these parks.

The Jerusalem Walls National Park (also known as the City of David National Park) and the Tzurim Valley National Park are officially declared national parks. The Mount Scopus Slopes National Park and the King's Valley National Park are in advanced stages of planning.[6] It is important to note that all INPA decisions regarding the preservation of archaeological remains within the confines of those parks and the way in which the antiquities are presented to the public are made in conjunction with the IAA.

Established in 1974, the Jerusalem Walls National Park covers some 1,100 *dunams* (ca. 270 acres).[7] It represents the city's most important national park and one of the country's most significant ones. This park spreads far beyond the area popularly known as the City of David, which has recently turned into a major tourist attraction. It encompasses the entire Ottoman city wall, including the gates giving access to the Old City as well as the Ophel Garden (also known as the Jerusalem Archaeological Park). This zone was originally designed by the British to form a ring around the Old City, separating the ancient and medieval nucleus from the

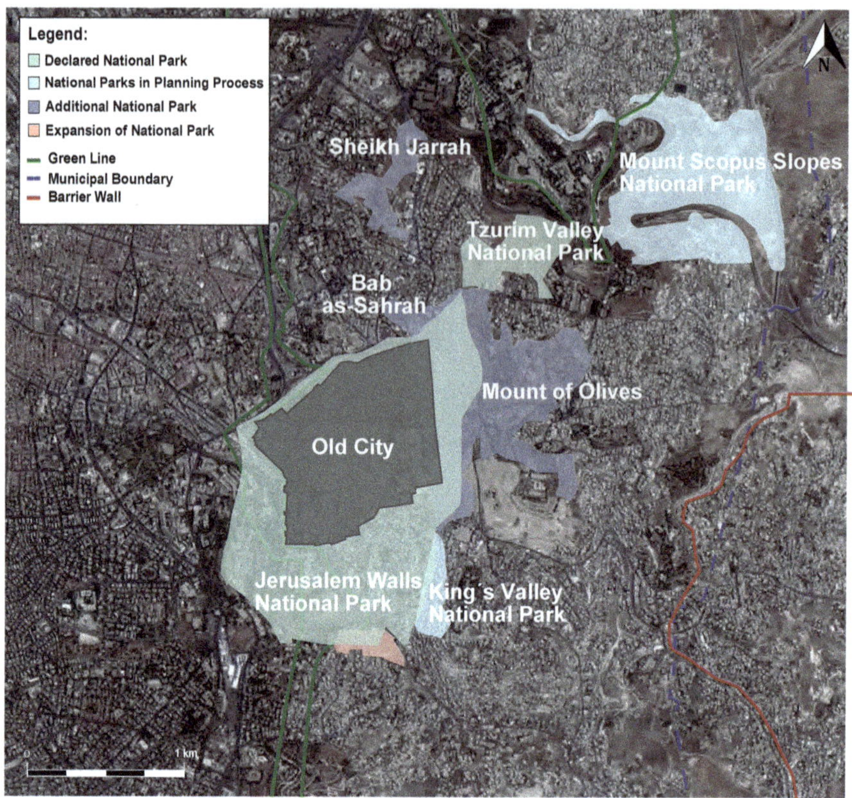

FIGURE 15. Map showing national parks. Redrawn by Franziska Lehmann, after: *Bimkom: From Public to National. National Parks in East Jerusalem*, Map 1.

new constructions outside the walls. The combined use of modern design ideas and the preservation of the ancient "biblical city" is yet another concept that Israel inherited from the British, rooted in much wider instances of colonial visual culture and modern cityscape and landscape visions.[8] Beyond fostering a sacred landscape, the park established under Israeli rule has also prevented new construction near the walls' exterior face and has served as a territorial link between disconnected areas captured by Israel in 1967, now encompassing the Jerusalem Walls National Park and the Tzurim Valley National Park.

Significant efforts and funds have been invested in the preservation of the archaeological remains, their presentation to the public, and in the overall development of the area for the city's expanding tourist industry. Excavations and surveys within the confines of Jerusalem Walls National Park have been carried out under Ottoman, British, and Jordanian rule, and they were intensified and expanded significantly under Israeli rule, beginning in 1967. Important heritage sites and monuments include the archaeological remains in Silwan and around the southwestern corner of the Temple Mount / Haram al-Sharif, as well as numerous historic buildings that spread to the east, south, and west of the Old City. Most significant among these are the Church of St. Peter in Gallicantu on the eastern slope of Mount Zion; the Tombs of Absalom, Jehoshaphat, Bnei Hezir, and Zechariah aligned in the Kidron Valley; the Tomb of the Prophets, the Grotto of Gethsemane, and the Churches of Dominus Flevit, St. Mary Magdalene, the Assumption, and the Basilica of the Agony spread throughout the western slope of the Mount of Olives; and, finally, the Tombs of Ketef Hinnom and Akeldama, St. Andrew's Church, and the Monastery of St. Onuphrius in the Hinnom Valley.[9] Major conservation and development efforts initiated in 1994 were carried out by the Ministry of Tourism, the Jerusalem Municipality, the IAA, and the East Jerusalem Development Company (PAMI), with increased investment in excavation and publication presentation efforts after 2002. These efforts have been largely dedicated to the two large-scale excavations carried out in Silwan (City of David excavations) and in the Ophel Garden around the southwestern corner of the Haram (Southern Temple Mount excavations), turning this general area into one of the most frequently visited national parks in the country. Exposed ruins range in date between the Chalcolithic period and the Mamluk era.[10] Conservation efforts and periods highlighted for public presentation, however, almost exclusively focus First and Second Temple period structures and layers.[11]

Declared a national park in 2000, the Tzurim Valley National Park is located northeast of the Old City on the slopes of Mount Scopus and the Mount of Olives, spreading toward the Kidron Valley. Extending over 165 *dunams* (ca. 40 acres), it was designed to recreate the "biblical landscape." The park includes and is surrounded by agricultural terraces and olive groves. Though no major archaeological remains have been uncovered within the confines of the park, the so-called Temple Mount Sifting Project—also known as the Temple Mount Antiquities Salvage Operation—has been hosted on its grounds since 2004.[12] The project is dedicated to examining construction debris from the Haram compound.

The Mount Scopus Slopes National Park is located between the Old City and the urban settlement of Ma'aleh Adumim, located in the West Bank. The area designated for the park measures approximately 730 *dunams* (ca. 180 acres). Archaeological remains in the area are relatively insignificant and poorly preserved and include a Roman- and Byzantine-period burial ground, agricultural installations, quarries, industrial facilities for the production of stone vessels, and a Byzantine church that was transformed into a roadside *khan* (inn) during the early Islamic period.[13] Another park in an advanced state of planning is the King's Valley National Park. Excavations carried out by Tel Aviv University since 2013 have not yet achieved any noteworthy results.[14] The park comprises some 50 *dunams* (ca. 12 acres) in the al-Bustan neighborhood of Silwan and is planned as an integral part of the Old City Historic Basin.[15]

Jerusalem is the first city in which the Israeli government planned and declared built environments as national parks. Given the limited nature and heritage value for most of the surface enclosed within the areas designated or planned as national parks, and only minor enclaves of archaeological remains, the establishment of these parks is clearly linked with other known efforts of the Israeli government and the Jerusalem Municipality to prevent the development of Palestinian neighborhoods.[16] These efforts are tied to the larger goal of fostering a Jewish territorial continuity around the Old City and in East Jerusalem, preventing any possibility of dividing the city, and circumventing clear-cut US governmental and international opposition to settlement.[17]

THE JEWISH QUARTER

Additional antiquities sites integrated into Jerusalem's urban fabric are featured in the Jewish Quarter. Located in the southeastern sector of the Old City, it represents one of its four traditional quarters. Its area stretches from the Zion Gate in the south, borders the Armenian Quarter to its west, runs parallel to the Street of the Chain in the north, and extends and incorporates the Western Wall, marking its eastern boundary.

Following the 1967 war, the government of Israel established the Jewish Quarter Development Company (JQDC) with the goal of developing it as a "national, religious, historic and cultural site, stressing its unique style and character."[18] This historic sector of the Old City, the planning and reconstruction of which was completed in 1975, was intended to be one of Israel's main heritage tourism attractions.[19]

The poor condition of the quarter prior to these refurbishment efforts was a result of destruction and neglect of the historic buildings during Jordanian rule, aggravated by damage incurred during the war of 1967. After the first archaeological discoveries in 1969, a decision had to be made regarding the excavation and development efforts. Two options were considered: to preserve the neighborhood as a "living museum" inhabited by real people or to establish the area as an archaeological park.[20] Ultimately, the decision was taken to systematically raze most of the dilapidated quarter.[21] This destruction provided opportunities for both archaeologists and developers, whose overlapping efforts and needs were managed by architects, planners, and archaeologists working jointly under the aegis of the JQDC and the IDAM. The 1978 Antiquities Law, prohibiting what Israel would later regard as illegal destruction and construction, had not been passed yet, thus enabling the demolition of countless historic buildings. At the time of the restoration project, the only convention that Israel had inherited from the British, stipulated that before new construction could begin in the ruined Jewish Quarter, preliminary excavations had to be carried out.[22]

The Jewish Quarter excavations were conducted by Nahman Avigad between 1969 and 1982.[23] Spreading over an area of 20 *dunams* (ca. 5 acres), representing about 20 percent of the total surface of the neighborhood and one of the largest excavations in the State of Israel, some twenty-five trenches were opened. Discoveries included fortifications and buildings from the Iron Age and the Hellenistic and early Roman periods, as well as the Byzantine Cardo and Nea Church complex. Archaeological and architectural remains from the early and late Islamic periods were almost completely erased and only few of them were recorded. A selection of excavated sites and monuments, featuring the First and Second Temple periods and reflecting the Jewish narrative of the city, were preserved and incorporated into the urban fabric of the Jewish Quarter. The archaeological highlights representing the First Temple period are the Israelite Tower and the Broad Wall; those representing the Second Temple period are the Wohl Archaeological Museum and the Burnt House.

The Israelite Tower (part of the Iron Age fortification system), located in the basement of a modern building in the outskirts of the quarter, is presented to the visitor as "one of the most impressive testimonies to the strength and might of Jerusalem during the First Temple period."[24] The full height of this tower is not known, but 8.2 meters of it have survived above ground. The display also includes the lower courses of an adjacent tower from the late Hellenistic (Hasmonean) period.[25]

An additional remainder of the city's Iron Age fortification is the so-called Broad Wall (see figure 16); sixty-five meters of the wall survives, and it is preserved in places to a height of 3.3 meters. This find disproves the view that Jerusalem was a relatively small settlement confined to the Eastern Hill in the eighth century B.C.E.; it shows that by this time the city had expanded to the Western Hill and was an important capital of the Southern Kingdom of Judah, well prepared for an attack by the Assyrian enemy.[26] The open-air display of a segment of the wall can be viewed from street level (looking down about two meters) and is accompanied with explanatory labels and an enormous panel showing the location of the wall within the context of Jerusalem in the Second Temple period—the decades preceding the destruction of the Herodian Temple and the city in 70 C.E.

The Wohl Archaeological Museum, located in the basement of the modern Yeshivat HaKotel building—three to seven meters below street level—features the remains of several buildings from the late Second Temple period. The remains are of "an upper class quarter, where the noble families of Jerusalem lived, with the High Priest at their head."[27] These include buildings identified as the Western House, the Middle Complex, and the Palatial Mansion. The display features the basement levels with storage and water installations, many of which were used as ritual pools

FIGURE 16. Broad Wall in Jewish Quarter, looking south. Photo by Katharina Galor.

(miqva'ot). The lower and upper levels of the houses, some of which indicate a second story above ground, are decorated with stucco, polychrome frescoes, and mosaic floors (see figure 17).[28] Display cases and platforms show architectural details, fragments of stone furniture, stone objects, glassware, and ceramics, evocative of the luxurious lifestyle of the Upper City's residents. Evidence of fire damage was left in place as a reminder of the destruction caused by the Romans in 70 C.E. Labels and holograms supplement the display and facilitate and enhance the visit of this underground museum.

Visitors to the Wohl Archaeological Museum are encouraged to explore the Burnt House, which is also preserved in the basement level of another modern building, located five minutes' walking distance away. Based on the findings, including a stone weight with an inscription reading "son of Kathros," the Burnt House was identified as belonging to a wealthy family of high priests, mentioned by name in the Babylonian Talmud, written between the third and fifth centuries C.E. This find brings to life the direct link between the residential areas exposed in the Jewish Quarter and the Herodian Temple on the other side of the Central Valley. In addition to the architectural remains, several pieces of furniture and other objects found during the excavation can be seen. A sound

FIGURE 17. Mosaic floor, stone tables, and vessels in Palatial Mansion, Wohl Archaeological Museum. Photo by Katharina Galor.

and light show dramatically recreates the fall of Jerusalem under the Romans and presents the archaeological discovery as part of the Jewish Quarter's restoration program.[29]

Significant remains from the Byzantine period include the Nea Church and the Cardo (the main road in Roman and Byzantine eras). Despite the fact that the Nea Church is known as one of most important churches built by the emperor Justinian and the largest church in all of ancient Palestine, most of its remains are located in a locked building situated in a poorly accessible, neglected corner of the Jewish Quarter, with no signs indicating its location or significance.[30] The Cardo, however, is incorporated as one of the major highlights of the neighborhood.[31] The original stretch of the Cardo (today located in the Christian and Muslim Quarters) was built in late Roman period as the major thoroughfare bisecting the city from north to south, but its southern extension (partially restored in the Jewish Quarter) was built during the time of the emperor Justinian in the sixth century, possibly to facilitate pilgrims traveling between the Church of the Holy Sepulchre (erected under the emperor Constantine in the fourth century) and the newly built Nea Church. Segments of this southern extension were exposed during Avigad's excavation. From the restored open-air section of the Byzantine Cardo, visitors can continue northward along a still later section of the Cardo, built in the Crusader period. This latter section has been remodeled, covered, and transformed into an upscale shopping area featuring souvenirs and Judaica (in this context, mostly Jewish religious artifacts and ritual items).[32] The original Christian context of this principal Jerusalem thoroughfare was thus effectively redesigned without distorting the Jewish narrative of the quarter's exposed and highlighted antiquities.

The original goal of the Jewish Quarter restoration project was to blend it functionally and architecturally into the rest of the city. This initiative was intended as the first step in a large-scale restoration of the entire Old City.[33] The nature of this program deviated from the British Mandatory policy, which excluded the Old City from the modernization process. According to William McLean's town plan of 1918, the Historic Basin was to be maintained as a religious, historical, and architectural preserve.[34]

In spite of the general consensus that the JQDC project neglected numerous aspects of heritage conservation and presentation, as reflected in the Venice Charter of UNESCO (1964) and the National Historic Preservation Act of the United States (1966), it is debated whether this defiance of official regulations was unique to Israel or reflected the international norm at the time.[35] Further disagreements concern the authorities and professionals involved in the planning and execution of the project and whether other countries would also have appointed an exclusively national team (without including any international experts) to coordinate and implement a major restoration project.[36]

One of the obvious shortcomings of the project is the fact that no overall architectural and archaeological survey of the quarter's historic buildings was carried out prior to their destruction. The history of different ethnic groups living in or passing through the quarter during the medieval, Ottoman, and British Mandate periods, as well as under Jordanian rule and during the 1948 and 1967 wars, were barely documented and studied. Sites and monuments representing religious or ethnic groups other than Jewish are only minimally represented in public installations.[37] The excavated ruins highlight periods of significance to the Jewish narrative, but few remains of importance to the Christian and Muslim traditions were preserved.

Surprisingly though, the Jewish remains preserved are primarily from the First and Second Temple periods; later periods are poorly represented. Although the Protection of Holy Places Law of 1967 stipulated the renewal of desecrated synagogues, most of them were left in a state of ruin and only a few select Ottoman-period synagogues and yeshivot were restored.[38] The failure to implement the recommended renovations can be linked, at least partially, to the lack of funding. But another reason for the failure was the prevailing attitude among many Israelis at the time that medieval and early modern synagogues were of little interest to the mostly secular aspirations of the new Zionist state, an attitude which for some reason did not affect their interest in Jewish antiquities.[39] The overall excavation, preservation, and presentation policies, as designed and implemented by the JQDC, thus reflect the broader ideological goals of the State of Israel prevalent during the early decades of its existence, which only took into account a very narrow perspective with regard to the city's cultural and religious heritage. The recent ambitious reconstruction project (2000–10) of the nineteenth-century Jewish Quarter Hurva Synagogue suggests that Jewish heritage priorities have shifted since.

A NEW ARCHAEOLOGICAL CIRCUIT

Since the mid-1990s, the IAA—in cooperation with several other governmental and various private establishments, including the INPA, the East Jerusalem Development Company (PAMI), the Western Wall Heritage Foundation, and Elad—has initiated a number of new large-scale excavations in East Jerusalem. These will be transformed into cultural-heritage sites for the public. Two of these excavation projects, the Western Wall Plaza excavations (see figure 18) and the Givati Parking Lot excavations (see figure 19), are tied to the planned construction of two building complexes that will serve the administration and display of archaeological sites and finds. Some of the new discoveries, along with previously exposed remains, have been incorporated into an archaeological circuit linking a number of dispersed sites that until 2012 were disconnected (see figure 20).

The Western Wall Plaza excavations, begun in 2005 and completed in 2009, was initiated in preparation for the construction of the Beit Haliba Building, an office and conference complex for the Western Wall Heritage Foundation, which will oversee prayer and tourism at the plaza and in the Western Wall Tunnels.[40] The planned building was originally designed to be identical in height to the Western Wall and would have completely transformed the current landscape, an initiative that contravenes UNESCO rules.[41] After objections were raised by planners, Jewish Quarter residents, and archaeologists, it was decided that the size of the building would be reduced.[42] The second complex, the Kedem Center, to be built on the site of the current Givati Parking Lot excavations—which were initiated in 2003 and resumed in 2007—will incorporate offices for the City of David Visitors Center and its Megalim educational institute, as well as a Bible Museum displaying artifacts from the excavations conducted in the City of David and other sites in the city.[43] As with the case of the Beit Haliba Building, the seven-story Kedem Center will have a significant impact on the surrounding landscape, which until the establishment of the City of David Visitors Center was largely defined by residential buildings and public structures that served the local community.[44] Since the beginning of the twentieth century, some Bronze and Iron Age water installations, fortification system, and domestic complexes had been accessible to visitors. These had been presented modestly, with interconnected trails and simple explanatory labels and several display cases featuring locally found artifacts. The new infrastructure of the City of David Visitors Center, incorporating more recent discoveries from the Bronze and Iron Ages, however, completely transformed the site's profile and turned it into the city's most popular archaeological attraction. The

FIGURE 18. Western Wall Plaza excavations. Photo by Katharina Galor.

original modest presentation was replaced by a state-of-the-art tourist complex, radically transforming the residential character of the area into a magnet for the expanding tourist industry. Along with the standard labels explaining artifacts and remains, the City of David Visitors Center now offers a variety of instructional and entertaining support media, including an auditorium for the screening of a 3-D sound and light show, cafeterias, souvenir shops, well-paved pathways, rest areas, and display sections, located both above and below ground. This newly created infrastructure provides scattered archaeological remains with a unified modern architectural framework surrounded by flowers and olive trees evocative of the biblical landscape. As the original presentation did, the City of David Archaeo-logical Park highlights the biblical narrative of King David and his city built in place of the former Jebusite settlement.

In August of 2011, the so-called Herodian Street and Tunnel—created by linking several Roman street segments with a sewage channel over a 550-meter stretch—was opened to tourists.[45] The tunnel is presented by the IAA as a trail used in the Second Temple period by pilgrims climbing toward the Temple.[46] It conducts visitors from the Siloam Pool in Silwan to the Western Wall Plaza. The Western Wall Tunnels, ac-cessible from north of the plaza, lead visitors along the western enclosure wall of the Haram platform, debouching in the Muslim Quarter. Features highlighted in the underground tour date to various late Hellenistic (Hasmonean) and early Roman (Herodian) phases of construction and use of the Jewish Temple Mount.

FIGURE 19. Givati Parking Lot excavations, looking north. Photo by Katharina Galor.

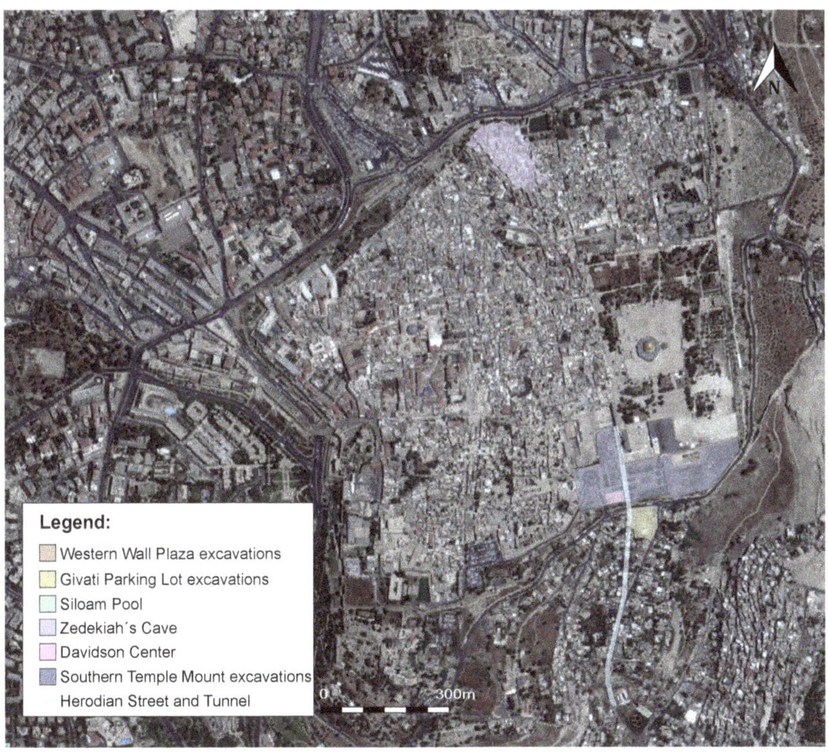

FIGURE 20. Map showing Western Wall Plaza, Mughrabi Gate, and Givati Parking Lot excavations, Herodian Street and Tunnel, Siloam Pool, Davidson Center, and Zedekiah's Cave. Drawn by Franziska Lehmann.

Another major destination accessible from the Western Wall Plaza is the Davidson Center, housed in the Ophel Garden. Significant finds in the open-air area include the southern Temple Mount staircase and entrances, Byzantine houses, and Umayyad palaces. Recently implemented changes facilitate a new route along the "Ritual Baths Lane," identified with the Jewish tradition of immersion in stepped pools *(miqva'ot)* prior to the visit at the Herodian Temple, as well as the visit of the "Ophel Walls" site, featuring several late Iron Age wall segments dating to the era of the Judean Kingdom.[47]

The Davidson Center is located within one of the Umayyad-period palaces uncovered during the Temple Mount excavations. The center's architectural design emphasizes the contrast between the modern materials used, such as wood, glass, and steel, and the massiveness of the original palace's stone walls. A short documentary film presents the story of the excavations conducted near the Temple Mount and provides the visitor with a brief historical overview. The building houses an exhibition gallery featuring artifacts from four main periods: the Second Temple, the Roman, the Byzantine, and the Islamic periods. Highlights include a digital 3-D simulation of the Herodian Temple as well as a high-definition digital video describing Jewish pilgrimage to Jerusalem during the Second Temple period.

Plans to extend the archaeological circuit to connect to further tourist sites within the Muslim Quarter of the Old City are in place.[48] Improved infrastructure in al-Wad Street will allow visitors to more easily reach Zedekiah's Cave, also known as Solomon's Quarries. This ancient limestone quarry stretches the length of five city blocks under the Muslim Quarter. It is believed to have served as the main quarry for the construction of the Herodian Temple Mount and for the Old City's walls built by Suleiman the Magnificent in the sixteenth century. Zedekiah's Cave is located between Damascus Gate and Herod's Gate in the Muslim Quarter. Excavations have been carried out at both gates. An ancient Roman gate, opened to tourists in the late 1980s, can be seen underneath the currently used Damascus Gate, built at the time of Suleiman's construction of the city wall.

Since 1967—and in particular after the First and the Second Intifadas—the main destination for Jewish and Israeli visitors in East Jerusalem has been the Jewish Quarter. The recent initiatives to link various sites in Silwan with the Jewish, Christian, and Muslims Quarters fulfills the goal to create a contiguous territory more readily accessible to both local and foreign visitors. All previous and recent excavation and conservation works in the Old City and Silwan in combination, clearly represent efforts "to fortify the Israeli hold on the Old City itself" and provide "a cover for the advancement of monumental building plans."[49] A remarkable escalation has taken place—from conducting excavations in open and accessible public areas in the immediate aftermath of Israel's capture of East Jerusalem to encroaching upon densely built residential areas, both above and below ground, since the mid 1990s. The only consistent aspect of the public presentation of archaeological finds appears to be the continued focus on the First and Second Temple periods, which together inform and remind visitors of Jerusalem's Jewish origin.

MUSEUMS

More than half a century separates Jerusalem's earliest excavations from the construction of its first museums. Originally, several significant artifacts had been shipped to Constantinople, following the standard established by the Ottoman Antiquities Law (originally passed in 1874 and revised in 1884) stipulating that finds discovered in Ottoman territory were the property of the Imperial Museum. Various factors contributed to the decision to establish facilities to store and display the region's antiquities locally. Among them was the desire to lay claim to Jerusalem's heritage and to prevent export of antiquities, reflecting a new awareness of cultural legacy prevalent during the Mandate period. Equally important was the objective to educate the public through exposure to the local and regional material culture, also a byproduct of other outreach efforts. Despite the focus on local cultures, collections and displays increasingly encompassed artifacts from other world cultures as well.[50]

Established in 1922, the Islamic Museum of the Haram al-Sharif was the first museum to be opened in Jerusalem and, in fact, in Palestine as a whole.[51] Originally located in the thirteenth-century Ribat al-Mansuri, west of the Haram near Bab al-Nazir, the collection was moved to its present location in 1929, inside the restored Crusader building additions to the west of the al-Aqsa Mosque. The museum is thus integrated into an architectural complex that houses, one of Islam's most venerated shrines. Three large halls accommodate the displays, storage facilities, and offices, all of which were formerly used as places of worship: the twelfth-century Jami' al-Magharibah, the Jami' al-Nisa in use during the Mamluk and Ottoman periods, and the fourteenth-century Madrassa al-Fakhriyah, later converted into a *zawiyyah* (Islamic monastery), whose mosque has been preserved and currently serves as an office for the museum administration. The museum was closed between 1974 and 1981, when renovations and a reorganization of the collection were carried out, under the auspices of the French Foreign Ministry. Owing to concerns over security, the museum was once again closed to the public in 1999 and has not been opened since. UNESCO, in collaboration with the Waqf administrations of Jordan and its Jerusalem branch, currently facilitates a safeguarding, refurbishment, and revitalization project, aiming to renovate the interior of the museum, to conserve, inventory, and store the collections, as well as to build capacity among the staff.[52] The reopening, however, will likely depend more on the political climate rather than on the state of the museum, the installations, and its personnel.

The collection features artifacts spanning a period of ten centuries, and encompassing many regions of the Islamic world: North Africa, Arab Asia, Turkey, Iran, and part of East Asia.[53] The vast array of Qur'an manuscripts and other objects represent endowments to the al-Aqsa Mosque, the Dome of the Rock, and other religious institutions in Jerusalem as well as several important Palestinian cities by Muslim rulers, sultans, princes, and other donors. Those gifts are indicative of the significant role the al-Aqsa Mosque and al-Quds (the Holy City) has held for Muslims from the early Islamic period onward. The collection also includes architectural details and various artifacts retrieved during restoration campaigns carried out on the Haram complex. The most notable objects from the al-Aqsa Mosque include carved wooden panels and painted architectural details from the original eighth-century structure, fragments of Nur al-Din's Ayyubid-period *minbar* as well as stained glass and gypsum windows from the Ottoman period. Among the materials collected from the Dome of the Rock are the carved and gilded marble panels from the original eighth-century construction and the glazed tiles from the Ottoman-period restorations to the exterior. Additional precious artifacts featured in the collection are incense burners, mosque lamps, candlesticks, caldrons, armor, weapons, coins, and textiles, primarily from the Mamluk and Ottoman periods.

As the most contested site in the city, and the most politically and religiously sensitive monument, the Haram and the museum, which forms an integral part of the complex, have suffered tremendously. Though under the official administration of the Waqf, the museum as all other Muslim establishments on the platform are caught in the midst of the power struggle between the local and Jordanian administrators and the Israeli government. As a focal point of tension between Muslims and Jews, Palestinians and Israelis, violent clashes on and near the Haram have led museum officials to take extreme measures with regard to display choices. Since the First Intifada, the torn and bloodied clothes of Palestinians were exhibited in a showcase near the museum entrance. This display was removed around the time the Second Intifada broke out, when access to the Dome of the Rock and the al-Aqsa Mosque became restricted to Muslim visitors only. Given the lack of coordination and adequate support, the museum—in spite of its prime location, the historic significance of the architectural setting, and the priceless nature of its collection—is not utilized to its fullest potential and advantage. Conservation and presentation standards are far below the level of Israeli museums in the city, and in spite of UNESCO's recent initiatives, much work and significant funds will be necessary to adequately preserve and present the museum's singularly important antiquities in the manner of a world-leading institution of Islamic heritage.

The establishment of the PAM was a landmark in the history of archaeology of Palestine. In 1917 the Ottoman authorities planned to transfer about six thousand antiquities from Jerusalem to Constantinople. This plan failed at the last moment, due to the declining fortunes of the Ottomans in the First World War. In the fall of 1917, the British took over Jerusalem, and the objects were ultimately left packed up and never left the city. Later, the British decided to exhibit the artifacts, which became the kernel of a museum for Palestine.[54] It was James Henry Breasted of the Oriental Institute in Chicago who, in 1925, initiated the construction of the first proper building to house and display the collection, and it was John David Rockefeller Jr. who financed the enterprise.[55] The collection was meant to represent the history of the region from the first appearance of humankind until the beginning of the eighteenth century, as reflected in archaeological finds.[56] On January 13, 1938, the doors of the museum were opened to the public. Known since as the Rockefeller Museum—in addition to its official name, PAM—it was built from quality materials in a neo-Gothic style, using a blend of Eastern and Western architectural traditions and conveying what archaeologist James Henry Breasted described as "the reverence felt by western civilization for the past of Palestine, a past which means more to the nations of the west than that of any other country."[57] Decades later, this colonial attitude found new meaning in the nationalistic goals, which the IAA promoted on a much larger scale, displaying archaeological collections in significantly grander contexts. The cornerstone of PAM was laid in 1930. The discovery of an ancient cemetery at the site, however, delayed the construction for three years. Excavations carried out on the grounds revealed tombs dating from the Hellenistic period through the Byzantine period, including a stone sarcophagus decorated in relief, funerary plaques bearing Greek inscriptions, as well as many burial gifts, such as ceramic and glass vessels, oil lamps, jewelry, and coins. The collection also features antiquities—ranging from prehistoric times through the Ottoman period—from excavations conducted during the time of the British Mandate throughout the region.[58] Highlights of the collection with a Jerusalem provenance include a third-century marble Aphrodite, several carved wooden panels and friezes from the original eighth-century al-Aqsa Mosque, and the twin portal lintels from the twelfth-century Church of the Holy Sepulchre. The current display of the collection almost fully reflects the format of the original exhibit, including the spatial organization and display cases.[59] According to the official policy adopted by Israel upon the museum's takeover in 1967, the collection was to be maintained in the state it was in.[60] In contravention of this stipulation, however, numerous artifacts have been removed to other museums, mostly on long-term loans.[61] Since Israel's occupation of East Jerusalem, the Rockefeller Museum is under the management of the Israel Museum and houses the head office of the IAA.

Hebrew University's Institute of Archaeology recently celebrated the seventieth anniversary of the Museum for Jewish Antiquities, which was established in 1941 on the Mount Scopus campus.[62] Just as the museum was going to open its door to the public, the 1948 war broke out, and the collection was removed from the campus. It was returned in 1967, when the university regained access to Mount Scopus. The original building of the Museum for Jewish Antiquities was built in the international style characteristic of Jerusalem architecture at the time. A stone brought from the excavations of the Third Wall in Jerusalem, the first archaeological project undertaken by Hebrew University, was incorporated in the facade north of the courtyard.

The creation of the museum was meant to reflect "the aspirations of the 1930s Jewish community in the pre-state Yishuv to establish cultural institutions and reinforce the link between the nation and its past."[63] An additional objective was to study other cultures in the country and its environs, including Transjordan, Egypt, Syria, Lebanon, Anatolia, Mesopotamia, Cyprus, and Greece. The collection is based on a core of artifacts from the private collections of Hebrew University archaeology professors Eliezer Sukenik and Benjamin Mazar. The original assortment of objects was supplemented by acquisitions and donations, including artifacts from the Baron Edmond de Rothschild collection and the Jewish Palestine Exploration Society. Thousands of additional pieces were acquired during the course of the institute's excavations in the country. Comprising today about thirty thousand objects, the collection includes pottery vessels, stone tools, glassware, ancient weapons, dozens of cuneiform clay tablets, Egyptian vessels, Hebrew seals, jewelry, ancient coins (with an emphasis on Jewish numismatics), and an extensive ethnographic collection. Among the most significant items from the Jerusalem area are ossuaries and burial gifts from tombs from the Second Temple period, including some discovered on the grounds of the Mount Scopus campus. Beyond those original objects, the collection also features replicas of significant finds relating to the history of the Jewish people. Other than a few objects currently on display and a few select artifacts on loan (mostly to local museums), the collection primarily serves study and research purposes. Though one of the city's earliest museums, access to the collection thus remains relatively restricted.

Of a completely different scale in terms of size, outreach, and public impact is the Israel Museum, founded in 1965 and located in Givat Ram in West Jerusalem.[64] Just a little over two years after the establishment of the State of Israel, Teddy Kollek, then director-general of the prime minister's office, conceived of a plan for an encyclopedic museum in Jerusalem that would join the ranks of the great national museums of the world's cultural capitals.[65] The original buildings, designed as a showcase of universal modernism, were recently renovated and expanded with the goal of creating a unified gallery space with improved display capacity. The archaeology, fine arts, and the Jewish art and life wings were completely redesigned, linking the original buildings with a new entrance pavilion.[66] The project was meant to reinforce the museum's "original spirit, both ideological and physically, by enhancing the power of its international modernist heritage and drawing strength from the equal power of its ancient landscape."[67] The new additions follow the same modular grid geometry of the original architectural complex. But rather than presenting opaque modular cubes clad with Jerusalem stone finishes on the exterior and concrete finishes on the interior, the new pavilions are made of glass curtain walls.

From the Israel Museum's inception, along with its exhibition halls, the grounds accommodated the offices of the IDAM, whose antiquities would be displayed for the first time rather than being kept in storerooms.[68] One of the original goals of the museum was to complement archaeological excavation and research by presenting the finds to the public, enabling the visitor to "acquire an understanding of the life of the people in ancient times and the development of the material and spiritual culture in all its aspects during their long history within the confines of the State of Israel."[69] As an attempt to counter the nationalistic tendency of Israel archaeology in the 1950s, the director of the IDAM suggested that "the national museum should include exhibitions of antiquities from other cultures, which would have 'an invaluable influence not only on the widening of the mental horizon of the Israeli public, but also on jolting it out of the rut of a national and cultural provincialism.' "[70]

The collection represents the most extensive holdings of biblical archaeology in the world, encompassing nearly half a million objects. The recently renovated and expanded Samuel and Saidye Bronfman Archaeology Wing consists of seven units.[71] The installations are organized chronologically from prehistory through the Ottoman period, weaving together significant historical events, cultural accomplishments, and technological advances, incorporating aspects of the everyday lives of the peoples of the region. Beyond the local material culture, the collection includes artifacts from Near Eastern, Greek, Roman, and Islamic cultures. In addition to the permanent collection, new discoveries and other thematic exhibits are displayed on a temporary basis. Finds uncovered in various locations in Jerusalem include several inscriptions, such as a Greek dedicatory plaque from the first-century B.C.E. Theodotos synagogue and a first-century Greek panel forbidding gentiles from entering the Temple.[72] Additional artifacts from the first century include several carved limestone ossuaries, a heel bone with an iron nail used for crucifixion still embedded in it, and fine pottery and stoneware from domestic contexts.[73] Byzantine finds include lead sarcophagi decorated with crosses, censers, and pilgrim's flasks.[74] The highlights of the local Islamic collection include a *mihrab* (a prayer niche, usually in mosques, indicating the direction of prayer toward Mecca) featured on a ninth- to tenth-century mosaic from Ramla, a Fatimid jewelry hoard from Caesarea, and a bronze hoard from Tiberias dating to the same period.[75] Relatively few artifacts from Jerusalem are displayed, all of which are minor-art objects. These include, two silver and gold jewelry assemblages from the Fatimid period and glass sprinklers and bowls from the Mamluk period.[76] Most of the Islamic artifacts featured in the galleries, however, come from regions outside Israel. This limited repertoire of local finds may be the result of earlier tendencies to discard finds and layers from early and late Islamic cultures. The inclusion of artifacts from other countries in the region may reflect the desire to compensate for this shortcoming in the recent reinstallation of the archaeological wing.

Other popular permanent exhibitions of ancient art at the Israel Museum are located in a separate building. These include the Dead Sea Scrolls, the Aleppo Codes, and other rare biblical manuscripts, which are housed in the Shrine of the Book. Furthermore, a 1:50 scale model of Jerusalem in the Second Temple period, originally constructed on the grounds of Jerusalem's Holyland Hotel, where it was displayed until 2006, can now be visited in the outdoor garden section of the Israel Museum. It replicates the city's topography and architectural features as they appeared prior to the destruction by the Romans in 70 C.E.

The museum also features temporary exhibits. The nine-month show on Herod the Great, the Jewish proxy monarch who ruled Jerusalem in the first century B.C.E., opened in February of 2013. It represented the museum's largest and most expensive archaeological project to date. The inclusion of numerous significant artifacts illegally removed from various West Bank locations, featured in Israel's national museum, brought forth severe criticism.[77] The Israel Museum thus serves both as a showcase for the region's multifaceted cultural makeup and no less as a hub for politically audacious exhibitions.

Adjacent to the Israel Museum, but built some thirty years later, stands the Bible Lands Museum, which opened its doors to the public in 1992.[78] The artifacts were donated by Batya and Elie Borowski, renowned collectors of ancient art who accumulated the collection over more than half a century and were recently implicated in the illicit trade of antiquities.[79] The permanent holdings encompass a vast array of ancient objects, revealing the numerous cultures of the ancient Near East from the "from the dawn of civilization through the roots of monotheism and early Christianity."[80] Scale models of ancient sites in Jerusalem, a Mesopotamian ziggurat, and Egyptian pyramids enhance the presentation. The galleries are organized chronologically, illustrating the technological and cultural changes that took place in lands mentioned in the Bible: from Egypt eastward across the Fertile Crescent to Afghanistan, and from Nubia northward to the Caucasian mountains. "The Biblical quotations throughout the galleries are intended to place the Biblical text into its historical context, thereby adding another dimension to our understanding of the world of the Bible."[81] Some of the themes featured in the temporary exhibits go beyond the biblical world and incorporate topics and objects from the Far East as well as classical Greece and Rome.

There is certain ambiguity in the translations of the name of the museum, all featured prominently on the entrance facade: the Bible Lands Museum in English, *Museon ha Mikrah* in Hebrew, and *Museon ha Ketub* in Arabic. Only the English version reflects the range of objects presented in its galleries, addressing the vast scope of the Judeo-Christian heritage. Both the Hebrew and the Arabic versions suggest that the museum features artifacts related to the ancient scriptures. The

Hebrew *Museon ha Mikrah* may be understood as focusing on the Hebrew Bible alone; the Arabic *Museon ha Ketub,* on themes related to the people of the books, that is, the three monotheistic religions. Other than in a small thematic exhibition called "The Three Faces of Monotheism," however, no objects pertaining to Islam are featured in the museum displays.[82]

The most recently established institution of significance is the Tower of David Museum, dedicated to the history of the city. Also known as the Jerusalem Citadel, it is located near Jaffa Gate, at a meeting point between the Old City and the New City. Apart from the Islamic Museum on the Haram al-Sharif, it is the only permanent exhibition housed in a historic building and thus represents an ideal setting for a history museum. The complex served as a citadel throughout most of its history, beginning in the Ayyubid period, with changes and additions made during the Crusader, Mamluk, and Ottoman eras. Among the most striking features are the Crusader moat surrounding the fortress and the Ottoman minaret, visible from afar and lending the whole a distinct shape that stands out as visitors approach the Old City from the east and the south (see figure 2). After initial renovations during the British Mandate period, the medieval citadel first served as a cultural center and then, from the late 1930s until 1948, as the Palestine Folk Museum. It was not until 1989 that the Tower of David Museum was opened to the public.[83] Unlike the city's publicly displayed archaeological collections, this museum never aspired to feature original artifacts. Instead, it uses a historic monument from the medieval and late Islamic periods—the building it is in—as the setting for illustrating Jerusalem's past in chronological order. Eight exhibition halls, each dedicated to a different period, are organized around an archaeological garden located in the courtyard of the medieval fortress (see figure 21). Replicas, models, reconstructions, dioramas, holograms, photographs, drawings, and audio and video recordings are used to recount the narrative.

The building in which the museum is housed is a significant documentation of the city's Islamic presence throughout the Ayyubid, Mamluk, and Ottoman periods, a timespan covering some seven hundred years, in addition to nearly hundred and fifty years of Christian rule during the Crusader period. But the structural and historical development of the building is barely documented in the museum. Other than a small-scale model on top of the roof, representing a palimpsest of Jerusalem, none of the original architectural features, details, and artifacts is adequately labeled. Those include Crusader-period capitals in the entrance hall, inscriptions from the Ayyubid and Mamluk periods, as well as the Ayyubid-period *mihrab* and Ottoman-period *minbar.* The labeling in the courtyard, featuring archaeological remains from the Iron Age through the Ottoman period, is kept to a minimum and fails to document the city's historical development on the very ground of the museum.[84]

FIGURE 21. Tower of David Museum courtyard. Photo by Katharina Galor.

The exhibit halls, which explicitly highlight the Jewish and Israeli heritage of the city, represent another curatorial decision that has invited criticism.[85] Though all major historical periods are featured, the primary focus is on events relevant to the Israelite and later Jewish presence in the city. Some of the periods represented are named according to Jewish textual sources (such as the First Temple, the Second Temple, and the Hasmonean periods), rather than conventional, neutral terminology. The last room is entirely devoted to Israel's capture of East Jerusalem, celebrating the achievement of a "united Jerusalem" under Israeli rule, with no attempt to present the Palestinian and international perspective of an occupied city.

The spatial organization and curatorial choices of the exhibition display direct the visitor's attention toward an illustrated history rather than the actual building, which merely serves as an aesthetically pleasing and atmospheric background. In the words of the museum's chief curator: "It is important to recognize that there is no such thing as an objective presentation. All presentations are based on interpretive choices, and these choices combine to tell a story. It is up to the presentation professional, in consultation with other specialists, to select which particular story will be told."[86]

And the stories told, not only in the Tower of David Museum, but in most museums throughout the city of Jerusalem, perhaps with the sole exception of the Islamic Museum of the Haram al-Sharif, seem to consistently reflect the primary interest in the Jewish narrative. The packaging, however, is increasingly sophisticated, multifaceted, and convincing.

THE CITY—A LIVING MUSEUM

The desire to preserve and display Jerusalem's archaeological heritage has always been linked to the colonial and nationalistic aspirations of fostering specific cultural and religious associations with the city and its larger region. The legal and administrative commitment to enhance the natural, built, and designed environment by projecting a certain narrative has been consistent, and has become increasingly efficient and professional, beginning with the British and acquiring new levels of excellence under Israeli rule. The first steps of increasing awareness of cultural heritage were taken during the British Mandate period, focused on the Historic Basin, speckled with monuments signaling the city's monotheistic traditions. These early initiatives were enhanced by the display of movable artifacts in Jerusalem's first museums. After a certain stagnation under Jordanian rule, the preservation and display of the city's visual and material legacies received increased attention under Israeli rule. Radical change occurred first upon Israel's capture of East Jerusalem, with the establishment of extensive archaeological and national parks, in particular in the occupied sectors of East Jerusalem and the display of artifacts in several new museums in all sectors of the city. Since the mid-1990s, this change established itself more solidly, seen in improved standards of Israeli policies, redefining rules and conventions of Jerusalem's cultural preservation and display modules. Both in the context of open-air and underground displays of archaeological sites and monuments, as well as in museum settings, conservation methods and display features have made significant progress. In recent years, the level of curatorial achievements can be compared to preservation and display modes used in major Western capitals, including Rome, London, and Paris. Thematically, however, as from the beginning of Israeli rule, presentations continue to highlight the Jewish and Israeli narrative of Jerusalem, which tend to be embedded in a seemingly multicultural setting, featuring periods that are also relevant for people of other faiths and nationalities. Thus, the general staging of antiquities over the past two decades has been committed to Zionist aspirations but is packaged in a progressively more sophisticated manner.

Exposing, presenting, and collecting antiquities that emphasize Jerusalem's Jewish legacy has clearly served the Israeli government as a most efficient means to strengthen its historical ties with the city, as well as to develop and maintain East Jerusalem and West Jerusalem as a unit. This focus on the Jewish narrative has been to the detriment of both the Christian and the Islamic heritage. In spite of financial support from UNESCO and several Arab countries, Palestinian preservation and display efforts have been modest compared to Israel's initiatives. Against the background of the existential struggle for survival and nationalist propaganda, the presentation of the city's archaeological heritage is not seen as a priority among Palestinians. Beyond some limited restoration projects of Ayyubid, Mamluk, and Ottoman buildings in the Old City's Christian and Muslim quarters—which are aimed at improving housing and living conditions for its Palestinian residents rather than educating and attracting visitors or making an explicit statement of cultural heritage and nationalism—very little investment is made in the preservation and display of Christian and Islamic sites, monuments, and artifacts.

When the Jewish archaeologists gathered in 1947 to discuss the collection of the PAM, their intent was to maintain the unity of its holdings and to use its contents for Jewish interests. The future of the museum itself did not play out as planned. The vision of those archaeologists found expression in a far more ambitious project. The entire city, not just merely the museum, was united and transformed into a living and thriving exhibition of Jewish antiquities, constantly expanding both horizontally and vertically, below and above the surface.

5

Archaeology in the Educational Systems

In July 1949, a group of nine senior scholars in the fields of cartography, archaeology, geography, and history gathered at the prime minister's office in Tel Aviv. Under the institutional umbrella of the Israel Exploration Society (IES), their mission was to foster research, publications, and education pertaining to *Eretz Israel* (Land of Israel) geared to the general public. The explicit objectives of the IES were to "lay claim to the ancestral homeland" and to "develop and to advance the study of the Land, its history, and pre-history, accentuating the settlement aspect of the sociohistorical connection between the People of Israel and *Eretz Israel*." The prime minister entrusted the assembled researchers with the task of providing "concrete documentation of the continuity of a historical thread that remained unbroken from the time of Joshua Ben Nun until the days of the conquerors of the Negev in our generation."[1] The meeting, called together by Prime Minister Ben-Gurion himself, would have a significant impact on the study and dissemination of knowledge of archaeology.[2]

As established in previous chapters, religiously and politically motivated agendas impacted the field of archaeology in Palestine and elsewhere long before 1948.[3] The challenge here is to discern to what extent ideology had an impact on the educational arena during the early decades of archaeological practice and study; how the situation has changed over time; and, most importantly, if improved methods of data and information acquisition, analysis, and transmission have been successful in countering ideologically charged procedures and interpretations. In order to fully appreciate the extent to which political ideology plays a role in the education of archaeological practice and in the knowledge access and distribution process in Jerusalem, both currently and in the past, it is essential to examine the city's

83

numerous centers of learning; the nature of the skills and knowledge imparted to students, scholars, and professionals; and the dissemination of the steadily growing corpus of information among the wider public.[4]

THE FIRST INSTITUTIONS OF ARCHAEOLOGICAL STUDY

With the exception of a few individuals motivated by the potential discovery of treasures of monetary and sensational value, a popular endeavor among European aristocrats, the majority of the earliest explorers dedicated to uncovering the mysteries of the Holy Land between the mid-nineteenth century through the last decades of Ottoman rule were educated in such fields as theology, biblical literature, ancient Semitic languages, archaeology, numismatics, geology, and botany.[5] Some of the late nineteenth-century British and American missions were headed and staffed by individuals trained in more practical fields, including engineering, cartography, and photography. Acquired skills and knowledge enabled those early explorers to examine their finds expertly and scientifically, placing them into a larger cultural, religious, theoretical, and technological context. Scientific curiosity, religious zeal, political ambitions, and a thirst for adventure all played a significant role. The first investigations were self-initiated, individual explorations, such as those by Edward Robinson, Melchior de Vogüé or Charles Clermont-Ganneau.[6] Wilson's 1864 survey of Jerusalem and its major monuments, conducted under the auspices of the Royal Engineers and the Ordnance Survey, introduced the beginning of organized operations, the success of which led to the founding of the PEF in 1865.[7] Establishing a formal framework for fieldwork and research started to have a clear impact on public education. The maps completed by Warren in 1867 were sold to educational establishments and museums in England, exemplifying the link between the work conducted in Jerusalem and Western education.[8]

With the exception of a few isolated incidents of protests by the local Jewish and Muslim communities, those early initiatives did not arouse much interest among the resident population. De Saulcy's second investigation of the Tomb of the Kings in 1863 caused the leaders of the Jewish community to lodge a complaint with the authorities in Constantinople, as they found that the tombs of their forefathers had been defiled. Before the grand vizier's instructions to halt the work reached Jerusalem, however, de Saulcy had already fled the region.[9] A few years later, in 1867, when Warren carried out his excavation against the southern wall of the Haram, the incessant pounding of sledgehammers used to clear a blocked passageway underneath the platform disturbed the daily prayers in the al-Aqsa Mosque. This apparently caused angered worshippers to hurl down showers of stones.[10]

It was not until the turn of the twentieth century that archaeological activity established itself as an institutionalized endeavor in Jerusalem.[11] Several permanent societies dedicated to archaeological exploration and study were created. Most of these institutions continue to play an active educational role in the city to this day.

In 1890 the Dominicans were the first to establish a foreign school, the École pratique d'études bibliques (Practical College of Biblical Studies), dedicated to exploring the region's Old and New Testament sites. In 1920 it became the École biblique et archéologique française de Jérusalem (EBAF, French Biblical and Archaeological School), moving to the ranks of other well established French research centers, such as the Écoles françaises in Athens (founded 1846) and Rome (1875). With the support of the Académie des inscriptions et belles lettres (Academy of Inscriptions and Literature), the school began to educate young scholars who eventually became the leaders of major French archaeological missions and establishments in the Near East.[12] Under the auspices of the École biblique, numerous surveys and excavations—such as the exploration on the grounds of their own school at the Basilica of St. Stephen (Saint-Étienne), in the City of David, near the Haram, on the Mount of Olives, in the Church of the Holy Sepulchre, and, more recently, at the Tomb of the Kings and at the churches of St. John and St. Anne. In addition, they carried out several comprehensive studies on ancient Jerusalem.[13] Educating scholars from various backgrounds—biblical, archaeological, and linguistic—has remained a central mission of the school to this day. The curriculum is designed for graduate students with the ability to obtain a doctorate in biblical studies. Courses and seminars cover a range of fields, including the Old and New Testament, early Judaism, archaeology, and geography, as well as Semitic languages. On a more practical level, students participate in field trips to museums and archaeological sites. The archaeological working museum *(musée)*, as well as the specialized library and the photo archives *(photothèque)*, considered the largest of their kind in the Near East, contribute to the high research profile of the École biblique. To this day, the school is a magnet for leading bible scholars and archaeologists as well as a center for learning and training. Regular field trips and popular lecture series geared toward the larger public have been in place since 1967. In spite of the clear biblical focus of the school, archaeological interests have encompassed an impressively large chronological, religious, and cultural scope, ranging from prehistory to early modern history.[14]

In 1895 J. Henry Thayer, a professor of biblical studies at Harvard, remarked that the "French Catholic School" had beaten the Americans to the punch and called for the establishment of an American school in Palestine, noting that this would hold great "promise of usefulness alike to biblical learning and missionary work."[15] Five years later, in 1900, the American Schools of Oriental Research (ASOR) was established, but it would take some twenty years before the school could move into a permanent home in the city. This was initially named the Jane Dows Nies Memorial Building, after its donor, and later, after completion of its construction in 1925, it was renamed ASOR's Jerusalem School. In 1970, major administrative changes led once more to the renaming of the school; it is now the W. F. Albright Institute.[16] W. F. Albright, often acknowledged for having "created the discipline of Biblical Archaeology," determined the scholarly direction of the institution far beyond his twelve-year tenure as director (between 1920 and 1929 and then again between 1933 and 1936).[17] Unlike other foreign schools (with the exception of the Kenyon Institute), the Albright Institute is not a religious institution, but its chronological and thematic focus is (and has always been) on the biblical world. The institute hosts and sponsors international scholars for extended research stays, and it offers regular workshops and field trips to its fellows. Its public lecture series is open to other members of Jerusalem's archaeological community.

Following Kaiser Wilhelm II's visit in Jerusalem in 1898, the Deutsches Evangelisches Institut für Altertumswissenschaft des Heiligen Landes (German Protestant Institute of Archaeology of the Holy Land) was founded in 1900.[18] The institution was clearly inspired by previously established German centers in Rome (1829) and Athens (1874) dedicated to archaeological research.[19] The German school followed the research model of the PEF in London (1865) and the Deutscher Palästina-Verein in Wiesbaden (1877), and it inspired the creation of several other foreign schools in Jerusalem. It was openly in competition with the École biblique (1890). Despite the fact that the school was denominational, its educational goal was to produce "scientific research not restricted by religious considerations."[20] Its first residence (1902–18) was in the Nashashibi House on Ethiopia Street, the former Austrian Consulate. After World War I (1920–64), it was moved to the guesthouse of the Redeemer Church in the Muristan in the Old City, then (in 1964) to the Nashashibi mansion in Sheikh Jarrah in East Jerusalem, and finally (in 1982) to the Canaan House, the former gardener's residence, of the Augusta Victoria Complex on the Mount of Olives. In 1975, an Amman branch opened, which cooperates with the Jerusalem branch. In 2007, both branches were formally recognized as research units of the Deutsches Archäologisches Institut (DAI, German Institute of Archaeology).[21] Other than hosting visiting students and scholars, the *Lehrkurs* (an archaeological course)—one of the institute's major educational initiatives, put in place one year after Gustaf Dalman was appointed as its first director, in 1902— offers young researchers the opportunity to explore the antiquities of the region, including visits to Jordan, Lebanon, and Syria. This annual two-month study-tour is primarily designed for German graduate students in theology and Middle Eastern studies.

Building upon a long presence of British explorers in the region, the British School of Archaeology in Jerusalem (BSAJ) was established in 1919, formally linked with its London office of the PEF for some fifty years. John Garstang served as its first director, overlapping for a few years with his position of director of the new DAP beginning in 1920.[22] The school's original role was to serve as an educational and professional training ground for the DAP; it also offered seminars, which were attended by members of the American school and the École biblique as well. Before moving to its current premises in Sheikh Jarrah, the former residence of the British consul in East Jerusalem, the school was housed in the Husseini Building. Other than Kenyon's significant contributions to the archaeology of Jerusalem, whose primary focus was the city's biblical past, the British school has dedicated much of its scholarship to the exploration of the city's Islamic monuments, beginning with the Dome of the Rock and the al-Aqsa Mosque and continuing with more comprehensive surveys of Ayyubid, Mamluk, and Ottoman Jerusalem.[23] Since 1998, following a review conducted by the Council for British Research in the Levant (CBRL) of various British research institutions, the British school in Jerusalem started to be managed by the CBRL. At that time, institutional changes broadened the scholarly scope of its affiliated researchers and projects to subjects across the humanities and social sciences. In 2003 the school was renamed in honor of biblical archaeologist Kathleen Kenyon. The Kenyon Institute currently is the only foreign school in Jerusalem hosting and sponsoring Palestinian scholars conducting field studies and research projects in the city.

After a failed attempt to establish a local school in the late nineteenth century, the Studium Biblicum Franciscanum (SBF, Franciscan Biblical School) officially opened in 1923.[24] Dedicated to the study of the Holy Land using biblical literature and archaeological methodologies as a basis, the school has focused its fieldwork and research projects on sites and monuments significant to the Christian tradition. Excavations have been conducted at the Church of the Holy Sepulchre and numerous other Byzantine and medieval churches in the city, including Dominus Flevit and the Imbomon on the Mount of Olives, St. Saviour on Mount Zion, the Tomb of the Virgin and the Grotto of the Apostles in Gethsemane, and finally the Monastery of Flagellation in the Old City, which is the original (and current) premises of the school.[25] The SBF, affiliated with the Studium Theologicum Jerosolymitanum, the Custody of the Holy Land's school of theology, offers degree and non-degree programs of studies in biblical interpretation and in archaeology. In a decree issued in 2001, the Vatican Congregation for Catholic Education declared the SBF a Faculty of Biblical Sciences and Archaeology.[26]

Beginning as a private endeavor of individuals, archaeological exploration and education in Jerusalem transitioned quickly into an institutionalized endeavor, with representatives from various Western nations. From the founding of these foreign institutions to the present, their activities have contributed to the intellectual and professional growth of a field in which national identity, religious interests, and scientific rigor continue to determine the production and distribution of archaeological knowledge to this day. Their impact on Israeli society, however, in particular the non-scholarly public, is negligible, if not completely absent.

JEWISH AND ISRAELI ESTABLISHMENTS

The opening of the first foreign schools in the city prompted the local Jewish population to establish their own institution dedicated to the historical, geographical, and archaeological research of the region. Scholarly, ideological, and political ambitions determined the nature of this mission. The Hebrew Society for the Exploration of Eretz-Israel and Its Antiquities, founded in 1920 (since 1948, called the Israel Exploration Society—IES), stated its objectives clearly:

> Establishing a Hebrew institution is desirable not only from a cultural-Hebrew point of view, but also for national political reasons. When we are set to build our national home and turn it into a center of Israeli culture, we cannot subject passively to the diligent and valuable efforts of scholars representing the world's nations, our competitors, to study our forefather's land. It is our holy duty to establish in our holy city of Jerusalem, next to the British, American, Dominican [i.e., the French] and German institutions, a Hebrew institution, in which Hebrew scholars and their disciples will focus on the study of our land. . . . We have to hurry, to double and triple our forces, to achieve in the future what we have neglected in the past.[27]

The first sites to be excavated in Jerusalem under the auspices of the newly established Jewish organization were the Tomb of Absalom in the Kidron Valley and the Third Wall north of the Damascus Gate. More extensive excavations, initiated after 1967 in the Jewish Quarter, near the Temple Mount, and in the City of David, were carried out under the auspices of the IES in conjunction with the Hebrew University.[28] The IES was established as a nonprofit organization governed by an executive committee and a council representing all of Israel's major institutes of archaeology and museums. The society has sponsored, supported, and administered archaeological excavations, surveys, and research projects in other parts of the country, spanning all periods from antiquity to the present. Since its inception in the 1920s, the IES has been Israel's leading publisher of archaeological reports and research.

Other than the administration of fieldwork and publication, the IES's main mission has been the dissemination and promotion of archaeological knowledge to the larger public, both in Israel and abroad. From the beginning, the society organized public lectures and tours. The first Hebrew Archaeological Conference was held in 1943, and it has been an annual event since then, supplemented in more recent years by three international conventions, each of which has attracted hundreds of attendees. In 1989, in recognition of its unique contribution to society and to the State of Israel, the IES was awarded the prestigious Israel Prize.

In 1926, just a few years after the Hebrew Society for the Exploration of Eretz-Israel and Its Antiquities was founded, the department of archaeology (since 1967 called the Institute of Archaeology) of the Hebrew University was established, the first university research and education unit devoted to archaeology in the city.[29]

The department was originally housed on Mount Scopus. After the division of the city in 1948, it was moved to the new campus on Giv'at Ram in West Jerusalem. It returned to the Mount Scopus campus after the capture of East Jerusalem in 1967. From its inception, the archaeology program at Hebrew University has had a close working relationship with the Hebrew Society for the Exploration of Eretz-Israel and Its Antiquities. The first faculty members represented three different fields of study: Moshe Stekelis, the prehistoric period; Eliezer Sukenik, the biblical and Second Temple eras; and Leo Aryeh Mayer, Islamic art and archaeology.[30] As the faculty of the institute expanded in the 1940s and 1950s, the original chronological distribution was gradually replaced by a more exclusive focus on the region's pre-Islamic cultures and periods, with the highest priority given to biblical studies. This focus has determined the research, teaching, and excavation curriculum throughout most of the institute's history. Since the 1970s, three principal teaching units have been devoted to the region's prehistoric, biblical, and classical cultures, with only a few classes offered in Islamic and medieval archaeology.[31] In 2009, the institute began the process of merging with the department of ancient Near Eastern studies; this merger has not yet been fully implemented, but nevertheless, it has broadened the thematic and geographical scope of the program.[32] Other than theoretical lectures and seminars, students attend workshops on pottery and other artifacts, making use of the extensive in-house collection. The accessibility of archaeological sites, either for study tours or excavations, is an important component of the undergraduate and graduate curriculum, as it enhances the practical experience of students' education and preparation for their careers. In 1991, the institute, in collaboration with the Hebrew University School of Education, created a track that prepares and qualifies students for teaching archaeology in high schools. Most of the institute's faculty were themselves educated at Hebrew University, as are most archaeologists working in the city's other public and private archaeological institutions and organizations.[33]

Since 1967, the IAA (or the IDAM before 1990) has played a significant role in archaeological education, both with regard to the scientific preparation of professionals and in the context of the dissemination of knowledge to the public. From the beginning, this governmental institution has invested significantly in the training of young professionals in the most advanced field methods, technical support systems, and research tools. A large number of specialists have been employed ensuring the quality of excavation, data processing, classification, analysis, interpretation, conservation, presentation, publication, dissemination, and public relations. Regular lecture and seminar series, workshops, field trips, and conferences have provided a dynamic platform for enhancing the employees' professional skills.[34] Scholarly accomplishments (grants, awards, publications, participation at national and international conferences, as well as the advancement toward higher degrees) have been encouraged, supported, and compensated. The numerous partnerships and collaborative projects the IAA has with other academic institutions (both Israeli and international) are indicative of the high professional and scholarly profile IAA has enjoyed.[35] Geared toward the nonspecialists, IAA's education department has made a marked contribution to the distribution of knowledge and the promotion of the field among the general public.[36] Jerusalem represents one of four regional centers administered by the education department, with activities geared toward participants coming from varied backgrounds. There are programs designed for children (preschool through high school), for teachers, and for adults and senior citizens. Currently, approximately half of the interested public comes from the religious sector, not including the ultra-Orthodox community.[37] The chronological and thematic foci are diverse, though there is an emphasis on periods and subjects of significance to the Jewish narrative of the city (the First and Second Temple periods). Prehistoric periods are usually not included in educational activities geared toward the Orthodox population (who consider the discussion of prehistoric periods contrary to their religious beliefs and thus offensive). A unique one-year project to reach out to a small sector of the Palestinian population of the city entailed a more heightened Islamic focus of the educational program.[38] In addition to lectures, workshops, and field trips, the IAA organizes study digs.[39] The financial support of Elad has recently enabled the IAA education department to organize a study dig on Mount Zion, which was launched in 2013. This project had solidified already existing collaborative efforts and institutional ties between the IAA and Elad in the domain of archaeological field projects and education in Jerusalem.

The Yad Izhak Ben-Zvi Institute was established by a special law of the Knesset in 1963 with the goal of continuing the Zionist, educational, and cultural activities of President Izhak Ben-Zvi. It was envisioned as one of the leading institutions in Israel and abroad for the research and dissemination of knowledge relating to the Land of Israel, Jerusalem, and the Jewish communities of the East.[40] In 1972, it moved to its current location, a building that previously served as the residence of the president of Israel in Jerusalem. From the beginning, the Ben-Zvi Institute enjoyed strong ties with Israeli universities and scholars. However, beyond fostering and facilitating research and publications, the institute's main objective has been to spread knowledge among the larger Jewish and Israeli public. Some of the lecture series, mini-courses, field trips, and conferences have been focused on Jerusalem, and more specifically the archaeology of the city. Though many of the activities organized by the institute have been inclusive of other religions, cultures, and regions—particularly the Near East—the primary focus has remained the Jewish faith and its history and traditions in various places, with a particular emphasis on the Jewish narrative of Israel and Jerusalem. More than any other educational institution in Jerusalem, the Ben-Zvi Institute makes the results of professional and academic archaeological work accessible to the general public, and it is perceived by most Israelis as an authoritative voice that embraces an open and unbiased spectrum of ideas.

In 1992 the Israeli Ministry of Education established a new interdisciplinary program entitled the Land of Israel Studies and Archaeology to be taught as an elective in high schools. The educational goal is to facilitate both a "direct and value-ridden" encounter between the student and the Land of Israel to help him or her to learn about the country's sites and cultural legacy.[41] The program encompasses various disciplines, such as history, archaeology, geography, and linguistics. Two primary textbooks are used, and instruction in the classroom consists of lectures, readings, and discussions, supplemented by field trips to museums and sites and by participation in archaeological excavations. The curriculum highlights the Jewish heritage of the region from the Bronze Age through the present, with about two-fifths of the material being devoted to Jerusalem. About two-thirds of the students who select this field of study are from the Jewish Orthodox sector of Israeli society.[42] A nonelective program designed for all Israeli schools, entitled Let Us Ascend to Jerusalem *(na'aleh le Yerushalayim),* facilitates three field trips to the city (in the fifth, seventh, and tenth grades). Students prepare for these field trips in the classroom, and the trips almost always have an archaeological component, usually including a visit to the City of David. Almost every Israeli primary and secondary school student has thus had at least a minimal exposure to the archaeology of Jerusalem from the perspective of the state narrative.

Unlike most other Israeli institutions listed here, the City of David Institute for Jerusalem Studies (generally known by its Hebrew name Megalim, which means "Discover") is a privately funded, non-governmental organization. It was founded by Elad in 2001, and it has established itself as the leading educational center promoting the archaeological discoveries in Jerusalem, and more specifically in the City of David, among the general public. Its education program is designed to "enhance the knowledge of ancient Jerusalem in the areas of history, archaeology and the Bible." The institute supports research as well as publications for the nonspecialized reader, and it is engaged in a variety of educational activities designed to establish the Jewish connection between present-day Jerusalem and antiquity, between contemporary Jews and Israelis and the ancient Israelites. Activities, mostly focused on the archaeology of the City of David and the First and Second Temple periods, range from guided tours to lectures, workshops, and conferences. Special seminars are offered for children, educators, guides, and soldiers. The popularity of the guided tours is enhanced by what has been criticized as a theme-park atmosphere, involving a 3-D animated movie, heavy sales of souvenirs and snacks, and Segway rentals.[43] The institute sponsors two annual conferences, one on Jerusalem, covering a variety of fields, such as the Bible, geography, history, and archaeology, as well as one focused on archaeology, entitled "City of David—Studies of Ancient Jerusalem." In recent years, the latter has attracted more individuals than any other conference devoted to archaeology in the country.[44] Cooperation between Megalim and various establishments from both the private and public sector, such as the Western Wall Heritage Foundation, the IDF, and Bnei Akiva (a Zionist youth movement), enhance the success of its outreach program. Collaboration with the leading academic institutions in Israel—Haifa University, Hebrew University, and, most recently, Tel Aviv University—establishes a strong scholarly profile.[45] Thus, Megalim strategically combines scholarly and popular—indeed, entertainment—priorities. In recent years, every Israeli schoolchild and soldier has visited the City of David at least once and has been guided and informed by the institute's staff. And unlike all other educational initiatives dedicated to promoting Jerusalem's Jewish archaeological and cultural heritage among the wider public, Megalim has been able to reach out to Israel's ultra-Orthodox community.[46]

After the first Zionist initiatives, in competition with various Western efforts to invest in the scientific exploration of the city, Jewish interests made a significant leap with the establishment of the State of Israel. Since then, archaeology has penetrated the curriculum of an increasingly diverse body of governmental and nongovernmental organizations committed to investing in archaeology as it relates to the origins of Judaism and successful in reaching out to the majority of the Israeli public.

PALESTINIAN INITIATIVES

The Palestine Oriental Society was established in 1920 to investigate the folklore and customs of the country. This endeavor has been viewed as an early "expression of emerging Palestinian cultural nationalism," but at the same time, as yet another outgrowth of foreign anthropological interest in the survival of biblical customs.[47] Most members, after all, were nonresidents, and among the locals, Jewish memberships outnumbered the Arab ones.[48] Despite the fact that the Christian and Muslim population still made up three-quarters of the local population at the time, the only possibilities to participate in fieldwork and research lay in the British Mandate's Department of Antiquities and the British School of Archaeology in Jerusalem.[49] More than sixty years passed before the first independent Palestinian institution dedicated to the field was opened. In the 1990s the first Palestinian academic establishments fostering the study and research of archaeology were established. Those activities, however, never entailed excavations in Jerusalem.[50] Three centers of higher learning either dedicated to or including the discipline of archaeology have operated under the auspices of Al-Quds University since 1992.

In 1992 the Institute of Islamic Archaeology opened its doors in East Jerusalem, originally housed in the Dar al-Tifl school and orphanage. When the institute was adopted by Al-Quds University in 1996, it was first moved to the Ramallah campus and then back to East Jerusalem to the Beit Hanina campus the following year.

Originally part of the department of history, the archaeology program developed into an independent academic unit in 2000, offering both undergraduate and graduate degrees. An additional change occurred in 2005, when the name of the program was changed to the Institute of Archaeology; it made a final move—this time to the Abu Dis campus (located outside the Jerusalem municipal boundaries)—in 2006 to enable students and teachers living in the West Bank to access the facilities. Since then, Jerusalem residents have been able to attend classes, seminars, and lectures only at the more recently established Center for Jerusalem Studies and the Jerusalem Archaeological Studies Unit. In addition to its regular course offerings, the institute organizes workshops, field trips, public lectures, and conferences. As part of the training, students are required to participate in one of the institute's affiliated excavations. The curriculum encompasses the fields of archaeology, architecture, and cultural heritage in the Near East, with a particular emphasis on Palestine. As opposed to the early years, during which the emphasis was on Islamic cultures and periods, the current program (as of 2005) encompasses a wider chronological time span, ranging from the Bronze Age to the medieval and Islamic periods. Faculty and students benefit from a lecture series, sponsored by the Albright Institute, which, since the move to the Abu Dis campus, is transmitted online. In 2007, a specialized program in conservation and restoration—in collaboration with the Italian association the International Cooperation South South (CISS)—was introduced to the program.[51] Its goal has been to provide students with the opportunity to acquire the necessary professional skills and knowledge to restore historical buildings and archaeological sites, safeguarding the Palestinian cultural heritage.[52]

Located in Suq al-Qattanin (Market of the Cotton Merchants) in the Muslim Quarter of the Old City, the Center for Jerusalem Studies was established in 1998. Its mission is to foster and disseminate knowledge about the city's past and present, using a multidisciplinary approach. Knowledge is understood as a "tool to support the process of liberation from Israeli occupation, which imposes ethnic and religious segregation and discriminates against Arab Palestinian residents."[53] Incorporated into a curriculum that spans the fields of law, political science, religious studies, urban studies, sociology, and economics, the center's master's degree program also offers courses in history, archaeology, architecture, cultural heritage, and tourism. The center offers field trips designed to help students to explore the city's cultural heritage and its architectural and archaeological landscape, as well as to learn about various contemporary issues from a Palestinian perspective. These field trips are organized for three different groups: students enrolled in the MA program, who are primarily Palestinian, with only a few international students; the general public, mostly the international community visiting or temporarily living in or near Jerusalem; and schoolchildren from West Bank refugee camps who are under the age of sixteen (once they are over the age of sixteen, they are prohibited by Israeli law from entering the city).

The Jerusalem Archaeological Studies Unit, located near Bab al-Amud (the Damascus Gate) in the Muslim Quarter of the Old City, was established in 2011 to facilitate research on and education in the archaeology of Jerusalem. In addition to offering undergraduate and graduate courses, the unit organizes a seminar and workshop series, primarily attended by the local Palestinian and international archaeological academic community. Affiliated staff and researchers are preparing a publication series documenting archaeological sites discovered during the late nineteenth and early twentieth centuries. Other projects promoted by the unit are to study post-1967 Israeli archaeological activities in the city and to create a specialized library. The unit's mission is to "approach archaeology in a scientific manner, without presenting an exclusive archaeological narrative of Jerusalem" and without being "captured by one national, political or religious agenda."[54]

The investment in the discipline of archaeology among various Palestinian institutions has thus made significant progress since the 1990s. The field, however, is still relatively marginalized and is mostly taught in the context of institutions of higher learning. These institutions suffer from the political and geographical fragmentation, hampering knowledge access and distribution among Palestinians.

EDUCATIONAL PROGRAMS IN MUSEUMS

A different approach to studying and learning about archaeology is through the immediate contact with artifacts stored and displayed in museums, which are accessible to both scholars and the general public. The idea to use a museum collection for educational purposes was expressed during a meeting of senior archaeologists a few months prior to the declaration of the establishment of the State of Israel. Their goal, which was never achieved, was to preserve the PAM as a "unique center of knowledge."[55]

Since the mid-1960s, the Israeli government has established three major museums in Jerusalem with educational programs focusing on the archaeological heritage of the region: the Israel Museum, the Bible Lands Museum, and the Tower of David Museum. Those activities have facilitated the exposure to key artifacts and have enhanced the learning experience through guided tours, lectures, workshops, and various playful activities for school-age visitors. Most of the programs are held in Hebrew, with some in English and only in exceptional cases in Arabic and other languages. Jewish themes are featured prominently. In addition to the regular programs and temporary exhibits, special activities are organized around Jewish holidays and special celebrations, such as Bat and Bar Mitzvahs. Most programs accommodate the Jewish Orthodox public, avoiding themes or artifacts that may be considered offensive, such as prehistoric topics and artifacts displaying nudity.

Soon after the Israel Museum was opened, in 1965, its Ruth Youth Wing for Art Education was established. This wing organizes the education programs for all age groups, and the primary goal is to attract the public to the museum and to disseminate knowledge as it relates to various cultures embodied in the art and artifacts on display in the galleries. The staff of the Ruth Youth Wing includes roughly one hundred teachers, guides, docents, and administrators who share a common vision: "to serve as a center for the study and creation, which stimulates artistic and cultural dialogue and endeavor, inspired by the original works housed in the Israel Museum."[56] Enjoying the immediate access to the country's largest archaeological collection, many of the programs involve the study of ancient artifacts, sites, and cultures. Some of the activities are entirely focused on archaeological topics; others use objects from the archaeological wing to enhance various other themes and study foci, such as the display of ancient jewelry to explore the theme of fashion. Most activities are of an interactive nature, avoiding lectures and encouraging hands-on activities (see figure 22). Two innovative projects, geared toward children and youth, highlight this approach. In 1991, the wing reconstructed an archaeological tell (an artificial mound that is created over centuries by many successive settlements—each settlement building on top of the last one—with the hill eventually having deposits from various periods and cultures) in one of its courtyards, allowing visitors to experience the process of an excavation.[57] The following year, a prehistoric cave was built in another courtyard, enabling children to explore and reenact life in ancient times. Jewish themes are featured prominently in galleries and associated educational activities.

Established in 1989, as an institution committed to educating the public about the history of the city, the Tower of David Museum has the enormous advantage of being part of an ancient monument and incorporating an archaeological site in its midst.[58] Its educational programs, however, focus on chronologically organized rooms and open spaces featuring modern media and technology rather than authentic ancient artifacts. A dynamic educational department organizes tours, lectures, sound-and-light shows, and hands-on activities for children. The goal is to teach history through enactment, taking advantage of the setting, but not so much learning about the excavated site or the actual building. Visitors, primarily children, explore the museum in guided groups, learning through conversation and exploration of the didactic material on display in the enclosed and open spaces or featured in booklets. A more flexible approach in reaching out to museum visitors is apparent in the organization of guided tours and instructional programs geared toward different communities. In addition to the Hebrew-speaking educators who work primarily with the secular population, one educator is designated for the Jewish Orthodox public and another one for Arabic-speaking groups. Educators design their programs mostly according to their own preferences, adjusting the content and perspective to the specific groups.[59] In recent years, in addition to Christian and Muslim children attending schools administered by the Israeli Ministry of Education, children from the other Arabic-speaking school systems in

FIGURE 22. The so-called archaeological tell in the Ruth Youth Wing of the Israel Museum. Courtesy of the Israel Museum, Jerusalem.

Jerusalem began to attend the tours.[60] In spite of the relatively open curriculum of the educational-support material and the guided tours, the curated sections of the museum displays unequivocally showcase a Jewish and Israeli narrative of the city.

As the only museum dedicated to the history of the Bible and the Ancient Near East, the chronological and thematic focus of the Bible Lands Museum is primarily of interest to the Jewish and Christian public, including both local and foreign visitors. The museum's mission, since its establishment in 1992, has been "to create an institution of learning, a unique resource of universal stature, where people of all faiths would come to learn about biblical history. In the shadow of the Holocaust, this concept began to take shape as a way to encourage future generations to understand the morals and ethics of the Bible."[61] In spite of the wide chronological and regional scope, Islamic artifacts and cultures are not included in the permanent exhibits, either within the gallery displays or in the educational programs.[62] Tours, lectures, courses, and other creative programs focusing on biblical studies, geography, art history, art, and archaeology are designed for children and adults. Since 1999, an externally funded program entitled "The Image of Abraham" facilitates meetings between Arab and Jewish children from East and West Jerusalem schools, promoting learning and understanding of their shared cultural heritage. Though a successful experience, the limited funding does not allow for it to have a significant impact.

Integrating an archaeological curriculum into the museum world thus shifts the process of knowledge acquisition and distribution beyond the intimate space of the library and classroom and into the public realm. Rather than being limited to students and scholars, archaeology as a field of exploration thus becomes accessible to a much larger audience and interest group. Since the 1960s, the education on archaeology has increasingly taken place in museums built throughout the city that cater primarily to the Jewish and Israeli public, with an emphasis on subjects related to Judaism.

CONTESTED HERITAGE

Knowledge acquired through excavation, survey, and research in Jerusalem between the mid-nineteenth until the mid-twentieth century was shaped by Western imperial interests in the region, scientific curiosity, and the desire to establish the "physical reality" of the biblical narrative. These motivations are still apparent in most of the leading educational establishments in the city today. The actors involved in the early years of colonial rule were primarily students and citizens of the Western European and Anglo-American world. It was not until the British established the Department of Antiquities in 1920 that locals, including Palestinians and Jews, were intentionally hired as staff.[63] Though the governance of the department was officially committed to "making active preparation for the training of [local] archaeologists . . . no Arab students benefitted from this educational opportunity."[64] Efforts to train Jewish scholars were likely linked to the goal of the British to establish a Jewish national home.

Before the first graduates from Hebrew University took leadership roles in archaeological exploration and research after the creation of the State of Israel, most Jewish archaeologists were educated abroad, typically with degrees from European universities.[65] Since the 1960s, almost all archaeologists active in the city have been Israeli, and the large majority has been locally trained and educated, mostly in Jerusalem.

Promoting the knowledge of archaeology among the local public was not on the agenda before the Hebrew Society for the Exploration of Eretz-Israel and Its Antiquities became active in the 1920s, catering specifically to the Jewish population of Palestine. When, less than thirty years later, Ben-Gurion called the legendary meeting with a group of senior scholars to encourage research on the region's antiquity with the goal to "lay claim to the ancestral homeland," the foundations had already been established for merging the most advanced scientific methods of archaeological practice and research; of learning, training, and teaching; and above all, of reaching out to and instructing the society as a whole. The nationalistic outlook of Israeli archaeology was thus combined with the highest standards of a successful educational protocol. Other than in the context of schools and institutions of higher learning, archaeology under Israeli rule has increasingly penetrated various additional public platforms of education (such as the IES, the IAA, the Yad Izhak Ben-Zvi Institute, and Megalim, as well as the numerous museums built throughout the city), which more often than not are combined with leisure and entertainment programs. These programs have been particularly successful in the context of tourism initiatives in East Jerusalem, which since the 1990s strategically combine an archaeological curriculum with settlement policies.

Since 1948, and in particular after 1967, Israeli archaeology has indeed penetrated a large number of didactic fora, reaching out to all age groups and to individuals coming from various cultural, religious, and political backgrounds representing the full spectrum of Israeli society, though almost exclusively Jewish, with a significant representation of the Orthodox community. The subject of archaeology, with a consistent emphasis on the city's and nation's Jewish origins—specifically the First and Second Temple periods—and a more peripheral interest in other cultures and religions, has played and continues to play an important role in shaping a shared identity among Israelis and, to some extent, among Jewish visitors from around the world.

For Palestinians, archaeology has played a distinctly more marginal role in education. After the active and successful participation of a number of Arab scholars in the archaeological exploration of Jerusalem during the early years of the British Mandate, their numbers gradually diminished in comparison to their Jewish colleagues.[66] The political and economic reality of the region's Palestinian population following the 1948 and 1967 wars, in addition to the lack of local academic institutions supporting their involvement in archaeological activity and related scholarship, severely restricts Palestinian contributions to the field. The territorial segmentation of the Palestinian academic community, as well as the compromised socioeconomic and political status of Jerusalem's Arab residents, are further contributing factors to the diminished profile of their scholarly and educational involvement in the field. The modest and only relatively recent efforts of the Palestinian academic community in Jerusalem, beginning in the 1990s, face substantial obstacles in establishing themselves among—or on the margins of—a network of well-established, heavily funded, and mostly government-supported Israeli educational establishments. Unlike in the Jewish Israeli sector of society, on the Palestinian side, archaeology has hardly penetrated the public educational fora, both those serving Palestinian residents of Jerusalem, as well as those catering to Palestinians from other cities within Israel and throughout the region.

With regard to cooperation or joint enterprises between Israeli and Palestinian archaeologists, there have only been a few isolated attempts, most of which were initiated prior to the outbreak of the Second Intifada. An exception to this is the Jerusalem Virtual Library, an academic database on historic Jerusalem, a joint project of Hebrew University and Al-Quds University, launched in 2001. As the academic boycott of Israel expanded—a movement that originated in England in 2001, leading to the first Palestinian initiatives in 2004—official collaboration between Israeli and Palestinian scholars and institutions in Jerusalem ceased entirely.

Today there are only a few personal and non-institutionalized contacts between archaeologists representing the two sides.[67]

A review of the entire history of archaeological education in the city allows us to see a marked continuity between the first colonial investment in the education of biblical archaeology and the nationalistic endeavors of the Jewish State focusing on the material culture of the First and Second Temple periods. The change lies in the increasingly heightened professional excellence of students, field archaeologists, teachers, and researchers, along with the tremendous growth and speed of data and knowledge production and distribution. Under colonial rule, only a few select fell under the educational orbit of archaeology, but today, by contrast, almost the entire Israeli public has been exposed, in one way or the other, to knowledge produced by or channeled through archaeological finds. Israeli institutions, however, cater primarily to the city and country's Jewish citizens and largely ignore the Christian and Muslim populations—marginalized in most other domains of public life as well.

6

———

Archaeological Ethics

Moshe Dayan, celebrated by many Israelis as one of the country's greatest military heroes and political leaders, is also remembered for his great passion for antiquities. In a recent biography, he is featured as a learned explorer of archaeological sites and as someone who saved antiquities from destruction.[1] His daughter, Yael, describes her father's interest in archaeology and the collection featured in his home and garden: "My father resumed his ardent interest in archaeology, and whenever he could, he went digging or sat in the garden putting shards together. His collection grew, and the garden acquired a special near-magic when among the shrubs and flowers he placed Corinthian pillars and ancient millstones. The delight he took in his discoveries was still childlike and appealing, totally free of materialistic considerations."[2]

In contrast to this romanticized depiction of Dayan's relationship with antiquities, most evaluations of his publicly known interest in ancient artifacts are rather harsh, accusing him of robbing and trading antiquities; of abusing his status by using army personnel and equipment to satisfy his greed and private pleasures; and of repeatedly denying his ethical and legal transgressions.[3] Most of Dayan's collecting and looting activity—and the lack of legal sanction—would be considered unthinkable today.[4] The academic discourse on archaeological ethics has evolved since his lifetime, and the laws regulating the excavation, trading, and handling of ancient burials are no longer the same. Some of Dayan's rather compulsive habits, however, have left their mark on Jerusalem's current antiquities scene and thus invite a critical analysis of ethical norms as they evolved over the last four decades. Some customs and rulings have clearly changed or developed; other traits have persisted.

How do we best create a baseline for moral principles in the field of archaeology? Numerous ethical codes and standards have been formulated by different societies worldwide. Differences rarely concern the nature of the proclaimed principles, but rather the emphasis on certain values, which depend on two things: first, the specific experiences, circumstances, and concerns of the groups served by the organization, and second, the cultural and political framework in which the archaeological work is being conducted. Despite the fact that most ethical standards in the profession have universal value, some regulations pertain only to specific geographical and national contexts. Certain recommendations or rules, widely respected by professionals in other regions, can be of limited concern or of no relevance at all to the case of Jerusalem. A further singularity in the city is that archaeological practice—in spite of UNESCO's presence as representative of the international community—relies almost exclusively on Israeli legislation, which, for the most part, ignores and bypasses international rulings.

To better appreciate the development of archaeological norms in Jerusalem, it is useful to consider how the concern for ethical questions in the field emerged and evolved elsewhere. The academic interest in archaeological ethics first established itself in North America and Western Europe in the 1960s and 1970s, which resulted in the formulation of several codes of ethics.[5] The discourse, largely theoretical in the beginning, was influenced by a new archaeology movement that began in the late 1950s, when researchers started to shift their attention away from the study of artifacts to the study of human behavior.[6] Another factor was the establishment of public archaeology (also known as *community archaeology,* which is the dissemination of academic scholarship among the larger public) in the United States, following federal legislation.[7] A more direct incentive to formulate and implement ethical standards came in 1970, through a UNESCO ratification to protect world culture.[8]

In Israel, the Association of Archaeologists in Israel (AAI), founded in 1984, established the first local ethics committee. Their initiatives, however, were of relatively short duration and of minor impact on the archaeological community.[9] A code, written between 1990 and 1992, included nine guidelines focusing primarily on the standards of fieldwork and publication, on professional relationships, and on the antiquities trade.[10] Some of the issues addressed in the code had already been formulated in the much more authoritative 1978 Antiquities Law, incorporating rules for both excavation and publication. Though the intent of the ethics committee was to give "practical and ethical guidelines" to all archaeologists in Israel, their efforts never received much attention.[11] One reason was that the initiatives of the AAI overlapped with the creation and fast expansion of the IAA, which, soon after its establishment in 1990, took on a leadership role in the profession and overshadowed the activities and academic profile of the AAI.[12] In addition, some important issues were not addressed in the ethics committee's code, such as the rights of local communities over sites and finds and over the reburial of human remains. Thus, the code neglected numerous social, religious, and political dimensions that impact the divides among Jewish Israelis, as well as the rifts between Jews and Palestinians.[13]

Archaeological ethics encompass, indeed, an extremely wide spectrum of issues pertaining to how the profession is practiced, to the role of sites and artifacts, and also to the people whose heritage is being investigated. Central to this rapidly growing field are several widely circulated questions, such as: Who owns the past? Whose heritage is being investigated? Which remains should be documented, preserved, and presented to the public? How does the past tie into the present? And how do political agendas and identity formation interact with archaeological practice? All these questions are relevant to the discussion of archaeological ethics in Jerusalem. Some, however, are also being addressed either explicitly or implicitly in other chapters of this study. This chapter focuses on three select topics that have a particularly timely relevance and show how ethical standards have been significantly compromised in the past two decades. The first relates to professional standards; the second to acquisition, collection, and display policies; and the third to the excavation and desecration of tombs.

PROFESSIONAL STANDARDS

Excavation, documentation, and interpretation procedures have undergone important changes since the beginning of archaeological excavation in Jerusalem, regionally, and worldwide. What was considered acceptable practice in the nineteenth or mid-twentieth century is different from what conforms to ethical standards in the twenty-first century. By and large, the archaeological community in Jerusalem has fairly consistently held to the highest professional standards. Even prior to the academic discourse on the ethical necessity of employing the most advanced scientific methods in the field, excavations conducted in Jerusalem conformed to standard international practice. Since 1967, however—and in more drastic ways since the mid-1990s—the ideological pursuit of establishing a continued Jewish presence in East Jerusalem has compromised this positive trend.

Since the beginning of Israeli rule, first under the IDAM and with increased rigor under the IAA, professional standards have been formulated, regulated, and even sanctioned by a number of explicit rules and laws. These have insured that all excavations are conducted by professional archaeologists, for the most part with an academic degree in archaeology and extensive field experience. Fieldwork can be carried out only with proper survey and excavation licenses. The most meticulous recording and documentation procedures have to be followed. Preliminary and final excavation reports have to be published in a regular and timely manner. Specialized teams cooperate in the most effective ways. Regular training sessions, workshops, and conferences ensure the knowledge and use of up-to-date excavation, publication, and research methods, and they facilitate a continued education. The preservation of finds and their public display and dissemination among the general public are considered high priorities. All those rules have been and still are strictly governed and implemented by the IAA.

Despite of these high professional standards, however, one obvious shortcoming of Israeli archaeology, also discussed in other parts of this study, is the preferential treatment of remains from the First and Second Temple periods, highlighting finds of relevance to the city's Jewish narrative, to the neglect of other cultures and periods. This clear deviation from ethical standards has been the subject of much criticism, and it is seen in most public displays of excavations conducted since 1967. One thing that has changed since the mid-1990s is that medieval and Islamic layers are no longer bulldozed. Instead, most IAA excavations now meticulously record and dutifully document the remains that span the entire spectrum of pre-1700 periods, as stipulated by the AL. Some select projects even document and record more recent layers, including the late Ottoman period, the time of the British Mandate, and, in some cases, the destruction layers associated with the 1948 and 1967 wars. At least in that respect, they are following the standard protocol of salvage excavations.[14] Today, it is only the public presentation and dissemination of information that continues to focus on the Jewish narrative. Thus, professional archaeological practices—increasingly conscientious in other ways—do not really stand in the way of the continued commitment to the Zionist ideology, which emphasizes the continuity of a Jewish presence since antiquity and the entitlement of return to the Jewish homeland.

One issue discussed in the AAI codes of ethics but not commonly addressed in codes from other countries or continents concerns professional relations between colleagues, as well as between mentors and students. In Israel, there is an expectation that university archaeology students will assist their teachers and advisors in fieldwork and research projects—often for years and even decades—without receiving proper credit. This appears to be a tradition that will be difficult to break. For instance, the Hebrew University Institute of Archaeology's almost exclusive hiring of internally trained students is likely linked to this trend and is, without doubt, problematic.[15] An equally neglected problem is the uneven professional distribution of Ashkenazi, Sephardic, and female employees, as well as the predomination of Jewish versus Palestinian Israeli archaeologists in higher-ranked positions, not only in academia, but also in most relevant governmental and nongovernmental institutions.[16]

In addition to this professional and academic exploitation and discrimination, there are ethical transgressions in Jerusalem's archaeological arena that affect significantly larger segments of populations, with direct implications for the political reality of Israel's occupation of East Jerusalem. Several underground explorations—beginning relatively modestly with the Western Wall Tunnels immediately after 1967, and expanding significantly after the mid-1990s, including in the area below the Southeast Hill (City of David / Silwan)—are of relevance here. Both projects have been conducted under the auspices of the IAA, the former in collaboration with the Western Wall Heritage Foundation, the latter in collaboration with Elad.[17] One of the shortcomings of these projects is that they rely heavily on excavation methods that undermine the stability of existing dwellings and public structures and thus necessitate the use of elaborate steel and concrete support systems. Steel pillars and scaffolding are problematic as they are excessively costly and compromise the appearance of the archaeological landscape.

Another shortcoming is that the excavations target select layers and features of the archaeological record, making it difficult or impossible to make an objective assessment of chronological and multicultural developments. Tunnel or shaft and gallery excavations were used commonly in excavations conducted before the British Mandate period.[18] Warren, for instance, was trained in the art of military mining, which at the time was almost indistinguishable from standard archaeological methodology.[19] Toward the end of the nineteenth century, the stratigraphic method of excavation was introduced in Egypt and Palestine by Flinders Petrie and gradually replaced tunnel excavations.[20] By the 1960s, this method was implemented in Jerusalem to the highest degree of rigor by Kathleen Kenyon, and it was established henceforth as the norm. Stratigraphic excavations expose accumulated layers of deposits of material culture and natural deposits layer by layer from top to bottom, enabling the archaeologists to define various phases of occupation. It prevents archaeologists from prioritizing specific features or periods and establishes a multilayered reconstruction of past cultures. The IAA's return to the use of tunnel and underground excavations is thus outdated and does not conform to current scientific methods.

Furthermore, the targeted exposure of remains that highlight the Jewish narrative, exemplified best in some of the excavations conducted on the Southeast Hill, thus compromises current archaeological practice, which aims to expose all the cultural aspects of one particular place over the course of many centuries. This method therefore represents an attempt to legitimize the Jewish presence in Silwan and obscure the ties of the neighborhood's current residents to the place. This approach has been aptly compared to early archaeological endeavors in Jerusalem, which were shaped by "[W]estern imperialist ambitions."[21] Recovering the material remains of the biblical past, understood as the foundations of Western civilization, undermined the Islamic heritage as well as the Islamic presence in the city. In the nineteenth and early twentieth centuries, the biblical world was understood as a superior reality that was misunderstood and ignored by the oriental, backward-living locals.[22] Notable parallels exist between this early colonial approach to the city's cultural heritage and the IAA's recent archaeological projects that have clear nationalistic aspirations, motivated by the desire to historically and archaeologically justify the Israeli occupation of East Jerusalem. According to current archaeological ethical standards, as advocated by professional organizations as well as by individual scholars publishing on related issues, the inclusion of local communities—in particular when excavations are conducted in residential areas—is strongly recommended. The local residents in Silwan are predominantly Palestinian—other than the growing settler community—and they should be involved in the excavation and interpretation process, partially in compensation for the disruption of their daily routines and living conditions, but, more importantly, to establish their connection to the area's cultural heritage, which should be recognized primarily as theirs.[23] Several isolated attempts of community-based excavations conducted in other parts of the city could serve as a model for integrating Jerusalem Palestinian and Israeli residents in the process of exposing and understanding multicultural layers. Their impact, however, has been negligible.[24]

Another endeavor conducted under the auspices of Elad, which also fails to meet current archaeological ethical and professional standards, is the Temple Mount Sifting Project. After the construction of the Marwani Mosque inside "Solomon's Stables" between 1996 and 1999, the debris material was dumped at Abu Dis, on the western slope of the Kidron Valley, and at various other locations outside of the Old City. In 2005 it was moved to the Tzurim Valley National Park, and since then it has been systematically sifted (see figures 15 and 23).[25] Since the finds do not come from a proper archaeological context and the debris has been moved at least twice since the renovations of the mosque, the procedure lacks scientific value. Chronological and typological observations do not contribute to our current knowledge of the city's material culture, and, most importantly, no stratigraphic or contextual conclusions can be drawn.[26]

The common denominator among these recent government-endorsed archaeological endeavors, other than the transgression of ethical and professional standards, is the manipulation of archaeological sites and finds and the resulting justification of Israel's occupation of East Jerusalem.

ACQUISITION, COLLECTION, AND DISPLAY POLICIES

The earliest documented interest in digging up artifacts in Jerusalem and other cities in the Holy Land and trading these objects locally and regionally is from the fourth century. After Empress Helena, the mother of Constantine, visited the Holy Land in 326, pilgrims began to flock to the region and acquired relics imbued with biblical meanings, including bones, shrouds, and the garments of saints and New Testament figures, thus contributing to the economy of the local religious establishments.[27] In the eighteenth century, the continued demand for religious relics and icons was coupled with the newly emerging interest in acquiring

FIGURE 23. Temple Mount Sifting Project inside tent. Photo by Katharina Galor.

artifacts for scientific purposes.[28] The Ottoman AL passed in 1874, which was revised and enhanced in 1884, was the first attempt to regulate the trade in local antiquities.[29] Albeit largely unenforced, this law stipulated that all artifacts discovered in Ottoman territory were the property of the Imperial Museum in Constantinople. In this period, however, a complex smuggling network encompassing the region of Palestine and Syria was established, which has been linked to this Ottoman attempt to control European access to local cultural heritage.[30] The 1920 Antiquities Ordinance, formulated by John Garstang, director of the Department of Antiquities in Mandate Palestine, and enacted by the high commissioner in 1929, introduced a much more professional and bureaucratic legal system of protecting cultural heritage, administered locally for the first time.[31] The department issued licenses for the trade in antiquities, enabling dealers to officially engage in the business of buying and selling antiquities for the purpose of trade.

To this day, the 1929 Antiquities Ordinance still forms the basis for all domestic legislation concerning protection of cultural property in Israel and Palestine.[32] An official Israeli Antiquities Law was not enacted until 1978. Though adequate regarding its regulation of excavation and the requirement of full scientific publication, the legal precepts of the antiquities trade are, in many ways, regressive, in particular in comparison with other Mediterranean countries rich in archaeological remains, such as Italy, Greece, Turkey, and Egypt. According to the Israeli Antiquities Law, it is legal to buy and sell artifacts from pre-1978 collections and inventories. Numerous loopholes in this law, however, enable a continuous supply of illegally looted artifacts, which are sold by legally sanctioned dealers (both Israeli and Palestinians), almost all of whom are based in Jerusalem.[33] The laundering chain is known to begin with the overseers and middlemen—Bedouin, Israelis, and Palestinians—who often finance the looting and then transfer the artifacts to legally sanctioned dealers. In Jerusalem, mostly in the Old City and East Jerusalem, but also in West Jerusalem, licensed IAA dealers are able to sell the material by using register numbers of similar, previously sold inventoried items, thus turning the objects into legally purchasable goods (see figure 24). The buyers are mostly tourists, some high-end collectors, educational institutions, and museums.[34] Opinions regarding the legal trade and its impact on looting are divided between those who believe that legalized trade increases the market demand, which leads to more looting, and those who believe that if the selling of antiquities is banned, the market will go underground, as it has done in many other archaeologically rich countries.[35] Proponents of a legal market have recently suggested to sell finds from the IAA storage facilities. Though it would temporarily provide extra income, the storage facilities would be depleted in less than a year and, according to some, rather than prevent the looting of sites and subsequent illegal sales, it would stimulate the market even further.[36]

The scientific and ethical concerns regarding the marketing of unprovenanced artifacts stem from the belief that removing an archaeological object from its find spot without professional supervision results in the irretrievable loss of context documentation and knowledge—and thus the displacement and destruction of local cultural heritage.[37] As it is widely acknowledged that market demand fuels the incentive for looting, every individual and institution directly or indirectly involved in the trade of artifacts has a share in the ethical violation. Though not everybody involved in the chain—the looters, the dealers, the buyers, and the appraisers, who are often museum professionals or academic archaeologists—has equal responsibility in the legal transgression, all steps contribute in one way or the other to the trading, and thus the looting, of ancient artifacts.[38] From an archaeologically ethical point of view, no amount of money obtained from the sale of an unprovenanced artifact can justify the irretrievable loss of cultural and historical knowledge.

Though it is commonly agreed upon that economic incentive drives most of the pillaging of archaeological sites, largely located in the West Bank, there are also other reasons. Looting is a leisure activity for some, undertaken in the evenings and on weekends, and for others, looting is a traditional activity, based on experience the looters gained as laborers on archeological excavations.[39] Looting, however, can also be understood as a form of political resistance to the Israeli

FIGURE 24. One of the many licensed antiquities dealers in Jerusalem's Christian Quarter. Photo by Katharina Galor.

occupation and subjugation of the Palestinian people. Other than realizing that there is a higher gain to be made from artifacts with a Jewish or Israeli connection, Palestinians often believe that by pillaging archaeological sites that are thought to bolster a Jewish claim to the land, this association can be erased.[40] The looters perceive the cultural heritage of the artifacts as Israeli rather than Palestinian, which is a result of the prevailing public image projected by both foreign and local archaeologists, Israeli governmental institutions, and the media.[41] In 1985, in response to the growing public debate on looted antiquities, the IAA established the Theft Prevention Unit with the goal of limiting the robbery of archaeological sites and supervising the sale of antiquities.[42] The effectiveness of policing this underground activity is questionable, however, as the risk of being caught and penalized is relatively minor in comparison to numerous other criminal acts, and the potential financial gains are higher.[43]

A market survey indicates that most objects traded are associated with the Judeo-Christian heritage. Particularly popular among tourists, the primary customers in Jerusalem's antiquities shops, are Herodian oil lamps and Bar Kokhba coins.[44] Only in recent years has there been interest in objects related to the region's Islamic heritage; this market, however, is still underdeveloped.[45]

situation in Jerusalem will almost always compromise professional conscientiousness and progress. It is true that today university professors can no longer collect, as Avigad and Yadin did in the past, and today politicians cannot rely on the public endorsing private collections of looted antiquities, as Teddy Kollek or Moshe Dayan did in the 1960s and 1970s. Trading, however, is still legal, displaying looted and unprovenanced artifacts is the accepted norm, and transferring objects from occupied Palestinian territories, including East Jerusalem, and exhibiting them in the city's national museum is a celebrated achievement.

Along with admiring Jerusalem's exposed ruins and viewing artifacts in public museums, collectors, tourists, and pilgrims can legally purchase antiquities and take them home. The focus on Judeo-Christian artifacts that determines the nature of Jerusalem's numerous markets and collections indicates the prevailing and persistent interest in biblical artifacts, and to some extent the overlapping taste and ideological confluence of Zionist and Evangelical Christian consumer groups. The proliferation and accessibility of this relatively narrow chronological spectrum of antiquities in recent years exemplifies how commerce, religious beliefs, ideological perceptions, and political agendas are intertwined and feed each other.

THE EXCAVATION AND DESECRATION OF TOMBS

Our knowledge about early human activity is derived to a large extent from the material remains of burials. The exploration of tombs has always played an important role in the study of ancient civilizations, providing valuable insights on funerary customs and the belief in an afterlife, as well as on cultural developments, changes, and affiliations more generally. Furthermore, anthropological studies of burials can offer much helpful information on gender, ethnicity, DNA, genetic disorders, diseases, and nutrition.

It may come as a surprise that scholars as well as archaeological and anthropological societies have only recently initiated formal codes of ethics addressing the complexity of digging up and studying the mortal remains of the dead. The Vermillion Accord on Human Remains, adopted in 1989 at the World Archaeological Congress, advocates for respect to be paid to human remains "irrespective of origin, race, religion, nationality, custom and tradition." It further stipulates that the value of scientific research of skeletal, mummified, and other human remains should be demonstrated and should not be taken for granted.

In Jerusalem, and in Israel more broadly, major controversies regarding the excavation and study of ancient burials have gained wide public attention. Heated debates and actual conflicts have erupted around perceived cultural, ethnic, and religious links between past and present communities, particularly sensitive in the context of Jewish and Muslim tombs and cemeteries. Surprisingly, however, the AAI code of ethics has not addressed the issue of excavating burials, and formal restrictive policies regarding the excavation and scientific study of ancient burials were not established until 1994.

The very first excavation conducted in Jerusalem, in 1850–51, was devoted to the exploration of an ancient burial complex. De Saulcy had obtained an official firman from the Ottoman authorities to explore the so-called Tomb of the Kings. This endeavor caused turmoil among the local Jewish community, who complained that the graves of their ancestors had been desecrated.[57] Despite the anger, which forced de Saulcy's escape from the region, the excavation of ancient tombs in Jerusalem proceeded in a relatively undisrupted manner for nearly a century.

Since 1967, as a result of the dramatic proliferation of urban development projects in and around Jerusalem, a number of particularly controversial incidents have led to heated debates among archaeologists, other scholars, and the general public, some of which were brought before the Israeli Supreme Court. Several cases have caught the attention of local and international media.

Among the most contentious cases in Jerusalem are excavation projects that were interrupted by protests led by Atra Kadisha (Aramaic for *holy place* or *holy site*), an ultra-Orthodox fringe group invested in protecting ancient Jewish tombs.[58] Their goal is to prevent the desecration of Jewish graves, and in most cases, their opposition to archaeological excavations is linked to major development projects. In their view, opening and penetrating ancient tombs represents a violation of Jewish law as it pertains to the respect to be paid to the dead.[59] Though exclusively concerned with Jewish burials, their resistance also affects burials associated with other cultures and religions.[60]

Atra Kadisha was first established between 1957 and 1959, as a response to excavations carried out at Beit Shearim, a Jewish town and cemetery from the Roman and Byzantine periods in southwestern Galilee. Their interference with archaeological excavations in Jerusalem, often entailing violent and destructive behavior, only started to have significant professional and legal implications in the 1990s, following protests and demonstrations in French Hill and Mamilla near Jaffa Gate.[61] Unlike the salvage excavation carried out in French Hill, which exposed primarily Jewish tombs from the Second Temple period, the excavations conducted in Mamilla exposed a Christian mass grave from the time of the Persian capture of Jerusalem in 614 C.E.[62]

These and other cases were brought before the Israeli Supreme Court, leading to a directive issued by attorney general Michael Ben-Yair on July 22, 1994, that stated that archaeologists must show proper "respect . . . in handling the bones of corpses," and that human bones must "be forwarded, after their examination, to the Ministry for Religious Affairs for burial."[63] Protests led by Atra Kadisha, however, have continued regardless of the new regulations and despite the fact that the IAA has limited the exposure of tombs and cemeteries—not only Jewish, but also pagan, Christian, Muslim, and even prehistoric ones to a minimum. In 1998, in an attempt to calm the situation, the Israeli government appointed five Orthodox rabbis to the Archaeological Council, a body that consists of thirty-eight archaeologists and other experts who advise the IAA on granting excavation permits. Unlike Atra Kadisha, who argue that any disturbing of burials goes against Jewish law, Orthodox rabbis have mostly agreed that bones can be removed so that excavations can proceed.[64] Nevertheless, even the Ministry of Religious Affairs representing the Orthodox community insists that bones must be reburied without being studied by anthropologists, the procedure that was followed in Israel before the clashes in the 1990s. The more recent structure introduced in 1998 has been conditioned by Atra Kadisha's continued opposition to the excavation of burials, who not only disregard the directives of the Supreme Court but also the authority of the Ministry for Religious Affairs. Despite the fact that not all Orthodox and ultra-Orthodox individuals and communities agree with Atra Kadisha's position on the excavation of burials, their body has an indirect influence on religious groups and parties active within the government and the Knesset.[65]

Another highly controversial case is the late Ottoman (and more recent) construction on top of Jerusalem's largest Muslim cemetery in Mamilla, located to the west of the Old City and within the boundaries of the Historic Basin.[66] The burial ground is centered around a shallow rectangular water reservoir, known as the Mamilla Pool. According to popular tradition, the cemetery holds the remains of several of the Prophet Muhammad's companions. Numerous religious, political, and military leaders, eminent scholars, and various other Jerusalem notables are known to have been buried there over the last millennium.[67] The burial grounds were once densely covered with tombstones and memorials, most of which are now gone. Among the few remaining are several Mamluk and Ottoman burial plaques and monuments, and most notable among them are the thirteenth-century mausoleum al-Qubba al-Kubakiya for 'Ala' al-Din Aidughdi al-Kubaki (see figure 25), the governor of Safed in the Mamluk Sultanate and the sixteenth-century tomb of Sheikh Dajani.[68]

The boundaries of the cemetery were established during Ottoman rule in the 1860s.[69] The Mamilla Cemetery was declared an antiquities site in 1944 by the British Mandatory authorities, a status that was twice reconfirmed under Israeli rule, first in 1964 and then again by the IAA in 2002.[70] Recent excavations conducted in sporadic areas have established four archaeological strata and hundreds of burials ranging in date from the eleventh century to the beginning of the twentieth century.[71] Ever since the expansion of the city beyond the Ottoman walls in the 1860s, modern roads and buildings started to slowly encroach upon the cemetery. It was not until the 1950s, however, that significant areas of the burial grounds were appropriated for the construction of residential and commercial or other public spaces and buildings. In 1986 this led to a petition by Palestinians to UNESCO. The most controversial case has been the recent construction of the so-called Center

FIGURE 25. Al-Qubba al-Kubakiya. Photo by Katharina Galor.

for Human Dignity—Museum of Tolerance, initiated in 2004. The first Museum of Tolerance was established in Los Angeles, California, in 1993, designed as the educational arm of the human rights organization the Simon Wiesenthal Center. Like its American counterpart, the Jerusalem museum was also to examine racism and prejudice around the globe, with a focus on the Holocaust. Following the standard procedure for new development, salvage excavations were carried out that established the density of human burials. The excavation and building activity has generated heated debates and resulted in numerous lawsuits as well as public protests in both Israel and around the world. Several petitions were filed urging Israel to halt the construction of the Museum of Tolerance and to honor the "cultural and archaeological importance of the cemetery to the history of the Holy City of Jerusalem."[72] In 2011, the Supreme Court granted permission to go forward with the construction, based on a report submitted by the IAA, though that report has been challenged for its accuracy, including by the archaeologist originally assigned to direct the excavation.[73] The project disinterred significant numbers of graves, estimated at least in the hundreds. Additional construction on top of the Muslim Cemetery and adjacent to the site of the Museum of Tolerance, consisting of 192 housing units, a 480-room hotel, commercial spaces, and parking, was approved in July of 2015 by the Jerusalem Planning and Building Committee.[74]

This gradual encroachment upon the Mamilla Cemetery and the disrespect paid toward the human remains buried in this area is particularly striking in comparison with another historic burial ground in Jerusalem. The Jewish cemetery on the Mount of Olives, which, according to tradition, goes back to the time of King David and includes tombs that date back hundreds of years, has not fallen victim to modern development.

BONES AND BURIALS OF CONTENTION

In many ways, the controversies and confrontations surrounding the excavation and study of human remains in Jerusalem reflect the tensions between the Jewish secular and religious sectors of Israeli society, as well as the conflict between Jewish and Muslim communities, Israeli governmental establishments and Palestinian national entities. Opposition to the excavation and desecration of ancient tombs and cemeteries mostly stems from the desire to protect religious communities—their beliefs and practices—rather than the individual. In contrast to the actual act of excavating tombs, however, very few ethical concerns have been voiced regarding the use of burial goods as cultural, educational, or commercial commodities, once they have left the ground.

Two displays at the Israel Museum reflect the complexity and evolving perception of archaeological ethics as they affect changing professional standards, past and current acquisition and display policies, and finally the exploration of ancient burials. The ethical concerns in these and most other cases dealing with funerary remains are intricately linked with the always sensitive and often explosive social and political climate in Jerusalem.

Several anthropoid Canaanite coffins from Deir al-Balah, which greet visitors as they enter the newly renovated archaeology wing at the Israel Museum (see figure 26), are widely known to have been looted by Dayan at a time when the Gaza Strip was under Israeli military administration.[75] They were dug up and transported to Dayan's home sometime in the 1970s, using military equipment, and were then sold to the museum in 1982 by his widow.[76] Thus, both the process in which the artifacts were uncovered, as well as their acquisition and display are highly questionable with regard to professional standards, as officially professed by Israeli archaeologists and museum professionals.

Perhaps equally blatant in its politically and ethically compromised curatorial choice was the focus of the Israel Museum's Herod exhibit on the latter's alleged sarcophagus and funerary monument.[77] Though the artifacts on display were excavated by applying the most up-to-date scientific methods, the show defied international law—as well The Hague's convention—by incorporating finds from occupied territory.[78] Herod, this man who was both feared and hated by his Jewish contemporaries, has risen to become Israel's most illustrious king. It appears that the legacy he has left behind is more palpable than that of Kings Saul, David, and Solomon, whose only traces consist of the biblical narrative. Hundreds of thousands of enthusiastic visitors, mostly Jewish, arrived to circumambulate his tomb in the galleries of the Israel Museum, recalling the motion of millions of Christian pilgrims paying homage to the tomb of Christ at the Holy Sepulchre. Herod would most likely have taken great satisfaction in knowing that his tomb was given so much honor and attention, and by no one less than the Jewish people. This, in the end, was his goal when he planned his funerary monument to be set up at Herodium. The question, however, is whether displacing and appropriating funerary monuments by completely altering their original functions impinges on the deceased's ethical rights, perhaps no less severely than the exhumation of one's bones.

FIGURE 26. Canaanite coffins from Deir al-Balah at entrance of Israel Museum's archaeological wing. Photo by Katharina Galor.

The transgressions of ethical norms in the professional, educational, and commercial realms of archaeological practice in post-1967 Jerusalem, with significantly higher impact after the mid-1990s, do not appear to have significantly influenced the public image of archaeology. The general perception, among most Israelis and tourists, has been and continuous to be that engaging in archaeology is an overall virtuous endeavor.

My hope, though, is that by exposing some of the existing and persistent misconceptions on archaeological practice and its role in the public sphere, and by creating awareness of what is professionally viable and ethically defendable, we can have a better understanding of how issues of cultural heritage play themselves out in the following case studies. How has archaeological fieldwork and research contributed to our knowledge of some of Jerusalem's most venerated sites and monuments? Who and what has impacted the specific explorers and explorations involved? And how did these together shape public information and opinion? Can we untangle the elements that contribute to the confluence of science, religion, and ideology?

Three Controversies

THREE CASE STUDIES—the City of David / Silwan, the Church of the Holy Sepulchre, and the Temple Mount / Haram al-Sharif—lead us through the journey in which scientific procedures and religious aspirations have led to the binary forces of scholarly agreement and dissonance, as well as of political alliance and conflict. First, as the place where Jerusalem's earliest settlement has been documented, the City of David has been turned into a stage where the Hebrew Bible is reenacted, using archaeology as a tool. Below the houses of Palestinian residents of Silwan, its numerous cavities and tunnels—and their alleged holiness—have recently evolved into one of Jerusalem's most contested sites. Second, above the ground, the standing monument of the Church of the Holy Sepulchre has served as Jerusalem's primary Christian place of worship and pilgrimage, as well as one of the most desired places of scientific exploration. It has been on the front line of Christian denominational disputes, as well as a locus of negotiations with the Jewish, Muslim, and, more recently, the Israeli and Palestinian communities. Finally, Jerusalem's main acropolis and the city's focal holy site, the Temple Mount, or the Haram al-Sharif, has served as an active place of worship and pilgrimage from antiquity to the present. Here we can retrace how the Jewish, Christian, and Muslim faiths continue to build upon each other physically and spiritually, and how these interdependent communities have been caught up in the religio-political struggle. More so than any other holy compound, the Temple Mount / Haram al-Sharif has been used as a stage to manipulate heritage for the purpose of religious and nationalistic agendas of regional and international impact. These three controversies encapsulate the challenges of Jerusalem's archaeological heritage and demonstrate the entanglement of science and ideology.

7

The City of David / Silwan

On top of Wadi Hilwe Street, two signs direct the visitor to explore the neighborhood. One of them reads Silwan; the other, City of David. Both names appear in three different languages, Hebrew, Arabic, and English, an apparent attempt to balance or disguise a completely unruly situation. Amid a population of about fifty thousand Palestinian villagers live some seven hundred Jewish settlers, a cohabitation that is facilitated through barbed wires, electric fences, guard booths, and towers, as well as dozens of security cameras and personnel, which may occasionally help prevent some violent confrontation, but more surely emphasize and deepen the rift and animosity between the original residents and the Jewish settlers, who started to move into the neighborhood in 1991.[1]

Silwan is the name of the village. It originated on Ras al-Amud, on the southwest slope of the Mount of Olives, and at the beginning of the twentieth century, gradually began expanding across the Kidron Valley (to locals also know as Wadi Sitti Maryam or the Valley of St. Mary). It eventually incorporated all of the Southeast Hill, which today is considered the Wadi Hilwe neighborhood (see figure 27). The village of Silwan is hundreds of years old; according to tradition, it originated at the time of Salah al-Din in the twelfth century.[2] City of David—in Hebrew, Ir David, a biblical epithet (2 Samuel 5:9), which most likely indicated David's citadel—was a term introduced by French archaeologist Raymond Weill, who conducted the first open-air excavations on the Southeast Hill, in 1913–14. The name was rarely used, however, until Yigal Shiloh began to direct the first Israeli exploration of the hill, in 1978. Most excavators till then preferred the name Ophel, another biblical name used to describe the area immediately to the south of the Temple Mount platform.[3]

FIGURE 27. The densely built-up area of the Palestinian neighborhood Silwan, in the midst of which the City of David Archaeological Park was established. Courtesy of the Institute of Archaeology, The Hebrew University of Jerusalem.

Silwani villagers live in modest, often improvised housing—a mix of stone, concrete, and steel construction—built alongside lanes and roads, some of which are unpaved. The City of David Visitors Center, the surrounding archaeological park, as well as the settlers' houses, in contrast, are beautifully built and maintained, speckled amid the Palestinian village and connected by newly paved streets. The gardening and numerous Israeli flags make for additional unmistakable attributes of the recent urban transformations initiated and financed by both the Jerusalem municipality and Elad. Tourist trails lead visitors through well-designed spaces, some of which are above ground, but most of which are expanding underneath the private and public buildings of the Silwan neighborhood. Since the mid-1990s, millions of visitors have explored the excavated features, treading in the footsteps of dozens of adventurous explorers on a journey to discover physical remains embodying the biblical narrative.[4] Two realities seem to be ignored, however, by most visitors: the many centuries of historical legacy that link the Palestinian Silwani to this place and the lack of archaeological data on the Southeast Hill supporting the biblical narrative of King David's conquest and rule in the city.

DIGGING UP THE BIBLE

The Southeast Hill is the most excavated place in Jerusalem, with a history of more than 150 years of exploration. Ironically, the most extensive and intrusive excavations coincided with the most significant and rapid growth of the modern village, following Israel's 1967 capture of East Jerusalem. The archaeological exploration has been motivated from the beginning by the desire to find physical traces of the biblical narrative, prioritizing this mission over the concern for the residents who live on the land. The quality of private and public life in Silwan, particularly over the last two decades, has been increasingly compromised by excavation and the development of the tourist industry. Though highly successful in attracting millions of visitors, much of this recent activity is ideologically and politically motivated and cannot be justified on scientific grounds. This entanglement of archaeology, religion, and ideology has fueled the tension between the Jewish settlers and the original Silwani residents, between the Israeli and the Palestinian public.

An ongoing debate about the significance of the continuous flow of supposedly important discoveries related to the biblical narrative, the political implications of the growing settler presence, and the eviction of Palestinian residents has flooded the media and produced numerous erudite articles. One of the lacunae in the scholarly discourse is the apparent lack of communication between archaeologists and professionals or researchers in other fields. The literature that addresses the social and political aspects of the issue—the impact of archaeological activities and tourism development on Silwan's residents, the political conflict, and the territorial and demographic realities of Jerusalem—is mostly written by social and political scientists or by architects and urban planners, but it doesn't pay much attention to the actual archaeological data. The scholarly discourse of archaeologists focuses primarily on the tangible data—or lack thereof—of their work, but without discussing the practical and political implications of the excavation, preservation, and development initiatives that are being carried out, both above and below ground.[5]

What have 150 years of archaeological survey and excavation on the Southeast Hill revealed? Which were the most significant expeditions and the most important discoveries? The countless excavations, the innumerable finds, and finally the discrepancy between scholarly consensus and media coverage make it difficult, even sometimes for the experts themselves, to differentiate between sensational discoveries and genuinely significant finds.

Numerous excavations have been carried out on the Southeast Hill since the beginning of exploration in the mid-nineteenth century (see figure 28). Our knowledge has expanded greatly, and scientific methods have made tremendous progress. Yet the primary motivation to dig up the relatively small area has not changed since the Ottoman period: uncovering the physical traces of the biblical narrative.

Some of the most significant discoveries on the Southeast Hill were made under Ottoman rule, during the first decades of archaeological activity. Those include the water systems of the Bronze and Iron Age and the Siloam Tunnel and its inscription, the Herodian Siloam Pool, the Theodotus synagogue inscription, and the Byzantine Siloam Church.[6] It is interesting to note that at the beginning of the twentieth century, both scholarly circles and the wider public were alike able to differentiate between scientific endeavors and aimlessly conducted and spiritually motivated treasure hunts. The legendary Parker expedition, which sought to uncover the Ark of the Covenant and Solomon's treasures, invited Father Vincent from the École biblique to provide a scientific framework to an otherwise unreasonable project. The irrational nature of the enterprise, however, was quite transparent to

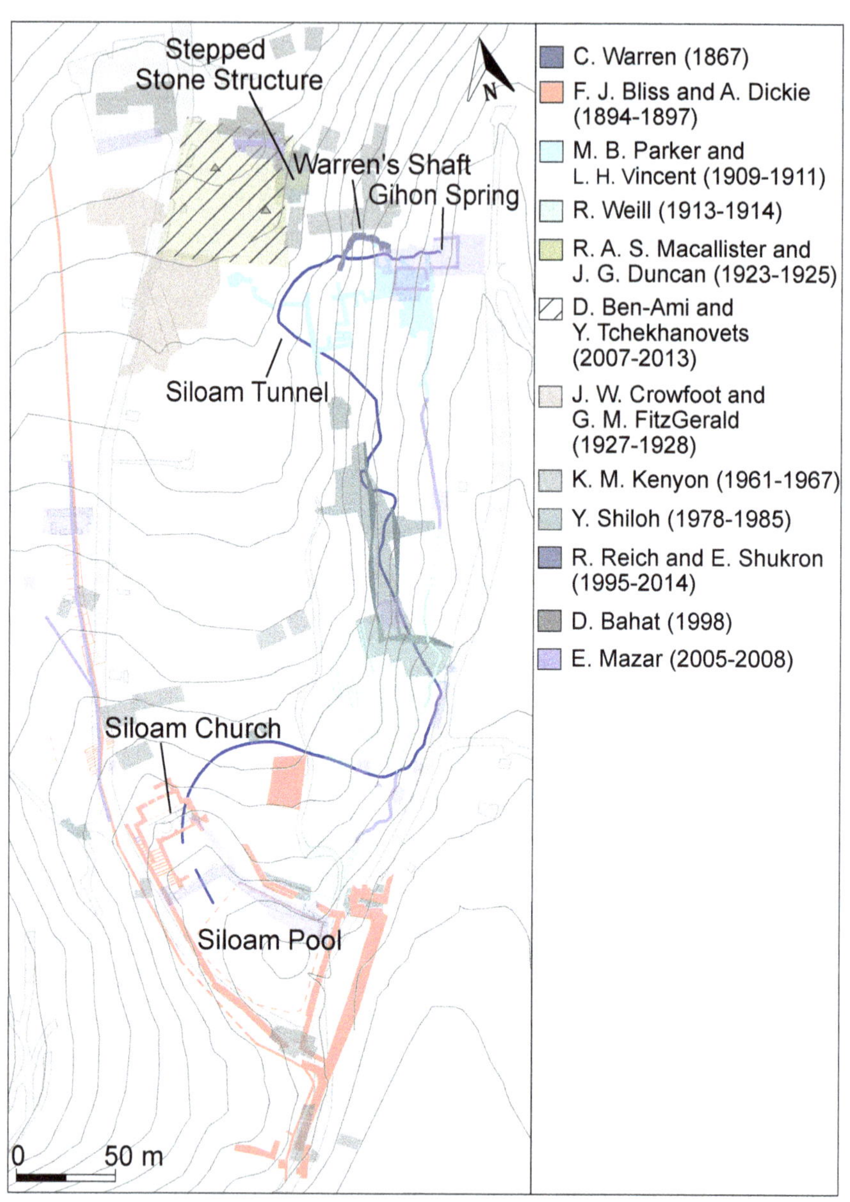

FIGURE 28. City of David, areas of excavation. Redrawn by Franziska Lehmann, after: Reich, *Excavating the City of David. Where Jerusalem's History Began,* plates 11, 57, 74 and 83.

all. Given local and even international pressures, the excavation could ultimately not be completed.[7] Expeditions conducted by Warren and by Bliss and Dickie under the auspices of the PEF, and even Weill's work, carried out on behalf of Baron Edmond de Rothschild, on the other hand, gained wide acclaim and some of their results have impacted our understanding of Jerusalem's early history.

The two theories established during those early years of exploration that had a significant influence on all further archaeological work carried out in the city were that Jerusalem's earliest settlement began on the Southeast Hill, outside of the Old City boundaries, and that King David used the underground tunnel system linked to a vertical sinkhole known as Warren's Shaft to conquer the city from the Jebusites. Recent excavations established that the earliest finds documenting a prehistoric presence on the Southeast Hill can be dated to as early as the Epipaleolithic period (22,000 B.P.–9,500 B.C.E.).[8] But these excavations also proved that Warren's Shaft had been inaccessible during the period attributed to David's conquest of Jerusalem.[9]

Under British rule, there were two especially significant expeditions, one led by R. A. S. Macalister and J. G. Duncan in 1923–25, and the other by J. W. Crowfoot and G. M. FitzGerald in 1927.[10] The chief discovery made during this period pertains to the Stepped Stone Structure, which at the time was only partially exposed. It was believed to represent the fortress of Zion mentioned in the Bible (2 Samuel 5:7), built by the Jebusites and taken over by the Israelites around 1000 B.C.E.[11] As a result of the excavations carried out in the 1960s and 1970s, which gradually exposed the remainder of the structure, numerous chronological assessments and interpretations have been proposed. Chronological distinctions are made between the core (the substructural terraces) and the surface, commonly referred to as the Stepped Stone Mantle. Suggested dates range between the Bronze Age (fourteenth to thirteenth centuries B.C.E.) and the Hellenistic period (second century B.C.E.).[12] Though the original function and appearance of the structure remain unresolved, most scholars are reluctant to detach themselves completely from the biblical reference to the fortress of Zion, suggesting that the Stepped Stone Structure served as a substructure of a public building, possibly a palace or administrative complex.[13]

Despite the fact that Kathleen Kenyon's work, which was carried out during the period of Jordanian rule, is usually associated with significant scientific advances, including the introduction of stratigraphic excavation, it is often ignored that she had little interest in post-biblical periods. In addition to exposing various sections of the Bronze and Iron Age defense system, as well as changes or additions introduced during the Hellenistic period, she excavated an area that she assumed to be cultic in nature, including two *masseboth* (standing stones), a *favissa* (repository pit of votive objects), and a libation altar.[14] Though still recognized for her meticulous and progressive work, many of her interpretations have been refuted over the years, most importantly, her view that the city remained small throughout the Iron Age.[15]

The most intensive period of exploration on the Southeast Hill began shortly after Israel captured East Jerusalem in 1967. Since then, numerous excavations have been carried out involving faculty from most major Israeli universities (Hebrew University, Haifa University, and Tel Aviv University) as well as employees from the IAA.[16] The first major project was directed by Yigal Shiloh, which exposed further components of the Bronze and Iron Age water and defense system, dwellings from the Iron Age that document the last period of occupation prior to the Babylonian conquest of the city in the sixth century B.C.E. and traces of the fire that both destroyed and preserved various features of Iron Age II material culture.[17] Eilat Mazar excavated the so-called Large Stone Structure, which she thought formed part of King David's palace, a theory that has not gained support in the academic community.[18] The longest and most extensive excavation was conducted by Ronny Reich and Eli Shukron, which provided a completely new understanding of the city's early water and defense system. This not only disproved Warren's long-standing theory of David's conquest but also showed that during the Middle Bronze Age II, the Gihon Spring was located within the city boundaries and was protected by a monumental wall and tower.[19] Another noteworthy discovery was the so-called Siloam Pool, a large stepped pool, built and used prior to the destruction of the Second Temple.[20] According to the excavators, it was used by pilgrims for ritual purification before visiting the Temple and served as the site of Jesus's healing of the blind man mentioned in the New Testament (John 9); neither interpretation has gained much recognition among scholars.[21]

Another large-scale project, still ongoing, are the Givati Parking Lot excavations directed by Doron Ben-Ami and Yana Tchekhanovets. These excavations have shown that the area served as a residential neighborhood, with only short interruptions, from the eighth century B.C.E. through the tenth century C.E. The most important architectural finds include a Roman peristyle villa (late third to fourth centuries C.E.) and a large building (dated to the fifth to seventh centuries C.E.) that is presumably the "seat of the Byzantine official representative."[22]

SCHOLARLY CONSENSUS AND CONTROVERSY

Though the majority of archaeologists digging on the Southeast Hill have been in agreement about the desired focus of exploring the Southeast Hill—bringing the written narratives of the Hebrew Bible, Flavius Josephus, and the New Testament into dialogue with the material remains—most discoveries, in particular those potentially relevant to the biblical accounts, have resulted in a disarray of interpretations. There are, however, several noteworthy discoveries whose meaning scholars agree about. The location of Jerusalem's earliest settlement on the Southeast Hill is quite clear, as is the dating of the earliest flint tools, the first dwellings, and the city walls. No one seems to challenge the results of the excavations exposing Jerusalem's Middle Bronze Age fortification and water system. No major discrepancies exist in scholarly interpretations regarding the late Iron Age settlement and dwellings destroyed during the Babylonian conquest in the late sixth century B.C.E. It is also unlikely that the recent discoveries of the Roman peristyle villa, the Byzantine mansion, and Abbassid dwellings will lead to scholarly controversies. These facts seem straightforward, and no major historical revisions are necessary.

It is documented that the Gihon Spring and Siloam Pool remained important landmarks throughout the early Islamic, medieval, and late Islamic periods.[23] The Siloam Pool is depicted on several Crusader maps of the city, and there is archaeological evidence that the Gihon Spring was unblocked sometime during the twelfth or thirteenth century.[24] Despite the fact that even the earliest excavations documented artifacts from the Mamluk period, archaeologists have paid remarkably little attention to post-Byzantine structures.[25] It is difficult to assess how many of these later finds were discarded and perhaps bulldozed, a situation that would not be so different from other areas within the city and more generally in the region.

Less unison seems to exist among scholars regarding religious sites and monuments. In spite of the numerous late Iron Age figurines and other possible cult paraphernalia uncovered, there is no real agreement about the cultic use of this area, as the Southeast Hill does not appear to have ever served a central role in the city's religious public life. No concrete evidence for the existence of a house of worship, other than the first-century C.E. synagogue inscription, which was not found in situ, has been documented.

Among the more controversial discoveries are sites or monuments that have been linked to biblical descriptions, such as the Stepped Stone Structure, the Large Stone Structure, Warren's Shaft, and the Siloam inscription. The most debated issue in the context of the Southeast Hill, however, concerns the limited amount of material remains dating to the eleventh and tenth centuries B.C.E. (the time of the transition between Iron Age I and Iron Age II), the period believed to correspond to the reigns of Kings David and Solomon, the time of the United Kingdom of Judah and Israel. One may easily understand how an unusual artifact or structure can lead to heated discussions and conflicting reconstructions and theories, so it is peculiar that, in fact, the most disputed topic about the Southeast Hill excavations is the *lack* of finds. Of course, one of the main principles of the field of archaeology is that the absence of evidence is no evidence for absence. That is, if something was not found, that doesn't mean that it was never there. The possibilities of interpretation are more varied and flexible when no tangible remains have survived. Beyond the limited extant material data for the tenth century B.C.E., the difficulty in reconstructing the city during this period stems from the absence of contemporary historical records. The biblical passages describing David's and Solomon's Jerusalem were written hundreds of years after the events they describe, portraying the monarchy from a later perspective. At one extreme, some scholars believe that the historicity of these accounts is minimal or even completely absent.[26] They argue that the biblical narrative was influenced by religious perceptions and political agendas, largely inflating the narrative to portray a more glorious and powerful rule.[27] On the other extreme are those conservative scholars who rely on the biblical account as their primary guidance in understanding historical events and identifying archaeological remains.[28] They put forth various explanations as to why the material records are so limited. One is the argument that the people of the late Iron Age continued to use the well-built Middle Bronze Age structures, and since the period was relatively peaceful, there was no need to construct new fortifications and water systems. Another explanation is that the numerous destructions that the city suffered throughout the centuries, each one followed by reconstruction, sometimes completely eliminated earlier layers and traces of occupation. An additional argument is that in Jerusalem buildings are made of stone and thus each new construction is built directly on bedrock, rather than on earlier courses of brick, as is the case at most biblical tells in the region. A variety of valuable arguments have been put forward to explain the paucity of archaeological remains, and many thoughtful theories have been developed regarding Jerusalem in the eleventh and tenth centuries B.C.E. and the relationship between the Southeast Hill and the biblical narrative. No ultimate proof, however, has been presented, and the discourse continues.

ARCHAEOLOGY, RELIGION, AND POLITICS ENTANGLED

The professional and ideological zeal of most archaeologists who have explored the Southeast Hill often impeded productive contact with the local Jerusalem communities— especially the inhabitants of Silwan. A distinct tone of disdain can be perceived in Warren's account of the condition of the village and his description of its residents as "a lawless set, credited with being the most unscrupulous ruffians in Palestine."[29] Throughout the early decades of archaeological activity, the interaction between Western archaeologists and locals was quite limited and often unfriendly.

It was not until 1981, however, that tensions between archaeologists and Jerusalem residents—this time not the local villagers, but members of the ultra-Orthodox community—escalated to the point that police had to interfere and legal action had to be taken. The battle waged by excavation director Yigal Shiloh against Atra Kadisha, which claimed that Jewish graves were being dug up, was perceived by many not only as the struggle of Israel's archaeologists advocating the freedom of science and knowledge but also as exemplary of the great rift between the objectives of Israel's secular segment of society versus the religious and ultra-Orthodox sectors.[30]

The conflict resulting from archaeological activity would reach entirely new dimensions when the objectives of the excavation and associated tourism initiatives started to be part of an official municipal program in which religious and political agendas rather than scientific inquiries began to dictate the scope and nature of the work. In 1995, the Jerusalem Municipality celebrated the three thousandth anniversary of David's conquest of the city, initiating a new chapter in the archaeological exploration of the hill.[31] The decision was made to conduct even more massive excavations to connect the different sites and to develop them into a major tourist attraction.

At this point, Elad turned into one of the main actors involved in facilitating this overhaul. One fact that is ignored by many, however, is that Elad—which is the primary sponsor of the excavations conducted in Silwan today—was established as a foundation several years prior to its involvement with archaeology.[32] Originally, Elad's exclusive goal was that of renewing the Jewish presence in Silwan and East Jerusalem more generally, particularly through the acquisition of Palestinian homes. Their early years of activity in the neighborhood, in fact, caused major clashes with the archaeological community, who opposed their ambitious building projects, which would unavoidably endanger archaeological heritage. The intended construction of two hundred housing units for Jewish citizens in Silwan, planned by Elad jointly with the Ministry of Housing in 1992, led to protests by a group of Israeli archaeologists—including Israeli academics and employees of the IAA—and several legal battles, which ultimately prevented the construction.[33]

Following these initial hostilities, instead of building new homes, Elad's strategy began to shift more heavily toward appropriating homes of Palestinian families. Furthermore, rather than endangering the area's antiquities and thus operating in opposition to the archaeological community, Elad transformed itself into Silwan's primary archaeological sponsor, financing most of the excavations as well as the associated tourism and education activities, gradually turning itself into the city's most powerful NGO. Since 2002, Elad has managed the City of David Archaeological Park, an authority that has been sanctioned by the Jerusalem Municipality, the IAA, and the INPA.[34] Cooperation between Elad and the different governmental institutions has been smooth and thriving ever since. In recent years, the City of David Archaeological Park has indeed turned into Jerusalem's most popular heritage site and one of the country's most visited tourist attractions (see figure 29). In spite of Elad's increasing success in terms of fund raising, home appropriations, excavation, conservation and reconstruction projects, education and outreach activities, tourist development, and—perhaps most importantly—full governmental approval, support, and cooperation, numerous individuals as well as communities and organizations have voiced criticism regarding its activities.[35]

FIGURE 29. Entrance to the City of David Archaeological Park. Photo by Katharina Galor.

The most active and effective group to challenge Elad's mission in the City of David is Emek Shaveh, which is invested in informing the public of how political and religious ideology is implicated in the current excavation and tourist initiatives in Silwan to the detriment of its Palestinian inhabitants.[36] Established and directed by two Israeli archaeologists, this group interacts closely with the Wadi Hilwe Information Center, a Palestinian organization whose mission is to build a strong, well-informed, and involved Palestinian community and to provide educational and recreational courses for young people.[37]

In its criticism of Elad's activities, Emek Shaveh states that "an archaeological find should not and cannot be used to prove ownership by any one nation, ethnic group or religion over a given place. Moreover the term 'archaeological site' does not only refer to excavated layers of a site but also to its present day attributes—the people living in it or near it, their culture, their daily life and their needs."[38] In numerous publications, Emek Shaveh has established how various recent initiatives conducted under the sponsorship of Elad have manipulated archaeological findings in Silwan to highlight the Jewish narrative, while ignoring both the historical and cultural legacy—as well as the human rights—of its Palestinian residents. Emek Shaveh has further demonstrated how Elad has compromised scientific and professional standards for its ideological goals, entailing the Judaization of a Palestinian neighborhood.[39]

Emek Shaveh's outreach efforts, including alternative archaeological tours of the City of David, booklets, regular newsletters, and an active website, are mostly geared toward educators, journalists, and politicians, some local, but most international. Their activities have gained some momentum among the general public, but they are at a clear disadvantage in comparison to Elad's outreach efforts, as Elad has millions of dollars at their disposal, as well as marketing strategies that have proved most effective in the development of other entertainment parks, both nationally and internationally. Additionally, Elad creates facts on the ground that can be consumed, by excavating and restoring antiquities, by acquiring Palestinian homes, by building homes for Jewish citizens, and by constructing residential and tourist infrastructure. Emek Shaveh, on the other hand, is mostly limited to raising awareness among the public and providing information to those willing to examine the state of affairs critically. Reaching the masses with popular myth and tradition by using effective and highly entertaining visual and sound stimuli—as practiced by Elad—is generally more appealing than Emek Shaveh's approach of focusing on analytical and critical commentaries that deal with the distressing local and regional conflict.

It is undeniable that, since the mid-1990s, archaeological initiatives on the Southeast Hill can no longer be separated from the political conflict between Israelis and Palestinians, as reflected in the latter's struggle to maintain or appropriate land and to ascertain their entitlement to living in Silwan. No one living, working, or even visiting Silwan can be indifferent to the ideological weight of archaeology and tourism in this sector of the city.

Since the mid-1990s, all archaeological excavations in Silwan have been linked directly with various other municipally and governmentally controlled activities, including tourist development, discriminatory housing and building policies for Palestinians, house demolitions, and the procurement of homes for Jewish settlers. These activities have progressed simultaneously and with a common goal: to mark the ground of a continued Jewish presence, both historically and territorially, and to justify Israeli's occupation of East Jerusalem. And since 2002, when Elad took on the official role of managing the City of David Archaeological Park, these investments have seemed to be more efficiently coordinated and irrevocably entangled, despite efforts to disguise excavation and tourist development as scientifically framed and culturally motivated.

LIGHT AT THE END OF THE TUNNEL?

In 1999 Reich and Shukron published an article in a popular archaeology journal entitled "Light at the End of the Tunnel: Warren's Shaft Theory of David's Conquests Shattered."[40] This publication, and the excavations on which it was based, had the potential to liberate the Southeast Hill from its longstanding burden to provide the physical proof of the biblical narrative of King David's conquest. For nearly 150 years, Warren's theory that a vertical sinkhole in proximity of the Gihon Spring was used by the Israelites to conquer Jerusalem from the Jebusites was widely accepted among scholars and was a magnet for anyone visiting Silwan. Reich and Shukron's excavations established that Warren's Shaft, was not accessible until about two hundred years after the legendary conquest, dated to around 1000 B.C.E. They also showed that the site's most impressive features, including fortifications and water installations, were built during the Middle Bronze Age, long before King David's and King Solomon's reigns. But despite the fact that the theory of David's conquest via Warren's Shaft has lost its credibility, the rapidly expanding underground facilities have met with growing interest and enthusiasm among tourists and visitors. Those facilities, consisting of natural cavities and fissures as well as of built tunnels and halls, many of them carved out only in recent years, have proved to be suitable grounds for physically reenacting the adventurism of the city's past and present explorers and experiencing the mysteries of the biblical and historical narratives set in Jerusalem.

This potential has been recognized and used in the context of the new archaeological circuit that provides a direct link between the City of David in Silwan and the Western Wall Plaza in the Jewish Quarter. Referred to as the Herodian Street and Tunnel,[41] the underground route begins at the Siloam Pool near the southern tip of the City of David and resurfaces at the Givati Parking Lot. From there, visitors can continue through another underground segment leading under the Old City walls and emerge via a Herodian street running under Robinson's Arch and leading to the southwest corner of the Temple Mount. Other than the area near the Siloam Pool, which consists of a paved esplanade and two parallel segments of stepped streets, most of the route consists of a drainage channel, which had been exposed (in short sections) in various expeditions conducted over the last century.[42] This system was designed to carry the wastewater—rainwater runoff and sewage—first down to the Central Valley and then southward, debouching outside the city. Though the circuit is advertised as the path trod by pilgrims of the Second Temple period ascending from the City of David to the Temple Mount, only few sections of the original pavement overlying the channel are preserved (see figure 30).[43] Neither the original path nor its date can be fully and accurately reconstructed.[44] The clearing of this channel necessitated the construction of extremely complicated and powerful support structures made of cement and steel piles—no doubt at the cost of millions of dollars—and yet the futility of this project from an archaeological point of view is obvious, perhaps more so than any other excavation conducted in Jerusalem. The recent excavations have revealed nothing that was not known prior nor did they promise to provide any useful data or enhance the knowledge regarding the chronology, function, or topography of the area. Its purpose was to strengthen the Jewish narrative of pilgrimage to the Holy City, as well as to create both a tangible and ideological link between the First and Second Temple periods, between the City of David and the Temple Mount, and finally between the Israelite and Jewish past and the Israeli present. Strengthening the Jewish ties to the neighborhood and undermining the position of Palestinian residents, their historical roots and their current civic rights, are interrelated realities that lead to tangible facts both below and above the ground, sealing the irreversible reality of Israeli occupation.

What does the light we see at the end of the recently excavated tunnels illuminate? Which scholarly riddles were elucidated, if the theory of David's legendary

FIGURE 30. Herodian street section with artist reconstruction of Second Temple period pilgrimage scene. Photo by Katharina Galor.

conquest was debunked? And how do these mobilize the interest and attention among hundreds and thousands of tourists annually? The archaeological findings in Silwan certainly carry an intrinsic value and are instructive in relation to Jerusalem's early history, in particular regarding the city's water and fortification systems. But in spite of the expeditions' persistent focus on early periods and their minor engagement with post-Byzantine remains, the significance of the discoveries with regard to the biblical narrative is limited, if not completely absent, for the periods associated with the rules of David and Solomon. It appears that the holiness that the City of David holds for some is recent, ideologically motivated, and not anchored in the tradition of an ancient sanctuary.

8

The Church of the Holy Sepulchre

Following the narrow alleys of the Muristan in the Christian Quarter, heading toward Christian Quarter Road, one ultimately faces the Parvis, the enclosed courtyard with its twin portal and main entrance of the Church of the Holy Sepulchre, a rather clustered access often overwhelmed by the relentless movement of visitors (see figure 31). Other than the relative calm on the rooftop compound occupied by the Ethiopian monks, the place is mostly filled with the hustle and bustle of thousands of clergy and pilgrims, creating one of the liveliest scenes in the Old City.[1] The Church of the Holy Sepulchre represents one of Christendom's holiest sites, venerated as the place of Jesus's crucifixion, burial, and resurrection. Originally built under Constantine the Great in the fourth century C.E., most of the surviving structure is a testimony to the reconstruction programs of the eleventh and twelfth centuries.

The spatial intricacy and complexity of the compound results from the multiple destruction and rebuilding campaigns that have, over centuries, incorporated surviving architectural features into new additions and overall building designs. Housing numerous chapels, niches, and altars shared and administered by six denominations, the church has an atmosphere of spirituality mingled with a mostly manageable chaos, though it frequently gives away to conflicts among the different religious communities. The first attempt to regulate the recurrent frictions was a firman issued by the Sublime Porte in 1767, establishing a division of the church among the claimants. The territorial partition, as well as the rights and privileges of the communities involved, were reconfirmed by the Status Quo of the Christian Holy Places in 1852. A visual reminder of this partition is the Immovable Ladder (see figure 32), leaning against a window ledge of the church's facade. Except for

FIGURE 31. Aerial view of the Church of the Holy Sepulchre, looking northwest. Photo by Hanan Isachar.

FIGURE 32. The Immovable Ladder of the Church of the Holy Sepulchre. Photo by Katharina Galor.

two occasions, the wooden ladder has remained in the same location since the eighteenth century, due to an understanding that no community members may move, rearrange, or alter any property without the consent of all six orders.[2]

With the exception of the relatively brief interlude of the Byzantine period, when the church reflected the imperial program of creating a magnet for Christian pilgrims, this monument has existed as an island under Muslim and, most recently, Jewish dominion. A reminder of the long-term Muslim governance of Jerusalem is the fact that the responsibility to open and lock the door of the Holy Sepulchre rests in the hands of Muslims. The keys to the church's main door are held by the Joudeh and Nuseibeh families, allegedly entrusted as custodians by Salah al-Din in the Ayyubid period.[3]

In spite of the sustained tension among the different Christian communities who hold a share in the building, external religious and political pressures have created some kind of unity, a complex situation reflected also in the architectural and archaeological exploration of the site, as well as in its conservation program.

EXPLORATION AND FINDINGS

Scholarly interest in the Church of the Holy Sepulchre began in the nineteenth century with preliminary studies conducted by George Williams, Melchior de Vogüé, and Charles Wilson, followed by more comprehensive investigations of the history and archaeology of the site by Louis-Hugues Vincent and Félix-Marie Abel at the beginning of the twentieth century.[4] The severe dilapidation of the church, the result of centuries of neglect, combined with the damage caused by an earthquake in 1927 as well as two fires, one in 1934 and another in 1949, led to the decision to undertake major restoration projects. These initiatives also provided the opportunity for excavations, which were begun in the church complex in 1960. Between 1960 and 1969, Virgilio Corbo, a Franciscan friar working on behalf of his order, explored various areas within the Anastasis, the Chapel of the Apparition to the Virgin, the Franciscan monastery, the gallery over the Virgin's Pillars, and, finally, the Chapel of the Finding of the True Cross.[5] Additional work was conducted at the invitation of the Greek Orthodox Patriarchate. In 1970 Anastasios Ekonomopoulos supervised the excavation in the area of the Katholikon , and in 1977 Christos Katsimbinis led the work carried out at the Rock of Golgotha.[6] In 1975 the Armenian Orthodox Patriarchate initiated excavations in the Chapel of St. Vartan, which were originally carried out by untrained clergy of their order and later continued and documented by Israeli archaeologist Magen Broshi.[7] In 1997, the Coptic Metropolitan of Jerusalem and the Near East invited Israeli archaeologists Gideon Avni and Jon Seligman to work in their section of the church, focusing on the subterranean spaces in between the church and the al-Khanqah al-Salahiyya Mosque and al-Khanqah Street.[8]

Excavations conducted underneath the floors of the Church of the Holy Sepulchre and other buildings in its proximity have established that throughout most of the Iron Age, the site was used as a stone quarry. Toward the end of the Iron Age, the area was abandoned and replaced by sporadic domestic construction.[9] Several late Hellenistic and early Roman burials, cut into the walls of the former quarry, including the so-called Tomb of Joseph of Arimathea, indicate that the area remained outside the city walls until at least through the period associated with the time of Jesus's execution.[10] Most scholars have interpreted this evidence as support of the description in the Gospel accounts, which concur that Jesus was buried in a newly cut, rock-hewn tomb (John 19:38–41; Luke 23:50–53; Matthew 27:51–61).[11]

According to Eusebius (*Vita Constantini* 3.26), as part of his newly designed forum, Hadrian built a temple dedicated to Aphrodite on the site of Jesus's burial. The raised podium of the temple was apparently designed to hide the tomb, which left it intact until it was again revealed under Constantine. Late Roman building remains uncovered below the grounds of the church have been associated with the temple and the civic basilica of the city's forum.[12] When Constantine the Great decided to erect a commemorative church on Jesus's burial site, the first act was to demolish Hadrian's temple. Once the tomb was revealed, the surrounding rock mass was hewn away with the goal of isolating the tomb within a circular plaza. This plaza was then used as a starting point to develop a larger complex known as the Church of the Holy Sepulchre, which originally included four major components (from east to west): the atrium or entrance courtyard, where holy relics were kept; the Martyrium, a large basilica featuring a central nave and four side aisles; the Triportico, an open courtyard incorporating Golgotha, the place mentioned in the Gospels as the site of the crucifixion (Matthew 27:33; Mark 15:22, John 19:17); and finally the Rotunda, also known as the Anastasis (resurrection in Greek) enclosing the Sepulchre or holy tomb (see figure 33).[13] The church incurred damage during the Persian conquest of Jerusalem in 614, and some renovations were made after Emperor Heraclius retook the city in 629.

In 1009 Fatimid Caliph al-Hakim bi-Amr Allah ordered the demolition of the large basilica. From then onward, the Sepulchre and Golgotha became the prime focus of restoration projects, the first major one begun in 1030, under Emperor Constantine IX Monomachus, and the second completed on the fiftieth anniversary of the Crusader conquest in 1149.[14] The eleventh-century renovation design turned the Rotunda into a circular church with an apse on the east and the main entrance on the south. It was at this point that access to the church was facilitated through the Parvis, still in use as the main entrance into the church to this day. The Crusaders removed the apse and enclosed the Rock of Golgotha, thus incorporating it and the Sepulchre into one coherent structure for the first time, which was built in a typical Romanesque style.[15] At the same time, a monastery for the Augustinian Order was established on the site of the former Constantinian basilica. The

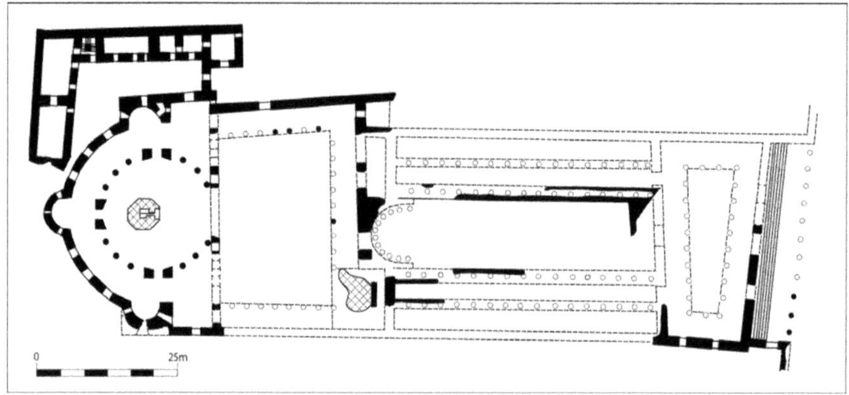

FIGURE 33. Plan of the Constantinian Church of the Holy Sepulchre. Redrawn by Franziska Lehmann, after: Corbo, *Il Santo Sepolcro*, pl. 3.

present Church of the Holy Sepulchre is primarily a result of these eleventh-and twelfth-century restorations, which incorporated minor traces of the earlier building stages as well as some recent additions and modifications made both within the complex and on the exterior.[16]

During the course of the nineteenth and twentieth centuries, a number of incoherent restoration initiatives were carried out by the different communities responsible of the various subsections of the church. Some of these changes appear to reflect the ethnic origins of the communities in charge. The areas remodeled by the Franciscans, for instance, clearly reflect the architectural and artistic principles of the Western churches, while the sections under the control of the Greek Orthodox order replicate the style of Orthodox churches.[17] Thus, the architectural history of the Holy Sepulchre reflects the theological and cultural intricacies of the development of Jerusalem's historic churches, their role within the larger Christian world, and finally their relationships with local governance and politics.[18]

BETWEEN FAITH AND SCIENCE

The desire to validate the site of Jesus's crucifixion and burial and to confirm that the Constantinian church built three centuries later commemorated the authentic location of the events described in the Gospel accounts determined most of the eventual scientific exploration of the Church of the Holy Sepulchre. The resulting scholarship was largely an attempt to understand the physical remains in light of the textual traditions, both the New Testament account and extra-canonical sources. Much of the site's physical development has been explored by members of the church's own communities, but there have also been several recent attempts to appoint external and impartial professionals to oversee conservation and restoration initiatives and to conduct and evaluate archaeological excavations. One such initiative was an international conference of architects in 1955 and the creation of a group called the Common Technical Bureau in 1959, bringing together Armenian, Greek, and French architects to oversee surveys and excavation and restoration projects.[19] The professional and scholarly engagement with the ecclesiastic complex, however, never aroused much interest among the Protestant or Evangelical communities.

In the late nineteenth century, another site was suggested as the place of Jesus's crucifixion and burial. This site, known as the Garden Tomb (see figure 34), is located outside the Old City boundaries, just north of Damascus Gate. Discovered in 1867, it was first documented by Conrad Schick and other early Jerusalem scholars.[20] On the occasion of his visit in Jerusalem in 1883, General Charles George Gordon, a British military hero, identified the rock scarp adjacent to the tomb as the hill of Golgotha. Soon after Gordon's visit, his interpretation gained popularity, and a controversy emerged over which site was the legitimate burial place of Jesus. The Church of the Holy Sepulchre was supported mostly by Catholics, the Garden Tomb mainly by Protestants.[21] Much of the desire to provide an alternative to the traditional site stemmed from the rapidly growing interest of Westerners in visiting the Holy Land and, more specifically, their lack of a proprietary share in the Church of the Holy Sepulchre, as well as their distaste for its gloomy and often filthy spaces, crowded primarily with priests, monks, and pilgrims from Eastern countries.[22] Most of the literature defending the Garden Tomb as the authentic site of Jesus's burial published since then, however, is based on theological beliefs rather than on scientific arguments.[23] A renewed archaeological investigation of the tomb initiated in 1974 established that it was hewn and first used during the Iron Age II (eighth to seventh centuries B.C.E.). During the Roman period—that is, when Jesus was crucified and buried—the structure was abandoned and not used again for burial purposes until the Byzantine period.[24] Other than the Garden Tomb, numerous additional burial structures dating from the Iron Age have been excavated and documented in the area to the north of Damascus Gate, thus supporting a coherent picture for the area in which the Protestant contender of Jesus's burial site is located, both from a functional and a chronological point of view.[25] The only advantage the Garden Tomb holds over the area of the Church of the Holy Sepulchre is its location beyond the Old City walls; in antiquity, crucifixions and burials would have taken place outside the city boundaries. This advantage, however, does not hold true for the time of Jesus's crucifixion, when the site of the Holy Sepulchre was located outside the Second Wall. The Third Wall, which brought the site into the boundaries of the protected city, was built shortly after Jesus was executed, sometime between 41 and 44, under the reign of Herod Agrippa I, the grandson of Herod the Great.[26] Hadrian's attempt to obliterate the

FIGURE 34. Garden Tomb. Photo by Katharina Galor.

memory of Jesus's tomb at the beginning of the second century by erecting a pagan temple on it, at which point the site was no longer outside the city walls, has thus been used as the strongest argument in support of preserving the authentic site of his burial. Given the discovery of several funerary structures dating from the general time period of Jesus's ministry and death, both underneath the Church of the Holy Sepulchre and in the adjacent areas, and the logical conclusion that the site was located outside the city boundaries at the time of the crucifixion, the claim of authenticity of the location of the church as the true burial site of Jesus can not be refuted on archaeological grounds. Thus, despite the lack of an ultimate physical proof, the Holy Sepulchre nevertheless holds an advantage over the site of the Garden Tomb. For the latter, archaeological evidence establishes unequivocally that the area had not been used as a burial ground at the time of Jesus's death.

The history of the Church of the Holy Sepulchre's Aedicule (the little structure enclosing what was believed to represent Jesus's actual burial), located within the heart of the Rotunda, has been far less contentious. Martin Biddle's recent study of the successive shrines that were built over the site of the purported tomb, from the time of Constantine to the present, has maintained its place as the most authoritative voice on the subject.[27] The present Aedicule was built in 1810 by the Greek Orthodox community but preserves the interior marble cladding from the sixteenth century.[28]

Beyond the controversy over the location of Jesus's burial place, only a few minor points regarding the architectural history of Church of the Holy Sepulchre have been debated among scholars. Of interest among these is the drawing of a ship with an inscription located on a wall of St. Krekor's Chapel. According to Magen Broshi, the drawing was executed during the construction of the foundations of the Constantinian basilica and represents the earliest documentation of a Christian pilgrim to the Holy Land. Shimon Gibson and Joan Taylor reject this view and argue instead for a second-century C.E. date.[29] Furthermore, various interpretations based on Eusebius's description of the Rotunda have been put forward. According to Corbo, the Anastasis was built as a roofed building at the time of Constantine. In Charles Coüasnon's view, there were two stages, both of them dating to the fourth century; during a first phase, the Sepulchre was a simple mausoleum standing in an open courtyard, surrounded by columns; then, during a second stage, the building was covered, enclosing the tomb.[30] Various other discrepancies regarding the structural and architectural history of the ecclesiastic complex fill the pages of numerous scholarly publications.[31] These do not, however, affect the denominational conflicts, which persist to this day.

THE COMMUNITIES: COOPERATION AND FRICTION

Several different communities currently coexist in the Church of the Holy Sepulchre. These include the three major shareholders: the Greek Orthodox, the Latins (Roman Catholics), and the Armenians. The three minor communities are the Copts, the Syrian-Jacobites, and the Ethiopians. The development of the religious rights and allotments in the church reflects the history of Christianity in the city as it evolved over the course of some seven hundred years. The first significant split between the Orthodox and the Monophysite communities (Armenians, Coptics, Syrian-Jacobites, and Ethiopians) occurred in 451, when the Council of Chalcedon declared that Christ had two natures, one divine and the other human. These theological differences soon transpired in spheres that determined religious practice, social and economic opportunities, as well as cultural and artistic preferences.

In spite of the lack of concrete documentation for a regulated coexistence of various denominations worshipping in the Church of the Holy Sepulchre during the Byzantine and early Islamic periods, it is generally assumed that some informal agreements with regard to conducting different services were in place even from the very beginning.[32] It appears that it was not until 1054, when Michael Cerularius, patriarch of Constantinople, refused to accept the supreme authority of the pope in Rome, that the division between the Eastern (later Greek Orthodox) and the Western (later Roman Catholic or Latin) branches of Christianity were formally recognized.[33] With the Crusader conquest of the city, in 1099, and the founding of the Latin patriarchate in Jerusalem, the rift between the Latin and Greek Orthodox communities within the context of the Church of the Holy Sepulchre was firmly established.[34]

Beginning with Salah al-Din's conquest of Jerusalem, in 1187, the divisions among different communities were exploited by imposing taxes for the rights of possession within the church. Another means of establishing the polarity between the new religious authority and the inferior status of the tolerated Christian communities living within the city and sharing the church was by handing the keys to the Holy Sepulchre to two Muslim families, a tradition that has survived to the present.[35]

The current spatial distribution in the church originated in the thirteenth century, with minor changes introduced between the fourteenth and sixteenth centuries (see figure 35). Additional modifications were made after the Ottoman conquest in 1516 when the Orthodox, Latins, and Armenians increased their possessions, to the detriment of the smaller communities, who no longer could afford the steadily increasing taxes imposed by the new rulers.[36] In the mid-nineteenth century, the most significant areas within the church were turned into common property, including the Aedicule, the Rotunda, the Stone of Unction, the south transept, the Parvis, and the entrance to the church. The remaining spaces, many of which are used as chapels, remained divided among the different denominations and include the following: the Katholikon, two of the three chapels in the ambulatory, the northern part of Calvary, the Prison of Christ, most rooms surrounding the Rotunda, various buildings bordering the Parvis, the monastery of St. Abraham and the belfry belong to the Greek Orthodox community; the south part of Calvary, the Chapel of Apparition, the Chapel of Mary's Agony, and the Chapel of the Invention of the Cross are owned by the Latins; the Chapel of St. Helena, the Chapel of the Parting of the Raiment, the Chapel of St. John, the Station of the Holy Women, and one of the rooms bordering the Rotunda belong to the Armenians; the Chapel of Nicodemus and the adjacent Tomb of Joseph of Arimathea are under Syrian ownership; the chapel to the west of the Aedicule, the two rooms south of the Chapel of Nicodemus, as well as a building west of the main entrance belong to the Copts; and finally, the Chapel of St. Michael and the Chapel of the Four Beasts to the east of the Parvis, as well as the courtyard of Dair as-Sultan belong to the domain of the Ethiopians.[37] Various subsections of the church have changed hands repeatedly over the centuries, intricate allocation processes too complex to review here. Indicative of the volatility of ownership is the Calvary, which was reappropriated five times—going back and forth between the Armenians and Georgians—in a period of only thirty years in the 1400s.[38]

The first official declaration freezing the rights of worship and possession of the religious denominations within the church was issued in 1852 by Sultan Abdul Mejid, in a decree known as the Status Quo.[39] The following year, the sultan transferred the power of jurisdiction over the Holy Sepulchre and other holy places of worship from Palestine to the Sublime Porte. In 1878, Article LXII of the Treaty of Berlin incorporated the decrees into international law. The Status Quo, frequently but often inappropriately referenced even today, represents a customary set of

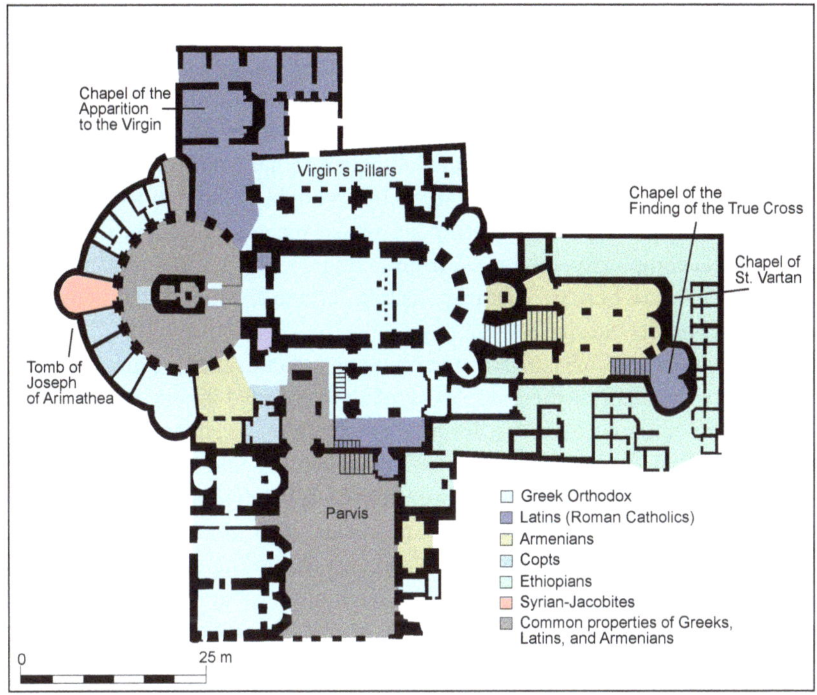

FIGURE 35. Plan showing denominational distribution of space in the Church of the Holy Sepulchre. Drawn by Franziska Lehmann.

practices defining possessions, usage, and liturgy within the church, enabling the different communities to live and worship side by side. Rather than being a definitive code, it consists of a number of overlapping understandings of conventions, with each community holding to its own singular compilation of rules. And it is this flexibility—or rather discrepancy between the different versions—that have maintained the tension and conflicts among the different church orders.[40]

During the first half of Ottoman rule, the more serious conflicts were solved in the Muslim religious courts. After the 1852 firman, most disagreements were handled by the governor. Under British Mandatory administration, efforts were made to both maintain and update the Ottoman system of adjudicating internal church conflicts, a method that itself proved problematic.[41] Given the lack of official documents codifying established customary rights, it was often difficult, if not impossible, to judge disputes fairly and authoritatively. In an attempt to overcome these difficulties, the administrative complexities increased over time, and authorities of various ranks were consulted, including the district commissioner, the high commissioner, the chief secretary, and sometimes the colonial secretary of state.[42] In certain ways, the Status Quo of 1852 was maintained even more meticulously during Mandatory rule than during the Ottoman period. Pro forma Israeli policy on the issue of the holy places followed the rules defined by the

British, which, in the case of the Church of the Holy Sepulchre, became relevant only after Israel's capture of East Jerusalem in 1967. Though Israel acknowledged "its international responsibility for the deep spiritual attachment of other peoples to the Holy City," the government did not assume any legal obligation to honor any of the Status Quo rights.[43] As a result, any internal conflicts among different religious communities of the Holy Sepulchre brought before the Israeli Supreme Court were relegated to the government, which repeatedly—given the religious and political complexity—refrained from taking decisions.[44] The tendency under Israeli rule has thus been to defer responsibility and to encourage the communities to resolve conflicts internally.

Disagreements among the various religious communities within the Church of the Holy Sepulchre—the complexity of their internal affairs as well as their tenuous dependencies on the frequently changing legal and governmental policies—have impacted the structural development and maintenance of the building complex. Despite the improvements of the Status Quo system regarding spatial usage and worship regulations, one of its major drawbacks concerns the lack of provision for carrying out repair works. According to Ottoman property law, payment for repair of a structure indicated possession. As a result, whenever one community was willing to cover renovation or construction costs—which would confer to them ownership—the other communities would do their utmost to block the initiative.

Several successful renovations, such as those carried out in the Aedicule in 1555, on the dome in 1719, or more globally after the fire of 1808, provided opportunities to lay proprietary claims on certain sections of the church and consolidate existing proprietary rights. At the same time, however, numerous necessary repairs, which transpired over the centuries, were blocked at the outset, a situation that contributed to the substantial architectural dilapidation of the Holy Sepulchre.

In 1933, British architect William Harvey reported the danger of imminent collapse of the Holy Sepulchre and argued that emergency scaffolding had to be erected, a result of centuries of neglect, enhanced by a major earthquake that struck Jerusalem in 1927. Various political events over the next twenty years, including the Arab revolt, World War II, and the 1948 Arab-Israel conflict, delayed immediate action. Among the most absurd proposals was the complete replacement of the entire church complex and half of the Christian Quarter, a solution proposed and endorsed by the Roman Catholic custodianship in 1949, a plan that incorporated a chapel for Anglican use. Fortunately, it was unanimously rejected by both the Greek Orthodox and the Armenian communities.[45]

It was not until 1954 that architects—appointed on behalf of the Greek Orthodox, the Latins, and the Armenians—drew up a joint report documenting the precarious structural condition of the building complex and gave recommendations for feasible solutions. Major restorations were carried out between 1961 and 1980, including repair work on foundations, cisterns, walls, ceilings, domes, vaults, columns, and various architectural details.

After the death of the Greek Orthodox Patriarch Benedict of Jerusalem in 1980, the restoration work of the church temporarily came to a halt, and the Common Technical Bureau, originally established in 1952, ceased to operate. The Aedicule, the paving throughout the church, and the electrical and sewage systems were left in a state of disrepair. The 1997 agreement to restore the dome, signed by the three religious communities administering the church in 1994, enabled the scaffolding that had covered the dome since 1970, to be removed. Armenian Patriarch Manoogian referred to the agreement as "a turning point for all Christendom" providing "telling evidence of the new spirit of ecumenical rapprochement" in both the Western and Eastern Christian worlds.[46] The renovations of the latrine facilities, however, originally agreed upon in 2007, partially as a result of the improved relations between the Latin and Greek communities, have not yet been implemented. The delay is due to a dispute regarding the sewage line, which runs under the contested grounds of the Coptic patriarchate. The unresolved conflict impacts the Greek Orthodox and Armenian protocols of the miracle of the Holy Fire, an Easter ceremony key to both denominations.[47] Various other minor gestures and disruptions of established procedures continue to disturb the daily coexistence of the communities, indicative of the denominational rivalry that taints the atmosphere inside the Holy Sepulchre.[48]

BETWEEN RELIGIOUS RIVALRY AND POLITICAL UNITY

For most of the history of the Church of the Holy Sepulchre, and even during the three centuries that preceded its erection, Christians represented a minority in the city, with limited social and political powers.[49] Throughout centuries of Muslim and, most recently, Jewish rule, the church persevered as an island of Christian faith, in which different denominations vied for a role in guarding the site for believers from around the world. The building history of the Holy Sepulchre reflects the tumultuous evolution of the Christian presence in Jerusalem and its relationship with the region's ruling powers, which have had varying sympathy toward the church's cause. This history is displayed in the physical signs of multiple destruction and reconstruction programs.[50] In spite of internal schisms and conflicts between the communities of the church and those conflicts' often negative impact on necessary conservation measures, the architectural and archaeological study of the site has progressed in a relatively coherent direction. One of the primary goals of all involved clergy, professionals, and researchers has been to trace the church's role in preserving the memory of the site of Jesus's burial and crucifixion and how the building complex has adjusted to the ever-changing political and cultural context. Other than the objections voiced by the Anglican and Protestant communities with regard to the authenticity of the site, which were based on theological and political rather than on scientific grounds, none of the architectural or archaeological work undertaken in and near the Church of the Holy Sepulchre has threatened the religious and historical validity of the monument in the eyes of the universal church. Indicative of this overall confidence is the fact that, since the 1980s, Israeli archaeologists have been invited by the clergy to contribute to the scientific exploration of the church, serving in some ways as an unbiased professional body, capable of providing an external confirmation of an established tradition.

In contrast to the church's reliance on professional support from Israeli archaeologists, the overall political climate has led to distrust of and opposition to the Israeli government. Since Israel's capture of East Jerusalem in 1967, the clergy of the Holy Sepulchre and, more generally, of the historic churches in the city—which, unlike the local Christian laity, is mostly non-Palestinian—have become more involved politically. Mayor Teddy Kollek's investment in good relations with the Christian communities in the early years after Israel's capture of East Jerusalem started to fall apart in the late 1980s. Since then, various efforts on the part of the Israeli government to discourage the creation of a united Christian front against Israeli policies in Jerusalem and to prevent any possibility of a Muslim-Christian religious coalition, which would strengthen and protect the Palestinian nationalist leadership, have had limited impact. Israel's covert support for settler penetration into the Christian quarters of the Old City has, in fact, led to an unprecedented degree of coordination among the different church denominations. The occupation of St. John's Hospice in April 1990 by a settler movement was a defining event and was indicative of the more recent rapport between the Israeli government and the established Christian communities of Jerusalem. The immediate response of the Church of the Holy Sepulchre was to close its doors to visitors for twenty-four hours, the first time the church had done so in eight hundred years.[51] A more lasting response, indicative of the growing rift between the historic churches and the Israeli government, was the publication of the "Statements by the Heads of Christian Communities In Jerusalem" between 1988 and 1992.[52] The document implied that the Christian religious leadership would likely have more influence in a bicommunal Palestinian state than in an exclusivist Zionist one in which settlers are given free rein. In this regard, the 1994 Memorandum (another declaration written by the heads of the Christian communities in Jerusalem), a vital document on the significance of Jerusalem for Christians, is the ultimate reference point for any discussion of the Christian role in the city.[53] It reaffirms the importance of the Status Quo arrangements in their present form.[54]

In spite of the numerous impairments and destructions that the Church of the Holy Sepulchre has suffered, this monument has survived for more than 1,600 years.

The communities in charge of its upkeep and maintenance have faced numerous internal conflicts, accentuated by the struggles that Christianity has faced more globally. It appears that there are two factors that have allowed the communities and, as a result, the building to survive: first, the need to overcome internal differences and disputes so as to face the threat of external political and religious powers as a united force; and second, the continuity of tradition, which venerates the site and associated building complex as the authentic burial place of Jesus. Unlike numerous, or even most, other Christian holy sites, architectural surveys and archaeological work conducted in and near the Holy Sepulchre have provided additional validation for a centuries-old religious conviction regarding the location of the burial of Jesus.

9

The Temple Mount / Haram al-Sharif

The best view overlooking the Temple Mount (in Hebrew, *Har Ha-Bayit*), or the Haram al-Sharif (Noble Sanctuary), is either from the Mount of Olives to its east or from the Haas Promenade on the so-called Hill of Evil Counsel to its south. The raised platform, crowned by the golden cupola of the Dome of the Rock *(Qubbat as-Sakhrah),* as well as various monuments built throughout the 1,300 years of the city's Islamic rule, visually dominate the Old City (see figures 1 and 36). Its sheer size and solid appearance compensate for its inferior elevation in comparison to the Western Hill—today's Armenian, Jewish, and Christian Quarters, which are some twenty-five meters higher—thus still deserving of the term *acropolis,* usually a town's or city's most elevated ground. More so than any other monument in the city, new or old, contradictory impressions emanate from this place, blending a sense of sanctity, peace, and salvation with hatred, tension, and violence.

The hill on which the platform sits is traditionally identified with Mount Moriah (Genesis 22:2). According to the biblical narrative, David bought the property from Araunah the Jebusite and erected an altar (2 Samuel 24:16–25 and 1 Chronicles 21:15–22), which his son, Solomon, replaced with the First Temple (2 Chronicles 3:1). The same location is also associated with the Binding of Isaac (Psalm 24:3; Isaiah 2:3 and 30:29; and Zechariah 8:3). Tradition holds that the site of the Second Temple, built after the Babylonian exile, and the restored Herodian Temple were erected in exactly the same spot as the First Temple. Though ancient sanctuaries were often built in place of earlier holy sites or monuments, even as divinities were substituted or religions replaced, no physical traces of either temple has survived, and thus speculations and opinions regarding the exact location are numerous and diverse.[1] The choice to build the Dome of the Rock on the assumed spot of the

146

FIGURE 36. Aerial view of the Haram al-Sharif, looking east. Photo by Hanan Isachar.

destroyed Jewish Temple, however, is documented in historical sources from the early Islamic period.[2] Subsequently, the same site has been venerated by Muslims as the location of the "Farthest Mosque" mentioned in the Qur'an (17:1), marking the place of Muhammad's miraculous Night Journey to heaven *(Surah al-Isra)*. In Muslim tradition, it was Ishmael, the ancestor of the Arab people, rather than Isaac, whom Abraham prepared to sacrifice (Qur'an 37:100–106).

For Jews, the location of the former temples has determined the direction of worship throughout the world from antiquity to the present. For Muslims, the original *qiblah* (direction of prayer) was toward the Haram al-Sharif; this was replaced by the Holy Kaaba in Mecca in the second year of the migration of the Prophet Muhammad to Medina, in 624 C.E. (Qur'an 2:142–44).[3]

Other than a few subterranean building components, consisting primarily of cisterns and water channels, many of which date to the Hellenistic period, the most substantial remainders of the enclosure wall can be linked to the renovations initiated under King Herod the Great in the second half of the first century B.C.E. and completed shortly before the outbreak of the First Jewish Revolt in 66 C.E. The most significant damage to the Herodian complex, in particular to the Jewish Temple and the Royal Stoa located on top of the platform, was suffered during the destruction caused by the Romans in the year 70 C.E. Whether, during the late Roman period, a pagan temple or simply a statue dedicated to Jupiter took the place of the former Jewish Temple is unclear.[4] But it is generally agreed upon that, during Byzantine rule, there was a desire to eradicate the memory of the Jewish Temple and that the site was used as a quarry and garbage dump.[5]

The revival of the site as a major sanctuary occurred after the city's Muslim conquest in 638 C.E., first with the construction of a rudimentary mosque at the southern extremity of the platform and, most significantly, under Umayyad rule, with the building of the Dome of the Rock under Abd al-Malik in 691 C.E. and the al-Aqsa Mosque under his son Abd al-Walid in 715 C.E.[6] Renovations and reconstructions, as well as numerous new building initiatives on top of the platform throughout the city's Islamic rule, testify to the important role the monument retained as an active place of worship, upholding its position as the third holiest pilgrimage site in Islam after Mecca and Medina.[7]

Though the destruction of the Herodian Temple in Jerusalem represents an important turning point in Jewish worship, not only eliminating the priesthood and animal sacrifice, but also affecting other significant religious, political, and cultural changes, the memory of the abolished ritual practice and vanished physical presence of the Temple has retained a central role in Judaism to this day. Sacred space in Herod's sanctuary was restricted to the Temple itself, including the various courtyards within the boundaries of the *soreg* (a low fence), thus segregating this area from most of the platform and enclosure wall, which remained accessible to Gentiles. After the destruction under the Roman general Titus in 70 C.E., the substructure gained sanctity, blurring the Temple's original barriers from the rest of the complex as early as the Roman and Byzantine periods.[8]

Throughout most of Islamic rule in the city, access to the platform itself was limited to Muslims. During the first few centuries of Ottoman rule, the policy of prohibiting non-Muslims from accessing the Haram was maintained, but the restriction was loosened in the early nineteenth century, when a few Westerners started to be permitted to visit and study the monument. During the Mandatory period, non-Muslims were officially granted access to the Haram for the first time, and the Ottoman Status Quo was extended to the Western Wall, allowing Jews to worship in this location. Under Hashemite rule, Jews were no longer able to enter East Jerusalem, but the platform remained accessible to Christian visitors and explorers.

Since the 1967 capture of East Jerusalem, Israel claimed political sovereignty over the compound, but granted the Waqf custodianship of the platform.[9] The same Palestinian and Jordanian officials and clergymen who had administered the site before Israel's occupation continued to do so from Amman, with Israel's implicit consent.[10] Though prayer has remained restricted to Muslims only—a rule imposed by the Israeli government, which is often challenged by religious and nationalistic Jewish fringe groups—access was opened to people of other faiths.[11] Since then, regulations and disputes concerning the Temple Mount, including the platform and the Western Wall, have remained under the jurisdiction of the government and Israel's Supreme Court, requiring constant police and military surveillance.[12]

Given the fact that the compound is not only considered a holy place but also an antiquities site, it falls under both the Preservation of the Holy Places Law of 1967 and the Antiquities Law of 1978.[13] Since Israel's rule over East Jerusalem is contested, however, both locally by the Waqf and most of the region's Muslim and Palestinian population, as well as internationally, its authoritative bodies are frequently challenged and dismissed and many of its regulations are unenforceable. The most volatile interrelation among Israeli, Palestinian, and Jordanian authorities, and their dealings with extremist activist groups who view the compound as a symbol of their respective religious and national aspirations, impacts not only the daily rulings as they pertain to visitors and worshippers but also the physical maintenance of a historic key monument—one that requires constant attention and care.

The site of the Temple Mount / Haram al-Sharif therefore embodies a contradiction between a continued veneration transcending religious and national boundaries and the desire either to disrupt the memory of Jewish hegemony or to infringe on the religious freedom and legal entitlements of Muslim worshippers and administrators.

EXCAVATIONS AND SURVEYS

Architect Frederick Catherwood was the first Westerner known to have made detailed drawings of the Haram and the Dome of the Rock in 1833 (see figure 37).[14] Between 1865 and 1869, Charles Wilson and Charles Warren conducted their survey of the complex, including numerous underground installations and various features of the enclosure wall. The results of their work, both the physical and published components, are still used as guidelines for archaeologists and researchers investigating the compound.[15]

The first important contributions to our knowledge of Islamic architecture and building chronology conducted during the last years of Ottoman rule are Keppel Archibald Cameron Creswell's studies of the Dome of the Rock and the al-Aqsa Mosque and Max van Berchem's collection of the Haram's Arabic inscriptions.[16] Following the damage that was caused to the southern area of the platform during the earthquake of 1927, Robert Hamilton conducted a detailed investigation of the al-Aqsa Mosque and opened several excavation trenches within and near the building (see figure 38).[17] Hamilton was at the time director of the British Mandate's Department of Antiquities and the work was thus conducted on behalf of the department, in coordination with the Waqf. His study of the mosque, including numerous plans, sections, and elevations, was published, but it unfortunately lacks

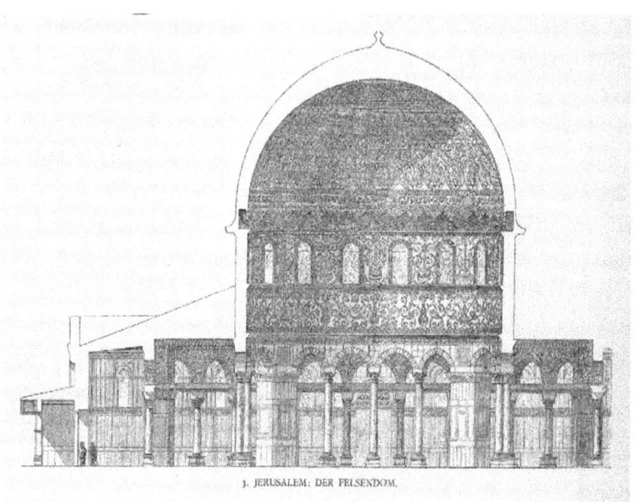

FIGURE 37. Cross section of the Dome of the Rock (print after the first
detailed drawings made by Frederick Catherwood in 1833 from Dehio
and von Bezold, *Die kirchliche Baukunst des Abendlandes,* 1887, Pl. 10).

any detailed documentation of the excavated trenches, which exposed numerous
fragments of mosaic floors. Whether their seemingly late Byzantine style points to
the presence of an undocumented church on top of the platform, as was recently
suggested—a thesis that would completely alter our understanding of the site during the years preceding the Muslim conquest—or whether they were from the
early Umayyad mosque remains unresolved.[18] One could state, though, that Hamilton's venture was a rare and lost opportunity to properly document an excavation
on top of the Haram.

The most extensive excavations to be carried out near the Temple Mount
(Southern Temple Mount excavations), surrounding the southwestern corner of
the enclosure wall and extending all the way to the southeastern corner, were initiated immediately after Israel's capture of East Jerusalem. Benjamin Mazar of Hebrew University directed the campaigns between 1967 and 1982.[19] His work was
continued under the supervision of Ronny Reich and Yaacob Billig and more recently under the directorship of Eilat Mazar.[20] The latest discoveries are related to
the so-called Herodian Street and Tunnel excavations on the Southeast Hill and
encroach upon the area near the southern end of the Western Wall.[21] Documented
remains range in date between the Iron Age and the early Islamic period. The most
significant structures uncovered include various Iron Age installations, building,
and fortification walls; several Herodian-period access facilities to the platform
from the south and the west, as well as cisterns and ritual pools from the same

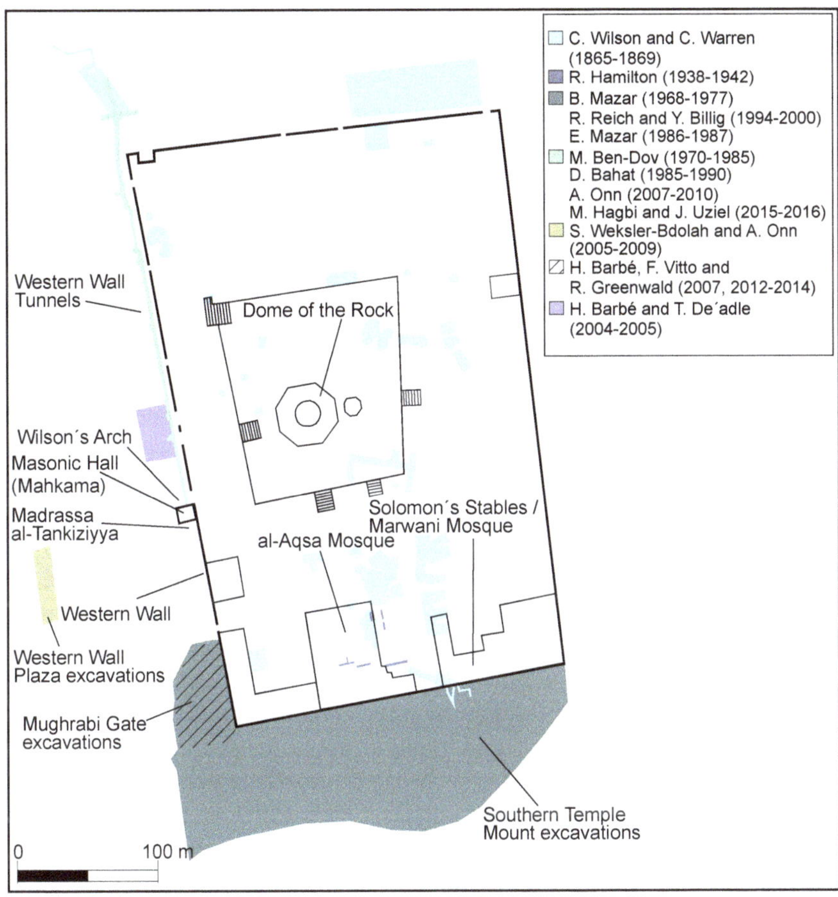

FIGURE 38. Plan of the Haram al-Sharif, with areas of excavation. Drawn by Franziska Lehmann.

period; Byzantine dwellings, workshops, and industrial installations; and, finally, a monumental Umayyad palace complex.

Another project initiated immediately after 1967 was the excavation along the western enclosure wall (Western Wall Tunnels excavations), constituting an extension of the work begun by several scholars of the PEF in the nineteenth century.[22] Some of the early initiatives were supervised and published by archaeologist Meir Ben-Dov. He was replaced by Dan Bahat in 1985.[23] Between 2007 and 2010, Alexander Onn continued the excavations on behalf of the IAA.[24] The exposed remains, ranging in date between the late Hellenistic period and the modern era, are located within a strip, approximately one hundred meters long and eleven meters wide, which extends north of the Western Wall Plaza along the enclosure wall. Most significant are the remains of a Herodian-period arch bridge, sometimes referred to as the Great Causeway, beginning in the east, at Wilson's Arch and stretching westward across the Central Valley. Noteworthy among several buildings located in proximity to the bridge are the Masonic Hall from the Herodian period and the Madrassa al-Tankiziyya, built in 1329 and used as a courthouse during the Mamluk and Ottoman periods.[25]

In spite of the Haram's continued use as a religious sanctuary throughout the history of scientific exploration—and despite the fact that no comprehensive excavations have ever been conducted on top or under the platform—an astonishing amount of documentation has been assembled over the years that allows us to reliably reconstruct the history of this architectural complex, its various building sequences, alterations, destructions, and restorations. This understanding has helped us to trace not only the site's changing interrelationship with various surrounding buildings and access routes but also its impact on Jerusalem's urban profile as it evolved from antiquity to the present. Unlike the Southeast Hill, where conflicting chronologies and interpretations—to a large extent resulting from the use of biblical narratives as a reference to reconstruct cultural changes—still overwhelm the scholarship, very few controversies exist with regard to the structural history of the Temple Mount / Haram al-Sharif. No other monument in Jerusalem has been accompanied by such detailed and regular descriptions provided by contemporaries who visited or lived at the place or who were directly or indirectly involved in the changes that affected its physical appearance and its use.

Flavius Josephus provides us with two very detailed descriptions of Herod's construction of the Temple Mount complex.[26] Early Christian and later medieval pilgrims documented first its use as a Muslim shrine, then its conversion into a Crusader stronghold, and then again back into a Muslim sanctuary. These accounts are complemented by numerous contemporary texts written by historians, geographers, theologians, and government officials.[27] Inscriptions written in Hebrew, Greek, Latin, and Arabic, most of them found in situ, as well as countless manuscripts stored over hundreds of years at the Haram, supplement the data that archaeologists, art historians, and historians have at their disposal.[28] There are a few controversies surrounding some features of the site, but these are relatively minor. For example, there is a lack of support for the dating and interpretation of the so-called Solomonic Wall in the Southern Temple Mount excavations, there are the minor disagreements concerning the date of the renovations of the Herodian enclosure wall extensions and entrance routes and gates, and the dating of Ayyubid versus Crusader constructions are in dispute. These controversies, however, pale in comparison to the disputes that affect our understanding of the early history of the Southeast Hill.[29] The clashes surrounding the Temple Mount or the Haram al-Sharif are indeed of a completely different nature.

CONSTRUCTION, DESTRUCTION, AND SALVAGE CAMPAIGNS

Given the fact that the Haram has functioned continuously as an active place of worship, archaeological surveys and investigations have always been conducted under particularly difficult conditions.[30] Before Israel's capture of East Jerusalem, there was repeated tension and occasional clashes between the guardians of the compound and scholars investigating the site. These problems, however, did not much affect the structural maintenance of the monument and the relationship among the various institutional representatives involved in it. Any conflicts or tensions they had were relatively minor.

Beginning in 1967, however, with the major physical alterations—involving destruction, construction, and excavation—affecting the Haram compound and its immediate surroundings, the conflicts between the different religious and national groups took on new forms. This made it difficult, if not impossible, to undertake any kind of scientific investigation without impacting the highly sensitive and easily explosive nature of the political situation. Two initiatives immediately following the 1967 war set the stage for how Israel's transformation of the Haram's surrounding landscape would permanently alter not only the physical nature of the site but also the sociopolitical interactions among all involved religious groups who share an interest in the monument. The first was the destruction of the historic Mughrabi Quarter for the purpose of creating the Western Wall Plaza; the second was the continued large-scale excavation conducted along the southern and western enclosure walls. Despite the different nature of these actions, both efforts have been at the root of recurrent tensions between Israelis and Palestinians, often escalating from demonstrations and protests to violence and death, with regional as well as international repercussions.

The spatial modifications made by those two initiatives invited the Jewish and Israeli public to participate in this urban transformation in different dimensions—culturally, by experiencing the exposed antiquities within the context of the archaeological park; religiously, by visiting and praying at the Western Wall; and, finally, politically, by observing or partaking in IDF induction ceremonies on the plaza as well as other commemorations and ceremonies, often in the presence of Israel's president.[31] Palestinian Muslims, in contrast, perceived these initiatives as aggressive and explicit attempts to undermine their religious, historical, and cultural ties with one of Islam's holiest sites—a site that had been under their exclusive governance for nearly 1,400 years—as well as the first irreversible steps toward physically encroaching upon or destroying some or even all of the complex.

Surprisingly, however, despite the general discontent within the Muslim world regarding the physical transformations around the Haram area, and notwithstanding the numerous conflicts and even violent clashes between Israelis and Palestinians around issues directly related to the governance and use of the compound, during the first three decades of Israeli occupation in East Jerusalem, there was some degree of cooperation among the various administrative bodies concerned with the site's archaeological and conservation efforts.[32] Both the First Intifada, which broke out in December 1987, and the al-Aqsa Massacre of October 1990, referred to as the stormiest event in the history of Palestinian-Israeli violence at the compound, had already turned the sacred esplanade into a central locus of the national conflict.[33] It was not until 1996 that the informal contacts between the Waqf and the IAA, which had existed since 1967, came to an end. The three key events that most significantly impacted this change were Prime Minister Netanyahu's decision to open the northern end of the Western Wall Tunnels in 1996; the construction of the Marwani Mosque, between 1996 and 1999; and, finally, Likud Party leader Ariel Sharon's visit to the Temple Mount in 2000. The first and third events were perceived by Palestinians as reinforcing the Jewish claim to the Temple Mount and more generally to the city of Jerusalem; the second, in contrast, was perceived by Israelis as an expression of Palestinian denial of Israel's sovereignty over the Haram and East Jerusalem. Since then, as a result of the heightened political tensions between Israelis and Palestinians, combined with the increased awareness, locally and internationally, that archaeology is being used as a political tool, the IAA has reiterated their classification of all new and all continued archaeological projects near the Haram as salvage work. In other words, rather than being conducted purely for the sake of exploring a site's archaeological and historical sequence for the purpose of knowledge construction—as could be easily argued in the case of the Southern Temple Mount excavations—all projects initiated after 1996 have been elaborately justified and broadly publicized by the IAA as necessary prerequisites for required maintenance, repair, or development work.

The opening of the northern end of the Western Wall Tunnels in 1996 led to a chain of catastrophic events and was likely the turning point that led to the IAA applying more scientifically and methodologically conscientious professional procedures and using more carefully designed public communication. Understood by Palestinians as an intentional and provocative act, meant not only to create a physical link between the Jewish and Muslim Quarters but also to encroach upon and potentially destroy a Muslim holy site, the opening of the tunnel led to several outbursts of protest. More publicly than ever, various Israeli governmental agencies—Netanyahu's Likud Party, the Western Wall Heritage Foundation, and the IAA—appeared to conflate political and archaeological interests. This intensified the perceived dual insult of deception and provocation. Verbal condemnations by Palestinian Muslims eventually evolved into gun battles, first in East Jerusalem and then spreading to the West Bank and Gaza Strip, killing a total of fifty-seven Palestinians and fifteen Israelis.[34] The Palestinian activities in reaction to the opening of the Western Wall Tunnels are commonly referred to as the "al-Aqsa Intifada," highlighting the significant role archaeology and religion have played in the popular uprising against Israel's occupation. Following these fatal clashes, the Islamic Movement in Israel organized the first convention *(mihrajan)* under the banner "al-Aqsa is in danger," informing the Palestinian public that Israeli excavations constitute a physical threat to the al-Aqsa Mosque and that Israel is seeking, in a deliberate and systematic manner, to destroy the mosque in order to build the Third Temple in its place.[35] Though excavations had never been carried out with the goal of physically undermining the compound, several Jewish fringe groups have repeatedly called for plans and initiatives to destroy the al-Aqsa Mosque and replace it with a Third Temple, which has contributed to this misunderstanding and the escalating fear among Muslims.[36]

Directly linked to the Western Wall Tunnels through a recently built underground passage and also administered by the Western Wall Heritage Foundation is the Ohel Yitzhak Synagogue, originally established in 1904, abandoned in the 1936–39 Arab revolt, and destroyed during the 1948 war.[37] In conjunction with the renovations and reconstruction of the synagogue, which opened in 2008, excavations were conducted on the ground between 2004 and 2005, directed by Hervé Barbé and Tawfik De'adle from the IAA. Other than providing valuable information on the Roman and Byzantine street network, a well-preserved *hammam* (public bath house) from the Mamluk period, which was identified as Mustahamm Daraj al-Ayn, was exposed.[38] This project establishes the unabashed and continued commitment of the IAA to conduct archaeological work adjacent to the Haram while ignoring Muslim sensitivities and fears about their restricted access to their holy site and their constrained ability to worship.

A further recent project claiming to prepare a necessary development initiative is the Western Wall Plaza excavations. The planned development concerns the Beit Haliba Building, designed to oversee prayer and tourism on the plaza and in the Western Wall Tunnels, as well as to provide office and conference space for the Western Wall Heritage Foundation. The salvage excavation, conducted between 2005 and 2009, was directed by Shlomit Weksler-Bdolah and Alexander Onn of the IAA and is located in the northwestern part of the prayer plaza, at about one hundred meters distance from the enclosure wall. Significant structural remains include an Iron Age dwelling of the four-room type (seventh century B.C.E.), a section of the colonnaded eastern Cardo from the Roman and Byzantine periods, a late Islamic building decorated with a unique *ablaq*-style fresco and equipped with a bakery (thirteenth to fifteenth centuries), and finally a late Ottoman building with a *mihrab* (nineteenth to twentieth centuries). It is noteworthy that the archaeological documentation includes reference to the layers of the recent 1967 destruction of the Mughrabi Quarter initiated to establish the Western Wall Plaza.[39] The delay in the construction of the new building is a result of protests by the public and legal complaints filed by Israeli archaeologists. Criticism concerns the fact that the Beit Haliba Building will transform the current landsape of the Old

City. As is the case with most other ambitious development efforts connected to archaeology and tourism in East Jerusalem, the building is considered a necessity exclusively from the viewpoint of Israel's occupation policy.

The most recent controversial excavation in East Jerusalem, initiated in 2007, is located near the Mughrabi Gate, the only access to the Haram used by non-Muslims (see figure 39).[40] According to a public statement issued by the IAA on the Israel Ministry of Foreign Affairs website on February 12, 2007, the motivations for conducting the excavations were in the interest of all involved parties—Israelis, Palestinians, as well as foreign visitors to the Temple Mount.[41]

> The collapse of the ramp [in 2004] posed a danger to tourists ascending to the Temple Mount and to the worshippers in the Women's Area in the Western Wall plaza below. The site was declared hazardous by the City Engineer immediately after the collapse. Greater Jerusalem, in its entirety, is a declared antiquities site. According to the Antiquities Law, the Israel Antiquities Authority is required to excavate every archeological site that has been damaged, willfully or by natural causes, so that any engineering plan (construction of a new bridge or strengthening of the existing ramp) requires a full archeological salvage excavation. The strengthening of the existing ramp or the construction of a new bridge necessitates construction of engineering infrastructures which in turn require a full archeological excavation. The importance of preserving the appearance of the Western Wall plaza as a holy site, dictates a suitable reconstruction of the damaged Mughrabi gate access. The new access should provide convenient and safe passage for visitors to the Temple Mount, including disabled persons.

Fully aware of the highly sensitive and inflammatory nature of the situation, the IAA proceeded in a most conscientious manner, publicizing that "professional work of the highest standard will be guaranteed." Committing to their "guiding principles" and "inter-religious considerations," IAA issued a declaration, which was also posted on the Israel Ministry of Foreign Affairs website.

> The antiquities authority has never excavated, nor will it ever permit excavation, in the Temple Mount compound. It is a site of supreme historical value in which excavations are prohibited. All construction is to take place outside the Temple Mount, and care taken to preserve the status quo. The distance between the columns of the bridge and the Temple Mount will be 80m. The construction is being carried out in an area under Israeli sovereignty and under the responsibility of the Jerusalem Municipality and the Government of Israel. The parties responsible for religious affairs on the Temple Mount, including the Moslem Wakf, were kept informed of Israel's intention to restore the access, in the ongoing dialogue which exists between them. All care is taken that the construction of the new bridge does not harm religious sensitivities, the holy places, or other religious interests.

The continued overlap of Israel's occupation policies and their expanding investment in public archaeology and tourist sites in East Jerusalem, which have

FIGURE 39. Mughrabi Gate ramp and excavations. Photo by Katharina Galor.

increasingly impinged on Palestinian entitlements to live in the city and claim a part in its historical and religious heritage, has completely blurred the lines between archaeological projects that are to the benefit of all religious and national communities and projects that are politically motivated. The painstaking nature of the planning procedures and the assurance to follow the highest professional standards have done little or nothing to quench the distrust of Palestinian residents, which is based on numerous prior so-called salvage excavations carried out in the occupied sector of the city.

Once again, the excavations were condemned, by both Hamas and Fatah, who called for Palestinians to unite in protest. Additional opposition was voiced by Jordan, Syria, Saudi Arabia, Malaysia, as well as the fifty-seven-member organization of the Islamic Conference, viewing these actions as a grave threat to one of Islam's three holiest mosques. Israel denied the charges and installed cameras to film the excavation, a further effort to be fully transparent in this endeavor. The footage was broadcast live on the web, which they hoped would ease the widespread anger. Despite the fact that UNESCO cleared the Israeli team of wrongdoing, confirming that no harm was being done to the Haram and that excavations were being carried out according to professional standards, their report recommended the cessation of the work. As a result of the local and international protest, the work was interrupted soon after it was launched, though it was resumed in 2013, to be completed in 2015.[42]

In response to the imposed political sovereignty and related archaeological activities touching upon the Haram compound, Palestinian efforts to physically claim the Muslim holy shrine culminated in the construction of the Marwani Mosque. Though widely covered in the local, mostly Israeli media, relatively little international attention was dedicated to this affair. Between 1996 and 1999, an ancient vaulted structure—which is popularly referred to as Solomon's Stables, though it is commonly dated to the Herodian period—located underneath the southeastern corner of the Haram platform, was converted into an underground mosque that can accommodate some ten thousand worshippers. The construction was officially carried out by the Islamic Waqf, with financial sponsorship and logistical assistance from the Islamic Movement in Israel under the stewardship of Shaykh Ra'id Salah, mayor of Umm al-Fahm—and leader of the movement's northern branch. A central tenet of the movement's activism within Israel has been its commitment to rehabilitate and restore holy places. It also champions the renovation of the al-Aqsa Mosque, popular protests against occupation, and the celebration of religious festivals at the compound. Other than refurbishing the underground vaulted structure, a new access ramp and staircase were built to facilitate entrance and egress.[43] The clearing and construction process has been severely criticized by a group of Israeli archaeologists (who support continued occupation) for using bulldozers and for damaging and eliminating antiquities without proper archaeological supervision.[44]

On several occasions in 1999 and again in 2000, the construction material was dumped at various locations outside of the Old City. In 2000, archaeologists from the IAA began to examine the debris material for ancient artifacts.[45] It was not until 2005, however, that the Temple Mount Sifting Project was formed, as a platform for Israeli archaeologists and activists dedicated both to protesting the construction inside a historic monument without archaeological supervision and to recovering additional artifacts from the dumps.[46] After moving the discarded construction debris to the Tzurim Valley National Park, the material has been systematically sifted by Elad staff members, volunteers, and tourists.[47]

For the most part, religious and ideological perceptions and agendas with regard to the compound's historical legacy on the Jewish Israeli and the Palestinian Muslims fronts are thus either in support of occupation (for the former) or in reaction to occupation (for the latter). In response to the gradually increased scale of Israeli excavations at and near the Haram, beginning in 1967, and their growing public commitment to archaeological professional standards since the mid-1990s, UNESCO's attempts to reprimand and Palestinian efforts to counter have been largely ineffective.

ONE MONUMENT, TWO HERITAGE NARRATIVES

The Temple Mount / Haram al-Sharif epitomizes the continuity of sacred space and represents a monument that transcends the change of religious affiliation and practice, having evolved from a Jewish sanctuary to a Muslim shrine—and temporarily into a Christian holy site along the way. But since Israel's occupation of East Jerusalem, it has turned into the city's main locus of religious and national tension, conflict, and repeated violence between Jews and Muslims, and more recently between Israelis and Palestinians, a situation that has impacted both the study and the preservation of a monument of shared value.

For over a millennium, its primary use as a Muslim place of worship had not been challenged other than during Crusader rule. Throughout the early and late Islamic periods, the region's religiopolitical convergence assured the platform's unquestioned function as a Muslim place of prayer, study, and legal and civic activity. Jewish worship—relegated, for the most part, to the Western Wall—did not interfere or threaten its exclusive usage (see figure 40). The transfer of holiness from the Temple to its enclosure had occurred centuries before the Muslim conquest in 638, having begun as a result of the destruction of the Jewish sanctuary by the Romans in 70 C.E. The first incidents of tension between Muslims and Jews did not occur until the British Mandate. These religious frictions were closely related to the emerging territorial conflict between Jews and Arabs, particularly heated in the context of shared holy places. Hostilities intensified during the period of Jordanian rule but were only rarely enacted on the grounds of the compound, mostly as a result of the Temple Mount's inaccessibility to Jews. A new chapter in the history of the compound and its role in the Israel-Palestine conflict began after Israel's capture of East Jerusalem, which placed all of the site's Muslim shrines and buildings under Israel's political authority, as well as police and military surveillance. Since 1996, the Temple Mount / Haram al-Sharif has indeed turned into the region's focal point, where the reciprocal traumas and violent expressions of Palestinian resistance to Israeli occupation have come to their fore in the most militant forms. The intense archaeological activity conducted by Israeli professionals, the lack of adequate archaeological supervision during construction and renovation initiatives by the Waqf authorities, and the absence of a coordinated plan for conservation and preservation efforts for the entire complex are the result of the site's deep implication in the Israel-Palestine conflict. Competing narratives of past traditions and current activities surrounding the Temple Mount / Haram al-Sharif have played a particularly powerful role in the increasingly violent clashes between Jews and Muslims, between Israelis and Palestinians.

One of the most controversial points of the compound is the Western Wall, a short section—about seventy meters—of the southern portion of the western enclosure wall, whose total length is 488 meters. Literary sources suggest that Jewish attachment to the Western Wall goes back to the tenth and eleventh centuries C.E., though there is a certain ambiguity regarding the exact location of that early attachment.[48] The earliest Muslim tradition associating the Western Wall with al-Buraq dates to the fourteenth century.[49] It was not, however, till the rise of the Zionist movement in the early twentieth century that the wall became a source of significant friction between the Jewish and Muslim communities, leading to outbreaks of violence in 1928 and 1929 and the appointment of an international commission in 1930 by the British government to determine the rights and claims of Muslims and Jews in connection with the site.[50] The idea to purchase and demolish the adjacent Mughrabi Quarter to facilitate Jewish worship at the wall was

FIGURE 40. Western Wall. Photo by Katharina Galor.

first raised by Baron Rothschild in 1887, a plan that was only executed in 1967.[51] In contrast to the minor attention that the neighborhood adjacent to the wall received from residents, visitors, and scholars of ancient Jerusalem, an area which housed buildings ranging in date from the early Ayyubid period through the late Ottoman period, including houses of worship, the wall itself started to absorb the concern and care of the local communities and professionals as early as the beginning of the twentieth century. In 1920, Muslim authorities began conducting minor repairs to the Western Wall's upper courses. Though the Jewish community agreed that the work was necessary, they appealed to the British authorities, requesting that the conservation initiatives be carried out under the supervision of the newly established Department of Antiquities, recognizing the wall as part of a historic monument requiring specialized treatment.[52] A decision was then taken to place the maintenance of the small, upper stone courses under the authority of the Supreme Muslim Council (SMC), while the lower Herodian and Umayyad masonry was to be preserved by the Department of Antiquities, a decision challenged by the Mufti of Jerusalem. This partition of responsibilities was reiterated a number of times but has rarely proved itself as a viable means to adequately solve conservation problems.[53]

For Jews, the Temple Mount marks the site of the destroyed First and Second Temples. Despite the fact that the city's early Muslim conquerors and the builders of the Dome of the Rock intended to mark the exact spot of the former Jewish Temple, in recent decades, the Temple's existence has been contested in the Muslim world, a view that is fed by the threat presented by Israel's sovereignty over

Islam's third holiest place. For Israelis, the reclaiming of the Temple Mount in 1967 goes far beyond recovering the physical structure. It represents the reclaiming of Judaism's holiest site, which, according to the biblical narrative, came into being some 1,600 years before Islam was born. It is the Jewish antecedence to Islam, visually and physically encapsulated at this very location, that is regarded by Israelis as the ultimate proof for their right to resettle the land, to occupy East Jerusalem, and to reclaim the monument some two thousand years after the destruction of the Temple. And it is those very consequences, rather than the facts in isolation, which Palestinian Muslims consider a threat to their entitlement of continued worship and ownership. Therefore, a common statement within various Palestinian educational and media fora, is that the existence of a Jewish Temple is an ideologically motivated myth rather than a historical fact. This belief has found resonance even within scholarly circles, exemplified by Palestinian-Jordanian historian Kamil al-'Asali's statement that "modern archaeology has not succeeded in proving that the site on which the Temple stood is located in this place, since no remnants of the Temple have survived."[54] Though more accepting of the chronologies of Jewish temples and Muslim shrines, but certainly no less radical ideologically, is the argument among some Jewish fringe groups that the Jewish Temple should be restored. This vision, which would necessarily involve the destruction of the Dome of the Rock, has been advocated by the Temple Mount Faithful movement as well as other organizations established in recent decades.[55] This idea, though it comes from a radical element of Israeli society, has led to both preemptive and responsive actions among Palestinian Muslims, escalating the general atmosphere of mistrust and adversarial engagement, frequently involving violence on both sides.

In an effort to counter Israel's somewhat disguised efforts to solidify their political and military control of the Haram through archaeological excavations, Muslim leaders and the Arab media have repeatedly claimed that Israeli archaeologists are digging tunnels underneath the Haram to undermine the stability of the compound and destroy the al-Aqsa Mosque.[56] It is indeed the case that in recent decades there are cracks and bulges noticeable along the southern and western enclosure walls as well as damage in buildings situated above the Western Wall Tunnels. It should be stated, however, that even if the excavations abut directly the enclosure wall or platform, they do not extend underneath. Furthermore, all work is performed with extreme caution, using sophisticated reinforcement and support systems made of steel and concrete. The primary interest, beyond doubt, is to expose and emphasize elements associated with the Jewish Temples. But the physical destruction of the Haram would also cause the obstruction of Judaism's holiest site, making the destruction of the Haram a rather implausible motivation. Though excavations conducted adjacent to the Haram and underneath nearby buildings may have impacted their stability, it is impossible to assess to what extent the structural damages have been caused by the archaeological activity. The many centuries of use and wear, the often inadequate restoration measures employed in those buildings, and the repeated earthquakes are all contributing factors that have to be taken into account.

A further claim that affects the site's cultural heritage and the way it is perceived by various communities concerns recent construction and maintenance work undertaken on top of the Haram platform. The construction of the Marwani Mosque between 1996 and 1999, as well as electrical cable replacements in 2007, were condemned by the Temple Mount Sifting Project as efforts to obliterate traces of the First and Second Jewish Temples.[57] Though both the Islamic Movement in Israel and the Waqf are indeed concerned exclusively with the Islamic heritage of the site, these recent works only marginally affected archaeological remains from periods associated with the Jewish Temples.[58] Most of the material removed during the course of the Marwani Mosque construction and the cable work was debris and fill material from the Ayyubid and later periods, affecting—if at all—the Islamic layers and heritage of the site.[59] Given the highly questionable scientific contribution of the Sifting Project, the only significance of the endeavor is of a political nature, by calling attention to the negligence in which the Waqf recently carried out the work on the Haram.

Whether it is primarily the excessive nature of the archaeological work conducted near the enclosure wall conducted by Israelis or rather the inadequate enforcement of archaeological supervision during repair or construction initiatives by Palestinians does not really matter. In the end, it is the lack of coordination, along with the religious, ideological, and political differences of the various sides involved in the administration and execution of these endeavors, that is at the core of the compound's inadequate state of preservation. Rather than investing in the exposure and excavation of hidden elements, professionals and researchers should focus on the maintenance and study of the exposed and accessible areas, which, other than the Dome of the Rock, the al-Aqsa Mosque, and the enclosure wall, include hundreds of buildings and artifacts spanning more than two thousand years of history. Such a change in course of action, which would not only benefit all of the involved communities but also the monument itself, is, however, unthinkable in the context of Israel's occupation of East Jerusalem.

Conclusion

A main task of this book and its account of how Jerusalem's physical heritage is enmeshed in religious and national interests and struggles has been to persuade the reader of the severity of numerous entanglements of truth and fiction, of facts and interpretations, and thus of the elusive middle ground between science and ideology. We cannot simply differentiate between the scientific and ideological practice of inquiry to recover the city's actual physical reality, whether above the ground or below. Indeed, capturing and investigating scrupulously and expertly the material remainders of those who have passed through or settled in the city may bring us closer to some real untainted substance of past existence, a quality more easily associated with artifacts and buildings rather than with words or ideas. Yet, religious beliefs and political agendas have the ability to attach themselves as subtly to objects, monuments, and places as they do in written testimonies and spiritual manifestos. Therefore, regardless of the sources we use for a viable reconstruction of Jerusalem's past, our ideas will always remain partial and incomplete. It is the knowledge and admittance to this subjectivity, however, that constitutes a first step in building the necessary bridges to overcome the disparity in perception, opinion, and dogma at the root of most conflicts over Jerusalem. Exposing the idiosyncratic nature of archaeological practice in Jerusalem, rather than unraveling the mysteries of the past, can thus free us from the burden we often tend to impose on the city's cultural legacy.

CONTEXTUALIZING ISRAELI ARCHAEOLOGY

One of this study's goals was to expose the social, political, and ideological context of Jerusalem's first archaeological investigations to understand the historical and religious framework that produced and shaped the field of biblical archaeology, initially a matter of sporadic interest, but which quickly evolved into a regular affair of institutional and national profile. This query established how the discipline of excavation progressed slowly but steadily from a pursuit motivated no less by faith and adventure than by scholarly curiosity. At first this endeavor was governed rather chaotically by the Ottomans, then, later, more strictly and conscientiously under the British, and finally flourishing in a machinery of professional expertise under the Israelis. As demonstrated in this survey and analysis, professional and scientific standards made significant progress over time, with the control of excavations passing from independent explorers to institutions established abroad, and then from local establishments to governmental bodies, thus placing the power to shape the science of archaeology into the hands of an increasingly administratively and politically powerful entity. The field thus moved from the convictions of an individual to the beliefs of a community and the ideology of a state, in which institutionalization and operationalization of strategy have played an increasingly dominant role. The progressively structured, institutionalized, and legalized context of archaeological activity does not, however, diminish or eliminate the power and responsibility of the individual person or community implicated in the discovery, presentation, and even, to some extent, the consumption of archaeological discoveries. As we know, archaeology is not an exact science and, therefore, every individual who participates in the process of this knowledge and story producing mechanism, carries part of the responsibility, for better or worse.[1] In concrete terms, this means that an unnamed employee of the IAA who classifies coins from an excavation conducted in East Jerusalem is no less implicated in the ideological aspirations of his or her country than those PEF celebrities such a Charles W. Wilson or a Charles Warren, whose discoveries have trademarked the colonial mission of "digging for God and country" and still carry their names to this day.

Studying and understanding archaeology and its relation to Israel's policies of occupation can thus not be understood without examining how the field first evolved from its inception to the time of the Old City's capture by Israel in 1967 and then beyond to the present. The use of archaeology for religious and political agendas is clearly not an Israeli invention. Colonial models provided the necessary and persistent basis for the neocolonial or nationalist elaborations of early and current Zionist endeavors of archaeological exploration. Without the accomplishments—including trials, errors, and rectifications—of early excavations, Israeli archaeology would not have made the same undeniable contributions to professional standards, exemplified by the use of improved field methods, of superior levels of scientific documentation and analyses, and of increasingly powerful means of public presentation and dissemination tools. The persistent thread in archaeological practice in Jerusalem is thus the combined product of science and ideology, where one feeds the other, becomes dependent, and, in fact, reinforces the impact of persuasion exponentially.

JERUSALEM AS A CASE STUDY

The religious, social, and political complexities of archaeology and cultural heritage in a contested city like Jerusalem demands an evaluation that considers numerous fields of expertise and methods of inquiry, too vast a project to be summarized in just one book. In fact, the enormity of the task has led me to remain focused exclusively on this one city, which regrettably resulted in the exclusion of invaluable comparative investigations. Therefore, I would like to at least point out that the use or misuse of archaeology and cultural heritage for religious and nationalist agendas not only affects the city of Jerusalem. The phenomena of excavations, cultural heritage, and politics entangled—or the domains of archaeopolitics and religiopolitics intertwined—are known and have been debated and written on in various forms and venues, popular and scholarly. The bulldozing of archaeological layers and monuments and the discarding of artifacts is not exclusive to the city under scrutiny here. Intentional destruction and biased preservation, display, and presentation initiatives are known in nearly every place where antiquity and its legacy are valued. Ideologically motivated excavations and restorations, as well as manipulated narratives, have left their imprint in numerous other locations in the region and around the world. In spite of its unique history and complex ethno-religious and national makeup, Jerusalem is not the only place where cultural heritage has been caught up in a regional struggle.

Trends and developments of biblical archaeology in Jerusalem could be studied in light of other sites and areas of significance to this field of investigation, within the Jewish State and beyond, under the banner of one religion versus another. The role of archaeology in the Israeli educational systems could be contrasted to similar educational programs in Europe or the United States. Comparisons could be drawn with existing publications on colonial and nationalist frameworks of archaeological practice. A more nuanced distinction between colonial and postcolonial situations, between nationalist and post-nationalist, could be established. The relationship between governing and occupying forces with oppressed minorities in other domains of cultural or social studies could benefit the analysis of archaeological practice in Jerusalem and other regions of the Middle East. The impact of repatriation and restitution of cultural heritage in places that have a similar historical and political trajectory to Jerusalem could be examined. Parallels could be shown between Jerusalem and other equally contested cities in war or post-conflict situations. Placing the competing narratives of Jerusalem's antiquities into the larger context of the divides between Western and non-Western ideologies and the disparity of cultural priorities would be a most timely topic of inquiry; or, more specifically, the conflict of Western and Islamic perceptions of archaeology and its tragic outcomes could enhance the current interest of the present inquiry and provide an additional contemporary context of comparison. The possibilities are nearly endless, and the suggested comparanda may provide some inspiration for ideas for further investigations. Jerusalem, indeed, is not the only city that has fallen victim to the religious and political aspirations of individual explorers and their respective communities or nations. Yet, it is the locus we have selected for this study, and it may serve as a useful starting point for future research.

MEDIA AND MARKET

An additional domain not sufficiently explored in this study, but pertinent to the discussion of cultural heritage and ideology in Jerusalem, is the role of archaeology's popular and media portrayal, which capitalizes on the notion of Bible adventure and discovery. Administrative procedures and methodical progress have clearly imposed an increasingly structured protocol on archaeological endeavors. Yet, despite the scientific and technological advances in the field, there are still palpable traces of the original spirit of adventure and spirituality associated with digging up the city's biblical past. There may be a general consensus that Parker's grandiose quest to find King Solomon's treasures in Jerusalem was an unreasonable escapade too blatantly unscientific even to the uninitiated of the early 1900s. But so many of today's endeavors in Jerusalem are just as unabashedly motivated by finding relics of Kings David, Solomon, or Herod. This is perhaps best illustrated with the persistent interest in artifacts, monuments, and sites baring a biblical significance, the continued involvement and sponsorship of religious establishments in the excavation, interpretation, and showcasing of finds, as well as the ever more aggressive media coverage, which successfully promotes the excitement of discovering finds of relevance to the Jewish and Judeo-Christian narratives. Numerous projects involving dozens, if not hundreds, of local and international students and volunteers, the growing educational and tourism industry that has developed around the discoveries, and, lastly, the economic incentive and marketability of antiquities promoting this sense of a tangible link to the city's mundane and glorious past have all contributed to both preserve and promote the original spirit of the field and, most importantly, to lastingly and broadly impact the social and religious arena of Jerusalem politics. The relationship between media and market—indeed, the dependency and enhancement of archaeology's public profile in the context of a strategically placed tourist industry in occupied East Jerusalem—is of interest to the shared ideological and political ambitions of the Jewish State and Evangelical Christians, a connection established in numerous other contexts and well deserving of further inquiry beyond the present framework.

One of the most vivid examples that demonstrates best what I call the "public travesty of archaeology" is the tunnel excavation in Silwan and the City of David's Archaeological Park. Under the pretext of recovering Jerusalem's glorious biblical past, rigorously trained archaeologists revert to excavation methods that have been outdated for more than a century. Millions of dollars are invested in clearing underground spaces, including an ancient sewage channel, while the living conditions of the Palestinian villagers living above ground are radically compromised. Proper scientific excavation reports are missing, and valuable scholarly contributions or discoveries enhancing the current knowledge of Jerusalem's history are lacking. Though the scandalous nature of this enterprise and the misuse of archaeology for a purely ideologically motivated endeavor are widely acknowledged in the scholarly literature, its popular image has not been affected by it. The prominent role entertainment and theme-park packaging play make up effectively for the monotonous stones and dust. Business thrives on the spirit of the Bible reenacted. The City of David has indeed achieved the rank of Israel's most visited archaeological site, and despite international criticism regarding its obvious association with Israel's settlement policies, it was recently selected as the scenic film set for a new NBC series entitled *DIG*.[2]

MAIN ACTORS

In a topical study on Jerusalem, Craig Larkin and Michael Dumper have aptly described the current status quo of cultural heritage and the various players intertwined in the struggle. In their words, "Jerusalem remains both an occupied and a contested city claimed by two national groups, and subject to dynamic regional trends and global strategic interests. Heritage has becoming an increasing important weapon in the ongoing battle for Jerusalem; for Israelis it is a means of consolidating power and hegemonic control, for Palestinians it has become a rallying call for resistance and defiance. UNESCO is caught between two highly politicized agendas, and is therefore struggling to forge for itself an independent mediating role or indeed convince either side of the 'World Heritage' vision of 'unity in diversity' and 'the promotion of mutual understanding and solidarity among peoples.' "[3]

In this succinct description, Larkin and Dumper identify the three main actors who participate in the battle over Jerusalem and their diverging roles in cultural heritage. My study certainly tried to keep these different—indeed, opposing—perspectives, motivations, and agendas in constant focus. Examples that demonstrate Israel's attempts to consolidate power and hegemonic control through archaeological activities are numerous. These include recent development projects aggressively boosting the tourist industry through the construction of enormous architectural complexes such as the Beit Haliba Building or the Kedem Center in the heart of the Historic Basin, which impose the necessity to conduct so-called salvage excavations. An example illustrating Palestinian resistance and defiance to Israeli hegemony in East Jerusalem is their refusal to cooperate with the IAA in their restoration and construction efforts at the Haram al-Sharif. UNESCO's struggle to mediate between the two sides of the conflict is evident in the near absence of efforts to foster interreligious and intercultural dialogues among Israelis and Palestinians, in contrast to their more productive intervention in other regions of conflict.[4]

In my view, one important factor to consider when confronting these different actors, as Dumper and Larkin's and similar comparative studies on the conflict attempt to do, is not to impose a frame or model which projects symmetry. Almost in every aspect that touches upon archaeology and cultural heritage in Jerusalem, the impact of the involved players is disproportionate. Whereas Israel's control of the archaeological landscape, both below and above the surface, as well as of the narrative that is being projected, is nearly exclusive, Palestinian and international efforts to counter or even just balance these efforts are modest, if not completely impotent. This brings us to another aspect of asymmetry not explicitly touched upon in the body of this study, but transpiring throughout the chapters. It concerns the asymmetry or, perhaps more accurately, the disproportionate weight of the Palestinian Muslim and the Palestinian Christian heritage of the city. Without imposing a hierarchy on the value or significance of one versus the other cultural and religious legacy in the city, the impact of the different involved religious communities in question and their proclaimed legacies on their relationship with the Israeli government and the Jewish sector of Israeli society more informally is quite different. And there are multiple reasons for this, not all of which are relevant to this study. Of bearing to archaeological practice and issues of cultural legacy is the fact that, given the longer duration of Islamic rule versus Christian governance in Jerusalem, it is the Muslim heritage that dominates the city's landscape, at least quantitatively. Furthermore, since the end of the Crusades, the Muslim community remained the largest population, a situation that changed only toward the end of the Ottoman period or the beginning of the British period, when Jews became the dominant religious community. Relative to the Christian presence, however, the Muslim community continued to maintain its majority. The most recent radical change in the demography and the Muslim/Christian ratio occurred after 1967. When Israel captured East Jerusalem, there were 56,795 Muslims living in Jerusalem, as opposed to 10,813 Christians.[5] According to the Israel Central Bureau of Statistics in 2006, 32 percent of the city's population was Muslim; only 2 percent was Christian. In other words, the role of Palestinian Christians in matters touching upon cultural heritage in the city, in comparison to Palestinian Muslims, has been relatively minor. And, despite the fact that in recent years there has been a significant increase in the "Palestinianization of clergy," most of the city's church leaders still belong to nonlocal communities.[6] This important numerical distinction between the city's Muslim and Christian presence in Jerusalem clearly has implications on the role cultural heritage plays in the Israel-Palestine conflict. There are certainly some parallels between Israel's battles with Palestinian Muslims and the ones fought with Palestinian Christians. One similarity would be Israel's imposed military and policing presence at the city's major worship sites, namely the Haram al-Sharif and the Church of the Holy Sepulchre. The undeniable distinction, however, is the difference in the scale, the severity, and the frequency of the clashes of the numerous authorities and communities implicated in the struggle and representing the different sides of the conflict. The list of recent incidents imposing access restrictions to Muslim worshipers involving armed violence and terror on and near the Haram would be too long to include here. The last major incident of tension related to Israel's security measures controlling the access to the Holy Sepulchre occurred in 2000, in preparations for the millennium celebrations, for which large crowds of pilgrims were expected. The repercussions for the Israel-Palestine conflict of this and other similar incidents, however, are negligible compared to the local, regional, and international implications of clashes and violence surrounding access restrictions to the Haram al-Sharif. Notwithstanding these important distinctions between the different religious communities that make up Palestinian society, there is nonetheless a shared identity and solidarity on numerous issues that inform matters of cultural heritage. Though related to many of the issues examined here, these topics go beyond the scope of my study and are outside my expertise.

GRASSROOT INITIATIVES

The ongoing battle among the different parties involved in the safekeeping of the city's cultural heritage is—apart from numerous other reasons raised in this study—a result of the differing perceptions of what constitutes Jerusalem's most significant periods and cultures. One of the more effective ways of overcoming this disparity would be to invest in a more diverse and flexible interpretation of the city's past, where the narrative is not dominated or controlled by one religious or national group, but coordinated among all local resident communities, with input from international participants, third-party specialists, as well as arbitration professionals. The concept of heritage belonging to all humankind is not one that can be imposed and regulated according to a specific protocol that implements merely physical actions and changes. It requires long-term investment and intervention at various levels across the different social, religious, demographic, and educational sectors of society. And most importantly, it requires participation and involvement of all local groups implicated in the religio-national conflict.

Among the first efforts to overcome the disparity of views regarding archaeological and cultural heritage in the region was the establishment of an Israeli

Palestinian Archaeology Working Group (IPAWG), facilitated by the University of California Institute of Archaeology. During a series of meetings, which took place between 2005 and 2009, Israeli and Palestinian archaeologists started to tackle issues of archaeology and cultural-heritage management in Israel-Palestine. One of the main goals of the group was "to consider various aspects of the role of archaeology in the Israeli-Palestinian conflict, including public perceptions of archaeology, the status of archaeological sites and finds in case of the implementation of a two-state solution, and Jerusalem as a World Heritage Site." A jointly drafted document made recommendations regarding the role of archaeological heritage in a final-status agreement. Furthermore, a complete inventory of Israeli archaeological activity in the West Bank between 1967 and 2007, the so-called West Bank and East Jerusalem Archaeological Database (WBEJAD) was established.[7] Efforts to renew these initiatives have been underway, such as, for example, Emek Shaveh's steering committee, which just (in June of 2016) released a comprehensive plan for managing ancient sites in Jerusalem's Historic Basin, entitled Guiding Principles for a Jerusalem Antiquities Master Plan.[8]

Even if issues of cultural heritage are often considered a relatively minor point in the much larger Israeli-Palestinian conflict, and relegated to marginal matters of disaccord, they do affect surprisingly large segments of the local population and are major players in the shaping of public opinion. Consequently, if these issues can be nuanced appropriately, and the problems around them resolved, the possibilities of negotiations in other areas will have a better chance to advance.

WHAT NEXT?

With over 1,700 sites having been excavated in Jerusalem, and the considerable fortunes spent on archaeological fieldwork, interpretation, conservation, and presentation, our knowledge on the city's cultural development from prehistory to the present is tremendous. Archaeological sites, ancient monuments, and artifacts dominate and indeed overwhelm the landscape. Despite the significant investment in archaeological practice, most ancient buildings, particularly in the Old City and the Historic Basin, are neglected and would benefit from a complete overhaul and restoration program. Moreover, most completed excavations have not been properly published. It would take decades or perhaps even a century of research, employing dozens of archaeologists, to make up for the lacking final reports, a debt that should haunt the profession and alarm those concerned about Jerusalem's cultural heritage. Conducting further excavations will not only increase the debt, but it will ultimately widen the gap between actual data and knowledge. The already-exposed layers, monuments, and artifacts provide us with almost unparalleled data to reconstruct Jerusalem's history through the millennia. Rather than illuminating exiting questions, newly excavated material often increases the riddles and produce new unresolved problems. It is time to halt this activity and invest in other sectors of the city's cultural heritage—most importantly, in the domains of education and professional training as well as the conservation of exposed ruins and standing monuments. Let us find what is already there, rather than look for something that may only further complicate both the mysteries of the past and the conflicts of the present!

NOTES

PREFACE

1. I conducted most of the interviews during the summers of 2012 and 2013, the former supported by a RISD Professional Development Fund and the latter by a Brown University Middle East Studies Research Travel Grant. Some of the individuals listed may no longer hold the positions or titles mentioned here.

INTRODUCTION

1. For different opinions regarding the exact limits of the Historic (or Holy) Basin, see R. Lapidoth, *The Historic Basin of Jerusalem: Problems and Possible Solutions* (Jerusalem: Jerusalem Institute for Israel Studies, 2010), 16. On how this concept has become central to planning policy and political interests, see W. Pullan and M. Sternberg, "The Making of Jerusalem's 'Holy Basin,' " *Planning Perspectives* 27, no. 2 (2012): 225–48.

2. In contrast to the concept of legal continuity between archaeological fieldwork in East and West Jerusalem, the administrative framework of East Jerusalem residents is far more complex. Whereas the Israeli government maintains an administrative distinction between Israeli citizens and noncitizens in East Jerusalem, the Jerusalem municipality does not.

3. Abu El-Haj focuses primarily on the first two decades of fieldwork conducted after 1967. See N. Abu El-Haj, *Facts on the Ground: Archaeological Practice and Territorial Self-Fashioning in Israeli Society* (Chicago: University of Chicago Press, 2001), 2, 8, 16, 19, 45, 74; T. Oestigaard, *Political Archaeology and Holy Nationalism: Archaeological Battles over the Bible and Land in Israel and Palestine from 1967–2000*, Gotarc Series C, no. 67 (Gothenburg, Sweden: Gothenburg University Press, 2007); and N. Masalha, *The Zionist Bible: Biblical Precedent, Colonialism, and the Erasure of Memory* (London: Routledge, 2013). Similar

tendencies of colonial and state-building efforts have been associated with archaeological work in Jordan. See E. D. Corbett, *Competitive Archaeology in Jordan: Narrating Identity from the Ottomans to the Hashemites* (Austin, University of Texas Press, 2014).

4. According to Seligman, the recently improved professional standards counter the argument that Israeli archaeology is "motivated by colonial, nationalist, and exclusivist agendas." See J. Seligman, "The Archaeology of Jerusalem—Between Post-Modernism and Delegitimization," *Public Archaeology* 12, no. 3 (2013): 181–99.

5. The Waqfs are Islamic religious and charitable foundations created by endowed trust funds. The word *waqf* means "pious endowment" or "pious foundation." Waqfs is the plural form of the name more commonly used in English, though Awqaf is also used, which is the Arabic form of the plural.

6. On the political and administrative structures of the Palestinian Authority, the local and the Jordanian Waqfs, see M. Dumper, "The Palestinian Waqfs and the Struggle over Jerusalem, 1967–2000," *Annuaire Droit et Religions* 3 (2008/09): 199–221; M. Dumper, "The Role of Awqaf in Protecting the Islamic Heritage of Jerusalem, 1967–2010," in *Hamam Al Ayn / Hamam Al Hana': Essays and Memories in Celebration of a Historic Public Bath House in Jerusalem's Old Arab City. Al-Quds University, Jerusalem*, ed. D. Emtiaz (Jerusalem: Al-Quds University, 2011); and C. Larkin and M. Dumper, "In Defense of Al-Aqsa: The Islamic Movement inside Israel and the Battle for Jerusalem," *Middle East Journal* 66 (2012): 31–52.

7. The literature on the subjectivity of archaeological interpretations is too extensive to review here. It is based on the post-processual movement, which originated in England in the late 1970s and early 1980s, associated mostly with Ian Hodder. For his most recent publication relevant to the subject, see I. Hodder, *Entangled: An Archaeology of the Relationships between Humans and Things* (Malden, MA: Wiley-Blackwell, 2012).

8. "Science as a Vocation" was originally published as "Wissenschaft als Beruf," *Gesammelte Aufsätze zur Wissenschaftslehre* (Tübingen 1922), 524–55.

9. The formal name of Jordan (since 1949) is the Hashemite Kingdom of Jordan; between 1946 and 1949, the country was known as the Hashemite Kingdom of Transjordan.

1. BOUNDARIES, BARRIERS, WALLS

1. The construction of the Barrier Wall (also referred to as Israeli West Bank Barrier, Security Barrier, Separation Barrier, Racial Segregation Wall, and the Apartheid Wall) began in 2000, during the Second Intifada. Israel considers it a defense mechanism against terrorism; Palestinians identify it as yet another tool of racial segregation or as an expression of apartheid policies. Most sources don't distinguish between the name of the Jerusalem segment and other segments of the longer wall. Some refer to the East Jerusalem section as the Jerusalem Envelope. The International Court of Justice refers to it as the "Wall" (www.icj-cij.org/docket/index.php?pr=71&code=mwp&p1=3&p2=4&p3=6); in Hebrew, it is generally referred to as Chomat ha-Hafrada (Separation Wall), and in Arabic, mostly as Jidar (Wall).

2. For a slightly more detailed description of Jerusalem's Old City topography, see K. Galor and H. Bloedhorn, *The Archaeology of Jerusalem: From the Origins to the Ottomans* (New Haven, CT: Yale University Press, 2013), 10–15.

3. Regarding the location of Jerusalem, see J. Simons, *Jerusalem in the Old Testament: Researches and Theories* (Leiden: Brill, 1952), 6–26; and W. H. Mare, *The Archaeology of the Jerusalem Area* (Grand Rapids, MI: Baker Book House, 1987), 21–23.

4. On Jerusalem's role as a capital city, from antiquity to the present, see C. F. Emmett, "The Capital Cities of Jerusalem," *The Geographical Review* 86 (1996): 233–58.

5. See G. Dalman, *Jerusalem und sein Gelände* (Gütersloh, Germany: Bertelsmann, 1930), 21–151.

6. Regarding the size of Jerusalem throughout history, see K. J. Asali, *Jerusalem in History: From 3,000 B.C. to the Present Day*, rev. ed. (London: Kegan Paul International, 1997), 204; and F. E. Peters, *Jerusalem: The Holy City in the Eyes of Chroniclers, Visitors, Pilgrims, and Prophets from the Days of Abraham to the Beginnings of Modern Times* (Princeton: Princeton University Press, 1985), 408, 564–65.

7. For pagan and Jewish burials, the separation between the "city of the living" and the "city of the dead"—the necropolis—was strictly observed. Changes occurred during the Byzantine and early Islamic periods. See G. Avni, "The Urban Limits of Roman and Byzantine Jerusalem: A View from the Necropoleis," *Journal of Roman Archaeology* 18 (2005): 373–96.

8. See Galor and Bloedhorn, *Archaeology of Jerusalem*, 14–17. For different versions of maps featuring Jerusalem throughout the periods under discussion, see D. H. K. Amiran, A. Shachar, and Kimhi, *Atlas of Jerusalem* (Jerusalem: Massada, 1973); D. Bahat, *The Illustrated Atlas of Jerusalem* (London: Simon and Schuster, 1990); and M. Ben-Dov, *Historical Atlas of Jerusalem* (New York: Continuum, 2002).

9. According to E. A. Knauf, "Jerusalem in the Late Bronze and Early Iron Ages. A Proposal," *Tel Aviv* 27 (2000): 75–90, Mount Moriah may have been included within the city wall as early as the Middle Bronze Age.

10. In 586 B.C.E., Jerusalem was destroyed by the Babylonians under king Nebuchadnezzar II.

11. The interpretation of the Sukenik-Mayer Wall and its implications for the extent of Herodian period Jerusalem are discussed by Galor and Bloedhorn, *Archaeology of Jerusalem*, 52–55.

12. A. Boas, *Jerusalem in the Time of the Crusades: Society, Landscape, and Art in the Holy City under Frankish Rule* (London: Routledge, 2001), 35–40, 83–93.

13. D. Gold, *The Fight for Jerusalem: Radical Islam, the West, and the Future of the Holy City* (Washington, DC: Regnery Publishing, 2009), 111; and A. Arnon, "The Quarters of Jerusalem in the Ottoman Period," *Middle Eastern Studies* 28 (1992): 5.

14. Arnon, "The Quarters of Jerusalem," 7.

15. Mujir ad-Din first used the term, in 1495, some twenty years before the Ottoman conquest, to describe various quarters and streets named after particular populations and communities who settled in the city.

16. Arnon, "The Quarters of Jerusalem," 13.

17. Arnon, "The Quarters of Jerusalem," 5.

18. R. Kark and M. Oren-Nordheim, *Jerusalem and Its Environs: Quarters, Neighborhoods, Villages, 1880–1948* (Detroit: Wayne State University Press, 2001), 45.

19. Y. Ben-Arieh, "The Growth of Jerusalem in the Nineteenth Century," *Annals of the Association of American Geographers* 65 (1975): 252.

20. A. Schölch, "Jerusalem in the 19th Century (1831–1917)," in *Jerusalem in History* (New York: Olive Branch Press, 1990), 254.

21. J. McCarthy, *The Population of Palestine: Population History and Statistics of the Late Ottoman Period and the Mandate* (New York: Columbia University Press, 1990); and R. A. Davis, "Ottoman Jerusalem," in *Jerusalem: 1948: The Arab Neighborhoods and Their Fate in the War*, ed. S. Tamari, 30–67 (Jerusalem: Institute of Jerusalem Studies and Badil Resource Center, 1999), 11.

22. See U. O. Schmelz, "Notes on the Demography of Jews, Muslims and Christians in Jerusalem," *Middle East Review* 13 (1981): 17; R. Kark and S. Landman, "The Establishment of Muslim Neighbourhoods in Jerusalem, Outside the Old City, during the Late Ottoman Period," *Palestine Exploration Quarterly* 112 (1980): 131; Y. Ben-Arieh, *Jerusalem in the 19th Century: Emergence of the New City* (New York: St. Martin's Press, 1986), 241, 354, and 366; and Y. Ben-Arieh, *Jerusalem in the 19th Century: The Old City* (New York: St. Martin's Press, 1984), 354–55.

23. The Ottoman millet system allowed different confessional communities to judge according to their own religious rulings, including the laws of the Muslim Sharia, the Christian Canon law, and the Jewish halakha.

24. R. Kark, "The Traditional Middle Eastern City: The Cases of Jerusalem and Jaffa during the Nineteenth Century," *Zeitschrift des Deutschen Palästina-Vereins* 97 (1981): 99–100.

25. Kark and Oren-Nordheim, *Jerusalem and Its Environs*, 45.

26. See Davis, "Ottoman Jerusalem," 17; Ben-Arieh, *New City*, 241 and 354; and Kark and Landman, "Establishment of Muslim Neighbourhoods," 131.

27. Arnon, "Quarters of Jerusalem," 26.

28. The land west of the Jordan River remained under direct British rule until 1948 and was known as Palestine, while the land east of the Jordan became a semiautonomous region known as Transjordan, under the rule of the Hashemite family from the Hijaz, which gained independence in 1946.

29. On August 6, 1953, the Parliament of Jordan proclaimed Jerusalem as the alternative capital of the kingdom, probably in an attempt to keep Jordan's large minority population of Palestinians content. The Parliament voiced plans to meet in Jerusalem occasionally but in fact convened there only once. See Emmett, "Capital Cities of Jerusalem," 237.

30. See N. Krystall, "The De-Arabization of West Jerusalem 1947–50," *Journal of Palestine Studies* 27, no. 2 (1998); and M. Dumper, *The Politics of Jerusalem Since 1967* (New York: Columbia University Press and the Institute for Palestine Studies), 67.

31. B. Slae, R. Kark, and N. Shoval, "Post-War Reconstruction and Conservation of the Historic Jewish Quarter in Jerusalem, 1967–1975," *Planning Perspectives* 27 (2012): 380.

32. On how Jordan reconstituted a national identify following 1948, and on the role Christian and Muslim holy sites played in this context, see K. Katz, *Jordanian Jerusalem: Holy Places and National Spaces* (Gainesville: University Press of Florida, 2005), 121.

33. S. Ricca, *Reinventing Jerusalem: Israel's Reconstruction of the Jewish Quarter after 1967* (London: I. B. Tauris, 2007), 21–22; and N. al-Jubeh, "Bab al-Magharibah: Joha's Nail in the Haram al-Sharif," *Jerusalem Quarterly File* 18 (2003): 17–24.

34. Jerusalem's municipal borders have changed repeatedly in modern history. For more detailed surveys on the frequent changes, see S. Dellapergola, "Jerusalem's

Population, 1995–2020: Demography, Multiculturalism and Urban Policies," *European Journal of Population / Revue Européenne de Démographie* 17 (2001): 168–69.

35. On the destruction and expropriation of Waqf property by the Israeli state, see Dumper, "The Palestinian Waqf," 208–10.

36. Estimates for the number of people who were evicted range between six hundred and one thousand. In addition to some 135 houses, the al-Buraq and al-Afdaliya mosques were destroyed. See N. Abu El-Haj, "Translating Truths: Nationalism, the Practice of Archaeology, and the Remaking of Past and Present in Contemporary Jerusalem," *American Ethnologist* 25 (1998): 175; M. Dumper, "Israeli Settlement in the Old City of Jerusalem," *Journal of Palestine Studies* 21, vol. 4 (1992): 33–34; T. Abowd, "The Moroccan Quarter: A History of the Present," *Jerusalem Quarterly File* 7 (2000)."

37. According to Abu El-Haj, this marked difference between the Jewish and the other quarters of the Old City, as well as the clear boundaries separating the different quarters were introduced relatively recently. See Abu El-Haj, "Translating Truths," 180.

38. On the political implications of declaring those areas as national parks, see Y. Mizrachi, *Between Holiness and Propaganda: Archaeology and Political Claims over the Old City of Jerusalem* (Jerusalem: Emek Shaveh, 2011); and R. Greenberg, "Towards an Inclusive Archaeology in Jerusalem: The Case of Silwan/The City of David," *Public Archaeology* 8 (2009): 42.

39. For an overview on recent demographic changes in the city of Jerusalem, see Dellapergola, "Jerusalem's Population." On the policies regarding the demographic balance and the redrawing of municipal boundaries, see M. Benvenisti, *City of Stone: The Hidden History of Jerusalem* (Berkeley: University of California Press, 1996), 50–68.

40. For a list of all Basic Laws, including definitions, see www.knesset.gov.il/description/eng/eng_mimshal_yesod1.htm (English version); and http://main.knesset.gov.il/Activity/Legislation/Pages/BasicLaws.aspx (Hebrew version).

41. The international community, including the United States, maintains their embassies in Tel Aviv.

42. International bodies such as the United Nations have condemned Israel's Basic Law concerning Jerusalem as a violation of the Fourth Geneva Convention and therefore hold that the establishment of the city as Israel's capital is against international law. Unlike a treaty agreement, however, customary international law is usually not written. In its 2004 advisory opinion on the legality of the Barrier Wall, the International Court of Justice (the primary judicial branch of the United Nations) reiterated that the lands captured by Israel in the 1967 war, including East Jerusalem, are occupied territory. On the complexity of international law and its contested relevance, see E. Cotran, "The Jerusalem Question in International Law: The Way to a Solution," *Islamic Studies* 40 (2001); and Weiner, "The NGOs, Demolition of Illegal Building in Jerusalem, and International Law," *Jewish Political Studies Review* 17, no. 1–2 (2005).

43. The committee at its twenty-fifth session (Helsinki, 2001) endorsed the recommendation of the twenty-fifth session of its bureau (Paris, June 2001) "to postpone further consideration of this nomination proposal until an agreement on the status of the City of Jerusalem in conformity with International Law is reached, or until the parties concerned submit a joint nomination" (Jerusalem UNESCO World Heritage List, http://whc.unesco.org/en/tentativelists/1483).

44. The first segments of the Barrier Wall were built in 2000. On how the division of Jerusalem impacts the populations' ethnic, religious, and linguistic cleavages, see M. Dumper, "A False Dichotomy? The Binationalism Debate and the Future of Divided Jerusalem," *International Affairs* 87 (2011). On the political purpose of the wall in Jerusalem, countering its defensive or security role, which the Israeli government usually stresses, see M. Klein, "Jerusalem as an Israeli Problem—A Review of Forty Years of Israeli Rule over Arab Jerusalem," *Israel Studies* 13, no. 2 (2008): 66; and Ir Amim's statements regarding the "separation barrier": www.ir-amim.org.il/en/issue/separation-barrier. See also I. Kershner, *The Seam of the Israeli-Palestinian Conflict* (New York: St. Martin's Press, 2005); and F. Chiodelli, *Shaping Jerusalem: Spatial Planning, Politics and the Conflict* (New York: Routledge, 2017).

2. INSTITUTIONALIZATION

1. N. A. Silberman, "Power, Politics, and the Past: The Social Construction of Antiquity in the Holy Land," in *The Archaeology of Society in the Holy Land,* ed. by T. E. Levy (London and Washington: Leicester University Press, 1990), 12; N. A. Silberman, *Digging for God and Country: Exploration, Archeology and the Secret Struggle for the Holy Land, 1799–1917* (New York: Knopf, 1982), 10–27.

2. A. Glock, "Archaeology as Cultural Survival: The Future of the Palestinian Past," *Journal of Palestine Studies* 23, no. 3 (1994): 73.

3. Silberman, "Power, Politics, and the Past," 12.

4. Silberman, "Power, Politics, and the Past," 17.

5. Two significant artifacts from Jerusalem discovered during the Ottoman period, the so-called Orpheus mosaic and the Siloam inscription, were shipped to Constantinople and are among the prized pieces of the Istanbul Archaeological Museum.

6. Glock, "Archaeology as Cultural Survival," 73.

7. When Warren received a firman from Constantinople, he decided to keep the contents of the document secret and continued to excavate in the city (Silberman, *God and Country,* 92). To be able to conduct his treasure hunt, Parker offered two high-ranking members of the Young Turk government 50 percent of any treasure he might find in return for their official confidence and support (182). To excavate within the Haram, Parker offered twenty-five thousand dollars to Azmey Bey Pasha, the local official, who arranged that Sheikh Khalil, the hereditary guardian of the Dome of the Rock, would also be bribed (186).

8. Much of our knowledge regarding Robinson's life and professional achievements comes from Roswell D. Hitchcock, the president of the Union Theological Seminary. His account, *Edward Robinson,* was published shortly after Robinson's death. For a summary of and commentary on Robinson's contributions to the field of biblical archaeology, see Silberman, *God and Country,* 37–47.

9. J. B. Pritchard, *Archaeology and Old Testament* (Princeton: Princeton University Press, 1958), 57–58.

10. Silberman, *God and Country,* 47.

11. On de Saulcy's travels, see his *Voyage autour de la mer Morte* and *Voyage en Terre Sainte.* For a summary of his life and his explorations in Palestine, see Silberman, *God and*

Country, 63–72; and V. Lemire, *La soif de Jérusalem: Essai d'hydrohistoire (1840–1948)* (Paris: Publications de la Sorbonne, 2011), 31, 38–45.

12. L. Y. Rahmani, "Ancient Jerusalem's Funerary Customs and Tombs: Part Four," *The Biblical Archaeologist* 45 (1982): 112.

13. S. Gibson, "British Archaeological Work in Jerusalem between 1865 and 1967: An Assessment." In Galor and Avni, *Unearthing Jerusalem,* 26–29.

14. Silberman, *God and Country,* 79–88.

15. For his work in Jerusalem, Wilson was assisted by a team of sappers and miners, as well as the photographer James McDonald, R.E., who made an extremely important pictorial record of the city's buildings. Gibson, "British Archaeological Work," 26.

16. A detailed report of his work was published in his *Ordnance Survey of Jerusalem.*

17. Gibson, "British Archaeological Work," 37.

18. On Warren and his work in Jerusalem, see Silberman, *God and Country,* 89–99.

19. Gibson, "British Archaeological Work," 40–41.

20. After completion of their work, Walter Morrison, the PEF Treasurer, edited a book with chapters by Wilson and Warren entitled *The Recovery of Jerusalem,* which was followed by a popular account of Warren's work in Jerusalem entitled *Underground Jerusalem.* See C. W. Wilson and C. Warren, *The Recovery of Jerusalem: A Narrative of Exploration and Discovery in the Holy Land* (London: R. Bentley, 1871); and C. Warren, *Underground Jerusalem* (London: Palestine Exploration Fund, 1876).

21. C. Clermont-Ganneau, "Une stèle du Temple de Jérusalem," *Revue Archéologique* 2, no. 23 (1872).

22. C. Clermont-Ganneau, *Archaeological Researches in Palestine during the Years 1873–1874,* vols. 1–2 (London: Palestine Exploration Fund, 1899–96 [sic]); C. Clermont-Ganneau, *Recueil d'archéologie orientale,* vols. 1–8 (Paris: Leroux, 1888–1924); and C. Clermont-Ganneau, *Études d'archéologie orientale,* vol. 2 (Paris: Vieweg, 1880).

23. Among his numerous publications, see, in particular, *Beit el Makdas oder der alte Tempelplatz zu Jerusalem, wie er jetzt ist* (Jerusalem: Selbstverlag des Verfassers, 1887); "Recent Discoveries in Jerusalem," *Palestine Exploration Quarterly* 21 (1889), 62–63; and *Die Stiftshütte, der Tempelplatz der Jetztzeit* (Berlin: Weidmann, 1896).

24. H. Guthe, *Ausgrabungen bei Jerusalem* (Leipzig: K. Baedeker, 1883).

25. For an account of their excavations, see Silberman, *God and Country,* 147–70.

26. F. J. Bliss and A. C. Dickie, *Excavations at Jerusalem, 1894–1897* (London: Palestine Exploration Fund, 1898).

27. For a detailed account of the Parker expedition, see Silberman, *God and Country,* 180–88; and Silberman, "In Search of Solomon's Lost Treasures, *Biblical Archaeology Review* 6.4 (1980). Following Parker's escape from Jerusalem, the Palestine Exploration Fund Quarterly Statement published Dalman's ("Temple Treasure") and Warren's ("Recent Excavations") critics of the expedition.

28. Vincent devoted much of his career to the study of ancient Jerusalem. See L.-H. Vincent and F.-M. Abel, *Jérusalem nouvelle: Recherches de topographie, d'archéologie et d'histoire,* II, 1–4 (Paris: J. Gabalda, 1914–26); and L.-H.Vincent and M.-A. Steve, *Jérusalem de l'Ancien Testament: Recherches d'archéologie et d'histoire,* I–III (Paris: J. Gabalda, 1954–56). For Vincent's work for the Parker expedition, see his *Jérusalem sous terre: Les récentes*

fouilles d'Ophel (London: H. Cox, 1911), "Les récentes fouilles d'Ophel" [1], *Revue Biblique* 20 (1911), and "Les récentes fouilles d'Ophel" [2], *Revue Biblique* 21 (1912).

29. R. Weill, *La cité de David: compte rendu des fouilles exécutées à Jérusalem, sur le site de la ville primitive, campagne de 1913–1914* (Paris: P. Geuthner, 1920); and *La cité de David: compte rendu des fouilles exécutées à Jérusalem, sur le site de la ville primitive, II, campagne de 1923–1924* (Paris: P. Geuthner, 1947).

30. See J. S. Kloppenborg Verbin, "Dating Theodotos ('CIJ' II 1404)," *Journal of Jewish Studies* 51 (2000).

31. S. Gibson, "British Archaeological Institutions in Mandatory Palestine, 1917–1948," *Palestine Exploration Quarterly* 131, no. 2 (1999): 135; and Gibson, "British Archaeological Work," 48.

32. Gibson, "British Archaeological Work," 48; and C. R. Ashbee, *Jerusalem 1918–1920: Being the Records of the Pro-Jerusalem Council during the Period of the British Military Administration* (London: The Council of the Pro-Jerusalem Society, 1921), 15–18.

33. See Silberman, "Power, Politics, and the Past," 15.

34. It appears that the decision to select only Muslim and Jewish representatives from the local communities was motivated by the desire to compensate for the exclusive Christian representation of professionals on the British, American, and European side.

35. Glock, "Archaeology as Cultural Survival," 75.

36. J. Seligman, "The Departments of Antiquities and the Israel Antiquities Authority (1918–2006): The Jerusalem Experience," in Galor and Avni, *Unearthing Jerusalem*, 126.

37. Gibson, "British Archaeological Work," 48–49.

38. Silberman, "Power, Politics and the Past," 15.

39. Seligman, "Departments of Antiquities," 127.

40. Those salvage excavations exposed hundreds of ancient tombs (Seligman, "Departments of Antiquities" 127).

41. R. A. S. Macalister and J. G.Duncan, *Excavations of the Hill of Ophel, Jerusalem, 1923–1925: Being the Joint Expedition of the Palestine Exploration Fund and the "Daily Telegraph,"* Annual of the Palestine Exploration Fund 4 (London: Palestine Exploration Fund, 1926).

42. J. W. Crowfoot, "Excavations on Ophel, 1928," *Palestine Exploration Quarterly* 61 (1929); and "Ophel Again," *Palestine Exploration Quarterly* 77 (1945); and J. W. Crowfoot and G. M. Fitzgerald, *Excavations in the Tyropoeon Valley, Jerusalem, 1927* (London: Palestine Exploration Fund, 1929). The gate is generally thought to be Hellenistic, but Gibson relates it to the Middle Bronze Age ("British Archaeological Work," 49).

43. C. N. Johns, "Excavations at the Citadel, Jerusalem, Interim Report, 1935," *Quarterly of the Department of Antiquities of Palestine* 5 (1936)"; and C. N. Johns, "The Citadel, Jerusalem: A Summary of Work since 1934," *Quarterly of the Department of Antiquities of Palestine* 14 (1950)."

44. Flavius Josephus, in his description of Jerusalem's fortifications, names three walls: the First Wall, built by one of the Hasmonean kings around 130 B.C.E. on the lines of the Iron Age city wall; the Second Wall, in place during King Herod the Great's rule, between 37 and 4 B.C.E. (and possibly built by him); and the Third Wall, Jerusalem's northern-most wall, built by Herod Agrippa I between 41 and 44 C.E.

45. E. T. Richmond, *The Dome of the Rock in Jerusalem. A Description of Its Structure and Decoration* (Oxford, 1924); and R. W. Hamilton, *The Structural History of the Aqsa*

Mosque: A Record of Archaeological Gleanings from the Repairs of 1938–1942 (Jerusalem: Department of Antiquities of Palestine, 1949).

46. W. Harvey, *Church of the Holy Sepulchre, Jerusalem; Structural Survey, Final Report, William Harvey, with an Introduction by E. T. Richmond* (London: Oxford University Press, 1935).

47. R. Reich, "The Israel Exploration Society (IES)," In Galor and Avni, *Unearthing Jerusalem* 119.

48. In "Producing (Arti) Facts: Archaeology and Power during the British Mandate of Palestine," *Israel Studies* 7.2 (2002), N. Abu El-Haj discusses the political and ideological motifs and implications of focusing on the region's Jewish past, specifically during the period of the Mandate.

49. Silberman, "Power, Politics, and the Past," 18.

50. Silberman, "Power, Politics, and the Past," 18.

51. On the historical background of the Department of Antiquities in Jordan, see http://doa.gov.jo/en/inside.php?src=sublinks&SlID=5003&MlID=1.

52. R. Kletter, *Just Past? The Making of Israeli Archaeology* (London: Equinox, 2005), 190–92; and Seligman, "Departments of Antiquities," 131–35.

53. G. Avni and J. Seligman, *Temple Mount 1917–2001. Documentation, Research and Inspection of Antiquities* (Jerusalem: Israel Antiquities Authority, 2001), 22.

54. It was not until the 1990s and leading into the twenty-first century that Jordan became interested once again in the theme of biblical archaeology in the context of identity construction around newly excavated holy places. See Katz, *Jordanian Jerusalem*, 15. Kenyon published two popular versions of her excavations in Jerusalem: *Digging Up Jerusalem* (London: Praeger, 1974) and *Jerusalem: Excavating 3000 Years of History* (London: Thames & Hudson, 1967). Five volumes of the final report have been published since, see A. D. Tushingham and M. L. Steinger, *Excavations in Jerusalem, 1961–1967*, vol. 4 (Ontario: Royal Ontario Museum, 1985); H. J. Franken and M. L. Steiner, *Excavations at Jerusalem, 1961–1967*, vol. 2, *The Iron Age Extramural Quarter on the South-East Hill*, British Academy Monographs in Archaeology (Oxford: Oxford University Press, 1990); M. L. Steiner, *Excavations by Kathleen M. Kenyon in Jerusalem 1961–1967*, vol. 3, *The Settlement in the Bronze and Iron Ages* (Sheffield, England: Sheffield Academic Press, 2001); I. Eshel and K. Prag, *Excavations by K. M. Kenyon in Jerusalem*, vol. 4, *The Iron Age Cave Deposits*, British Academy Monographs in Archaeology (London: Council for British Research in the Levant, 1995); and K. Prag, *Excavations by K. M. Kenyon in Jerusalem, 1961–1967*, vol. 5, *Discoveries in Hellenistic to Ottoman Jerusalem*, Levant Supplementary Series 7 (London: Council for British Research in the Levant, 2008).

55. Though Flinders Petrie had introduced the methods of seriation analysis and stratigraphic excavation to the region as early as the 1920s, for Jerusalem, it is usually Kenyon who is associated with introducing the rigors of stratigraphic techniques and ceramic typology for dating of archaeological strata. See Silberman, *God and Country*, 176–79.

56. Kletter, *Just Past?* 124.

57. See M. Avi-Yonah, "Excavations at Sheikh Bader," *Bulletin of the Jewish Palestine Exploration Society* 15 (1949/50); and Seligman, "Departments of Antiquities," 133.

58. The Tombs of the Sanhedrin and the Tomb of Jason are among the more significant burial complexes discovered during this time frame. See Seligman, "Departments of Antiquities," 133.

59. This stipulation was formulated in the *Official Gazette* (the official journal of the United States Patent and Trademark Office) number 1390, 30.8.1967.

60. Silberman points out that those excavations were judged by some to go far beyond the legitimate and permitted function of protecting immediately endangered archaeological sites. Silberman, "Power, Politics, and the Past," 18–19.

61. Uzi Dahari served as interim director.

62. Shin Bet is the Israel Security Agency (ISA), similar to the British MI5 or the American FBI. Israel Hasson's appointment as director of the IAA was controversial because of his ties to Elad. See N. Hasson, "Israel Antiquities Authority Taps Politician with Ties to Rightist NGO," *Ha'aretz*, October 29, 2014.

63. In 2011, Avni was replaced by Jon Seligman and has since acted as academic director of excavations, surveys, research, laboratories, and scientific publications.

64. For an overview of the history of the IDAM and the IAA between 1967 and 2006, see Seligman, "Departments of Antiquities," 135–46.

65. The survey was published in three volumes. See A. Kloner, *Survey of Jerusalem, the Southern Sector* (Jerusalem: Israel Antiquities Authority—Archaeological Survey of Israel, 2000); *Survey of Jerusalem, the Northeastern Sector* (Jerusalem: Israel Antiquities Authority—Archaeological Survey of Israel, 2001); and *Survey of Jerusalem, the Northwestern Sector: Introduction and Indices* (Jerusalem: Israel Antiquities Authority—Archaeological Survey of Israel, 2003).

66. For a more extensive summary of excavations conducted in Jerusalem since 1967, see Seligman, "Departments of Antiquities," 135–45. Most excavations were published in reports published by the IAA in issues and volumes of the *'Atiqot* and *Hadashot Arkheologiyot* series.

67. For the École biblique excavations, see J.-B. Humbert, "Saint John Prodromos Restoration Project Jerusalem, Greek Orthodox Patriarchate property, Jerusalem," *Cabinet d'architects des monuments historiques, Michel Goutal (Paris) Excavation of the École biblique et archéologique française de Jérusalem* (2011), and for the German Protestant Institute excavations, see D. Vieweger and G. Förder-Hoff, *The Archaeological Park under the Church of the Redeemer in Jerusalem* (Jerusalem: German Protestant Institute of Archaeology, 2013).

68. See S. Gibson and J. Taylor, "New Excavations on Mount Zion in Jerusalem and an Inscribed Stone Cup/Mug from the Second Temple Period," in *New Studies in the Archaeology of Jerusalem and Its Region,* collected papers, vol. 4, ed. by D. Amit, O. Peleg-Barkat, and D. Stiebel (Jerusalem: Israel Antiquities Authority and Institute of Archaeology, Hebrew University of Jerusalem, 2010).

69. M. H. Burgoyne, *Mamluk Jerusalem: An Architectural Study* (London: World of Islam Festival Trust, 1987).

70. M. K. Hawari, *Ayyubid Jerusalem (1187–1250): An Architectural and Archaeological Study* (Oxford: British Archaeological Reports, 2007); Y. Natsheh, "The Architecture of Ottoman Jerusalem," in Auld and Hillenbrand, *Ottoman Jerusalem,* 583–655; and Y. Natsheh "Catalogue of Buildings," in Auld and Hillenbrand, *Ottoman Jerusalem,* 657–1085.

71. According to Seligman, a total of approximately twelve thousand sites have been excavated in the city since the beginning of archaeological exploration in the mid-nineteenth century. According to Galor and Avni, this number only reflects official expeditions. The number of illegal or undocumented excavations is around five hundred. See Seligman,

"Departments of Antiquities," 145; and G. Avni and K. Galor, "Unearthing Jerusalem: 150 Years of Archaeological Research," in Galor and Avni, *Unearthing Jerusalem,*" x.

72. See Seligman, "Departments of Antiquities," 145.

73. The term *illegal* in this context refers to excavations conducted without official governmental approval. Given the contested nature of the Israeli annexation of the Old City and East Jerusalem, the legality of excavation is internationally disputed. On Israeli and foreign law as it pertains to the archaeological activity and the preservation of its cultural heritage, see S. Berkovitz, *The Temple Mount and the Western Wall in Israeli Law,* The Jerusalem Institute for Israel Studies Series 90 (Jerusalem: JIIS and the Jerusalem Foundation, 2001); S. Berkovitz, *The Wars of the Holy Places: The Struggle over Jerusalem and the Holy Sites in Israel, Judea, Samaria and the Gaza District* (Jerusalem: Hed Arzi Publishing House and the Jerusalem Institute for Israel Studies, 2001); and G. Avni and K. Galor, "Unearthing Jerusalem," x.

74. Cultural heritage efforts under Jordanian rule focused mostly on the Islamic heritage. But in terms of fieldwork, Kathleen Kenyon's was the only excavation carried out during this period and thus shaped the focus on the biblical past.

3. FROM DESTRUCTION TO PRESERVATION

1. A few days later, Herzl changed his mind. He suggested building a new secular city outside the walls and leaving the holy shrines in an enclave of their own. It was a perfect expression of the secularist ideal: religion must be relegated to a separate sphere, where it will rapidly become a museum piece. T. Herzl, *The Complete Diaries of Theodor Herzl,* ed. R. Patai, 2 vols. (London and New York: Herzl Press with Thomas Yoseloff, 1960), 745. Two decades after Herzl, British archaeologist W. M. Flinders Petrie made a similar suggestion. He proposed to demolish much of the Old City, remove the medieval remains and restore the Jewish layers of habitation. *Palestine Exploration Quarterly Statement* 5, 1919, 3. See also S. Gibson, "British Archaeological Work in Jerusalem between 1865 and 1967: An Assessment," in Galor and Avni, *Unearthing Jerusalem,* 48.

2. Benvenisti, *City of Stone,* 136.

3. At the turn of the twentieth century, there were some fifty synagogues and *yeshivot* in the Jewish Quarter. Surprisingly, by 1975, only four of the destroyed buildings were wholly or partially renovated. In "Post-War Reconstruction and Conservation," (382), Slae, Kark, and Shoval point out that for many Israelis, the heritage value associated with religious institutions was perceived as obsolescent.

4. M. Dumper, *The Politics of Sacred Space: The Old City of Jerusalem in the Middle East Conflict* (Boulder, CO: Lynne Rienner, 2002), 175; and N. al-Jubeh, "Bab al-Magharibah."

5. In *Reinventing Jerusalem,* Ricca documents the process of the reconstruction and explains the cultural and ideological ramifications locally and internationally. He compares the Jewish Quarter reconstruction to other contemporary urban restoration initiatives and comes to the conclusion that if international standards had been followed and foreign experts had been consulted, the extent of destruction could have been avoided. According to Slae, Kark, and Shoval, only one hundred (a third) of the old structures in the quarter were deemed suitable for restoration ("Post-War Reconstruction and Conservation," 377).

6. See M. Inbari, *Jewish Fundamentalism and the Temple Mount: Who Will Build the Third Temple?* (Albany: State University of New York Press, 2009), 17–30. Some advocate for the return of the compound without building a temple.

7. M. Dumper and C. Larkin compare the situation of cultural heritage in Jerusalem to other cities with a complicated political and religious make up, such as Fez, Aleppo, Mostar, and Kosovo. See "The Role of UNESCO in Jerusalem's Old City," *Jerusalem Quarterly* 39 (2009): 16–28.

8. This quotation (as well as the quotations in the rest of this paragraph) are from "The Conservation of Jerusalem's City Walls," on the IAA website, www.antiquities.org.il/jerusalemwalls/default-eng.asp.

9. See www.iaa-conservation.org.il/article_Item_eng.asp?subject_id=42&id=118.

10. The literature is extensive. For a few select recent publications, see T. Webb, "Appropriating the Stones: The 'Elgin Marbles' an English National Taste," in Barkan and Bush, *Claiming the Stones,* 51–96. C. C. Coggins, "Latin America, Native America, and the Politics of Culture," in Barkan and Bush, *Claiming the Stones,* 97–115; L. Smith, *Archaeological Theory and the Politics of Cultural Heritage* (London: Routledge, 2004); and N. Moore and Y. Whelan, *Heritage, Memory and the Politics of Identity. New Perspectives on the Cultural Landscape* (Aldershot, England: Ashgate, 2008).

11. J. B. Scott, *The Hague Conventions and Declarations of 1899 and 1907* (New York: Oxford University Press, 1918). For a recent reevaluation of the conventions, see W. C. Banks, *New Battlefields/Old Laws: Critical Debates on Asymmetric Warfare* (New York: Columbia University Press, 2011).

12. K. Jote, *International Legal Protection of Cultural Heritage* (Stockholm: Jurisförlaget, 1994), 19; and Ricca, *Reinventing Jerusalem,* 129.

13. This was the first international legal framework for the fight against the illicit trafficking of cultural property in times of peace.

14. S. Titchen, *On the Construction of Outstanding Universal Value: UNESCO's World Heritage Convention and the Identification and Assessment of Cultural Places for Inclusion in the World Heritage List* (PhD diss., Canberra, Australian National University, 1995), 94.

15. The charter was prepared by the International Committee for the Management of Archaeological Heritage (ICAHM) and approved by the Ninth General Assembly in Lausanne.

16. Article 3, on Legislation and Economy.

17. On the contested nature of Jerusalem's holy sites, see Dumper, *Politics of Sacred Space;* Dumper, "The Palestinian Waqf"; S. Berkovitz, *The Wars of the Holy Places: The Struggle over Jerusalem and the Holy Sites in Israel, Judea, Samaria and the Gaza District.* (Jerusalem: Hed Arzi Publishing House and the Jerusalem Institute for Israel Studies, 2001); and D. E. Guinn, *Protecting Jerusalem's Holy Sites: A Strategy for Negotiating a Sacred Peace* (Cambridge: Cambridge University Press, 2006).

18. M. M. Kersel, "The Trade in Palestinian Antiquities," *Jerusalem Quarterly* 33 (2008): 24.

19. Kersel, "Trade in Palestinian Antiquities," 25–26.

20. Katz, *Jordanian Jerusalem,* 144.

21. Katz, *Jordanian Jerusalem* (1–15, 118–36), examines how the modern Jordanian state has invested sacred sites with national meaning and how this has impacted tourism and

pilgrimage to Jerusalem. She argues that the city's Muslim and Christian sites became a focal point of Jordan's identity. On the pre-state family contribution to the renovations of the Dome of the Rock, see Katz, chapter 4. On the Second Hashemite Restoration after the coronation of King Hussein, see www.kinghussein.gov.jo/islam_restoration.html.

22. Kersel, "Trade in Palestinian Antiquities," 27.

23. For a critical analysis of Israeli archaeological activity in Jerusalem between 1967–2007 and its ideological role in support of a 'unified' city, see R. Greenberg, "Extreme Exposure: Archaeology in Jerusalem 1967–2007," *Conservation and Management of Archaeological Sites* 11 (2009), 262–81. On the nationalistic and ideological roles of Israeli archaeology in Jerusalem, see Abu El-Haj, "Translating Truths," 168–85; and Abu El-Haj, *Facts on the Ground*, 130–62.

24. In addition to the significant resources made available by Elad and the regular IAA funds, the government has made available 1 billion ILS (ca. $270 million) to be spent on archaeological activity and tourist development in East Jerusalem between 2005 and 2013.

25. S. Berkovitz, *The Temple Mount and the Western Wall in Israeli Law,* The Jerusalem Institute for Israel Studies Series 90 (Jerusalem: JIIS and the Jerusalem Foundation, 2001), 13.

26. Though Israel considers itself as having inherited this right, and as having ultimate jurisdiction over all holy sites in the city, it tacitly ceded limited administrative autonomy over the Haram compound to the Waqf administration. This excludes, however, the physical control over and the security arrangements connected to the site.

27. See M. Dumper and C. Larkin, "The Politics of Heritage and the Limitations of International Agency in Divided Cities: The Role of UNESCO in Jerusalem's Old City," *Review of International Studies* 38 (2012): 30.

28. For the official current definition of the IAA, see www.antiquities.org.il. Dumper and Larkin, "The Politics of Heritage," 6–7.

29. The problematic nature of legally protecting only those antiquities that predate 1700 is discussed by N. al-Jubeh, "Palestinian Identity and Cultural Heritage," in *Temps et espaces en Palestine, Contemporain publications, no. 25,* ed. R. Heacock (Beirut, Lebanon: Institut français du Proche-Orient, 2005), 26.

30. Abu El-Haj comments on the exclusive focus on First and Second Temple periods but fails to acknowledge the change in Israeli archaeology since roughly the 1990s. See Abu El-Haj, "Translating Truths," 172, 174, 176; and Abu El-Haj, "Producing (Arti) Facts," Archaeology and Power during the British Mandate of Palestine." *Israel Studies* 7.2 (2002): 46–47). In spite of the general focus on Herodian structures in Benjamin Mazar's excavation, an early Islamic architectural complex, the Umayyad governmental complex at the foot of the southwestern corner of the Haram, was preserved and restored and is featured prominently in the archaeological park.

31. See, for example, B. Z. Kedar, S. Weksler-Bdolah, and T.Da'adli, "Madrasa Afdaliyya / Maqam Al- Shaykh 'Id: An Example of Ayyubid Architecture in Jerusalem," *Revue Biblique* 119 (2012): 271–87; A. Onn, S. Weksler-Bdolah, and R. Bar-Nathan, "Jerusalem, The Old City, Wilson's Arch and the Great Causeway. Preliminary Report," *Hadashot Arkheologiyot* 123 (2011); or S. Weksler-Bdolah, A. Onn, B. Ouahnouna, and S. Isilevitz, "Jerusalem, the Western Wall Plaza Excavations, 2005–2009. Preliminary Report,"*Hadashot Arkheologiyot* 121 (2009).

32. On the extended role of the conservation department of the IAA, see www.iaa-conservation.org.il (in Hebrew) or www.iaa-conservation.org.il/index_eng.asp (English version).

33. Dumper and Larkin, "Politics of Heritage," 26.

34. Ever since the Arab municipality was abolished by the Israeli government in 1967, there has been a Palestinian consensus to boycott Israeli municipal elections.

35. On the complex relationships between Israel, Jordan, the PLO (Palestine Liberation Organization), the PNA (Palestinian National Authority) and the Waqf administration, in particular in post-Oslo Jerusalem, see Larkin and Dumper, "In Defense of Al-Aqsa," 34–35.

36. On the role of the al-Aqsa Association, or Palestinian Islamists, under the leadership of Shaykh Ra'id Salah and their commitment to rehabilitate and restore "holy places" in Israel, and more specifically in East Jerusalem and on the Haram, see Larkin and Dumper, "In Defense of Al-Aqsa," 31–39.

37. According to Dumper ("The Palestinian Waqf," 203–5) the Waqf owns approximately 67 percent, or more than two-thirds, of Jerusalem's Old City. The recent survey of the Jerusalem Revitalization Program of the Welfare Association indicates that 21.4 percent of residential houses were recorded as Islamic or Christian Waqf, while another 24 percent were family Waqfs (Welfare Association, *Jerusalem: Heritage and Life: Old City Revitalization Plan* [Jerusalem and Ramallah: Welfare Association, 2004], 70 and 105–6). On the establishment of the Ministry of Islamic Affairs and Awqaf, see Katz, *Jordanian Jerusalem*, 6.

38. Dumper, "The Palestinian Waqf," 201.

39. On the administration of Waqf property in Jerusalem, see Y. Reiter, "The Administration and Supervision of Waqf Properties in 20th Century Jerusalem," *Varia Turcica* (Istanbul: Institut Français d'Études Anatoliennes 26, 1994), 169–82; Y. Reiter, *Islamic Endowments in Jerusalem under British Mandate* (London: Frank Cass, 1996), 146–206; and Y. Reiter, *Islamic Institutions in Jerusalem: Palestinian Muslim Administration under Jordanian and Israeli Rule* (The Hague, London and Boston: Kluwer Law International, 1997), 23–45.

40. The Waqf administration's Department of Islamic Archaeology had informal contacts with Israeli academics. See Reiter, *Islamic Institutions in Jerusalem*, 208; Avni and Seligman, *Temple Mount*, 24–42.

41. As Larkin and Dumper have correctly pointed out, "Beyond the preservation of monuments and religious sites, heritage conservation must be linked to urban revitalization, with the improvement of social amenities such as housing, sanitation and water supply. See Larkin and Dumper, "UNESCO and Jerusalem," 21.

42. See General Conference of UNESCO Resolution on protection of cultural property in Jerusalem 15C/Resolutions 3 342 and 3.343; 82 EX/Decision 4.4.2, 83 EX/Decision 4.3.1, 88 EX/Decision 4.3.1, 89 EX/Decision 4 4.1, 90 EX/Decision 4.3.1, and 17C/Resolution 3.422.

43. The nomination by Jordan was much debated, as the Hashemite kingdom was no longer ruling the Old City. The nomination has been perceived by some as a political step.

44. On Lemaire's relationship with the Israeli and Palestinian sides, see Ricca, *Reinventing Jerusalem*, 146–52.

45. Between 1971 and 1997, the first director-general representative on the cultural heritage of Jerusalem was Raymond Lemaire. Lemaire's supportive role of Israeli cultural heritage initiatives has been discussed in detail by Ricca, *Reinventing Jerusalem*, 119–20, 127, 140–53.

46. In his last report from 1997, Lemaire notes that the Israeli authorities built a metallic pergola in the middle of the former courtyard of one of the Umayyad palaces that disfigured the site. See Ricca, *Reinventing Jerusalem,* 142.

47. See Dumper, "The Palestinian Waqf."

48. The British Mandate planning regulations already identified an extended area as the Jerusalem archaeological zone, including the Kidron Valley, the Garden of Gethsemane, the Pool of Siloam, Mount Zion and the Valley of Hinnom and an extended zone to include the Mount of Olives and the village of Bethany.

49. Ricca outlined three phases of relation between Israel and UNESCO between 1967 and 1999. See Ricca, *Reinventing Jerusalem,* 153–54. Dumper and Larkin identified a fourth phase since the start of the Second Intifada in September of 2000. See Dumper and Larkin, "Politics of Heritage," 37.

50. After Lemaire's death in 1997, appointments were either short or failed entirely. Professor Leon Pressouyre was sent on a mission in 1999, followed in 2000 and 2001 by Professor Oleg Grabar. In 2004 the task was entrusted to Francesco Bandarin, Director of UNESCO's World Heritage Centre.

51. UNESCO was the first UN agency the Palestinians joined since President Mahmoud Abbas applied for full membership of the United Nations on September 23, 2011. The motion to grant Palestinians membership to UNESCO was passed with 107 votes in favor, 14 against, and 52 abstentions. Elias Sanbar is currently the Palestinian representative to UNESCO.

52. Ricca, *Reinventing Jerusalem,* 127–55.

53. Dumper and Larkin, "Politics of Heritage," 42.

54. As opposed to Elad, which is an NGO, the Western Wall Heritage Foundation operates under the auspices of the office of the prime minister of Israel and the Government Companies Authority (GCA).

55. For the mission statement, see Emek Shaveh's website: www.alt-arch.org. The organization was founded by Raphael Greenberg, a professor of archaeology at Tel Aviv University, and Yonathan Mizrachi, a former employee of the IAA.

56. On the role of the al-Aqsa Association, or Palestinian Islamists, under the leadership of Shaykh Ra'id Salah and their commitment to rehabilitate and restore "holy places" in Israel, and more specifically in East Jerusalem and on the Haram, see Larkin and Dumper, "In Defense of Al-Aqsa," 31–39.

57. These include the General Assembly Resolutions 181 and 303, UN Security Council Resolution 476 and UN Human Rights Council Resolution 13/8.

58. See ARCH's website: www.archjerusalem.com. Their aim is to challenge Israeli plans to "Disneyfy" the historic village site as a luxury residential/commercial neighborhood and to draft the First Geneva International Convention on Vulnerable Cultural Heritage of Outstanding Universal Value.

59. According to S. Scham and A. Yahya, "Heritage and Reconciliation," *Journal of Social Archaeology* 3 (2003): 403, heritage preservation in the Old City is a pragmatic tool for securing and legitimizing physical presence, ownership and right to the land.

60. Fostering the Palestinian cultural heritage contributes to an enriched Palestinian identity that shares many of its roots with the Jewish cultural heritage in the region, a fact that is often neglected. On the origins of the Palestinian identity, see al-Jubeh, "Palestinian

Identity," 5–20; and on the role of cultural heritage in identity formation, see al-Jubeh, "Palestinian Identity," 21–22.

4. DISPLAY AND PRESENTATION

1. The report (9GL44868/7) was summarized by someone identified only by the surname Mayer on August 1, 1948. It is unclear who the archaeologists were and where they met. See Kletter, *Just Past?* 175.

2. "Encyclopedic collections" or "universal museums" are large, mostly national, institutions that offer visitors a plethora of material from across the world and all periods of human culture and history. Recent criticism of encyclopedic collections addresses the removal of artifacts and monuments from their original cultural setting.

3. The ICOMOS charter for the protection and management of the archaeological heritage was prepared by the International Committee on Archaeological Heritage Management (ICAHM) and approved by the Ninth General Assembly in Lausanne.

4. Information on the City of David (Jerusalem Walls) National Park in English can be found on the INPA website. A complete list of declared national parks only appears in Hebrew. The political implications of the creation of national parks in Jerusalem are discussed in detail on the Emek Shaveh website (http://alt-arch.org/en) as well as in several booklets published by the organization. See Y. Mizrachi, *Archaeology in the Shadow of the Conflict: The Mound of Ancient Jerusalem (City of David) in Silwan* (Jerusalem: Emek Shaveh, 2010); Mizrachi, *Between Holiness and Propaganda;* and R. Greenberg and Y. Mizrachi, *From Shiloah to Silwan: Visitor's Guide to Ancient Jerusalem (City of David) and the Village of Silwan* (Jerusalem: Emek Shaveh, 2011).

5. This area, known as E1—or Mevaseret Adumim in Hebrew—is located within the municipal boundary of the Israeli city of Maale Adumin, adjacent to Jerusalem. Given international pressure, Israeli plans for construction were temporarily frozen in 2009. In response to the United Nations approving the Palestinian bid for "non-member observer state" status in December of 2012, Israel announced that it was resuming planning and zoning work in E1.

6. Three further national parks are in early stages of the planning process: the Mount of Olives National Park, the ash-Sheikh Jarrah (Simon the Righteous) National Park, and the Bab as-Sahrah National Park. See T. Kulka, E. Cohen-Bar, and S. Kronish, *Bimkom: From Public to National Parks in East Jerusalem* (Jerusalem: New National Fund, 2012), 14.

7. Dunams are a measure of land area used in parts of the former Ottoman empire, including Israel.

8. See W. Pullan et al. *The Struggle for Jerusalem's Holy Places* (New York: Routledge, 2013) 48–75.

9. For a complete list of sites and monuments and their detailed description, see R. Reich, G. Avni and T. Winter, *The Jerusalem Archaeological Park* (Jerusalem: Israel Antiquities Authority, 1999).

10. R. Reich, *Excavating the City of David: Where Jerusalem's History Began* (Jerusalem: Israel Exploration Society and Biblical Archaeology Society, 2011), 280, 318, 351–52.

11. For a description of the City of David National Parks and the ideological and political nature of Elad's role, see Kulka, Cohen-Bar, and Kronish, *Bimkom,* 14–18.

12. Two official websites exist: www.mountofolives.co.il/eng/article.aspx?id = 941 and http://templemount.wordpress.com.

13. A. Eirikh-Rose, "Jerusalem, the Slopes of Mount Scopus, Survey," *Hadashot Arkheologiyot* 122 (2010); D. Amit, J. Seligman, and I. Zilberbod, "Jerusalem, Mount Scopus (East)," *Hadashot Arkheologiyot* 111 (2000); and D. Amit, J. Seligman, and I. Zilberbod, "The 'Monastery of Theodorus and Cyriacus' on the Eastern Slope of Mount Scopus," in *One Land—Many Cultures: Archaeological Studies in Honour of Stanislao Loffreda OFM,* ed. G. C., Bottini, L. Di Segni, and L. D. Chrupcala, 139–48 (Jerusalem: Amitai Press, 2006).

14. The project has been criticized for using funding from Elad and for lacking a clear scientific purpose. See N. Hasson, "Petition Slams Tel Aviv University's Involvement in East Jerusalem's Dig," *Ha'aretz,* December 25, 2012.

15. See Kulka, Cohen-Bar, and Kronish, *Bimkom,* 26–27.

16. The Mount Scopus National Park is located on agricultural land used by residents of the Palestinian neighborhoods of Issawiya and a-Tur. Houses in Silwan's al-Bustan neighborhood, within the area planned as the King's Valley National Park, have been demolished. The original plans to demolish the houses were drafted in 2002.

17. Kulka, Cohen-Bar, and Kronish, *Bimkom,* 4, 31–32. The official U.S. position to Israeli settlements has clearly shifted since the beginning of Donald Trump's presidency. Within days after the inauguration, the Jerusalem Local Planning and Building Committee approved the construction of 566 housing units in the Pisgat Ze'ev, Ramot, and Ramat Shlomo neighborhoods. See N. Hasson, "After Trump's Swearing-In, Jerusalem Approves 566 Homes beyond Green Line," *Ha'aretz,* January 22, 2017.

18. See statement of the company on its official website: www.jewish-quarter.org.il/chevra.asp. The JQDC serves both as the contractor and landowner.

19. Slae, Kark, and Shoval, "Post-War Reconstruction and Conservation," 369.

20. E. Netzer, "Reconstruction of the Jewish Quarter in the Old City," in Yadin, *Jerusalem Revealed,* 118.

21. Architect and archaeologist Ehud Netzer designed a master plan, accepted in 1967, which prescribed that only about one hundred (a third) of the old structures were deemed suitable for restoration. See Slae, Kark, and Shoval, "Post-War Reconstruction and Conservation," 377.

22. Slae, Kark, and Shoval, "Post-War Reconstruction and Conservation," 380.

23. See N. Avigad, *Discovering Jerusalem* (Nashville, Camden, and New York: Thomas Nelson Publishers, 1983) for a preliminary narrative of the excavation. For the final reports, see H. Geva, *Jewish Quarter Excavations in the Old City of Jerusalem: Conducted by Nahman Avigad, 1969–1982,* vols. 1–4 (Jerusalem: Israel Exploration Society, 2000–10); and Gutfeld, *Jewish Quarter Excavations in the Old City of Jerusalem: Conducted by Nahman Avigad, 1969–1982,* vol. 5 (Jerusalem: Israel Exploration Society, 2012).

24. See the description on the website of the Company for the Reconstruction and Development of the Jewish Quarter in the Old City of Jerusalem: www.jewish-quarter.org.il/meida-migd.asp.

25. For a description of the Iron Age defenses, see Avigad, *Discovering Jerusalem,* 49–54.

26. Avigad, *Discovering Jerusalem,* 54–60.

27. Avigad, *Discovering Jerusalem,* 83.

28. For a detailed description of the architectural remains and artifacts dating to the Herodian period, see Avigad, *Discovering Jerusalem*, 83–202.

29. Avigad, *Discovering Jerusalem*, 120–39.

30. On its significance, see Y. Tsafrir, "Procopius and the Nea Church in Jerusalem," in *Antiquité Tardive* 8 (2001): 149–64.

31. On the neglect of the Nea Church, see Mizrachi, *Between Holiness and Propaganda*, 9.

32. For a summary of the Byzantine period remains, see Mizrachi, *Between Holiness and Propaganda*, 208–46.

33. Slae, Kark, and Shoval, "Post-War Reconstruction and Conservation," 375.

34. Kark and Oren-Nordheim, *Jerusalem and Its Environs*, 82–87.

35. Ricca compares the Jewish Quarter restoration to preservation initiatives in Safed, Jaffa, Acre, Hebron, and Bethlehem, which enables him to highlight the inescapable role of ideology in all urban plans. See Ricca, *Reinventing Jerusalem: Israel's Reconstruction of the Jewish Quarter After 1967*, 156–95. According to Slae, Kark, and Shoval ("Post-War Reconstruction and Conservation," 372), Israel's preservation efforts were in line with the prevailing approach in Europe and America.

36. Ricca discusses the implications of excluding international experts at a time when Israel had no prior experience in conservation and preservation. See Ricca, *Reinventing Jerusalem*, 56 and 73–80. Slae, Kark, and Shoval ("Post-War Reconstruction and Conservation," 372) instead suggest that most conservation teams were national, even outside of Israel.

37. Slae, Kark, and Shoval, "Post-War Reconstruction and Conservation," 386.

38. The only synagogues to be restored before 1975 were Metivta Tiferet, Or ha-Hayyim, and Habad, as well as the yeshivot of Yerushalayim, Hayyei Olam, Etz Hayyim, Toray Hayyim, Bet-El, and Gemilut Hasadim. See Slae, Kark, and Shoval, "Post-War Reconstruction and Conservation," 382.

39. Slae, Kark, and Shoval, "Post-War Reconstruction and Conservation," 382.

40. For the scientific excavation reports, see Weksler-Bdolah et al., "Jerusalem, The Western Wall Plaza Excavations"; and Y. Baruch and D. Weiss, "Jerusalem, the Western Wall Plaza. Final Report," *Hadashot Arkheologiyot* 121 (2009).

41. For the planned construction, see Plan 11053 of the *Western Wall Heritage Center, Kotel Plaza in the Old City*, posted temporarily on the Ministry of Interior website (www. moin.gov.il) under "district committee for building and planning" (in Hebrew). See also Mizrachi, *From Silwan to the Temple Mount: Archaeological Excavations as a Means of Control in the Village of Silwan and in Jerusalem's Old City—Developments in 2012* (Jerusalem: Emek Shaveh, 2012), 9, 14–16.

42. N. Hasson, "Western Wall Plaza Facilities Cut to Size," *Ha'aretz*, June 13, 2014.

43. Protocol of government meeting 151, May 20, 2012, development of the city of Jerusalem, appendix 812, revised version posted temporarily on the website of the office of the prime minister (www.pmo.gov.il) under "Governmental Decisions" (in Hebrew). See also Mizrachi, *From Silwan to the Temple Mount*, 24–25; and Y. Mizrachi, *Archaeological Activities in Politically Sensitive Areas in Jerusalem's Historic Basin* (Jerusalem: Emek Shaveh, 2015), 12–13.

44. In spite of harsh criticism voiced internationally, the Jerusalem District Planning and Building Committee is expected to approve the plans. See Y. Yifa, "Visitors' Center Planned for East Jerusalem Draws Criticism," *The Times of Israel*, January 3, 2014.

45. See Mizrachi, *From Silwan to the Temple Mount,* 6–7, 29–30.

46. "Herodian Road from Shiloah Pool to the Western Wall," YouTube video, 3:18, posted by "City of David," published on April 5, 2012, www.youtube.com/watch?v=Z5OaFxK14yc. See also K. Galor, "King Herod in Jerusalem: The Politics of Cultural Heritage," *Jerusalem Quarterly* 62 (2015), 71–72.

47. Mizrachi, *From Silwan to the Temple Mount,* 17–18.

48. Plans for this work were submitted by the Jerusalem Development Authority (JDA) in 2011, a project to be conducted under the aegis of PAMI. See also Mizrachi, *From Silwan to the Temple Mount,* 10–13.

49. Mizrachi, *From Silwan to the Temple Mount,* 9.

50. The rest of this section discusses many of the antiquities collections and museums in Jerusalem. It is not a comprehensive list. Excluded from the list, but marginal for a discussion of provenanced Jerusalem artifacts and their impact on scholars, students, and the general public, are the Dar Al-Tifel Al-Arabi Museum, the L.A. Mayer Museum of Islamic Art, as well as the collections of the École biblique, the White Fathers of St. Anne, the German Protestant Institute, and the Studium Biblicum Franciscanum.

51. On the history of the museum, see M. F. Abu Khalaf, *Islamic Art through the Ages* (Jerusalem: Emerezian Graphic and Printing Est., 1998), 3–6; and K. Salameh, *The Qur'an Manuscripts in the al-Haram al-Sharif Islamic Museum* (Reading, England: Garnet; Paris: UNESCO, 2001), vi–ix, 2–3. Antiquities documented in a catalogue written by Bliss were showcased for the first time in a wing of a new school building established in 1891 north of Herod's Gate (Rushaidiya). This collection was moved to the Citadel in 1920.

52. For more on this project, see www.unesco.org/new/en/culture/themes/museums/ museum-projects/safeguarding-refurbishment-and-revitalization-of-the-islamic-museum-of-the-haram-al-sharif-and-its-collections.

53. On the collection, see Abu Khalaf, *Islamic Art,* 5–89; and Salameh, *Qur'an Manuscripts,* 5–19.

54. See W. J. Phytian-Adams, *Guide Book to the Palestine Museum of Antiquities* (Jerusalem: The Department of Antiquities, 1924); and Kletter, *Just Past?* 174.

55. At the time, the department of antiquities featured a modest display of ancient artifacts. This presentation, however, only included a few recently discovered finds.

56. F. Ibrahim, *West Meets East: The Story of the Rockefeller Museum* (Jerusalem: Israel Museum, 2006), 6.

57. See A. R. Fuchs, "Austen St. Barbe Harrison: A British Architect in the Holy Land" (PhD diss., Haifa, Technion, Israel Institute of Technology, 1992), 113; and Ibrahim, *West Meets East,* 10–11.

58. Only a few artifacts postdate 1967, such as, for example, a recently acquired Crusader stela. Approximately half of the collection is in storage; the other half is on display. All objects are registered with the IAA, and thus any object requested for loan has to be approved by the IAA.

59. Ibrahim, *West Meets East,* 6. The first PAM guide was written by the first keeper of the museum. See Phytian-Adams, *Guide Book.* New labels are currently being designed.

60. For a detailed account of the history of the PAM between 1947 and 1967, see Kletter, *Just Past?* 174–92. During the brief period of Jordanian rule, an international board of trustees served Israel's interests. Shortly after Israel conquered the West Bank, the board of trustees

was dissolved, and Israel took over the management of the PAM. In Kletter's words: "the atmosphere of peace and scholarship was replaced by the industrious activity of the IAA Management, which now occupies most of the building" (*Just Past?* 191).

61. Several artifacts have been on display for a prolonged period at the Israel Museum in Jerusalem and the Hecht Museum in Haifa. Some of the most prized pieces were moved in 2010 to the new archaeological wing of the Israel Museum. In May of 2016, Emek Shaveh appealed to the Supreme Court to reverse the IAA's decision to transfer the library of the Rockefeller Museum as well as a collection of coins to West Jerusalem. The Supreme Court turned the appeal down, stating that the Israeli law in East Jerusalem overrides international law.

62. Information about the collection can be found on the Institute of Archaeology website: http://archaeology.huji.ac.il/exhibitions/exhibitions.asp. Regarding the exhibit, see Shapira,"Ruins from Ancient Syrian Synagogue Put on Display in Israel after 63-Year Delay," *Ha'aretz,* July 17, 2011.

63. See the Hebrew University Institute of Archaeology website: http://archaeology.huji.ac.il/exhibitions/exhibitions.asp.

64. On the origins of the Israel Museum and its early ties with the IDAM, see Kletter, *Just Past?* 193–213.

65. J. S. Snyder, *Renewed: The Israel Museum, Jerusalem Campus Renewal Project* (Jerusalem: The Israel Museum, 2011), 17.

66. The renovation was completed in July of 2010.

67. Snyder, *Renewed,* 20.

68. A new, independent complex for the IAA offices, which will include all centralized administrative offices in one structure, is currently being built between the Israel Museum and the Bible Lands Museum. It will be called the Jay and Jeanie Schottenstein National Campus for the Archaeology of Israel; the cornerstone-laying ceremony was held in 2006. Regarding the inclusion of the IDAM's antiquities collection, see Snyder, *Renewed,* 199.

69. It was Yeivin, IDAM director between 1948 and 1959, who expressed those intentions. See Kletter, *Just Past?* 200.

70. Kletter, *Just Past?* 201.

71. A catalogue, featuring many of the major artifacts on display in the new archaeology wing was published in 2010. See M. Dayagi-Mendels and S. Rozenberg, eds., *Chronicle of the Land: Archaeology in the Israel Museum Jerusalem,* Israel Museum Catalogue 557 (Jerusalem: The Israel Museum, 2010).

72. Dayagi-Mendels and Rozenberg, *Chronicle of the Land,* 112 and 114.

73. Dayagi-Mendels and Rozenberg, *Chronicle of the Land,* 110, 116–19, 121, and 123.

74. Dayagi-Mendels and Rozenberg, *Chronicle of the Land,* 151, 169, and 117. For a sixth-century stone ambo from the Church of St. Theodore at Khirbet Beit Sila, north of Jerusalem, see Israeli and Mevorah, *Cradle of Christianity,* 55.

75. Israeli and Mevorah, *Cradle of Christianity,* 196 and 211. For the gold jewelry hoard, see Mazar, *Temple Mount Excavations,* 112.

76. Mazar, *Temple Mount Excavations,* 187, 197–99. For Islamic-period jewelry, see M. Spaer, *Ancient Glass in the Israel Museum: Beads and Other Small Objects* (Jerusalem: Israel Museum, 2001), 196–212; and R. Gonen, *Jewelry through the Ages at the Israel Museum* (Jerusalem: Israel Museum, 1997), 34–39.

77. In April 2013, a model of Herod's tomb, the centerpiece of the exhibit's display, was unveiled at its original site, Herodium. Ministers, Knesset members, and settler leaders were present at the event. Knesset members Ze'ev Elkin (Likud) and Otniel Schneller (Kadima) explicitly addressed the connection between the site and local Jewish construction. See Y. Bronner and Y. Mizrachi, "King Herod, Long Reviled, Finds New Love Among Jewish Settlers," in *Forward*, March 19, 2013: http://forward.com/articles/173101/king-herod-long-reviled-finds-new-love-among-jewis.

78. For a brief history of the collection and a summary of objects displayed in the twenty galleries of the museum, see L. Taylor-Guthartz, *A Guide to the Collection* 3rd rev. ed. (Jerusalem: Bible Lands Museum Jerusalem, 2002).

79. See J. Felch, *Chasing Aphrodite: The Hunt for Looted Antiquities at the World's Richest Museum* (Boston: Houghton Mifflin Harcourt, 2011), 339.

80. See the museum website: www.blmj.org/en/template/default.aspx?PageId=12.

81. B. Borowski, Introduction to *Guide to the Collection*, ed. L. Taylor-Guthartz, 3d. rev. ed. (Jerusalem: Bible Lands Museum Jerusalem, 2002), 7.

82. Though planned as a temporary exhibit that opened in 2007, a room on the second floor of the museum still exhibits a small selection of the artifacts. See J. Goodnick Westenholz, ed., *Three Faces of Monotheism* (Jerusalem: Bible Lands Museum Jerusalem, 2007).

83. On the history of the museum and its curatorial concepts, see R. Sivan, "Le Musée d'Histoire, Jerusalem 5000 Years of History," *Les dossiers d'archéologie* 165 (1991), 132–37.

84. The minimal use of labels identifying various archaeological and architectural features reflects the philosophy of the museum's chief curator, Renée Sivan. "Presentations should keep intervention on the site to a minimum, keeping the remains as the principal 'actors' rather than using them simply as stage design. Some presentation techniques currently in fashion can overwhelm the archaeological remains." See R. Sivan, "Presentation of Archaeological Sites," in *The Conservation of Archaeological Sites in the Mediterranean Region. An International Conference Organized by the Getty Conservation Institute and the J. Paul Getty Museum, 6–12 May 1995*, ed. M. de la Torre (Los Angeles: The Getty Conservation Institute, 1997), 53. The absence of proper labeling for Islamic artifacts has been criticized by N. Abu al-Hadj, *Facts on the Ground: Archaeological Practice and Territorial Self-Fashioning in Israeli Society* (Chicago: University of Chicago Press, 2001), 173–74. See also M. K. Hawari, " 'Capturing the Castle' ": Archaeology, Architecture and Political Bias at the Citadel of Jerusalem," *Jerusalem Quarterly* 55 (2013): 46–67.

85. Benvenisti, *City of Stone*, 8–9; and Hawari, "Capturing the Castle."

86. Sivan, "Presentation of Archaeological Sites," 52. The emphasis on Jewish themes was not determined by Sivan; rather, it followed the recommendation of the museum board.

5. ARCHAEOLOGY IN THE EDUCATIONAL SYSTEMS

1. See M. Benvenisti, *Sacred Landscape: The Buried History of the Holy Land since 1948* (Berkeley: University of California Press, 2000), 11–12.

2. On the relationship between archaeology, education, and the dissemination of knowledge in the United States, see L. Wurst and S. Novinger, "Hidden Boundaries: Archaeology, Education, and Ideology in the United States," in *Ideologies in Archaeology* ed. R. Bernbeck and R. H. McGuire, 254–69 (Tuscon: University of Arizona Press, 2011).

3. The literature on the convergence of ideology, nationalism, and archaeology is vast. For a few select publications, see M. Diaz-Andreu, *A World History of Nineteenth-Century Archaeology: Nationalism, Colonialism, and the Past* (Oxford: Oxford University Press, 2007); J. Goode, *Negotiating for the Past: Archaeology, Nationalism and Diplomacy in the Middle East, 1919–1941* (Austin: University of Texas Press, 2007); M. Diaz-Andreu and T. Champion, *Nationalism and Archaeology in Europe* (Boulder, CO: Westview Press, 1996); Kohl and Fawcett, *Nationalism, Politics and the Practice of Archaeology;* P. Kohl, "Nationalism and Archaeology: On the Construction of Nations and the Reconstruction of the Remote Past," *Annual Review of Anthropology* 27 (1998): 223–46; B. Arnold, " 'Arierdämmerung': Race and Archaeology in Nazi Germany," *World Archaeology* 38 (2006): 8–31; and K. Abdi, "Nationalism, Politics, and the Development of Archaeology in Iran," *American Journal of Archaeology* 105 (2001): 51–76.

4. On the role of archaeology in public education in North America, the following all focus specifically on the education of children: P. Stone and R. MacKenzie, eds., *The Excluded Past: Archaeology in Education* (London: Unwin Hyman, 1990); P. G. Stone and B. L. Molyneaux, eds. *The Presented Past: Heritage, Museums and Education* (London: Routledge, 1999); J. M. Moe, "Project Archaeology: Putting the Intrigue of the Past in Public Education," in *The Public Benefits of Archaeology,* ed. B. J. Little, 176–86 (Gainsesville: University Press of Florida, 2002); K. Smardz and S. J. Smith, *The Archaeology Education Handbook: Sharing the Past with Kids* (Walnut Creek, CA: AltaMira, 2000); and H. Boothe, "Tools for Learning about the Past to Protect the Future: Archaeology in the Classroom," *Legacy* 11, no. 1 (2000): 10–12, 37.

5. In 1909, Montague Brownslow Parker, son of the Earl of Morley, initiated the legendary hunt for King Solomon's treasures. In 1913–14 and again in 1923–24, Baron Edmond de Rothschild, scion of the French branch of the international banking family, sponsored excavations on the Southeast Hill, which were directed by French archaeologist Raymond Weill. See Silberman, *God and Country,* 180–88.

6. Silberman, *God and Country,* 37–47, 106–11. More specifically on French explorers, see N. Chevalier, *La recherche archéologique française au Moyen-Orient, 1842–1947* (Paris: Éditions Recherche sur les Civilisations, 2002).

7. Gibson, "British Archaeological Work," 29–35.

8. Gibson, in "British Archaeological Work," 26, uses those terms to describe the missions of the Ordnance Survey of Jerusalem.

9. Silberman, *God and Country,* 72.

10. Silberman, *God and Country,* 90–91.

11. Already prior to the establishment of the PEF, the Palestine Association and the Jerusalem Literary (and Scientific) Society were dedicated to exploring the Holy Land scientifically. All their meetings, however, were held in England. See Gibson, "British Archaeological Work," 232–47.

12. D. Trimbur, "The École Biblique et Archéologique Française," in Galor and Avni, *Unearthing Jerusalem,* 95–98. For a brief history of the École biblique, see also B. T. Viviano, "Profiles of Archaeological Institutes: École Biblique et Archéologique Française de Jérusalem," *The Biblical Archaeologist* 54 (1991): 160–67.

13. On the early excavations, see Trimbur, "École Biblique," 99–100. For the more recent excavations, see Humbert, "Saint John Prodromos"; and Humbert, "Fouilles du tombeau

des Rois: Rapport préliminaire 2008–2009," *École biblique et archéologique française de Jérusalem* (2009): 1–14. Among the most significant surveys of archaeological discoveries in Jerusalem at the time, see Vincent and Abel, *Jérusalem nouvelle;* and Vincent and Steve, *Jérusalem de l'Ancien Testament.*

14. For the most significant project involving the excavation of early Islamic finds, see J.-B. Humbert, "El-Fedein-Mafraq," *Liber Annuus* 36 (1986), 354–58; and J.-B. Humbert "Le surprenant brasero omeyyade, trouvé à Mafraq," *Jordanie, sur les pas des archéologues* (Paris: Institut du Monde Arabe, 1997). The popular archaeological guidebook written by Murphy O'Conner includes sites from the Mamluk period. See J. Murphy O'Conner, *The Holy Land: An Archaeological Guide from Earliest Times to 1700*, 5th rev. and expanded ed. (London: Oxford University Press, 2008).

15. B. O. Long, *Imagining the Holy Land: Maps, Models, and Fantasy Travels* (Bloomington: University Press, 2003), 132; and P. J. King, *American Archaeology in the Mideast: A History of the American Schools of Oriental Research* (Philadelphia: ASOR, 1983), 25.

16. J. A. Blakely, "AIAR: Rebuilding the School that Albright Built: A History of the W. F. Albright Institute of Archaeological Research Jerusalem, Israel, Highlighting the Period from 1967 to 2000," in Seger, *An ASOR Mosaic*, 127; and J. Branham, "The American Archaeological Presence in Jerusalem: Through the Gates of the Albright Institute," in Galor and Avni, *Unearthing Jerusalem*, 82.

17. S. Gitin, "The House that Albright Built," *Near Eastern Archaeology* 65, no. 1 (2002): 5.

18. G. Dalman, "Entstehung und bisherige Entwicklung des Instituts," *Palästinajahrbuch* 1 (1905): 14

19. The Deutsches Archäologisches Institut Abteilung Rom and Abteilung Athen were opened in 1874.

20. U. Hübner, "The German Protestant Institute of Archaeology. Deutsches Evangelisches Institut für Altertumswissenschaft des Heiligen Landes," in Galor and Avni, *Unearthing Jerusalem*, 60.

21. Hübner, "German Protestant Institute," 64–66. Up until 2007, the DAI was hesitant to affiliate itself with the German Protestant Institute of Archaeology in Jerusalem. Given its numerous partner institutions and excavations in other regions of the Middle East, an associating with a Jerusalem-based research center could have led to potential conflicts with its Arab colleagues.

22. Gibson, "British Archaeological Work," 48–49.

23. See Kenyon, *Digging Up Jerusalem;* and Kenyon, *Jerusalem.* Early investigations of the city's Islamic monuments include Creswell's study of the Dome of the Rock and Hamilton's of the al-Aqsa Mosque. For recent surveys of Islamic monuments in the city, see Hawari, *Ayyubid Architecture;* M. K. Hawari, "The Citadel (Qal'a) in the Ottoman Period. An Overview," in *Ottoman Jerusalem*, I, ed. S. Auld and R. Hillenbrand (London: Altajir World of Islam Trust, 2000), 493–518; Burgoyne, *Mamluk Jerusalem;* Natsheh, "Architecture of Ottoman Jerusalem"; and Natsheh, "Catalogue of Buildings."

24. M. Piccirillo, "The Archaeology of Jerusalem and the Franciscans of the Studium Biblicum," in Galor and Avni, *Unearthing Jerusalem*, 110.

25. For a complete reference list of excavation projects and reports, see Piccirillo, "The Archaeology of Jerusalem," 111–16.

26. Piccirillo, "The Archaeology of Jerusalem," 109.

27. I. Press, "Compte-Rendu du Secrétaire," *Recueil publié par la Société Hébraïque d'Exploration et d'Archéologie Palestiniennes* 1, no. 1 (1921), 91–92; Reich, "Israel Exploration Society," 119–20.

28. Meir Ben-Dov filmed the Absalom tomb excavation conducted in 1924 by David Solomon Slouschz. This ten-second-long footage was part of a longer motion picture entitled *Shivat Zion (The Return to Zion)*. It has been suggested that this was the first excavation in Palestine to be recorded on film. The footage is part of the Steven Spielberg Archive of Jewish Films at the Hebrew University in Jerusalem. For the excavation of the Third Wall, see E. L. Sukenik and L. A. Mayer, *The Third Wall of Jerusalem: An Account of Excavations* (Jerusalem: University Press, 1930); and E. L. Sukenik and L. A. Mayer, "A New Section of the Third Wall, Jerusalem," *Palestine Exploration Quarterly* 76 (1944), 145–51.

29. There are several other important Israeli academic institutions and centers that promote the study of archaeology not included in this survey, in particular, the Martin (Szusz) Department of the Land of Israel Studies and Archaeology and the Ingeborg Rennert Center for Jerusalem Studies, both at Bar Ilan University. The Sonia and Marco Nadler Institute of Archaeology and Ancient Near Eastern Cultures at Tel Aviv University; the Zinman Institute of Archaeology at the University of Haifa; and the Department of Bible, Archaeology, and Ancient Near Eastern Studies at Ben-Gurion University of the Negev. Since 1995, the Ingeborg Rennert Center for Jerusalem Studies has organized an annual conference devoted to the archaeology of Jerusalem. See Z. Safrai and A. Faust, *Recent Innovations in the Study of Jerusalem: The First Conference, September 12th 1995* (Ramat Gan, Israel: Bar-Ilan University, Faculty of Jewish Studies, 1995).

30. For a brief history of the Institute of Archaeology and a description of its curriculum, see S. Gitin, A. Ben-Tor, and B. Sekay, "Profiles of Archaeological Institutes: The Institute of Archaeology of the Hebrew University of Jerusalem," *The Biblical Archaeologist* 56 (1993): 121–52.

31. In 2011, an international committee tasked with the evaluation of Israeli archaeology programs commented on the insularity of the Institute of Archaeology's program. Their report addressed the geographic, thematic, and chronological narrow focus of the curriculum, as well as the marked neglect of Islamic cultures and periods. See: http://che.org.il/wp-content/uploads/2012/04/Archaeology-HUJI.pdf.

32. For an up-to-date description reflecting the program's academic mission and curriculum, as designed by its former chair, Zeev Weiss, see the institute's website: http://archaeology.huji.ac.il.

33. The international committee reviewed the academic profiles and curricula of the relevant departments at the following institutions: the Hebrew University of Jerusalem, the Ben-Gurion University of the Negev, Bar Ilan University, and Tel Aviv University. For the reports see website link in n31.

34. Since 2007, the IAA has organized an annual Jerusalem conference, originally jointly with Bar Ilan University, then with Hebrew University.

35. Two important scholarly journals, *Hadashot Arkheologiyot* and *'Atiqot*, are published by the IAA.

36. The IAA education department has collaborated with the Jewish National Fund, the INPA, the Society for the Protection of Nature in Israel, the Israel Corporation of Community Centers, the Karev Foundation, the IDF, UNESCO, and others.

37. The ultra-Orthodox community has a separate system of education in Israel, called Chinuch Atzmai (independent education).

38. This project was supported by an external, nongovernmental funding source. Numerous other programs have received funding from various national and Zionist organizations.

39. A successful study dig supervised by the educational department of the IAA has been conducted in Adulam Park in the Judean foothills. It offers youth and adults the opportunity to participate in excavations for a day or longer. This activity is supported primarily by two Zionist organizations: Taglit-Birthright Israel and Keren Kayemeth Leisrael (Jewish National Fund).

40. On the history of the institute, see S. Rubinstein, "The Establishment and Beginnings of the Institute for the Study of Jewish Communities in the East," *Pe'amim* 23 (1985): 127–49.

41. The curriculum of the Land of Israel Studies and Archaeology is described in detail on the Israeli Ministry of Education website: http://cms.education.gov.il/educationcms/units/mazkirut_pedagogit/eretz/hodaotveidkunim/dvarmafmar.htm.

42. The Land of Israel Studies and Archaeology is also being taught in Druze schools. Israeli Arabs can study the subject in two of the country's mixed Arab/Jewish schools. One is the Weitzman School in Jaffa and the other the Hagar School in Beersheba.

43. W. Pullan and M. Gwiazda, " 'City of David': Urban Design and Frontier Heritage," *Jerusalem Quarterly* 39 (2009): 35.

44. Approximately six hundred people attend the Jerusalem conference and about 1,500 people attend the archaeology conference. Attendees outnumber individuals participating in the much more veteran archaeology conferences organized by Yad Izhak Ben-Zvi, the IES, the IAA, and the Hebrew University.

45. A petition initiated by several Israeli academics, which has gained support from about two hundred scholars from leading North American and European universities, objects to the recent decision taken by the Institute of Archaeology at Tel Aviv University to conduct excavations in the City of David under the auspices of Elad. This collaboration, according to those critics, would further strengthen Elad's scientific credibility and mask their primary interest, which is to strengthen the Jewish presence in East Jerusalem.

46. The Israeli Academy of Sciences and Humanities has established a committee to review the field of archaeology as it is being practiced in the field, how it is taught and studied in various establishments of higher learning, and how it is presented and disseminated to the public. Reports are published regularly and are accessible online at the academy's website (in Hebrew): www.academy.ac.il.

47. Silberman, "Power, Politics, and the Past," 18.

48. In 1932, out of 191 members, 10 were resident Palestinians, 22 were resident Jews, 42 were resident foreigners, and 117 were nonresidents. Palestinian membership fluctuated from a high of 19 in 1926 to a low of 5 in 1934. See Glock, "Archaeology as Cultural Survival," 75.

49. Glock, "Archaeology as Cultural Survival," 73.

50. After 1967, all archaeological fieldwork in East Jerusalem, which was condemned by UNESCO and most importantly by the Palestinian community as a result of the Israeli occupation, was either channelled through or conducted by the IAA. As Palestinians do not recognize Israeli sovereignty in East Jerusalem, obtaining a survey or excavation permit would entail acceptance of the normalization.

51. CISS, International Cooperation South South, is an NGO, founded in 1985. It was officially recognized by the Italian Ministry for Foreign Affairs in 1989 as a qualified organization to promote and carry out projects of cooperation in developing countries.

52. The funding period came to an end in 2000.

53. For the exact wording of the vision for the Jerusalem Studies MA program, see the Centre for Jerusalem Studies website: www.jerusalem-studies.alquds.edu.

54. See the mission statement of the Jerusalem Archaeological Studies Unit's website: www.jasu.alquds.edu.

55. The report (9GL44868/7) was summarized by someone identified only by the surname Mayer on August 1, 1948. It is unclear who the archaeologists were and where they met. See Kletter, *Just Past?* 175.

56. See the mission statement of the Ruth Youth Wing for Art Education: www.english.imjnet.org.il/page_1193.

57. Though referred to as an archaeological tell, the area looks like a Roman-Byzantine synagogue.

58. On a brief history of the museum, see Sivan, "Musée d'Histoire." Curator Renée Sivan, a leading Israeli curator of museums and archaeological sites, comments on her philosophy of how to optimally guide and instruct visitors at an archaeological site, without overwhelming the general public with too much specialized and abstract information. See Sivan, "Presentation of Archaeological Sites."

59. In 2009, historian and archaeologist Abir Zayyad, questioning the Jewish roots in the city, was fired from her position as the Arabic-speaking guide of the Tower of David Museum. Archaeologist Noor Rajabi, who replaced Zayyad, has been highly successful in reaching out to a significantly larger circle of Arabic-speaking children.

60. Schools that are not under the auspices of the Israeli Ministry of Education in Jerusalem are either administered by the Islamic Waqf, the UN Relief and Works Agency (UNRWA) for Palestinian refugees, or else are part of the private sector.

61. See museum website: www.blmj.org/en/template/default.aspx?PageId=2.

62. A few Islamic artifacts were displayed in the temporary show entitled The Three Faces of Monotheism. See Goodnick Westenholz, *Three Faces of Monotheism.*

63. See Glock, "Archaeology as Cultural Survival," 74.

64. Glock, "Archaeology as Cultural Survival," 74.

65. Glock, "Archaeology as Cultural Survival," 75.

66. Glock, "Archaeology as Cultural Survival," 76.

67. On various views and issues regarding the academic boycott, see "Academic Boycott of Israel: The American Studies Association Endorsement and Backlash," *Journal of Palestine Studies* 43, no. 3 (2014): 56–71; and M. Gerstenfeld, "The Academic Boycott against Israel," *Jewish Political Studies Review* 15, no. 3–4 (2003): 9–70.

6. ARCHAEOLOGICAL ETHICS

1. E. Ben-Ezer, *Courage: The Story of Moshe Dayan* (Jerusalem: Ministry of Defense Publications, 1997), 121, 218–19.

2. Y. Dayan, *My Father, His Daughter* (New York: Farrar, Straus and Giroux, 1985), 260.

3. Dan Ben-Amotz was among his early critics. See D. Ben-Amotz, *Reflections in Time* (Tel Aviv: Bitan, 1974), 29–34. For a more recent evaluation of Dayan's ethical and legal

transgressions, see R. Kletter, "A Very General Archaeologist—Moshe Dayan and Israeli Archaeology," *The Journal of Hebrew Scriptures* 4 (2002–03), Article 5. See also N. A. Silberman, *Between Past and Present: Archaeology, Ideology, and Nationalism in the Modern Middle East* (New York: Holt, 1989), 123–36.

4. Kletter, "Very General Archaeologist," 35.

5. R. Baker, "Codes of Ethics; Some History," *Perspectives on the Professions* 19, no. 1 (1999): 3–5.

6. R. Kletter and G. Solimani, "Archaeology and Professional Ethical Codes in Israel in the Mid-80s: The Case of the Association of the Archaeologists in Israel and Its Code of Ethics," *The Journal of Hebrew Scriptures* 10 (2010): Article 4, 21.

7. T. F. King, "Professional Responsibility in Public Archaeology," *Annual Review of Anthropology* 12 (1983), 144; and P. Pels, ed., *Embedding Ethics: Shifting Boundaries of the Anthropological Profession* (Oxford: Berg Publishers, 2005), 1–3.

8. K. Vitelli and C. Colwell-Chanthaphon, *Archaeological Ethics,* 2nd ed. (Walnut Creek, CA: Altamira, 2006), 5–6.

9. In 1994, the ethics committee was mentioned for the last time in an archive. See Kletter and Solimani, "Archaeology and Professional Ethical Codes," 13.

10. For a description, see AAI statues, Appendix 1: Document 2. See also Kletter and Solimani, "Archaeology and Professional Ethical Codes," 12.

11. A. Kempinski, editorial in *Archaeologya. Bulletin of the Israel Association of Archaeologists* 3 (1992), 5.

12. Kempinski, editorial, 20.

13. Employers were always governmental institutions. See Kempinski, editorial, 22.

14. See, for instance, Kedar, Weksler-Bdolah, and Da'adli, "Madrasa Afdaliyya." Other recent reports published in *Hadashot Arkheologiyot* document evidence of recent destructions, including military confrontations.

15. This shortcoming was pointed out in the external review conducted under the auspices of the Council for Higher Education: http://che.org.il/wp-content/uploads/2012/04/Archaeology-HUJI.pdf.

16. Tawfiq Da'adli is the only Palestinian archaeologist currently employed as a faculty member in an academic Israeli institution. He was appointed lecturer in the departments of Islamic and Middle Eastern studies and art history at the Hebrew University of Jerusalem in 2015.

17. Greenberg and Mizrachi, *From Shiloah to Silwan,* 39; Mizrachi, *Archaeology in the Shadow of the Conflict,* 27; Mizrachi, *Between Holiness and Propaganda,* 30–34.

18. R. Reich, *Excavating the City of David, Where Jerusalem's History Began* (Jerusalem: Israel Exploration Society and Biblical Archaeology Society, 2011), 17–25, 46, 63.

19. Silberman, *God and Country,* 90–94, 183.

20. The first site in Palestine where Flinders Petrie conducted a stratigraphic excavation was Tell el-Hesy. See Silberman, *God and Country,* 148–49. Bliss returned to the method of tunnel and shaft excavation. Silberman, *God and Country,* 156.

21. Mizrachi, *Between Holiness and Propaganda,* 30.

22. Mizrachi, *Between Holiness and Propaganda,* 30.

23. In 2014, estimates for Silwan's Palestinian residents ranged between 20,000 to 50,000, and for Jewish residents, between 600 to 700. See Hasson, "East Jerusalem Remains 'Arab' Despite Jewish Settlers, Experts Say," *Ha'aretz,* October 2, 2014; Mizrachi, *Between*

Holiness and Propaganda, 39; and Greenberg, "Extreme Exposure," 278; and Mizrachi, *Archaeology in the Shadow of the Conflict,* 17–19.

24. Emek Shaveh, in collaboration with an environmental group called Friends of the Earth, has organized several successful community-based excavations. See Hasson, "Archaeology without Conquest," *Ha'aretz,* May 30, 2012.

25. Avni and Seligman, *Temple Mount,* 34–39; Mizrachi, *Between Holiness and Propaganda,* 20–21.

26. Mizrachi, *Between Holiness and Propaganda,* 21–22. Some archaeologists argue that knowledge can be gained from looted artifacts, which, unlike the Kidron Valley dumps, lack provenance. For debates concerning the scientific value of looted artifacts, see C. Rollston, "Non-Provenanced Epigraphs I: Pillaged Antiquities, Northwest Semitic Forgeries, and Protocols for Laboratory Tests," *Maarav* 10 (2003), 135–93"; and C. Rollston, "Non-Provenanced Epigraphs II: The Status of Non-Provenanced Epigraphs within the Broader Corpus of Northwest Semitic," *Maarav* 11 (2004), 57–79"; and M. M. Kersel, "The Value of a Looted Object. Stakeholder Perceptions," in *The Oxford Handbook of Public Archaeology,* ed. R. Skeates, C. McDavid, and J. Carman (Oxford: Oxford University Press, 2012), 257.

27. Silberman, "Power, Politics, and the Past," 11; and Kersel, "Trade in Palestinian Antiquities," 22–23.

28. Kersel, "Trade in Palestinian Antiquities," 23.

29. The law was enacted soon after the Pergamon Altar was expropriated. See S. Marchand, *Down from Olympus: Archaeology and Philhellenism in Germany, 1750–1970* (Princeton: Princeton University Press, 1996).

30. Kersel, "Trade in Palestinian Antiquities," 24.

31. Garstang, "Eighteen Months Work of the Department of Antiquities for Palestine," *Palestine Exploration Quarterly* 54 (1922): 57–62.

32. See Kersel, "Trade in Palestinian Antiquities," 26; and J. Oyediran, *Plunder, Destruction and Despoliation: An Analysis of Israel's Violations of the International Law of Cultural Property in the Occupied West Bank and Gaza Strip* (Ramallah: Al-Haq, 1997).

33. According to Kersel ("Trade in Palestinian Antiquities," 33), in 2003–04, there were eighty dealers licensed by the IAA, most of whom (seventy-five) were located in Jerusalem's Old City.

34. Kersel describes the market chain in several articles: "Transcending Borders: Objects on the Move," *Archaeologies: Journal of the World Archaeological Congress* 3 (2007), 86–87; "From the Ground to the Buyer: A Market Analysis of the Illegal Trade in Antiquities," in *Archaeology, Cultural Heritage and the Antiquities Trade,* ed. N. Brodie, M. Kersel, C. Luke, and W. Tubb (Gainesville: University Press of Florida, 2006), 189, 195; and "When Communities Collide: Competing Claims for Archaeological Objects in the Market Place," *Archaeologies: Journal of the World Archaeological Congress* 7 (2011).

35. Those who support a legal trade in antiquities are primarily collectors, dealers, and market nations. Those who oppose it are predominantly archaeologically rich states, archaeologists, and governments. See M. Kersel and R. Kletter, "Heritage for Sale? A Case Study from Israel," *Journal of Field Archaeology* 31 (2006): 318. On the correlation between legal trade and looting, see also G. Biseh; "One Damn Illicit Excavation after Another: The Destruction of the Archaeological Heritage of Jordan," in Brodie, Doole, and Renfrew, *Trade in Illicit Antiquities,* 115–18; Merryman; "A Licit International Trade in Cultural Objects,"

International Journal of Cultural Property 4, no. 1 (1995): 13–60"; and N. Brodie, "Export Deregulation and the Illicit Trade in Archaeological Material," in Richman and Forsyth, *Legal Perspectives on Cultural Resources,* 85–99.

36. O. Blum, "The Illicit Antiquities Trade: An Analysis of Current Antiquities Looting in Israel," *Culture without Context* 11 (2002): 20–23; D. Ilan, U. Dahari, and G. Avni ("Plundered! The Rampant Rape of Israel's Archaeological Sites," *Biblical Archaeology Review* 15, no. 2 (1989): 38–42) argue that the sale of antiquities would empty the IAA storage facilities in less than a year. For the ethically controversial nature of a state-run sale of antiquities, see Kersel and Kletter, "Heritage for Sale?" 325. On how an additional competitor can stimulate the market, see I. Kirzner, "Competition, Regulating, and the Market Process: An 'Austrian' Perspective," *Cato Policy Analysis* No. 18 (Washington: Cato Institute, 1982).

37. *Unprovenanced* means that the artifact was looted rather than scientifically excavated and documented, and thus it has lost its original find spot and historical meaning.

38. The AAI ethical code of 1992, in addition to denouncing robbery, also disapproved of both the direct and indirect scholarly involvement in and support of the antiquities trade. See Kletter and Solimani, "Archaeology and Professional Ethical Codes," 13. Regarding the published version of the code, see Kletter and Solimani, "Archaeology and Professional Ethical Codes," 17.

39. Kersel, "Transcending Borders," 85–91.

40. Kersel, "Transcending Borders," 91–93; and Abu El-Haj, *Facts on the Ground,* 255.

41. On the complex relationship between archaeology and media, see E. Meyers and C. Meyers, *Archaeology, Bible, Politics, and the Media* (Winona Lake, IN: Eisenbrauns, 2012).

42. Blum, "Illicit Antiquities Trade."

43. On the ineffectiveness of the policing of the looting activities in Israel, see the 2003 documentary *Schatzsuche in Israel* by Peter Dudzik.

44. On the popularity of Herodian artifacts among the Judeo-Christian public, see Galor, "King Herod in Jerusalem: The Politics of Cultural Heritage," *Jerusalem Quarterly* 62 (2015): 65–80.

45. Kersel, "Trade in Palestinian Antiquities," 32–35.

46. Lemaire has argued that the inscription on the pomegranate is authentic in several articles: "Une inscription paléo-hébrqaïque sur grenade en ivoire," *Revue Biblique* 88 (1981): 236–39; "Probable Head of Priestly Scepter from Solomon's Temple Surfaces in Jerusalem," *Biblical Archaeology Review* 10, no. 1 (1984): 24–29; and "A Re-examination of the Inscribed Pomegranate: A Rejoinder," *Israel Exploration Journal* 56 (2006): 167–77. Most scholars, however, have argued that the inscription is a forgery. See Y. Goren et al., "A Re-Examination of the Inscribed Pomegranate from the Israel Museum," *Israel Exploration Journal* 55 (2005): 3–20; and S. Ahituv et al., "The Inscribed Pomegranate from the Israel Museum Examined Again." *Israel Exploration Journal* 57 (2007): 87–95.

47. Various scholars have argued that the inscription is authentic. See S. Ilani et al., "Archaeometric Analysis of the 'Jehoash Inscription' Tablet," *Journal of Archaeological Science* 35 (2008): 2966–72; and H. Shanks, "Assessing the Jehoash Inscription," *Biblical Archaeology Review* 22, no. 5 (1996): 48–53. For arguments supporting a forgery, see for example E. A. Knauf, "Jehoash's Improbably Inscription," *Biblische Notizen* 117 (2003): 22–26; and Y. Goren et al., "Authenticity Examination of the Jehoash Inscription," *Tel Aviv* 31 (2004): 3–16.

48. On the James ossuary controversy, see R. Byrne and B. McNary-Zak, *Resurrecting the Brother of Jesus: The James Ossuary Controversy and the Quest for Religious Relics* (Chapel Hill: University of North Carolina Press, 2009); and A. Ayalon, M. Bar-Matthews, and Y. Goren. "Authenticity Examination of the Inscription on the Ossuary Attributed to James, Brother of Jesus," *Journal of Archaeological Science* 31 (2004): 1185–89; and H. Shanks, " 'Brother of Jesus' Inscription Is Authentic!" *Biblical Archaeology Review* 38, no. 4 (2012): 26–33, 62–65.

49. E. M. Cook is one of the few scholars concerned with the unprovenanced nature of the above artifacts. See Cook, "The Forgery Indictments and BAR: Learning from Hindsight," *Near Eastern Archaeology* 68 (2005): 73–75. Brodie and Kersel specifically discuss the ethical concerns of focusing on the discussion whether artifacts are authentic or forgeries without paying any attention to lack of provenance. See N. Brodie and M. Kersel, "The Social and Political Consequences of Devotion to Biblical Artifacts," in *All The Kings Horses: Looting, Antiquities Trafficking, and the Integrity of the Archaeological Record,* ed. P. K. Lazrus and A. W. Barker (Washington, DC: Society for American Archaeology, 2012), 109–10.

50. P. Boylan, "The Ethics of Acquisition: The Leicestershire Code," *The Museums Journal* 75 (1976): 165–70.

51. On museum acquisition policies and ethics and the consequences of different scandals that occurred during the 1990s and their consequences, see P. Watson and C. Todeschini, *The Medici Conspiracy: The Illicit Journey of Looted Antiquities from Italy's Tomb Raiders to the World's Greatest Museums* (New York: PublicAffairs, 2007); S. Waxman, *Loot: The Battle over the Stolen Treasures of the Ancient World* (New York: New York Times Books, 2008); and Felch and Frammolino, *Chasing Aphrodite.*

52. For some of Dayan's looted artifacts, the original find spots are known, but since the objects were retrieved without proper archaeological documentation, most of the context is lost, and thus the scientific value of the finds is highly compromised.

53. Archaeologists were mostly concerned with the fact that the artifacts were sold rather than donated. Their objection was not related to the fact that they were looted. Silberman, *Between Past and Present,* 123–36.

54. See Watson and Todeschini, *The Medici Conspiracy,* 17–18, 74.

55. Several artifacts were removed from the premises of the Rockefeller Museum and are on "long-term loan" at other museums. Most significant and controversial was the removal of the Dead Sea Scrolls, for which the Israel Museum built the Shrine of the Book. For additional examples of removed artifacts, see O. Ilan, D. Tal, and M. Haramati, *Image and Artifact: Treasures of the Rockefeller Museum* (Jerusalem: The Israel Museum, 2000), 30, 42, 51, 62, 65–66.

56. See, for example, articles by J. Greenberg, "Museum Exhibit Becomes Front in Israeli-Palestinian Struggle," *Washington Post,* February 13, 2013; J. Rudoren, "Anger That a Herod Show Uses West Bank Objects," *New York Times,* February 13, 2013; B. Ziffer, "Herodium Turns into a Cultural Settlement, " *Ha'aretz,* February 22, 2013; Y. Bronner and Y. Mizrachi, "King Herod, Long Reviled, Finds New Love among Jewish Settlers," *Forward,* March 20, 2013; and Y. Mizrachi, "Exhibition on Loan: How Israel's Cultural Institutions Contribute to Occupation," *972 Magazine,* May 4, 2013.

57. See Silberman, *God and Country,* 72.

58. According to Breitowitz, the concern for ancient Jewish burials is not limited to the ultra-Orthodox community but is protested within Jewish religious and academic circles more broadly. See Y. Breitowitz, "The Desecration of Graves in Eretz Yisrael: The Struggle to Honor the Dead and Preserve Our Historical Legacy." *Jewish Law,* www.jlaw.com/Articles/heritage.html.

59. See Breitowitz, "Desecration of Graves"; and T. Einhorn, "Israeli Law, Jewish Law and the Archaeological Excavation of Tombs," *International Journal of Cultural Property* 6 (1997): 47–79.

60. The argument is that within Israel, there is always a chance that graveyards include Jewish burials, even for periods when Jews were a the minority. See Einhorn, "Israeli Law."

61. Amir Drori has been particular active in condemning and fighting Atra Kadisha. See Shanks, "Death Knell" Two particularly controversial cases in recent years concern the excavations near the Andromeda apartment complex in Jaffa and Ashkelon. See S. Fogelman, "Are the Ultra-Orthodox Digging Their Own Grave?" *Ha'aretz.* July 25, 2010; and Y. Yagna, "Haredi Group Fights Ashkelon Construction to Save Graves," *Ha'aretz,* December 25, 2012.

62. On the excavation in Mamilla, see R. Reich, "God Knows Their Names: Mass Christian Grave Revealed in Jerusalem," *Biblical Archaeology Review* 22 no. 2 (1996): 26–33, 60.

63. The directive is based on the 1978 Antiquities Law (the so-called dry-bones law), which does not include human remains within the category of antiquities. It is, in fact, explicitly stated that it is illegal to excavate known burial sites, Jewish or non-Jewish.

64. See M. Balter, "Archaeologists and Rabbis Clash over Human Remains," *Science,* January 7, 2000, 34–35; and Einhorn, "Israeli Law."

65. On the role of ultra-Orthodox communities in Israeli society, see Friedman, *The Haredi (Ultra-Orthodox) Society—Sources, Trends and Processes* (Jerusalem: The Jerusalem Institute for Israel Studies, 1991). On their impact on Knesset elections and governmental policies, see G. Rahat and R. Y. Hazan, "Candidate Selection Methods: An Analytical Framework," *Party Politics* 7 (2001): 297–322"; and G. Rahat, "Determinants of Party Cohesion: Evidence from the Case of the Israeli Parliament," *Parliamentary Affairs* 60 (2007): 279–96."

66. For a critical view, condemning the construction of the Museum of Tolerance, see S. Makdisi, "The Architecture of Erasure," *Critical Inquiry* 36 (2009/10): 519–59. In response to Makdisi, see R. Israeli et al., "Critical Response II: 'The Architecture of Erasure'—Fantasy or Reality?" *Critical Inquiry* 36 (2009/10), 563–94.

67. See Y. Mizrachi, *The Mamilla Cemetery in West Jerusalem: A Heritage Site at the Crossroads of Politics and Real Estate* (Jerusalem: Emek Shaveh, 2012), 1; and M. Dumper and C. Larkin, "Political Islam and Contested Jerusalem: The Emerging Role of Islamists from within Israel," *Divided Cities Contested States, Working Paper No. 12* (Exeter: School of Politics, University of Exeter, 2009), 17–18.

68. Mizrachi, *Mamilla Cemetery,* 2; and T. Daadli, "Mamluk Epitaphs from Mamilla Cemetery," *Levant* 43 (2011): 78–97. On the Kebekiyeh dia A-Din Aidughdi, see also F. Ollendorf, "Two Mamluk Tomb-Chambers in Western Jerusalem," *Israel Exploration Journal* 32 (1982): 245–50.

69. The Muslim Supreme Council declared the cemetery a historical site in 1927. However, after the cemetery fell under Israeli control and was taken over by the Custodian

for Absentee Property, Muslim authorities were no longer allowed to maintain the burial ground.

70. Makdisi, "Architecture of Erasure," 521.

71. See Mizrachi, *Mamilla Cemetery*, 1.

72. See "Campaign to Preserve Mamilla Jerusalem Cemetery, Petition for Urgent Action on the Desecration of Mamilla Cemetery, Jerusalem, 10 February 2010 (Excerpts)," *Journal of Palestine Studies* 39, no. 3 (2010): 188–92.

73. Mizrachi, *Mamilla Cemetery*, 1. See also newspaper coverage by N. Hasson: "Museum of Tolerance Special Report / Introduction," *Haaretz*, May 18, 2012); and "What to Do with the Graves?" *Haaretz*, May 20, 2010. Also see N. Dvir, "Grave Concerns," *Haaretz*, October 25, 2011.

74. See N. Hasson, "Jerusalem Proceeding with Plan to Build on Old Muslim Cemetery," *Haaretz*, July 13, 2015.

75. On the coffins, see T. Dothan, "Anthropoid Clay Coffins from a Late Bronze Age Cemetery near Deir el-Balah," *Israel Exploration Journal* 23 (1973): 129–48," and T. Ornan, *A Man and His Land: Highlights from the Moshe Dayan Collection*, Israel Museum Catalogue 270 (Jerusalem: Israel Museum, 1986).

76. See Silberman, *Between Past and Present*, 123–36.

77. See Dayagi-Mendels and Rozenberg, *Chronicle of the Land*.

78. See Greenberg, "Museum Exhibit Becomes Front"; and J. Cook, "Herod Exhibit Digs Up Controversy," *Aljazeera*, March 1, 2013.

7. THE CITY OF DAVID / SILWAN

1. On the recent demographic shift in Silwan, see Hasson, "East Jerusalem Remains 'Arab.' "

2. On the contrasting architecture and urban infrastructure, reflecting the spaces used by the Palestinian villagers and those maintained by the Jewish settlers and Jerusalem Municipality mostly for tourist development, see Greenberg and Mizrachi, *From Shiloah to Silwan*, 34–39.

3. See Greenberg, "Towards an Inclusive Archaeology," 38–41.

4. For the significant increase in numbers in recent years and various available statistics, see Pullan et al., *Struggle for Jerusalem's Holy Places*, 83.

5. The exception are archaeologists Yonathan Mizrachi and Raphael Greenberg, who have published extensively on the political implications of the recent archaeological activity in Silwan. See Mizrachi, *Archaeology in the Shadow of the Conflict*; Mizrachi, *From Silwan to the Temple Mount*; Greenberg, "Contested Sites: Archaeology and the Battle for Jerusalem," *Jewish Quarterly* 208 (2007): 20–26; Greenberg, "Extreme Exposure;" Greenberg, "Towards an Inclusive Archaeology;" and Greenberg and Mizrachi, *From Shiloah to Silwan*.

6. The Siloam Tunnel and inscription are traditionally dated to the reign of King Hezekiah (725–698 B.C.E.). See R. Amiran, "The Water Supply of Israelite Jerusalem," in Yadin, *Jerusalem Revealed*, 78; and Younger, "The Siloam Inscription," 145–46. Recent radiometric dating of the tunnel confirmed the traditional view. See A. Frumkin, A. Shimron, and J. Rosenbaum, "Radiometric Dating of the Siloam Tunnel, Jerusalem," *Nature* 425 (2003): 169–71. Galor and Bloedhorn (*Archaeology of Jerusalem*, 47) argue that the tunnel was built

during the rule of King Manasseh (696–642 B.C.E.). The suggestion that it was built during the Hasmonean period (J. Rogerson and P. R. Davies, "Was the Siloam Tunnel Built by Hezekiah?" *The Biblical Archaeologist* 59 (1996): 138–49) was refuted (R. S. Hendel, "The Date of the Siloam Inscription: A Rejoinder to Rogerson and Davies," *The Biblical Archaeologist* 59 (1996): 233–37). Regarding the excavation of the Church of Siloam, see Bliss and Dickie, *Excavations at Jerusalem,* 178–210. On the Theodotus inscription, see L. I. Levine, *Jerusalem: A Portrait of the City in the Second Temple Period (538 B.C.E.–70 C.E.* (Philadelphia: Jewish Publication Society, 2002), 272–73; and L. I. Levine, *The Ancient Synagogue: The First Thousand Years* (New Haven, Connecticut: Yale University Press, 2000), 52–85.

7. On scholarly and public opinions regarding the Parker expedition, see Silberman, *God and Country,* 180–98; and Silberman, "Solomon's Lost Treasures." For the scholarly documentation of the underground survey, still very much valued by scholars today, see Vincent, *Jérusalem sous terre.*

8. See Reich, *Excavating the City of David,* 13.

9. Reich, *Excavating the City of David,* 152–58; and R. Reich and E. Shukron, "Light at the End of the Tunnel," *Biblical Archaeology Review* 25, no. 1 (1999): 26–33.

10. See Macalister and Duncan, *Excavations of the Hill of Ophel;* and Crowfoot and FitzGerald, *Excavations in the Tyropoeon Valley.* Weill also conducted a second season of excavation financed by Rothschild.

11. See Macalister and Duncan, *Excavations on the Hill of Ophel,* 52.

12. Macalister and Duncan referred to the first apparent courses of stone as the "Jebusite Ramp," see Macalister and Duncan, *Excavations on the Hill of Ophel,* 52. Kenyon and Shiloh dated the substructural terraces to the fourteenth to thirteen centuries B.C.E. and various components of the mantel to the Hellenistic period, see Kenyon, *Jerusalem,* 115–33; Kenyon, *Digging Up Jerusalem,* 192–93; and Y. Shiloh, *Excavations at the City of David,* I: *1978–1982, Interim Report of the First Five Seasons* (Qedem 19; Jerusalem: Institute of Archaeology, Hebrew University, 1984), 16–17. According to Steiner, who published Kenyon's final report, the substructure should be dated to the twelfth century B.C.E. and the superstructural mantle to the tenth century B.C.E., see M. L. Steiner, "Redating the Terraces of Jerusalem," *Israel Exploration Journal* 44 (1994): 20; Steiner, "The Evidence from Kenyon's Excavations in Jerusalem: A Response Essay," in Vaughn and Killebrew, *Jerusalem in Bible and Archaeology,* 351–60; Steiner, *Excavations by Kathleen M. Kenyon,* 43–53. According to Cahill, who published Shiloh's final report, the entire Stepped Stone Structure was built as one architectural unit around the thirteenth to the twefth centuries B.C.E., see J. M. Cahill, "Jerusalem at the Time of the United Monarchy: The Archaeological Evidence," in Vaughn and Killebrew, *Jerusalem in Bible and Archaeology,* 42; J. M. Cahill, "Jerusalem in David and Solomon's Time. It Really Was a Major City in the Tenth Century B.C.E.," *Biblical Archaeology Review* 30, no. 6 (2004): 25–26. A. Mazar divided the Stepped Stone Structure into five components, see A. Mazar, "Jerusalem in the 10th Century B.C.E.: The Glass Half Full," in *Essays on Ancient Israel in Its Near Eastern Context: A Tribute to Nadav Na'aman,* ed. Y. Amit, E. Ben Zvi, I. Finkelstein, and O. Lipschits (Winona Lake, IN: Eisenbrauns, 2006), 257–59. According to E. Mazar, the Stepped Stone Structure was part of the same complex as the Large Stone Structure, which, in her view, represented King David's Palace, see E. Mazar, *Preliminary Report on the City of David Excavations at the Visitors Center Area* (Jerusalem: Shalem Press, 2007), 44–49. For a recent analysis of the Stepped Stone

Structure, see Finkelstein et al., "Has King David's Palace in Jerusalem Been Found?" *Tel Aviv* 34 (2007): 150–54.

13. See Cahill, "Jerusalem at the Time of the United Monarchy," 53.

14. See Kenyon, *Jerusalem*, 35, 65–66.

15. She adjusted her reconstruction of a small Iron Age city after Avigad's discovery of the Broad Wall, still insisting, however, that the Western Hill remained un-built. See Reich, *Excavating the City of David*, 115–16.

16. For a brief survey of Israeli excavations on the Southeast Hill, see Reich, *Excavating the City of David*, 118–42, 263–69. For more detailed descriptions, as well as other smaller-scale excavations, see preliminary reports in *Hadashot Arkheologiyot*.

17. See Shiloh, *Excavations at the City of David*; D. T. Ariel, *Excavations at the City of David 1978–1985*, vols. 2 and 5 (Jerusalem: Institute of Archaeology, Hebrew University, 1990); A. De Groot and D. Ariel, *Excavations at the City of David 1978–1985*, vols. 3, 4, and 5 (Jerusalem: Institute of Archaeology, Hebrew University, 1990)

18. See E. Mazar, "Did I Find King David's Palace?" *Biblical Archaeology Review* 32, no. 1 (2006): 16–27, 70; E. Mazar, *Preliminary Report.* Countering her view, see Finkelstein et al., "King David's Palace"; and A. Faust, "Did Eilat Mazar Find David's Palace?" *Biblical Archaeology Review* 38, no. 5 (2012): 47–52, 70.

19. See Reich and Shukron, "Light at the End of the Tunnel"; Reich, *Excavating the City of David*, 154–77.

20. Reich, *Excavating the City of David*, 225–244.

21. Reich, *Excavating the City of David*, 229.

22. A trial excavation was conducted by Reich and Shukron in 2003, see Reich and Shukron, "Jerusalem, City of David, the Giv'ati Car Park," *Hadashot Arkheologiyot* 117 (2005). D. Ben-Ami and Y. Tchekhanovets began their excavation in 2007, see their "Jerusalem, Giv'ati Parking Lot," *Hadashot Arkheologiyot* 120, (2008); and "Jerusalem, Giv'ati Parking Lot," *Hadashot Arkheologiyot* 122 (2010).

23. The Siloam Pool is mentioned on several medieval maps of the city, such as, for example, the Cambrai Map.

24. For a representation of the Siloam Pool, see, for example, the Cambrai Map. On unblocking the Gihon Spring during the Mamluk period, see Reich, *Excavating the City of David*, 341.

25. Macalister and Duncan and Crowfoot and FitzGerald published some medieval and Islamic pottery shards and vessels. See Macalister and Duncan, *Excavations on the Hill of Ophel*, 196–201; and Crowfoot and FitzGerald, *Excavations in the Tyropoeon Valley*, vol. 4, plates 22 and 23, and vol. 5, plates 14, 15, and 16. Warren published a large, decorated Mamluk period glass lamp, see C. Warren and C. R. Conder, *The Survey of Western Palestine: Jerusalem,* (London: Palestine Exploration Fund, 1884), 540.

26. On the compromised historical value of the biblical account, see I. Finkelstein and N. A. Silberman, *The Bible Unearthed: Archaeology's New Vision of Ancient Israel and the Origin of Its Sacred Texts* (New York and London: Free Press, 2001). More specifically on the period relevant to Kings David and Solomon, see J. Uziel and I. Shai, "Iron Age Jerusalem: Temple-Palace, Capital City," *Journal of the American Oriental Society* 127 (2007): 161–70.

27. The lack of archaeological remains has been viewed by some as evidence that Jerusalem was at best a very small site and certainly not an administrative center. According to

D. Ussishkin ("Solomon's Jerusalem: The Text and the Facts on the Ground," in Vaughn and Killebrew, *Jerusalem in Bible and Archaeology,* 103–15) the lack of archaeological evidence indicates that Jerusalem was at best a very small site. According to N. P. Lemche and T. L. Thompson ("Did Biran Kill David? The Bible in the Light of Archaeology," *Journal for the Study of the Old Testament* 64 (1994): 3–22), the United Monarchy and the Judean state until the eighth century (and to a certain extent even beyond) was a figment of the late biblical composer's imagination.

28. See E. Mazar, *The Complete Guide to the Temple Mount Excavations* (Jerusalem: Shoham Academic Research and Publication, 2002); E. Mazar, *Preliminary Report;* N. Na'aman, "The Contribution of the Amarna Letters to the Debate on Jerusalem's Political Position in the Tenth Century BCE," *Bulletin of the American Schools of Oriental Research* 304 (1996): 17–27; and Cahill, "Jerusalem in David and Solomon's Time."

29. C. Warren, *Underground Jerusalem* (London: Palestine Exploration Fund, 1876), 149.

30. Reich, *Excavating the City of David,* 140; Greenberg, "Towards an Inclusive Archaeology," 41; and M. Feige, "The Vision of the Broken Bones: Haredim vs. Archaeologists in the City of David, 1981," in *Israeli Haredim: Integration without Assimilation,* ed. E. Sivan and K. Kaplan, 56–81 (Jerusalem: Van-Leer Institute, 2003).

31. Reich, *Excavating the City of David,* 1–4.

32. Elad was established in 1986.

33. On the history of Elad's activities in Silwan, see the detailed report on the Emek Shaveh website: www.alt-arch.org/settlers.php.

34. Based on internal IAA documents, which Emek Shaveh recently made public, the close, collaborative ties between the IAA and Elad, and, in fact, the latter's supremacy over the former, was established. See R. Greenberg, *A Privatized Heritage: How the Israel Antiquities Authority Relinquished Jerusalem's Past* (Jerusalem Emek Shaveh, 2014), 6 and 51.

35. Greenberg has shown that Elad in recent years has, in fact, superseded the governmental agencies in power and that heritage is therefore in the hands of an NGO. See Greenberg, *A Privatized Heritage.*

36. Since Emek Shaveh was established in 2008, they have been involved in numerous legal battles with Elad, which, for the most part, were successful in slowing Elad's campaigns to evacuate Palestinians from the neighborhood and to construct the Kedem Center. See, for example, A. Selig, "Jerusalem Court Halts Silwan Construction" *The Jerusalem Post,* September 10, 2009; D. K. Eisenbud, "Appeal Sent to Attorney General to Halt Elad Acquisition of Jerusalem Archaeological Park" *The Jerusalem Post,* March 10, 2014; N. Hasson, "Legal Challenges Mounted Against Planned Visitor Center in East Jerusalem" *Ha'aretz,* January 1, 2014; and Eisenbud, "NGO Petitions High Court to Prevent Closure of Area in Silwan," *The Jerusalem Post,* September 6, 2015.

37. On Wadi Hilwe Information Center's missions and activities see: www.silwanic.net.

38. See Emek Shaveh's mission statement, in Mizrachi, *Remaking the City: Archaeological Projects of Political Import in Jerusalem's Old City and in the Village of Silwan* (Jerusalem: Emek Shaveh, 2013), 2; and at http://alt-arch.org/en/about-us. See also Noy, "Peace Activism in Tourism: Two Case Studies (and a Few Reflections) in Jerusalem," in *Peace through Tourism: Promoting Human Security Through International Citizenship,* ed. L. Blanchard and F. Higgins-Desbiolles (New York: Routledge, 2013), 211.

39. For additional highly critical commentaries of Elad's ideologically motivated settlement activities in East Jerusalem and their politically motivated use of archaeology, see Pullan and Gwiazda, "City of David"; J. Yas, "(Re)designing the City of David: Landscape, Narrative and Archaeology in Silwan," *Jerusalem Quarterly File* 7 (2000): 17–23; and Greenberg, "Towards an Inclusive Archaeology."

40. Reich and Shukron, "Light at the End of the Tunnel."

41. For a detailed description of the various sections exposed since the nineteenth century, as well as the recent excavations, see Reich and Shukron, "The Second Temple Period Central Drainage Channel in Jerusalem—Upon the Completion of the Unearthing of Its Southern Part in 2011," in *City of David Studies of Ancient Jerusalem. The 12th Annual Conference,* ed. E. Meiron, 68*–95* (Jerusalem: Megalim City of David Institute for Jerusalem Studies, 2011).

42. The northern section, near Robinson's Arch, was first discovered by Charles Warren and then later explored by Benjamin Mazar. The southern section was initially discovered by Bliss and Dickey. According to Reich and Shukron, the two parallel sections of streets may have been joined at their southern end, where the width would have spanned the paved esplanade near the Siloam Pool. See Reich and Shukron, "Second Temple Period," 82*.

43. See the IAA press release: www.antiquities.org.il/article_Item_eng.asp?sec_id = 25&subj_id = 240&id = 1782&module_id = #as as well as their promotional video: www.facebook.com/video/video.php?v=484268573692.

44. Regarding the difficulty in dating the channel, see Reich and Shukron, "Second Temple Period," 88*–89*.

8. THE CHURCH OF THE HOLY SEPULCHRE

1. The peaceful atmosphere on the rooftop is, in fact, deceptive, as it is one of the most contested areas of the church, claimed both by the Coptic and Ethiopian communities. See C. F. Emmett, "The Status Quo Solution for Jerusalem," *Journal of Palestine Studies* 26, no. 2 (1997): 22.

2. An engraving, dated by the Franciscan Custody of the Holy Land to 1728, shows the ladder in this specific location. Several lithographs from the 1830s and photographs from the 1850s also feature the ladder under the window. See G. Simmermacher, *The Holy Land Trek: A Pilgrim's Guide* (Cape Town: Southern Cross Books, 2012), 194–95.

3. M. Biddle et al., *The Church of the Holy Sepulchre* (New York: Rizzoli, 2000), 118 and 123.

4. G. Williams, *The Holy City: Historical, Topographical, and Antiquarian Notices of Jerusalem,* 2 vols. (Cambridge: J. W. Parker, 1849); M. de Vogüé, *Les églises de Terre Sainte: fragments d'un voyage en Orient* (Paris: Lib. De V. Didron, 1860); and C. W. Wilson, *Golgotha and the Holy Sepulchre* (London: Palestine Exploration Fund, 1906). For a more detailed survey of the history of research, see G. Avni and J. Seligman, "Between the Temple Mount / Haram el-Sharif and the Holy Sepulchre: Archaeological Involvement in Jerusalem's Holy Places," *Journal of Mediterranean Archaeology* 19 (2006): 271–72.

5. V. C. Corbo, *Il Santo Sepolcro di Gerusalemme,* vols. 1–3, Studium Biblicum Franciscanum, colletio maior 29 (Jerusalem: Franciscan Publishing Press, 1982).

6. A. Ekonomopoulos, "Il ritrovamento dell'abside del 'Martyrium' " *La Terra Santa* 47 (1971): 107–11; and C. Katsimbinis, "The Uncovering of the Eastern Side of the Hill of Calvary and Its Base," *Liber Annus* 27 (1977): 197–208.

7. M. Broshi, "Evidence of Earliest Christian Pilgrimage to the Holy Land Comes to Light in Holy Sepulchre Church," *Biblical Archaeology Review* 3, no. 4 (1977): 42–44; M. Broshi and G. Barkay, "Excavations in the Chapel of St. Vartan in the Holy Sepulchre," *Israel Exploration Journal* 35 (1985): 108–28.

8. Avni and Seligman, "Between the Temple Mount"; J. Seligman and G. Avni, "Jerusalem, Church of the Holy Sepulchre," *Hadashot Arkheologiyot* 111 (2000): 69*–70*; and J. Seligman and G. Avni, "New Excavations at the Church of the Holy Sepulchre Compound," in *One Land—Many Cultures: Archaeological Studies in Honour of Stanislao Loffreda OFM*, ed. G. C., Bottini, L. Di Segni, and L. D. Chrupcala, 153–62 (Jerusalem: Franciscan Printing Press, 2003).

9. S. Gibson and J. Taylor, *Beneath the Church of the Holy Sepulchre, Jerusalem: The Archaeology and Early History of Traditional Golgotha* (London: Palestine Exploration Fund, 1994), 51.

10. J. Patrich, "The Church of the Holy Sepulchre in the Light of Excavations and Restoration," in *Ancient Churches Revealed*, ed. Y. Tsafrir (Jerusalem: Israel Exploration Society, 1993), 102.

11. See, for example, Corbo, *Il Santo Sepolcro*, 30–31; Gibson and Taylor, *Beneath the Church of the Holy Sepulchre*, 61; and D. Bahat, "Does the Holy Sepulchre Church Mark the Burial of Jesus?" *Biblical Archaeology Review* 12, no. 3 (1986): 26–45.

12. A number of hypothetical reconstructions have been proposed for the layout of the northern part of the Hadrianic forum. See C. Coüasnon, *The Church of the Holy Sepulchre, Jerusalem*, The Schweich Lectures, 1972 (London: Oxford University Press, 1974), 12–13; Tsafrir, *Eretz Israel*, 60, 92; H. Geva, "The Camp of the Tenth Legion in Jerusalem: An Archaeological Reconsideration," *Israel Exploration Journal* 34 (1984): 250; Bahat, "Does the Holy Sepulchre Church Mark the Burial of Jesus?" 40; Bahat, *The Illustrated Atlas of Jerusalem*, 66.

13. For a detailed description of the Constantinian complex, see Corbo, *Il Santo Sepolcro*, 81–137; and Coüasnon, *Church of the Holy Sepulchre*, 38–53. For a summary, including different interpretations with regard to the archaeological and architectural remains, see Gibson and Taylor, *Beneath the Church of the Holy Sepulchre*, 73–85.

14. Corbo, *Il Santo Sepolcro*, 139–209; and Coüasnon, *Church of the Holy Sepulchre*, 54–57.

15. During the Middle Ages, Golgotha was often perceived as the center of the world and shown as such on maps, for example, on the Mappa Mundi of Hereford Cathedral. See M. Prior, "Holy Places, Unholy Domination: The Scramble for Jerusalem," *Islamic Studies* 40 (2001): 512–13; and M. Eliade, *Patterns in Comparative Religions* (London and New York: Sheed and Ward, 1958), 375.

16. Corbo, *Il Santo Sepolcro*, 233–35; and Coüasnon, *Church of the Holy Sepulchre*, 54–62.

17. Avni and Seligman, "Between the Temple Mount," 281.

18. The use of the term *historic churches* here follows M. Dumper's definition (in "Christian Churches of Jerusalem in the Post-Oslo Period," *Journal of Palestine Studies* 31, no. 2

(2002): 51). He makes the distinction between churches that existed prior to 1967 (the so-called historic churches) and the more recent evangelical arrivals associated with the International Christian Embassy, the Mormons, the Hebrew Christians, or the Russian "Jewish Christians."

19. I. H. Reith, "A Dome in Jerusalem," *Structural Engineer* 60A (1982): 23–28; I. H. Reith, "Discussion: A Dome in Jerusalem," *Structural Engineer* 61A (1983): 126–27; and R. Cohen, *Saving the Holy Sepulchre: How Rival Christians Came Together to Rescue Their Holiest Shrine* (New York and Oxford: Oxford University Press, 2009), 109–10, 112–16, 152.

20. C. Schick ("Gordon's Tomb" *Palestine Exploration Fund Quarterly* 24 (1892), 120–24) provides a list of articles on the topic. See also S. Goldhill, "Jerusalem," in *Cities of God. The Bible and Archaeology in Nineteenth-Century Britain*, ed. D. Gange and M. Ledger-Lomas (Cambridge: Cambridge University Press, 2013), 75, n. 22.

21. It was around the same time that the Anglicans renounced their claims to the Church of the Holy Sepulchre as well as other traditional holy places that their interest in the Garden Tomb arose. See J. R. Wright, "An Historical and Ecumenical Survey of the Church of the Holy Sepulchre, with Notes on Its Significance for Anglicans," *Anglican and Episcopal History* 64 (1995): 482.

22. On the development of new holy places in Palestine by Europeans and the purchase of "Gordon's Calvary" in 1894 by the Garden Tomb Association, see R. Kark and S. J. Frantzman, "The Protestant Garden Tomb in Jerusalem, Englishwomen, and a Land Transaction in Late Ottoman Palestine," *Palestine Exploration Quarterly* 142 (2010): 199–216. See also G. Barkay, "The Garden Tomb: Was Jesus Buried Here?" *Biblical Archaeology Review* 12, no. 2 (1986): 40–57

23. In support of the Garden Tomb as a viable site for Jesus's burial, see E. Hanauer, "Model of a Columbarium. An Alleged Model of a Sanctuary from the Garden Tomb Grounds," *Palestine Exploration Quarterly* 56 (1924): 143–45. More recently a similar conclusion was reached by W. S. McBirnie, *The Search for the Authentic Tomb of Jesus* (Montrose: Acclaimed Books, 1975). The opposing view was published for the first time by a Dominican scholar from the École biblique. See H. Vincent, "Garden Tomb: histoire d'un mythe," *Revue Biblique* 34 (1925): 401–31.

24. Barkay, "Garden Tomb."

25. See, for example, A. Mazar, "Iron Age Burial Caves North of Damascus Gate Jerusalem," *Israel Exploration Journal* 26 (1976): 1–8; and G. Barkay and A. Kloner, "Jerusalem Tombs from the Days of the First Temple," *Biblical Archaeology Review* 12, no. 2 (1986): 22–39.

26. For a discussion of the Second and Third Walls and the implications for the location of the Church of the Holy Sepulchre, see Galor and Bloedhorn, *Archaeology of Jerusalem*, 71–74.

27. M. Biddle, *The Tomb of Christ (Stroud, England: Sutton, 1999).*

28. The Aedicule is currently undergoing restoration. See K. Romey, "Exclusive: Christ's Burial Place Exposed for the First Time in Centuries," *National Geographic*, October 26, 2016.

29. See Broshi, "Evidence of Earliest Christian Pilgrimage"; Broshi, "Excavations in the Chapel of St. Vartan," 121–22; and Gibson and Taylor, *Church of the Holy Sepulchre*, 47–48.

30. See Corbo, *Il Santo Sepolcro*, 68–79, pl. 1; and Coüasnon, *Church of the Holy Sepulchre*, 21–36.

31. Some of the major scholarly discrepancies are summarized by Patrich, "Church of the Holy Sepulchre."

32. Biddle et al., *The Church of the Holy Sepulchre*, 86.

33. H. Chadwick, *East and West: The Making of a Rift in the Church: The Making of a Rift in the Church, from Apostolic Times until the Council of Florence* (Oxford: Oxford University Press, 2003), 200–218.

34. Boas, *Jerusalem in the Time of the Crusades*, 37–38.

35. Wright, "Historical and Ecumenical Survey," 488.

36. Biddle et al., *The Church of the Holy Sepulchre*, 87.

37. For a detailed description of the spatial distribution of the church, see Wright, "Historical and Ecumenical Survey," 490–503.

38. For a summary of the development of contested areas within the church, see Emmett, "Status Quo Solution," 19–22.

39. The Status Quo applied initially to five sacred sites: the Church of the Holy Sepulchre, Dayr al-Sultan on its rooftop, the Chapel of the Ascension on the Mount of Olives, the Tomb of the Virgin Mary in Gethsemane, and the Church of the Nativity in Bethlehem.

40. There is an extensive literature on the friction between the different communities. See, for example, G. S. P. Freeman-Grenville, "The Basilica of the Holy Sepulchre, Jerusalem: History and Future," *Journal of the Royal Asiatic Society of Great Britain and Ireland* (1987): 188.

41. On Jerusalem's British district officer Lionel G. A. Cust's failed attempt to codify the existing practice of the time, see M. Eordegian, "British and Israeli Maintenance of the Status Quo in the Holy Places of Christendom," *International Journal of Middle East Studies* 35 (2003): 310–11.

42. Eordegian, "British and Israeli Maintenance," 311.

43. Eordegian, "British and Israeli Maintenance," 320.

44. Eordegian, "British and Israeli Maintenance."

45. See Wright, "Historical and Ecumenical Survey," 489.

46. Emmett, "Status Quo Solution," 22 and no. 6.

47. T. Butcher, "Feuding Monks in Bad Odour over Sewage," *The Telegraph*, April 7, 2007.

48. In 2002, a Coptic monk moved his chair, located on Ethiopian territory. Perceived as a hostile move by the latter community, the resulting violence led to eleven people being hospitalized. See C. Armstrong, "Divvying Up the Most Sacred Place," *Christianity Today*, July 1, 2002. More generally on the conflict between Copts and Ethiopians at the church, see Emmett, "Status Quo Solution," 22. In 2004, a fistfight erupted between Greek Orthodox and Franciscan monks, responding to a door leading to the Franciscan chapel that was left open during the Orthodox celebrations of the Exaltation of the Holy Cross. See A. Fisher-Ilan, "Punch-Up at Tomb of Jesus," *The Guardian*, September 28, 2004.

49. Today, the Christian population of Jerusalem represents about 2 percent of the total population of the city. On recent and anticipated demographic trends, see Dellapergola, "Jerusalem's Population." On Jerusalem's Christian population throughout the ages, see R. Abu Jaber, "Arab Christians in Jerusalem," *Islamic Studies* 40 (2001): 587–600.

50. Around 50 percent of Palestinian Christians belong to the Orthodox Church of Jerusalem. There are also Maronites, Melkite-Eastern Catholics, Jacobites, Chaldeans, Roman

Catholics, Syriac Catholics, Orthodox Copts, Catholic Copts, Armenian Orthodox, Armenian Catholics, Quakers, Methodists, Presbyterians, Anglicans, Lutherans, Evangelicals, Pentecostals, Nazarene, Assemblies of God, Baptists, and other Protestants.

51. See Dumper, "Christian Churches of Jerusalem," 53–54; and Dumper, *The Politics of Sacred Space*, 124–27.

52. See G. Lindén, *Church Leadership in a Political Crisis: Joint Statements from the Jerusalem Heads of Churches, 1988–1992* (Uppsala: Swedish Institute of Missionary Research, 1994); and Dumper, "Christian Churches of Jerusalem," 56.

53. The heads of the Christian communities met on November 14, 1994, to discuss the status of the holy city and its Christian population. See Memorandum statement: www.al-bushra.org/hedchrch/memorandum.htm.

54. Dumper, "Christian Churches of Jerusalem," 58.

9. THE TEMPLE MOUNT / HARAM AL-SHARIF

1. L. Ritmeyer reviews twelve different theories with regard to the location of the pre-Herodian Temple Mount, see *The Quest: Revealing the Temple Mount in Jerusalem* (Jerusalem: Carta and The Lamb Foundation, 2006), 147. See also Humbert, "Aux racines cananéennes."

2. See A. Kaplony, *The Haram of Jerusalem 324–1099. Temple, Friday Mosque, Area of Spiritual Power* (Stuttgart: Franz Steiner Verlag, 2002), 23–31.

3. W. Montgomery, *Muhammad: Prophet and Statesman* (Oxford: Oxford University Press, 1974), 112–13.

4. For various theories, see Y. Z. Eliav, *God's Mountain: The Temple Mount in Time, Place and Memory* (Baltimore: John Hopkins University Press, 2005), 85–91.

5. For a detailed description of the Temple Mount during the Byzantine period, see Eliav, *God's Mountain* 125–188.

6. Kaplony, *Haram of Jerusalem*, 33–57.

7. On renovations during the Ayyubid period, see Hawari, *Ayyubid Jerusalem*; on Mamluk renovations, M. H. Burgoyne, "1260–1516: The Noble Sanctuary (al-Haram al-Sharif) under Mamluk Rule Architecture," in Grabar and Kedar, *Where Heaven and Earth Meet*, 188–209; on Ottoman period transformations, see A. Cohen, "1516–1917: Haram-i-Şerif—The Temple Mount under Ottoman Rule," in Grabar and Kedar, *Where Heaven and Earth Meet*, 210–29, 399–400.

8. Eliav, *God's Mountain*.

9. Berkovitz, *Temple Mount*, 12–13. According to the Israeli Regulations for the Preservation of Holy Places to the Jews, 1981, the Temple Mount, unlike the Western Wall, was not legally defined as a holy place. See Berkovitz, *Temple Mount*, 91.

10. Y. Reiter and J. Seligman, "1917 to the Present: Al-Haram al-Sharif / Temple Mount (Har Ha-Bayit) and the Western Wall," in Grabar and Kedar, *Where Heaven and Earth Meet*, 253. The change affected only the official administrative framework. The Ministry of Islamic Affairs and Awqaf was established in 1967. See Katz, *Jordanian Jerusalem*, 6.

11. Since the outbreak of the Second Intifada, access to the Dome of the Rock and the al-Aqsa Mosque by non-Muslims is extremely restricted.

12. The issue of the ownership of the Western Wall is particularly complex. Although Israel refrained from expropriating the western enclosure wall, except for the strip at its

base, neither the wall nor the Temple Mount is registered in the Land Registry Office. See Berkovitz, *Temple Mount,* 87–88.

13. Berkovitz, *Temple Mount,* 29, 57.

14. On his work in Jerusalem, see V. W. Von Hagen, *F. Catherwood, Architect-Explorer of Two Worlds* (Barre, MA: Barre Publishers, 1968), 35–45.

15. S. Gibson and D. M. Jacobson, *Below the Temple Mount in Jerusalem: A Sourcebook on the Cisterns, Subterranean Chambers and Conduits of the Haram al-Sharif,* BAR International Series 637 (Oxford: Tempus Reparatum, 1996); and E. Mazar, *The Walls of the Temple Mount* (Jerusalem: Shoham Academic Research and Publication, 2011).

16. K. A. C. Creswell, *The Origin of the Plan of the Dome of the Rock* (Jerusalem: British School of Archaeology, 1924); and M. van Berchem, *Matériaux pour un Corpus Inscriptionum Arabicarum. 2, Syrie du Sud, 2, Jérusalem "Haram"* (Cairo: l'Institut français d'archéologie orientale, 1927).

17. Hamilton, *Structural History of the Aqsa Mosque.*

18. E. Lefkovits, "Was the Aksa Mosque Built over the Remains of a Byzantine Church?" *Jerusalem Post,* November 16, 2008.

19. E. Mazar and B. Mazar, *Excavations in the South of the Temple Mount: The Ophel of Biblical Jerusalem* (Qedem 29; Jerusalem: Institute of Archaeology, Hebrew University, 1989); and M. Ben-Dov, *In the Shadow of the Temple: The Discovery of Ancient Jerusalem* (New York: Harper and Row, 1982).

20. R. Reich and Y. Billig, "Jerusalem, Robinson's Arch," *Excavations and Surveys in Israel* 20 (2000): 135*; E. Mazar, *Discovering the Solomonic Wall: A Remarkable Archaeological Adventure* (Jerusalem: Shoham Academic Research and Publication, 2011).

21. D. Bahat, *The Jerusalem Western Wall Tunnel* (Jerusalem: Israel Exploration Society, 2013); Onn, Weksler-Bdolah, and Bar-Nathan, "Jerusalem, The Old City"; and Weksler-Bdolah et al., "Jerusalem, The Western Wall Plaza Excavations"; M. Hagbi and J. Uziel, "Jerusalem, The Old City, The Western Wall Foundations," *Hadashot Arkheologiyot* 128 (2016).

22. Warren and Conder, *Survey of Western Palestine,* 193–209; C. W. Wilson, *Ordnance Survey of Jerusalem* (Southampton: Ordinance Survey Office, 1865), 28–29, plate 12; C. W. Wilson, "The Masonry of the Haram Wall," *Palestine Exploration Quarterly* 12 (1880): 9–65.

23. The first ten years of work were conducted without archaeological supervision—a source of tension between the religious authorities and the Israel Department of Antiquities. See Reiter and Seligman, "1917 to the Present," 256. M. Ben-Dov, "The Underground Vaults West of the Western Wall," *Qardom* 21–23 (1982), 102–5"; M. Ben-Dov, *The Fortifications of Jerusalem: The City Walls, the Gates and the Temple Mount* (Tel Aviv: Zmora Bitan, 1983), 146; D. Bahat, "The Western Wall Tunnels," *Qadmoniot* 27 (1994): 38–48; D. Bahat, *The Jerusalem Western Wall Tunnel;* D. Bahat and A. Solomon, "Innovations in the Excavations of the Western Wall Tunnels," *Judea and Samaria Research Studies* 11 (2002): 175–86.

24. Onn, Weksler-Bdolah, and Bar-Nathan, "Jerusalem, The Old City."

25. Burgoyne, *Mamluk Jerusalem,* 223–40.

26. Josephus provides two only slightly different narratives of the Herodian Temple Mount construction, one in *The Jewish War* (5.5.184–227) and the other in the *Antiquities of the Jews* (15.11.380–425).

27. F. E. Peters, *Jerusalem: The Holy City. in the Eyes of Chroniclers, Visitors, Pilgrims, and Prophets from the Days of Abraham to the Beginnings of Modern Times* (Princeton: Princeton University Press, 1985).

28. For a complete survey of all Haram inscriptions, see van Berchem, *Corpus Inscriptionum Arabicarum.* For the manuscripts, see Salameh, *Qur'an Manuscripts.*

29. For the so-called Solomonic fortification in the Ophel, see E. Mazar, *Discovering the Solomonic Wall.* Regarding the differences in dating the Herodian enclosure wall and entrances, see Bahat, *The Jerusalem Western Wall Tunnel;* Ben-Dov, *The Fortifications of Jerusalem;* E. Mazar, *The Walls of the Temple Mount.* For the discrepancies on the dating of medieval remains, see Bahat, *The Jerusalem Western Wall Tunnel;* and Hawari, *Ayyubid Jerusalem.*

30. After a sustained period of neglect of the monuments on the Haram throughout the last phase of Ottoman rule, numerous restoration works were carried out under British, Jordanian, and Israeli rule. The relationship between the Muslim religious establishment and the official archaeological and architectural organs of the British Mandatory government were of a professional and friendly nature. See Reiter and Seligman, "1917 to the Present," 237.

31. Reiter and Seligman, "1917 to the Present," 258.

32. On significant incidents between 1967 and 1987, see Reiter and Seligman, "1917 to the Present," 254. On the First Intifada and the "al-Aqsa Massacre," see Reiter and Seligman, "1917 to the Present," 260. For the relationship between the Waqf and various Israeli governmental bodies, see Reiter and Seligman, "1917 to the Present," 255.

33. The riots, which resulted in the death of about twenty and the injury of more than 150 Palestinians, broke out after a decision by the Temple Mount Faithful to lay a cornerstone for the construction of the Third Temple on the platform. See Inbari, *Jewish Fundamentalism,* 79–80.

34. K. Romey, "Jerusalem's Temple Mount Flap," *Archaeology* 53, no. 2 (2000): 20.

35. Reiter and Seligman, "1917 to the Present," 258.

36. Inbari, *Jewish Fundamentalism;* Inbari, "The Oslo Accords and the Temple Mount, A Case Study: The Movement for the Establishment of the Temple," *Hebrew Union College Annual* 74 (2003): 279–323"; Inbari, "Religious Zionism and the Temple Mount Dilemma—Key Trends," *Israel Studies* 12, no. 2 (2007): 29–47.

37. The site was purchased by Ateret Cohanim, a religious Zionist organization, who encouraged Irving Moskowitz, a regular donor to Jewish settlements in East Jerusalem, to buy the building.

38. H. Barbé and T. De'adle, "Jerusalem, Ohel Yizhaq Synagogue," *Hadashot Arkheologiyot* 119 (2007).

39. Weksler-Bdolah et al., "Jerusalem, Western Wall Plaza Excavations."

40. See H. Barbé, F. Vitto, and R. Greenwald, "When, Why and by Whom the Mughrabi Gate Was Opened? Excavations at the Mughrabi Gate in the Old City of Jerusalem (2007, 2012–2014)," in *New Studies in the Archaeology of Jerusalem and Its Region: Collected Papers,* ed. G. D. Stiebel, O. Peleg-Barkat, D. Ben-Ami, and Y. Gadot, vol. 8, 32*–44* (Jerusalem: Tel Aviv University, Israel Antiquities Authority, and Hebrew University, 2014).

41. For this statement, see the Ministry of Foreign Affairs website: http://mfa.gov.il/MFA_Graphics/MFA%20Gallery/Powerpoint/MUGRABI-ENG.pps.

42. UNESCO, Report of the Technical Mission to the Old City of Jerusalem (February 27–March 2, 2007).

43. It has recently been argued that the arched underground structure was built in 640, at the very beginning of the Umayyad dynasty. See B. St. Laurent and I. Awwad, "The Marwani Musalla in Jerusalem: New Findings," *Jerusalem Quarterly* 54 (2013): 7–30. On the dating of various construction phases of Solomon's Stables, see J. Seligman, "Solomon's Stables, the Temple Mount, Jerusalem: The Events Concerning the Destruction of Antiquities 1999–2001," *'Atiqot* 56 (2007): 38*–40*; D. Bahat, "Re-Examining the History of Solomon's Stables," *Qadmoniot* 34 (2001): 128–29; and M. Ben-Dov, "Solomon's Stables," in *The Mosque of al-Aqsa, the Double Gate and Solomon's Stables,* ed. E. Schiller (Jerusalem, 1978); and Ben-Dov, *In the Shadow of the Temple,* 346. On the rehabilitation of Solomon's Stables, see N. al-Jubeh, "1917 to the Present: Basic Changes, but Not Dramatic: Al-Haram al-Sharif in the Aftermath of 1967," in Grabar and Kedar, *Where Heaven and Earth Meet,* 288–89.

44. Reiter and Seligman, "1917 to the Present," 269;" Seligman, "Solomon's Stables," 50*–51*.

45. Y. Baruch, "The Archaeological Finds in the Soil Debris Removed from the Temple Mount, Jerusalem, 1999–2000," *'Atiqot* 56 (2007): 55*.

46. G. Barkay and Y. Zweig, "New Objects Found While Sifting the Rubble from the Temple Mount," *Ariel* 175 (2005): 6–46."

47. Sine 2010, approximately twenty thousand volunteers are recruited annually to assist with the sifting.

48. D. M. Gitlitz and L. K. Davidson, *Pilgrimage and the Jews* (Westport, CT: Praeger, 2006), 42; R. Bonfil, *History and Folklore in a Medieval Jewish Chronicle: The Family Chronicle of Ahima'az Ben Paltiel* (Leiden: Brill, 2009), 336; Y. Levanon, *The Jewish Travellers in the Twelfth Century* (Lanham: University Press of America, 1980), 259; S. Goldhill, *Jerusalem: City of Longing* (Cambridge: Harvard University Press, 2010), 74–75. According to al-Jubeh ("Bab al-Magharibah"), the Western Wall was not venerated by Jews before the Ottoman period.

49. Ricca, *Reinventing Jerusalem,* 212

50. Reiter and Seligman, "1917 to the Present," 240.

51. D. Rossoff, *Where Heaven Touches Earth: Jewish Life in Jerusalem From Medieval Times to the Present* (Jerusalem: Guardian Press, 1988), 330–31.

52. R. Gonen, *Contested Holiness* (Jersey City: KTAV Publishing House, 2003), 135–37.

53. Reiter and Seligman, "1917 to the Present," 239.

54. Reiter and Seligman, "1917 to the Present," 265; and K. J. al-'Asali, *Jerusalem in Arab and Muslim Travel Narratives,* 39–40.

55. Reiter and Seligman, "1917 to the Present," 258.

56. Reiter and Seligman, "1917 to the Present," 258.

57. See their first three preliminary reports, as well as mission statement, on their website: http://templemount.wordpress.com.

58. Al-Jubeh, "1917 to the Present: Basic Changes, but Not Dramatic," 282.

59. According to Avni and Seligman, most of the finds were dated to the Byzantine period and thereafter. See Avni and Seligman, *Temple Mount,* 36. According to Bahat, the remains postdate the Ayyubid period. See D. Bahat, "Re-Examining the History of Solomon's Stables," *Qadmoniot* 34 (2001), 125–130 [Hebrew].

CONCLUSION

1. The refusal to assume full responsibility, as an individual who is directly implicated in this entanglement of archaeology and politics, as well as its public success, is perhaps best documented with two recent statements by one of Israel's leading archaeologists, who was active until recently in Jerusalem. Ronny Reich, whose career has received a significant boost through his position as chief archaeologist of the City of David and generous funding from Elad, has reiterated his indifference to the political use of the site's discoveries. In a 2012 interview with Nir Hasson from *Ha'aretz* ("In Jerusalem's City of David Excavation, Politics Is Never Absent," *Ha'aretz*, December 25, 2012), he repeatedly referred to himself as being "a little indifferent." Asked how his "worldview can be reconciled with [his] extensive scientific activity—that has effectively helped a rightist organization Judaize parts of Silwan"—he responded: "Some will say I'm playing into Elad's hands. . . . Yes, they use what I do. . . . I have no agenda to find any particular thing. Besides, if I wasn't doing it, someone else would be. And he would uncover the same artifacts. So what's the difference? . . . What excites me is contributing new knowledge, coloring in another blank area on our map of knowledge. I don't take the political side of things to heart. I'm not that way. What can I do?" Only after his retirement did his position become more critical, as stated in another *Ha'aretz* interview with the same journalist in 2016 ("Jerusalem, The Descent. A Voyage in the Underground City," *Ha'aretz*, April 21, 2016 [Hebrew]; my translation). In reference to the Herodian Street and Tunnel, the most recent archaeological project in Silwan, he stated, "This is an excavation in the service of tourism, and then of politics, or perhaps first politics and then tourism. . . . In terms of information, it doesn't add much. It may be a nice contribution as a monument, but it will not particularly add to our knowledge. We know the course of the wall, we know what it looks like and when it was built."

2. S. Levy, "Human Rights Groups Accuse NBC of Deceit about DIG Filming Locations in Occupied East Jerusalem," *Jewish Voice for Peace*, June 5, 2014.

3. Larkin and Dumper, "UNESCO and Jerusalem."

4. See Pullan et al., *Struggle for Jerusalem's Holy Places*, 142.

5. These numbers follow the Census of Population and Housing conducted by the Central Bureau of Statistics of the State of Israel. See also D. Tsimhoni, "Demographic Trends of the Christian Population and the West Bank 1948–1978," *Middle East Journal* 37 (1983): 55.

6. Dumper, "Christian Churches of Jerusalem," 53.

7. A. Yahya, "The Palestinian-Israeli Draft Agreement on Archaeological Heritage," *Present Pasts* 2, no. 1 (2010): 72–74.

8. See http://alt-arch.org/en/wp-content/uploads/2016/07/Principles-Eng-A4-dbl-sided_2.pdf.

BIBLIOGRAPHY

Abdi, K. "Nationalism, Politics, and the Development of Archaeology in Iran." *American Journal of Archaeology* 105 (2001): 51–76.

Abowd, T. "The Moroccan Quarter: A History of the Present." *Jerusalem Quarterly File* 7 (2000): 6–16.

Abu El-Haj, N. "Translating Truths: Nationalism, the Practice of Archaeology, and the Remaking of Past and Present in Contemporary Jerusalem." *American Ethnologist* 25 (1998): 166–88.

———. *Facts on the Ground: Archaeological Practice and Territorial Self-Fashioning in Israeli Society.* Chicago: University of Chicago Press, 2001.

———. "Producing (Arti) Facts: Archaeology and Power during the British Mandate of Palestine." *Israel Studies* 7, no. 2 (2002): 33–61.

Abu Jaber, R. "Arab Christians in Jerusalem." *Islamic Studies* 40 (2001): 587–600.

Abu Khalaf, M. F. *Islamic Art through the Ages.* Jerusalem: Emerezian Graphic and Printing Est., 1998.

"Academic Boycott of Israel: The American Studies Association Endorsement and Backlash." *Journal of Palestine Studies* 43, no. 3 (2014): 56–71.

Ahituv, S., A. Demsky, Y. Goren, and A. Lemaire. "The Inscribed Pomegranate from the Israel Museum Examined Again." *Israel Exploration Journal* 57 (2007): 87–95.

Amiran, R. "The Water Supply of Israelite Jerusalem," in Yadin, *Jerusalem Revealed*, 75–78.

Amiran, D. H. K., A. Shachar, and I. Kimhi. *Atlas of Jerusalem.* Jerusalem: Massada, 1973.

Amit, D., J. Seligman, and I. Zilberbod, "Jerusalem, Mount Scopus (East)." *Hadashot Arkheologiyot* 111 (2000): 66*–88* [Hebrew].

———. "The 'Monastery of Theodorus and Cyriacus' on the Eastern Slope of Mount Scopus," in *One Land—Many Cultures: Archaeological Studies in Honour of Stanislao Loffreda OFM*, edited by G. C. Bottini, L. Di Segni, and L. D. Chrupcala, 139–148. Jerusalem: Amitai Press, 2006.

Ariel, D. T. *Excavations at the City of David 1978–1985, Directed by Yigal Shiloh,* vol. 2, *Imported Stamped Amphora Handles, Coins, Worked Bone and Ivory, and Glass.* Qedem 30. Jerusalem: Institute of Archaeology, Hebrew University, 1990.

———. *Excavations at the City of David 1978–1985, Directed by Yigal Shiloh,* vol. 6, *Inscriptions.* Qedem 41. Jerusalem: Institute of Archaeology, Hebrew University, 2000.

Armstrong, C. "Divvying Up the Most Sacred Place." *Christianity Today.* July 1, 2002.

Arnold, B. " 'Arierdämmerung': Race and Archaeology in Nazi Germany." *World Archaeology* 38 (2006): 8–31.

Arnon, A. "The Quarters of Jerusalem in the Ottoman Period." *Middle Eastern Studies* 28 (1992): 1–65.

Al-'Asali, K. J. *Jerusalem in Arab and Muslim Travel Narratives.* Amman, 1992. [Arabic].

Asali, K. J., ed. *Jerusalem in History: From 3,000 B.C. to the Present Day.* Rev. ed. London: Kegan Paul International, 1997.

Ashbee, C. R., ed. *Jerusalem 1918–1920: Being the Records of the Pro-Jerusalem Council during the Period of the British Military Administration.* London: The Council of the Pro-Jerusalem Society, 1921.

Auld, S., and R. Hillenbrand, eds. *Ottoman Jerusalem: The Living City, 1517–1917.* 2 vols. London: Altajir World of Islam Trust, 2000.

Avigad, N. *Discovering Jerusalem.* Nashville, Camden, and New York: Thomas Nelson Publishers, 1983.

Avi-Yonah, M. "Excavations at Sheikh Bader." *Bulletin of the Jewish Palestine Exploration Society* 15 (1949/50): 19–24. [Hebrew].

Avni, G. "The Urban Limits of Roman and Byzantine Jerusalem: A View from the Necropoleis," *Journal of Roman Archaeology* 18 (2005): 373–96.

Avni, G., and K. Galor. "Unearthing Jerusalem: 150 Years of Archaeological Research." In Galor and Avni, *Unearthing Jerusalem,* ix–xix.

Avni, G., and J. Seligman, *Temple Mount 1917–2001. Documentation, Research and Inspection of Antiquities.* Jerusalem: Israel Antiquities Authority, 2001.

———. "Between the Temple Mount / Haram el-Sharif and the Holy Sepulchre: Archaeological Involvement in Jerusalem's Holy Places." *Journal of Mediterranean Archaeology* 19 (2006): 259–88.

Ayalon, A., M. Bar-Matthews, and Y. Goren. "Authenticity Examination of the Inscription on the Ossuary Attributed to James, Brother of Jesus." *Journal of Archaeological Science* 31 (2004): 1185–89.

Bahat, D. "Does the Holy Sepulchre Church Mark the Burial of Jesus?" *Biblical Archaeology Review* 12, no. 3 (1986): 26–45.

———. *The Illustrated Atlas of Jerusalem.* London: Simon and Schuster, 1990.

———. "The Western Wall Tunnels." *Qadmoniot* 27 (1994): 38–48. [Hebrew].

———. "Re-Examining the History of Solomon's Stables," *Qadmoniot* 34 (2001): 125–30. [Hebrew].

———. *The Jerusalem Western Wall Tunnel.* Jerusalem: Israel Exploration Society, 2013.

Bahat, D., and A. Solomon. "Innovations in the Excavations of the Western Wall Tunnels." *Judea and Samaria Research Studies* 11 (2002): 175–86. [Hebrew].

Baker, R. "Codes of Ethics; Some History." *Perspectives on the Professions* 19, no. 1 (1999): 3–5.

Balter, M. "Archaeologists and Rabbis Clash over Human Remains." *Science,* January 7, 2000, 34–35.

Banks, W. C. *New Battlefields/Old Laws: Critical Debates on Asymmetric Warfare.* New York: Columbia University Press, 2011.

Barbé, H., and T. De'adle. "Jerusalem, Ohel Yizhaq Synagogue," *Hadashot Arkheologiyot* 119 (2007).

Barbé, H., F. Vitto, and R. Greenwald. "When, Why and by Whom the Mughrabi Gate was Opened? Excavations at the Mughrabi Gate in the Old City of Jerusalem (2007, 2012–2014)." In *New Studies in the Archaeology of Jerusalem and Its Region: Collected Papers,* edited by G. D. Stiebel, O. Peleg-Barkat, D. Ben-Ami, and Y. Gadot, vol. 8, 32*–44*. Jerusalem: Tel Aviv University, Israel Antiquities Authority, and Hebrew University, 2014.

Barkan, E., and R. Bush, eds. *Claiming the Stones, Naming the Bones: Cultural Property and the Negotiation of National and Ethnic Identity.* Los Angeles: Getty Research Institute, 2002.

Barkay, G. "The Garden Tomb: Was Jesus Buried Here?" *Biblical Archaeology Review* 12, no. 2 (1986): 40–57.

Barkay, G., and A. Kloner. "Jerusalem Tombs from the Days of the First Temple." *Biblical Archaeology Review* 12, no. 2 (1986): 22–39.

Barkay, G., and Y. Zweig. "New Objects Found While Sifting the Rubble from the Temple Mount." *Ariel* 175 (2005): 6–46. [Hebrew].

Baruch, Y. "The Archaeological Finds in the Soil Debris Removed from the Temple Mount, Jerusalem, 1999–2000," *'Atiqot* 56 (2007): 55*–64*.

Baruch, Y., and D. Weiss. "Jerusalem, the Western Wall Plaza. Final Report." *Hadashot Arkheologiyot* 121 (2009).

Ben-Ami, D., and Y. Tchekhanovets. "Jerusalem, Giv'ati Parking Lot." *Hadashot Arkheologiyot* 120 (2008).

———. "Jerusalem, Giv'ati Parking Lot," *Hadashot Arkheologiyot* 122 (2010).

Ben-Amotz, D. *Reflections in Time.* Tel Aviv: Bitan, 1974. [Hebrew].

Ben-Arieh, Y. "The Growth of Jerusalem in the Nineteenth Century." *Annals of the Association of American Geographers* 65 (1975): 252–69.

———. *Jerusalem in the 19th Century: The Old City.* New York: St. Martin's Press, 1984.

———. *Jerusalem in the 19th Century: Emergence of the New City.* New York: St. Martin's Press, 1986.

Ben-Dov, M. "Solomon's Stables." In *The Mosque of el-Aqsa, the Double Gate and Solomon's Stables,* edited by E. Schiller, 68–70. Jerusalem, 1978. [Hebrew].

———. *In the Shadow of the Temple: The Discovery of Ancient Jerusalem.* New York: Harper and Row, 1982.

———. "The Underground Vaults West of the Western Wall." *Qardom* 21–23 (1982): 102–5 [Hebrew].

———. *The Fortifications of Jerusalem: The City Walls, the Gates and the Temple Mount.* Tel Aviv: Zmora Bitan, 1983. [Hebrew].

———. *Historical Atlas of Jerusalem.* New York: Continuum, 2002.

Ben-Ezer, E. *Courage: The Story of Moshe Dayan.* Jerusalem: Ministry of Defense Publications, 1997. [Hebrew].

Benvenisti, M. *City of Stone: The Hidden History of Jerusalem.* Berkeley: University of California Press, 1996.

——. *Sacred Landscape: The Buried History of the Holy Land since 1948.* Berkeley: University of California Press, 2000.

Berchem, M. van. *Matériaux pour un Corpus Inscriptionum Arabicarum, 2, Syrie du Sud, 2, Jérusalem "Haram."* Cairo: l'Institut français d'archéologie orientale, 1927.

Berkovitz, S. *The Wars of the Holy Places: The Struggle over Jerusalem and the Holy Sites in Israel, Judea, Samaria and the Gaza District.* Jerusalem: Hed Arzi Publishing House and the Jerusalem Institute for Israel Studies, 2001. [Hebrew].

——. *The Temple Mount and the Western Wall in Israeli Law.* The Jerusalem Institute for Israel Studies Series 90. Jerusalem: JIIS and the Jerusalem Foundation, 2001.

Bernbeck, R., and R. H. McGuire, eds. *Ideologies in Archaeology.* Tucson: University of Arizona Press, 2011.

Biddle, M. *The Tomb of Christ.* Stroud, England: Sutton, 1999.

Biddle, M., G. Avni, J. Seligman, and T. Winter. *The Church of the Holy Sepulchre.* New York: Rizzoli, 2000.

Biseh, G. "One Damn Illicit Excavation after Another: The Destruction of the Archaeological Heritage of Jordan." In Brodie, Doole, and Renfrew, *Trade in Illicit Antiquities,* 115–18.

Blakely, J. A. "AIAR: Rebuilding the School that Albright Built: A History of the W. F. Albright Institute of Archaeological Research Jerusalem, Israel, Highlighting the Period from 1967 to 2000." In Seger, *An ASOR Mosaic,* 125–237.

Bliss, F. J., and A. C. Dickie. *Excavations at Jerusalem, 1894–1897.* London: Palestine Exploration Fund, 1898.

Blum, O. "The Illicit Antiquities Trade: An Analysis of Current Antiquities Looting in Israel." *Culture without Context* 11 (2002): 20–23.

Boas, A. *Jerusalem in the Time of the Crusades: Society, Landscape, and Art in the Holy City under Frankish Rule.* London: Routledge, 2001.

Bonfil, R. *History and Folklore in a Medieval Jewish Chronicle: The Family Chronicle of Ahima'az Ben Paltiel* (Leiden: Brill, 2009).

Boothe, H. "Tools for Learning about the Past to Protect the Future: Archaeology in the Classroom." *Legacy* 11.1 (2000): 10–12, 37.

Borowski, B. Introduction to *Guide to the Collection,* edited by L. Taylor-Guthartz, 7. 3rd rev. ed. Jerusalem: Bible Lands Museum Jerusalem, 2002.

Boylan, P. "The Ethics of Acquisition: The Leicestershire Code." *The Museums Journal* 75 (1976): 165–70.

Branham, J. "The American Archaeological Presence in Jerusalem: Through the Gates of the Albright Institute." In Galor and Avni, *Unearthing Jerusalem,* 73–94.

Breitowitz, Y. "The Desecration of Graves in Eretz Yisrael: The Struggle to Honor the Dead and Preserve Our Historical Legacy." *Jewish Law.* www.jlaw.com/Articles/heritage.html.

Brodie, N. "Export Deregulation and the Illicit Trade in Archaeological Material." In Richman and Forsyth, *Legal Perspectives on Cultural Resources,* 85–99.

Brodie, N., J. Doole, and C. Renfrew, eds. *Trade in Illicit Antiquities: The Destruction of the World's Archaeological Heritage.* Cambridge: McDonald Institute, 2001.

Brodie, N., and M. Kersel. "The Social and Political Consequences of Devotion to Biblical Artifacts." In *All The Kings Horses: Looting, Antiquities Trafficking, and the Integrity of the*

Archaeological Record, edited by P. K. Lazrus and A. W. Barker, 109–25. Washington, DC: Society for American Archaeology, 2012.

Bronner, Y., and Y. Mizrachi. "King Herod, Long Reviled, Finds New Love among Jewish Settlers." *Forward.* March 20, 2013.

Broshi, M. "Evidence of Earliest Christian Pilgrimage to the Holy Land Comes to Light in Holy Sepulchre Church." *Biblical Archaeology Review* 3, no. 4 (1977): 42–44.

Broshi, M., and G. Barkay. "Excavations in the Chapel of St. Vartan in the Holy Sepulchre." *Israel Exploration Journal* 35 (1985): 108–28.

Burgoyne, M. H. *Mamluk Jerusalem: An Architectural Study.* London: World of Islam Festival Trust, 1987.

———. "1260–1516: The Noble Sanctuary (al-Haram al-Sharif) under Mamluk Rule Architecture." In Grabar and Kedar, *Where Heaven and Earth Meet,* 188–209.

Butcher, T. "Feuding Monks in Bad Odour over Sewage," *The Telegraph,* April 7, 2007.

Byrne, R., and B. McNary-Zak, eds. *Resurrecting the Brother of Jesus: The James Ossuary Controversy and the Quest for Religious Relics.* Chapel Hill: University of North Carolina Press, 2009.

Cahill, J. M. "Jerusalem at the Time of the United Monarchy: The Archaeological Evidence." In Vaughn and Killebrew, *Jerusalem in Bible and Archaeology: The First Temple Period,* 13–80.

———. "Jerusalem in David and Solomon's Time. It Really Was a Major City in the Tenth Century BCE." *Biblical Archaeology Review* 30, no. 6 (2004): 20–31, 62–63.

"Campaign to Preserve Mamilla Jerusalem Cemetery, Petition for Urgent Action on the Desecration of Mamilla Cemetery, Jerusalem, 10 February 2010 (Excerpts)." *Journal of Palestine Studies,* 39, no. 3 (2010): 188–92.

Chadwick, H. *East and West: The Making of a Rift in the Church, from Apostolic Times until the Council of Florence.* Oxford: Oxford University Press, 2003.

Chevalier, N. *La recherche archéologique française au Moyen-Orient, 1842–1947.* Paris: Éditions Recherche sur les Civilisations, 2002.

Chiodelli, F. *Shaping Jerusalem: Spatial Planning, Politics and the Conflict.* New York: Routledge, 2017.

Clermont-Ganneau, C. "Une stèle du temple de Jérusalem," *Revue Archéologique* II 23 (1872): 214–34, 290–96.

———. *Recueil d'archéologie orientale.* Vols. 1–8. Paris: Leroux, 1888–1924.

———. *Archaeological Researches in Palestine during the Years 1873–1874.* Vols. 1–2. London: Palestine Exploration Fund, 1899–96 [sic].

———. *Études d'archéologie orientale.* Vol. 2. Paris: Vieweg, 1880.

Coggins, C. C. "Latin America, Native America, and the Politics of Culture." In Barkan and Bush, *Claiming the Stones, Naming the Bones,* 97–115.

Cohen, A. "1516–1917: Haram-i-Şerif—The Temple Mount under Ottoman Rule." In Grabar and Kedar, *Where Heaven and Earth Meet,* 210–29, 399–400.

Cohen, R. *Saving the Holy Sepulchre: How Rival Christians Came Together to Rescue Their Holiest Shrine.* New York: Oxford University Press, 2009.

Cook, E. M. "The Forgery Indictments and BAR: Learning from Hindsight." *Near Eastern Archaeology* 68 (2005): 73–75.

Cook, J. "Herod Exhibit Digs Up Controversy." *Aljazeera.* March 1, 2013.

Corbett, E. D. *Competitive Archaeology in Jordan: Narrating Identity from the Ottomans to the Hashemites.* Austin, University of Texas Press, 2014.

Corbo, V. C. *Il Santo Sepolcro di Gerusalemme. Aspetti archaeologici dalle origini al periodo crociato I–III.* Studium Biblicum Franciscanum, colletio maior 29. Jerusalem: Franciscan Publishing Press, 1982.

Cotran, E. "The Jerusalem Question in International Law: The Way to a Solution." *Islamic Studies* 40 (2001): 487–500.

Coüasnon, C. *The Church of the Holy Sepulchre Jerusalem.* The Schweich Lectures, 1972. London: Oxford University Press, 1974.

Creswell, K. A. C. *The Origin of the Plan of the Dome of the Rock.* Jerusalem: British School of Archaeology, 1924.

Crowfoot, J. W. "Excavations on Ophel, 1928." *Palestine Exploration Quarterly* 61 (1929): 9–16, 75–77, 156–66.

———. "Ophel Again." *Palestine Exploration Quarterly* 77 (1945): 66–104.

Crowfoot, J. W., and G. M. FitzGerald. *Excavations in the Tyropoeon Valley, Jerusalem, 1927.* London: Palestine Exploration Fund, 1929.

Daadli, T. "Mamluk Epitaphs from Mamilla Cemetery." *Levant* 43 (2011): 78–97.

Dalman, G. *Jerusalem und sein Gelände.* Gütersloh, Germany: Bertelsmann, 1930.

———. "Entstehung und bisherige Entwicklung des Instituts." *Palästinajahrbuch* 1 (1905): 14–20.

Davis, R. A. "Ottoman Jerusalem." In *Jerusalem: 1948: The Arab Neighborhoods and Their Fate in the War,* edited by S. Tamari, 10–29. Jerusalem: Institute of Jerusalem Studies and Badil Resource Center, 1999.

Dayagi-Mendels, M., and S. Rozenberg, eds. *Chronicles of the Land: Archaeology in the Israel Museum Jerusalem.* Israel Museum Catalogue 557. Jerusalem: The Israel Museum, 2010.

Dayan, Y. *My Father, His Daughter.* New York: Farrar, Straus and Giroux, 1985.

De Groot, A., and D. Ariel. *Excavations at the City of David 1978–1985, Directed by Yigal Shiloh,* vol. 3, *Stratigraphical, Environmental, and Other Reports.* Qedem 33. Jerusalem: Institute of Archaeology, Hebrew University, 1992.

———. *Excavations at the City of David 1978–1985, Directed by Yigal Shiloh,* vol. 4, *Various Reports.* Qedem 35. Jerusalem: Institute of Archaeology, Hebrew University, 1996.

———. *Excavations at the City of David 1978–1985, Directed by Yigal Shiloh,* vol. 5, *Extramural Areas.* Qedem 40. Jerusalem: Institute of Archaeology, Hebrew University, 2000.

Dellapergola, S. "Jerusalem's Population, 1995–2020: Demography, Multiculturalism and Urban Policies," *European Journal of Population / Revue Européenne de Démographie* 17 (2001): 165–99.

Diaz-Andreu, M. *A World History of Nineteenth-Century Archaeology: Nationalism, Colonialism, and the Past.* Oxford: Oxford University Press, 2007.

Diaz-Andreu, M., and T. Champion, eds. *Nationalism and Archaeology in Europe.* Boulder, CO: Westview Press, 1996.

Dothan, T. "Anthropoid Clay Coffins from a Late Bronze Age Cemetery near Deir el-Balah." *Israel Exploration Journal* 23 (1973): 129–48.

Dumper, M. "Israeli Settlement in the Old City of Jerusalem." *Journal of Palestine Studies* 21, no. 4 (1992): 32–53.

———. *The Politics of Jerusalem Since 1967*. New York: Columbia University Press and the Institute for Palestine Studies, 1997.

———. *The Politics of Sacred Space: The Old City of Jerusalem in the Middle East Conflict*. Boulder, CO: Lynne Rienner, 2002.

———. "The Christian Churches of Jerusalem in the Post-Oslo Period." *Journal of Palestine Studies* 31, no. 2 (2002): 51–65.

———. "The Palestinian Waqf and the Struggle over Jerusalem 1967–2000." *Annuaire Droit et Religions* 3 (2008/09): 199–221.

———. "A False Dichotomy? The Binationalism Debate and the Future of Divided Jerusalem." *International Affairs* 87 (2011): 671–85.

———. "The Role of Awqaf in Protecting the Islamic Heritage of Jerusalem, 1967–2010." In *Hamam Al Ayn / Hamam Al Hana': Essays and Memories in Celebration of a Historic Public Bath House in Jerusalem's Old Arab City. Al-Quds University, Jerusalem*, edited by D. Emtiaz. Jerusalem: Al-Quds University, 2011.

Dumper, M., and C. Larkin. "Political Islam in Contested Jerusalem: The Emerging Role of Islamists from within Israel." *Divided Cities Contested States, Working Paper No. 12*. Exeter: School of Politics, University of Exeter, 2009, 1–26.

———. "The Politics of Heritage and the Limitations of International Agency in Divided Cities: The Role of UNESCO in Jerusalem's Old City." *Review of International Studies* 38 (2012): 25–52.

Dvir, N. "Grave Concerns." *Ha'aretz*. October 25, 2011.

Einhorn, T. "Israeli Law, Jewish Law and the Archaeological Excavation of Tombs." *International Journal of Cultural Property* 6 (1997): 47–79.

Eirikh-Rose, A. "Jerusalem, the Slopes of Mount Scopus, Survey," *Hadashot Arkheologiyot* 122 (2010): [23/12/2010].

Eisenbud, D. K. "Appeal Sent to Attorney General to Halt Elad Acquisition of Jerusalem Archaeological Park." *The Jerusalem Post*. March 10, 2014.

———. "NGO Petitions High Court to Prevent Closure of Area in Silwan." *The Jerusalem Post*. September 6, 2015.

Ekonomopoulos, A. "Il ritrovamento dell'abside del 'Martyrium,' " *La Terra Santa* 47 (1971): 107–11.

Eliade, M. *Patterns in Comparative Religion*. London: Sheed and Ward, 1958.

Eliav, Y. Z. *God's Mountain: The Temple Mount in Time, Place and Memory*. Baltimore: John Hopkins University Press, 2005.

Emmett, C. F. "The Capital Cities of Jerusalem." *The Geographical Review* 86 (1996): 233–58.

———. "The Status Quo Solution for Jerusalem." *Journal of Palestine Studies* 26, no. 2 (1997): 16–28.

Eordegian, M. "British and Israeli Maintenance of the Status Quo in the Holy Places of Christendom." *International Journal of Middle East Studies* 35 (2003): 307–28.

Eshel, I., and K. Prag. *Excavations by K. M. Kenyon in Jerusalem*. Vol. 4, *The Iron Age Cave Deposits*. British Academy Monographs in Archaeology. London: Council for British Research in the Levant, 1995.

Faust, A. "Did Eilat Mazar Find David's Palace?" *Biblical Archaeology Review* 38, no. 5 (2012): 47–52, 70.

Feige, M. "The Vision of the Broken Bones: Haredim vs. Archaeologists in the City of David, 1981." In *Israeli Haredim: Integration without Assimilation*, edited by E. Sivan and K. Kaplan, 56–81. Jerusalem: Van-Leer Institute, 2003. [Hebrew].

Feige, M., and Z. Shiloni, eds. *Archaeology and Nationalism in Eretz-Israel*. Jerusalem: Ben-Gurion Research Institute, 2008.

Felch, J., and R. Frammolino. *Chasing Aphrodite, The Hunt for Looted Antiquities at the World's Richest Museum*. Boston: Houghton Mifflin Harcourt, 2011.

Finkelstein, I., Z. Herzog, L. Singer-Avitz, and D. Ussishkin. "Has King David's Palace in Jerusalem Been Found?" *Tel Aviv* 34 (2007): 142–64.

Finkelstein, I., and N. A. Silberman. *The Bible Unearthed: Archaeology's New Vision of Ancient Israel and the Origin of Its Sacred Texts*. New York and London: Free Press, 2001.

Fisher-Ilan, A. "Punch-Up at Tomb of Jesus" *The Guardian*, September 28, 2004.

Fogelman, S. "Are the Ultra-Orthodox Digging Their Own Grave?" *Ha'aretz*. July 25, 2010.

Franken, H. J., and M. L. Steiner. *Excavations at Jerusalem, 1961–1967*. Vol. 2, *The Iron Age Extramural Quarter on the South-East Hill*. British Academy Monographs in Archaeology. Oxford: Oxford University Press, 1990.

Freeman-Grenville, G. S. P. "The Basilica of the Holy Sepulchre, Jerusalem: History and Future." *Journal of the Royal Asiatic Society of Great Britain and Ireland* (1987): 187–207.

Friedman, M. *The Haredi (Ultra-Orthodox) Society—Sources, Trends and Processes*. (Jerusalem: The Jerusalem Institute for Israel Studies, 1991).

Frumkin, A., A. Shimron, and J. Rosenbaum. "Radiometric Dating of the Siloam Tunnel, Jerusalem." *Nature* 425 (2003): 169–71.

Fuchs, A. R. "Austen St. Barbe Harrison: A British Architect in the Holy Land." PhD diss. Haifa, Technion, Israel Institute of Technology, 1992. [Hebrew].

Galor, K. "King Herod in Jerusalem: The Politics of Cultural Heritage." *Jerusalem Quarterly* 62 (2015): 65–80.

Galor, K., and G. Avni, eds. *Unearthing Jerusalem: 150 Years of Archaeological Research in the Holy City*. Winona Lake, IN: Eisenbrauns, 2011.

Galor, K., and H. Bloedhorn. *The Archaeology of Jerusalem: From the Origins to the Ottomans*. New Haven, CT: Yale University Press, 2013.

Garstang, J. "Eighteen Months Work of the Department of Antiquities for Palestine." *Palestine Exploration Quarterly* 54 (1922): 57–62.

Gerstenfeld, M. "The Academic Boycott against Israel." *Jewish Political Studies Review* 15, no. 3–4 (2003): 9–70.

Geva, H. "The Camp of the Tenth Legion in Jerusalem: An Archaeological Reconsideration." *Israel Exploration Journal* 34 (1984): 239–54.

———. *Jewish Quarter Excavations in the Old City of Jerusalem: Conducted by Nahman Avigad, 1969–1982*, vol. 1, *Architecture and Stratigraphy: Areas A, W and X-2. Final Report*. Jerusalem: Israel Exploration Society, 2000.

———. *Jewish Quarter Excavations in the Old City of Jerusalem: Conducted by Nahman Avigad, 1969–1982*, vol. 2, *The Finds from Areas A, W, and X-2, Final Report*. Jerusalem: Israel Exploration Society, 2003.

———. *Jewish Quarter Excavations in the Old City of Jerusalem: Conducted by Nahman Avigad, 1969–1982*, vol. 3, *Area E and Other Studies. Final Report*. Jerusalem: Israel Exploration Society, 2006.

———. *Jewish Quarter Excavations in the Old City of Jerusalem: Conducted by Nahman Avigad, 1969–1982,* vol. 4, *The Burnt House of Area B and Other Studies. Final Report.* Jerusalem: Israel Exploration Society, 2010.

Gibson, S. "British Archaeological Work in Jerusalem between 1865 and 1967: An Assessment." In Galor and Avni, *Unearthing Jerusalem,* 23–57.

———. "British Archaeological Institutions in Mandatory Palestine, 1917–1948." *Palestine Exploration Quarterly* 131, no. 2 (1999): 115–43.

Gibson, S., and D. M. Jacobson. *Below the Temple Mount in Jerusalem: A Sourcebook on the Cisterns, Subterranean Chambers and Conduits of the Haram al-Sharif.* BAR International Series 637. Oxford: Tempus Reparatum, 1996.

Gibson, S., and J. Taylor. *Beneath the Church of the Holy Sepulchre, Jerusalem: The Archeology and Early History of Traditional Golgotha.* London: Palestine Exploration Fund, 1994.

———. "New Excavations on Mount Zion in Jerusalem and an Inscribed Stone Cup/Mug from the Second Temple Period." In *New Studies in the Archaeology of Jerusalem and Its Region,* edited by D. Amit, O. Peleg-Barkat, and D. Stiebel, 32*–43*. Collected papers, vol. 4. Jerusalem: Israel Antiquities Authority and Institute of Archaeology, Hebrew University of Jerusalem, 2010.

Gitin, S. "The House that Albright Built." *Near Eastern Archaeology* 65, no. 1 (2002): 5–10.

Gitin, S., A. Ben-Tor, and B. Sekay. "Profiles of Archaeological Institutes: The Institute of Archaeology of the Hebrew University of Jerusalem." *The Biblical Archaeologist* 56 (1993): 121–52.

Gitlitz, D. M., and L. K. Davidson. *Pilgrimage and the Jews.* Westport, CT: Praeger, 2006.

Glock, A. "Archaeology as Cultural Survival: The Future of the Palestinian Past." *Journal of Palestine Studies* 23, no. 3 (1994): 70–84.

Gold, D. *The Fight for Jerusalem: Radical Islam, the West, and the Future of the Holy City.* Washington, DC: Regnery Publishing, 2009.

Goldhill, S. *Jerusalem: City of Longing.* Cambridge: Harvard University Press, 2010.

———. "Jerusalem." In *Cities of God. The Bible and Archaeology in Nineteenth-Century Britain,* edited by D. Gange and M. Ledger-Lomas, 71–110. Cambridge: Cambridge University Press, 2013.

Gonen, R. *Jewelry through the Ages at the Israel Museum.* Jerusalem: Israel Museum, 1997.

———, *Contested Holiness.* Jersey City: KTAV Publishing House, 2003.

Goode, J. *Negotiating for the Past: Archaeology, Nationalism, and Diplomacy in the Middle East, 1919–1941.* Austin: University of Texas Press, 2007.

Goodnick Westenholz, J., ed. *Three Faces of Monotheism.* Jerusalem: Bible Lands Museum Jerusalem, 2007.

Goren, Y., S. Ahituv, A. Ayalon, M. Bar-Matthews, U. Dahari, M. Dayagi-Mendels, A. Demsky, and N. Lavin. "A Re-Examination of the Inscribed Pomegranate from the Israel Museum." *Israel Exploration Journal* 55 (2005): 3–20.

Goren, Y., A. Ayalon, M. Bar-Matthews, and B. Schilman. "Authenticity Examination of the Jehoash Inscription." *Tel Aviv* 31 (2004): 3–16.

Grabar, O., and B. Z. Kedar, eds. *Where Heaven and Earth Meet: Jerusalem's Sacred Esplanade.* Jerusalem: Yad Ben-Zvi Press; Austin: University of Texas Press, 2009.

Greenberg, J. "Museum Exhibit Becomes Front in Israeli-Palestinian Struggle." *Washington Post.* February 13, 2013.

Greenberg, R. "Contested Sites: Archaeology and the Battle for Jerusalem." *Jewish Quarterly* 208 (2007): 20–26.

———. "Extreme Exposure: Archaeology in Jerusalem 1967–2007," *Conservation and Management of Archaeological Sites* 11 (2009): 262–281.

———. "Towards an Inclusive Archaeology in Jerusalem: The Case of Silwan/The City of David," *Public Archaeology* 8 (2009): 35–50.

———. *A Privatized Heritage: How the Israel Antiquities Authority Relinquished Jerusalem's Past.* Jerusalem: Emek Shaveh, 2014.

Greenberg, R., and A. Keinan. *Israeli Archaeological Activity in the West Bank 1967–2007: A Sourcebook: The West Bank and East Jerusalem Archaeological Database Project.* Jerusalem: Ostracon, 2009.

Greenberg, R., and Y. Mizrachi. *From Shiloah to Silwan Visitor's Guide to Ancient Jerusalem (City of David) and the Village of Silwan.* Jerusalem: Emek Shaveh, 2011.

Guinn, D. E. *Protecting Jerusalem's Holy Sites: A Strategy for Negotiating a Sacred Peace.* Cambridge: Cambridge University Press, 2006.

Gutfeld, O. *Jewish Quarter Excavations in the Old City of Jerusalem: Conducted by Nahman Avigad, 1969–1982, V: The Cardo (Area X) and the Nea Church (Areas D and T). Final Report.* Jerusalem: Israel Exploration Society, 2012.

Guthe, H. *Ausgrabungen bei Jerusalem.* Leipzig: K. Baedeker, 1883.

Hagbi, M., and J. Uziel. "Jerusalem, The Old City, The Western Wall Foundations." *Hadashot Arkheologiyot* 128 (2016).

Hallo, W. W., and K. L. Younger, Jr., eds. *The Context of Scripture, II: Monumental Inscriptions from the Biblical World.* Leiden: Brill, 2000.

Hallote, R., and A. Joffe. "The Politics of Archaeology: Between 'Nationalism' and 'Science' in the Age of the Second Republic," *Israel Studies* 7, no. 2 (2002): 84–116.

Hamilton, R.W. *The Structural History of the Aqsa Mosque: A Record of Archaeological Gleanings from the Repairs of 1938–1942.* Jerusalem: Department of Antiquities of Palestine, 1949.

Hanauer, E. "Model of a Columbarium. An Alleged Model of a Sanctuary from the Garden Tomb Grounds." *Palestine Exploration Quarterly* 56 (1924): 143–45.

Harvey, W. *Church of the Holy Sepulchre, Jerusalem; Structural Survey, Final Report, William Harvey, with an Introduction by E. T. Richmond.* London: Oxford University Press, 1935.

Hasson, N. "What to Do with the Graves?" *Ha'aretz.* May 20, 2010.

———. "Museum of Tolerance Special Report / Introduction." *Ha'aretz.* May 18, 2012.

———. "Archaeology without Conquest." *Ha'aretz.* May 30, 2012.

———. "In Jerusalem's City of David Excavation, Politics Is Never Absent." *Ha'aretz.* March 29, 2012.

———. "Petition Slams Tel Aviv University's Involvement in East Jerusalem Dig." *Ha'aretz.* December 25, 2012.

———. "Legal Challenges Mounted Against Planned Visitor Center in East Jeruaslem." *Ha'aretz.* January 1, 2014.

———. "Western Wall Plaza Facilities Cut to Size." *Ha'aretz.* June 13, 2014.

———. "East Jerusalem Remains 'Arab' Despite Jewish Settlers, Experts Say." *Ha'aretz,* October 2, 2014.

———. "Israel Antiquities Authority Taps Politician with Ties to Rightist NGO." *Ha'aretz.* October 29, 2014.

———. "Jerusalem Proceeding with Plan to Build on Old Muslim Cemetery." *Ha'aretz.* July 13, 2015.

———. "Jerusalem, The Descent. A Voyage In The Underground City." *Ha'aretz.* April 21, 2016 [Hebrew].

———. "After Trump's Swearing-In, Jerusalem Approves 566 Homes beyond Green Line." *Ha'aretz.* January 22, 2017 [Hebrew].

Hawari, M. K. "The Citadel (Qal'a) in the Ottoman Period. An Overview." In Auld and Hillenbrand, *Ottoman Jerusalem,* 493–518.

———. *Ayyubid Jerusalem (1187–1250): An Architectural and Archaeological Study.* Oxford: British Archaeological Reports, 2007.

———. " 'Capturing the Castle': Archaeology, Architecture and Political Bias at the Citadel of Jerusalem." *Jerusalem Quarterly* 55 (2013): 46–67.

Hendel, R. S. "The Date of the Siloam Inscription: A Rejoinder to Rogerson and Davies." *The Biblical Archaeologist* 59 (1996): 233–37.

Herzl, T. *The Complete Diaries of Theodor Herzl.* 2 volumes. Edited by R. Patai. London: Herzl Press with Thomas Yoseloff, 1960.

Hodder, I. *Theory and Practice in Archaeology.* London: Routledge, 1992.

———. *Entangled: An Archaeology of the Relationships between Humans and Things.* Malden, MA: Wiley-Blackwell, 2012.

Hübner, U. "The German Protestant Institute of Archaeology. Deutsches Evangelisches Institut für Altertumswissenschaft des Heiligen Landes." In Galor and Avni, *Unearthing Jerusalem,* 59–72.

Humbert, J.-B. "El-Fedein-Mafraq," *Liber Annuus* 36 (1986): 354–58.

———. "Aux racines cananéennes du Temple de Jérusalem." *Dédales* 3–4 (1996): 249–254.

———. "Le surprenant brasero omeyyade, trouvé à Mafraq." *Jordanie, sur les pas des archéologues.* Paris: Institut du Monde Arabe, 1997.

———. "Fouilles du tombeau des Rois: rapport préliminaire 2008–2009." *École biblique et archéologique française de Jérusalem* (2009): 1–14.

———. "Saint John Prodromos Restoration Project Jerusalem. Greek Orthodox Patriarchate property, Jerusalem." *Cabinet d'architects des monuments historiques, Michel Goutal (Paris) Excavation of the École biblique et archéologique française de Jérusalem* (2011): 2–81.

Ibrahim, F. *West Meets East: The Story of the Rockefeller Museum.* Jerusalem: Israel Museum, 2006.

Ilan, D., U. Dahari, and G. Avni. "Plundered! The Rampant Rape of Israel's Archaeological Sites." *Biblical Archaeology Review* 15, no. 2 (1989): 38–42.

Ilan, O., D. Tal, and M. Haramati. *Image and Artifact: Treasures of the Rockefeller Museum.* Jerusalem: The Israel Museum, 2000.

Ilani, S., A. Rosenfeld, H. R. Feldman, W. E. Krumbein, and J. Kronfeld, "Archaeometric Analysis of the "Jehoash Inscription" Tablet." *Journal of Archaeological Science* 35 (2008): 2966–72.

Inbari, M. "The Oslo Accords and the Temple Mount, A Case Study: The Movement for the Establishment of the Temple." *Hebrew Union College Annual* 74 (2003): 279–323.

———. "Religious Zionism and the Temple Mount Dilemma—Key Trends." *Israel Studies* 12, no. 2 (2007): 29–47.

———. *Jewish Fundamentalism and the Temple Mount: Who Will Build the Third Temple?* Albany: State University of New York Press, 2009.

Israel Antiquities Authority. "The Conservation of Jerusalem's City Walls." www.antiquities.org.il/jerusalemwalls/about_eng.asp.

Israel, Y., and D. Mevorah, eds. *Cradle of Christianity.* Jerusalem: Israel Museum, 2000.

Israeli, R., S. Berkovits, J. Neriah, and M. Hier. "Critical Response II: 'The Architecture of Erasure'—Fantasy or Reality?" *Critical Inquiry* 36 (2009/10): 563–94.

Johns, C. N. "Excavations at the Citadel, Jerusalem, Interim Report, 1935." *Quarterly of the Department of Antiquities of Palestine* 5 (1936): 127–31.

———. "The Citadel, Jerusalem: A Summary of Work since 1934." *Quarterly of the Department of Antiquities of Palestine* 14 (1950): 121–90.

Jones, S. "Nationalism, Archaeology and the Interpretation of Ethnicity in Ancient Palestine." *Boletim do Centro de Estudos e Documentação Sobre o Pensamento Antigo Clássico, Helenístico e sua Posteridade Histórica* (1997): 49–80.

Jote, K. *International Legal Protection of Cultural Heritage.* Stockholm: Jurisförlaget, 1994.

al-Jubeh, N. "Bab al-Magharibah: Joha's Nail in the Haram al-Sharif," *Jerusalem Quarterly File* 18 (2003): 17–24.

———. "Palestinian Identity and Cultural Heritage." In *Temps et espaces en Palestine, Contemporain publications,* No. 25, edited by R. Heacock, 205–31. Beirut, Lebanon: Institut français du Proche-Orient, 2005.

———. "1917 to the Present: Basic Changes, but Not Dramatic: Al-Haram al-Sharif in the Aftermath of 1967." In Grabar and Kedar, *Where Heaven and Earth Meet,* 275–89.

Kaplony, A. *The Haram of Jerusalem 324–1099. Temple, Friday Mosque, Area of Spiritual Power.* Stuttgart: Franz Steiner Verlag, 2002.

Kark, R. "The Traditional Middle Eastern City: The Cases of Jerusalem and Jaffa during the Nineteenth Century." *Zeitschrift des Deutschen Palästina-Vereins* 97 (1981): 93–108.

Kark, R., and S. J. Frantzman. "The Protestant Garden Tomb in Jerusalem, Englishwomen, and a Land Transaction in Late Ottoman Palestine." *Palestine Exploration Quarterly* 142 (2010): 199–216.

Kark, R., and S. Landman. "The Establishment of Muslim Neighbourhoods in Jerusalem, Outside the Old City, during the Late Ottoman Period." *Palestine Exploration Quarterly* 112 (1980): 113–35.

Kark, R., and M. Oren-Nordheim. *Jerusalem and Its Environs: Quarters, Neighborhoods, Villages, 1880–1948.* Detroit: Wayne State University Press, 2001.

Katsimbinis, C. "The Uncovering of the Eastern Side of the Hill of Calvary and Its Base," *Liber Annus* 27 (1977): 197–208.

Katz, K. *Jordanian Jerusalem: Holy Places and National Spaces.* Gainesville: University Press of Florida, 2005.

Kedar, B. Z., S. Weksler-Bdolah, and T. Da'adli. "The Madrasa Afdaliyya / Maqam Al-Shaykh 'Id: An Example Of Ayyubid Architecture in Jerusalem." *Revue Biblique* 119 (2012): 271–87.

Kempinski, A. Editorial in *Archaeology. Bulletin of the Israel Association of Archaeologists* 3 (1992): 5 [Hebrew].

Kenyon, K. M. *Jerusalem: Excavating 3000 Years of History.* London: Thames & Hudson, 1967.

———. *Digging Up Jerusalem.* London: Praeger, 1974.

Kersel, M. M. "From the Ground to the Buyer: A Market Analysis of the Illegal Trade in Antiquities." In *Archaeology, Cultural Heritage and the Antiquities Trade,* edited by N. Brodie, M. Kersel, C. Luke, and W. Tubb, 188–205. Gainesville: University Press of Florida, 2006.

———. "Transcending Borders: Objects on the Move." *Archaeologies: Journal of the World Archaeological Congress* 3 (2007): 81–98.

———. "The Trade in Palestinian Antiquities." *Jerusalem Quarterly* 33 (2008): 21–38.

———. "When Communities Collide: Competing Claims for Archaeological Objects in the Market Place." *Archaeologies: Journal of the World Archaeological Congress* 7 (2011): 518–37.

———. "The Value of a Looted Object. Stakeholder Perceptions." In *The Oxford Handbook of Public Archaeology,* edited by R. Skeates, C. McDavid, and J. Carman, 253–72. Oxford: Oxford University Press, 2012.

Kersel, M., and R. Kletter, "Heritage for Sale? A Case Study from Israel," *Journal of Field Archaeology* 31 (2006): 317–27.

Kershner, I. *The Seam of the Israeli-Palestinian Conflict.* New York: St. Martin's Press, 2005.

King, P. J. *American Archaeology in the Mideast: A History of the American Schools of Oriental Research.* Philadelphia: ASOR, 1983.

King, T. F. "Professional Responsibility in Public Archaeology." *Annual Review of Anthropology* 12 (1983): 143–64.

Kirzner, I. "Competition, Regulating, and the Market Process: An 'Austrian' Perspective." *Cato Policy Analysis* No. 18. Washington: Cato Institute, 1982.

Klein, M. "Jerusalem as an Israeli Problem—A Review of Forty Years of Israeli Rule over Arab Jerusalem." *Israel Studies* 13.2 (2008): 54–72.

Kletter, R. "A Very General Archaeologist—Moshe Dayan and Israeli Archaeology." *The Journal of Hebrew Scriptures* 4 (2002–03): Article 5.

———. *Just Past? The Making of Israeli Archaeology.* London: Equinox, 2005.

Kletter, R., and G. Solimani "Archaeology and Professional Ethical Codes in Israel in the Mid-80s: The Case of the Association of the Archaeologists in Israel and Its Code of Ethics." *The Journal of Hebrew Scriptures* 10 (2010): Article 4.

Kloner, A. *Survey of Jerusalem, the Southern Sector.* Jerusalem: Israel Antiquities Authority—Archaeological Survey of Israel, 2000.

———. *Survey of Jerusalem, the Northeastern Sector.* Jerusalem: Israel Antiquities Authority—Archaeological Survey of Israel, 2001.

———. *Survey of Jerusalem, the Northwestern Sector: Introduction and Indices.* Jerusalem: Israel Antiquities Authority—Archaeological Survey of Israel, 2003.

Kloppenborg Verbin, J. S. "Dating Theodotos ('CIJ' II 1404)." *Journal of Jewish Studies* 51 (2000): 243–80.

Knauf, E. A. "Jerusalem in the Late Bronze and Early Iron Ages. A Proposal." *Tel Aviv* 27 (2000): 75–90.

———. "Jehoash's Improbable Inscription." *Biblische Notizen* 117 (2003): 22–26.

Kohl, P. "Nationalism and Archaeology: On the Construction of Nations and the Reconstruction of the Remote Past." *Annual Review of Anthropology* 27 (1998): 223–46.

Kohl, P., and C. Fawcett, eds. *Nationalism, Politics, and the Practice of Archaeology*. Cambridge: Cambridge University Press, 1995.

Krystall, N. "The De-Arabization of West Jerusalem 1947–50." *Journal of Palestine Studies* 27, no. 2 (1998): 5–22.

Kulka, T., E. Cohen-Bar, and S. Kronish, *Bimkom: From Public to National Parks in East Jerusalem*. Jerusalem: New National Fund, 2012.

Lapidoth, R. *The Historic Basin of Jerusalem: Problems and Possible Solutions*. Jerusalem: Jerusalem Institute for Israel Studies, 2010.

Larkin, C., and M. Dumper. "UNESCO and Jerusalem: Constraints, Challenges and Opportunities." *Jerusalem Quarterly* 39 (2009): 16–28.

———. "In Defense of al-Aqsa: The Islamic Movement inside Israel and the Battle for Jerusalem." *Middle East Journal* 66 (2012): 31–52.

Lefkovits, E. "Was the Aksa Mosque Built over the Remains of a Byzantine Church?" *Jerusalem Post*. November 16, 2008.

Lemaire, A. "Une inscription paléo-hébraïque sur une grenade en ivoire." *Revue Biblique* 88 (1981): 236–39.

———. "Probable Head of Priestly Scepter from Solomon's Temple Surfaces in Jerusalem." *Biblical Archaeology Review* 10.1 (1984): 24–29.

———. "A Re-examination of the Inscribed Pomegranate: A Rejoinder." *Israel Exploration Journal* 56 (2006): 167–77.

Lemche, N. P., and T. L. Thompson. "Did Biran Kill David? The Bible in the Light of Archaeology." *Journal for the Study of the Old Testament* 64 (1994): 3–22.

Lemire, V. *La soif de Jérusalem: Essai d'hydrohistoire (1840–1948)*. Paris: Publications de la Sorbonne, 2011.

Levanon, Y. *The Jewish Travellers in the Twelfth Century*. Lanham: University Press of America, 1980.

Levine, L. I. *The Ancient Synagogue: The First Thousand Years*. New Haven: Yale University Press, 2000.

———. *Jerusalem: A Portrait of the City in the Second Temple Period (538 B.C.E.–70 C.E.* Philadelphia: Jewish Publication Society, 2002.

Levy, S. "Human Rights Groups Accuse NBC of Deceit about DIG Filming Locations in Occupied East Jerusalem." *Jewish Voice for Peace*. June 5, 2014.

Lindén, G. *Church Leadership in a Political Crisis: Joint Statements from the Jerusalem Heads of Churches, 1988–1992*. Uppsala: Swedish Institute of Missionary Research, 1994.

Long, B. O. *Imagining the Holy Land: Maps, Models, and Fantasy Travels*. Bloomington: University Press, 2003.

Macalister, R. A. S., and J. G. Duncan. *Excavations of the Hill of Ophel, Jerusalem, 1923–1925: Being the Joint Expedition of the Palestine Exploration Fund and the "Daily Telegraph."* Annual of the Palestine Exploration Fund 4. (London: Palestine Exploration Fund, 1926.

Makdisi, S. "The Architecture of Erasure." *Critical Inquiry* 36 (2009/10): 519–59.

Marchand, S. *Down from Olympus: Archaeology and Philhellenism in Germany, 1750–1970*. Princeton: Princeton University Press, 1996.

Mare, W. H. *The Archaeology of the Jerusalem Area*. Grand Rapids, MI: Baker Book House, 1987.

Masalha, N. *The Zionist Bible: Biblical Precedent, Colonialism, and the Erasure of Memory.* London: Routledge, 2013.

Mazar, A. "Iron Age Burial Caves North of Damascus Gate Jerusalem." *Israel Exploration Journal* 26 (1976): 1–8.

———. "Jerusalem in the 10th Century B.C.E.: The Glass Half Full." In *Essays on Ancient Israel in Its Near Eastern Context: A Tribute to Nadav Na'aman,* edited by Y. Amit, E. Ben Zvi, I. Finkelstein, and O. Lipschits, 255–72. Winona Lake, IN: Eisenbrauns, 2006.

Mazar, E. *The Complete Guide to the Temple Mount Excavations.* Jerusalem: Shoham Academic Research and Publication, 2002.

———. "Did I Find King David's Palace?" *Biblical Archaeology Review* 32, no. 1 (2006): 16–27, 70.

———. *Preliminary Report on the City of David Excavations 2005 at the Visitors Center Area.* Jerusalem: Shalem Press, 2007.

———. *Discovering the Solomonic Wall in Jerusalem: A Remarkable Archaeological Adventure.* Jerusalem: Shoham Academic Research and Publication, 2011.

———. *The Walls of the Temple Mount.* Jerusalem: Shoham Academic Research and Publication, 2011.

Mazar, E., and B. Mazar. *Excavations in the South of the Temple Mount: The Ophel of Biblical Jerusalem.* Qedem 29. Jerusalem: Institute of Archaeology, Hebrew University, 1989.

McBirnie, W. S. *The Search for the Authentic Tomb of Jesus.* Montrose: Acclaimed Books, 1975.

McCarthy, J. *The Population of Palestine: Population History and Statistics of the Late Ottoman Period and the Mandate.* New York: Columbia University Press, 1990.

Meiron, E., ed. *City of David Studies of Ancient Jerusalem. The 12th Annual Conference.* Jerusalem: Megalim City of David Institute for Jerusalem Studies, 2011.

Merryman, J. H. "A Licit International Trade in Cultural Objects." *International Journal of Cultural Property* 4.1 (1995): 13–60.

Meyers, E., and C. Meyers *Archaeology, Bible, Politics, and the Media.* Winona Lake, IN: Eisenbrauns, 2012.

Mizrachi, Y. *Archaeology in the Shadow of the Conflict. The Mound of Ancient Jerusalem (City of David) in Silwan.* Jerusalem: Emek Shaveh, 2010.

———. *Between Holiness and Propaganda. Archaeology and Political Claims over the Old City of Jerusalem.* Jerusalem: Emek Shaveh, 2011.

———. *From Silwan to the Temple Mount: Archaeological Excavations as a Means of Control in the Village of Silwan and in Jerusalem's Old City—Developments in 2012.* Jerusalem: Emek Shaveh, 2012.

———. *The Mamilla Cemetery in West Jerusalem: A Heritage Site at the Crossroads of Politics and Real Estate.* Jerusalem: Emek Shaveh, 2012.

———. *Remaking the City. Archaeological Projects of Political Import in Jerusalem's Old City and in the Village of Silwan.* Jerusalem: Emek Shaveh, 2013.

———. "Exhibition on Loan: How Israel's Cultural Institutions Contribute to Occupation," *972 Magazine,* May 4, 2013.

———. *Archaeological Activities in Politically Sensitive Areas in Jerusalem's Historic Basin.* Jerusalem: Emek Shaveh, 2015.

Moe, J. M. "Project Archaeology: Putting the Intrigue of the Past in Public Education." In *The Public Benefits of Archaeology*, edited by B. J. Little, 176–86. Gainsesville: University Press of Florida, 2002.

Montgomery, W. *Muhammad: Prophet and Statesman*. Oxford: Oxford University Press, 1974.

Moore, N., and Y. Whelan, eds. *Heritage, Memory and the Politics of Identity: New Perspectives on the Cultural Landscape*. Aldershot, England: Ashgate, 2008.

Murphy O'Connor, J. *The Holy Land. An Archaeological Guide from Earliest Times to 1700*. 5th rev. and expanded ed. London: Oxford University Press, 2008.

Na'aman, N. "The Contribution of the Amarna Letters to the Debate on Jerusalem's Political Position in the Tenth Century BCE." *Bulletin of the American Schools of Oriental Research* 304 (1996): 17–27.

Natsheh, Y. "The Architecture of Ottoman Jerusalem." In Auld and Hillenbrand, *Ottoman Jerusalem, 583–655*.

———. "Catalogue of Buildings." In Auld and Hillenbrand, *Ottoman Jerusalem*, 657–1085.

Netzer, E. "Reconstruction of the Jewish Quarter in the Old City." In Yadin, *Jerusalem Revealed*, 118–21.

Noy, C. "Peace Activism in Tourism: Two Case Studies (and a Few Reflections) in Jerusalem." In *Peace through Tourism: Promoting Human Security Through International Citizenship*, edited by L. Blanchard and F. Higgins-Desbiolles, 204–216. New York: Routledge, 2013.

Oestigaard, T. *Political Archaeology and Holy Nationalism: Archaeological Battles over the Bible and Land in Israel and Palestine from 1967–2000*. Gotarc Series C, no. 67. Gothenburg, Sweden: Gothenburg University Press, 2007.

Ollendorff, F. "Two Mamluk Tomb-Chambers in Western Jerusalem." *Israel Exploration Journal* 32 (1982): 245–50.

Onn, A., S. Weksler-Bdolah, and R. Bar-Nathan. "Jerusalem, The Old City, Wilson's Arch and the Great Causeway. Preliminary Report." *Hadashot Arkheologiyot* 123 (2011): [15/8/2011].

Ornan, T. *A Man and His Land: Highlights from the Moshe Dayan Collection*. Israel Museum Catalogue 270. Jerusalem: Israel Museum, 1986.

Oyediran, J. *Plunder, Destruction and Despoliation: An Analysis of Israel's Violations of the International Law of Cultural Property in the Occupied West Bank and Gaza Strip*. Ramallah: Al-Haq, 1997.

Patrich, J. "The Church of the Holy Sepulchre in the Light of Excavations and Restoration." In *Ancient Churches Revealed*, edited by Y. Tsafrir, 101–17. Jerusalem: Israel Exploration Society, 1993.

Pels, P., ed. *Embedding Ethics: Shifting Boundaries of the Anthropological Profession*. Oxford: Berg Publishers, 2005.

Peters, F. E. *Jerusalem: The Holy City in the Eyes of Chroniclers, Visitors, Pilgrims, and Prophets from the Days of Abraham to the Beginnings of Modern Times*. Princeton: Princeton University Press, 1985.

Phytian-Adams, W. J. *Guide Book to the Palestine Museum of Antiquities*. Jerusalem: The Department of Antiquities, 1924.

Piccirillo, M., "The Archaeology of Jerusalem and the Franciscans of the Studium Biblicum." In Galor and Avni, *Unearthing Jerusalem*, 109–16.

Pollock, S., and R. Bernbeck, eds. *Archaeologies of the Middle East: Critical Perspectives.* Maiden: Blackwell, 2005.

Prag, K. *Excavations by K. M. Kenyon in Jerusalem 1961–1967,* V: *Discoveries in Hellenistic to Ottoman Jerusalem.* Levant Supplementary Series, Vol. 7. London: Council for British Research in the Levant, 2008.

Press, I. "Compte rendu du secrétaire," *recueil publié par la Société Hébraïque d'Exploration et d'Archéologie Palestiniennes* 1.1 (1921) : 91–94 [Hebrew].

Pritchard, J. B. *Archaeology and the Old Testament.* Princeton: Princeton University Press, 1958.

Prior, M. "Holy Places, Unholy Domination: The Scramble for Jerusalem," *Islamic Studies* 40 (2001): 507–30.

Pullan, W., and M. Gwiazda. " 'City of David': Urban Design and Frontier Heritage." *Jerusalem Quarterly* 39 (2009): 29–38.

Pullan, W., and M. Sternberg. "The Making of Jerusalem's 'Holy Basin.' " *Planning Perspectives* 27, no. 2 (2012): 225–48.

Pullan, W., M. Sternberg, K. Lefkos, C. Larkin, and M. Dumper. *The Struggle for Jerusalem's Holy Places.* New York: Routledge, 2013.

Rahat, G. "Determinants of Party Cohesion: Evidence from the Case of the Israeli Parliament." *Parliamentary Affairs* 60 (2007): 279–96.

Rahat, G., and R. Y. Hazan. "Candidate Selection Methods: An Analytical Framework." *Party Politics* 7 (2001): 297–322.

Rahmani, L. Y. "Ancient Jerusalem's Funerary Customs and Tombs: Part Four." *The Biblical Archaeologist* 45 (1982): 109–19.

Reich, R. "God Knows Their Names: Mass Christian Grave Revealed in Jerusalem." *Biblical Archaeology Review* 22, no. 2 (1996): 26–33, 60.

———. "The Israel Exploration Society (IES)." In Galor and Avni, *Unearthing Jerusalem,* 117–24.

———. *Excavating the City of David: Where Jerusalem's History Began.* Jerusalem: Israel Exploration Society and Biblical Archaeology Society, 2011.

Reich, R., G. Avni, and T. Winter. *The Jerusalem Archaeological Park.* Jerusalem: Israel Antiquities Authority, 1999.

Reich, R., and Y. Billig. "Jerusalem, Robinson's Arch." *Excavations and Surveys in Israel* 20 (2000): 135*.

Reich, R., and E. Shukron. "Light at the End of the Tunnel." *Biblical Archaeology Review* 25, no. 1 (1999): 22–33, 72.

———. "Jerusalem, City of David, the Giv'ati Car Park." *Hadashot Arkheologiyot* 117 (2005) [31/10/2005].

———. "The Second Temple Period Central Drainage Channel in Jerusalem—Upon the Completion of the Unearthing of Its Southern Part in 2011." In *City of David Studies of Ancient Jerusalem. The 12th Annual Conference,* edited by E. Meiron, 68*–95*. Jerusalem: Megalim City of David Institute for Jerusalem Studies, 2011.

Reiter, Y. "The Administration and Supervision of Waqf Properties in 20th Century Jerusalem." In *Varia Turcica,* 169–82. Istanbul: Institut Français d'Études Anatoliennes 26, 1994.

———. *Islamic Endowments in Jerusalem under British Mandate.* London and Portland: Frank Cass, 1996.

———. *Islamic Institutions in Jerusalem: Palestinian Muslim Administration under Jordanian and Israeli Rule.* The Hague, London, and Boston: Kluwer Law International, 1997.

Reiter, Y., and J. Seligman. "1917 to the Present: Al-Haram al-Sharif / Temple Mount (Har Ha-Bayit) and the Western Wall." In Grabar and Kedar, *Where Heaven and Earth Meet,* 231–73.

Reith, I. H. "A Dome in Jerusalem." *Structural Engineer* 60A (1982): 23–28.

———. "Discussion: A Dome in Jerusalem." *Structural Engineer* 61A (1983): 126–27.

Ricca, S. *Reinventing Jerusalem: Israel's Reconstruction of the Jewish Quarter After 1967.* London: I. B. Tauris, 2007.

Richman, J., and M. Forsyth, eds. *Legal Perspectives on Cultural Resources.* Walnut Creek, CA: Altamira Press, 2004, 85–99.

Richmond, E. T. *The Dome of the Rock in Jerusalem. A Description of Its Structure and Decoration.* Oxford, 1924.

Ritmeyer, L. *The Quest: Revealing the Temple Mount in Jerusalem* Jerusalem: Carta and The Lamb Foundation, 2006.

Rogerson, J., and P. R. Davies. "Was the Siloam Tunnel Built by Hezekiah?" *The Biblical Archaeologist* 59 (1996): 138–49.

Rollston, C. "Non-Provenanced Epigraphs I: Pillaged Antiquities, Northwest Semitic Forgeries, and Protocols for Laboratory Tests." *Maarav* 10 (2003): 135–93.

———. "Non-Provenanced Epigraphs II: The Status of Non-Provenanced Epigraphs within the Broader Corpus of Northwest Semitic." *Maarav* 11 (2004): 57–79.

Romey, K. "Jerusalem's Temple Mount Flap." *Archaeology* 53, no. 2 (2000): 20.

———. "Exclusive: Christ's Burial Place Exposed for the First Time in Centuries." *National Geographic,* October 26, 2016.

Rossoff, D. *Where Heaven Touches Earth: Jewish Life in Jerusalem From Medieval Times to the Present.* Jerusalem: Guardian Press, 1988.

Rubinstein, S. "The Establishment and Beginnings of the Institute for the Study of Jewish Communities in the East." *Pe'amim* 23 (1985): 127–49.

Rudoren, J. "Anger That a Herod Show Uses West Bank Objects." *New York Times,* February 13, 2013.

Safrai, Z., and A. Faust, eds. *Recent Innovations in the Study of Jerusalem: The First Conference, September 12th 1995.* Ramat Gan: Bar-Ilan University, Faculty of Jewish Studies, 1995.

Salameh, K. *The Qur'an Manuscripts in the al-Haram al-Sharif Islamic Museum.* Reading, England: Garnet; Paris: UNESCO, 2001.

de Saulcy, F. *Voyage autour de la mer Morte et dans les terres bibliques, exécuté de décembre 1850 à avril 1851.* 2 volumes. Paris: J. Baudry, 1853.

Scham, S. A. "Mediating Nationalism and Archaeology: A Matter of Trust?" *American Anthropologist* 100 (1998): 301–8.

Scham, S., and A. Yahya. "Heritage and Reconciliation." *Journal of Social Archaeology* 3 (2003): 399–416.

Schick, C. "Gordon's Tomb." *Palestine Exploration Quarterly* 24 (1892): 120–24.

———. *Beit el Makdas oder der alte Tempelplatz zu Jerusalem, wie er jetzt ist* (Jerusalem: Selbstverlag des Verfassers, 1887).

———. "Recent Discoveries in Jerusalem." *Palestine Exploration Quarterly* 21 (1889): 62–63.

————. *Die Stiftshütte, der Tempelplatz der Jetztzeit* (Berlin: Weidmann, 1896).

Schmelz, U. O. "Notes on the Demography of Jews, Muslims and Christians in Jerusalem." *Middle East Review* 13 (1981): 62–68.

Schölch, A. "Jerusalem in the 19ᵗʰ Century (1831–1917)," in *Jerusalem in History*, 228–48. New York: Olive Branch Press, 1990.

Scott, J. B., ed. *The Hague Conventions and Declarations of 1899 and 1907, Accompanied by Tables of Signatures, Ratifications and Adhesions of The Various Powers and Texts of Reservations.* New York: Oxford University Press, 1918.

Seger, J. D., ed. *An ASOR Mosaic: A Centennial History of the American Schools of Oriental Research, 1900–2000.* Boston: ASOR, 2001.

Selig, A. "Jerusalem Court Halts Silwan Construction." *The Jerusalem Post*, September 10, 2009.

Seligman, J. "Solomon's Stables, the Temple Mount, Jerusalem: The Events Concerning the Destruction of Antiquities 1999–2001." *'Atiqot* 56 (2007): 33*–53*

————. "The Departments of Antiquities and the Israel Antiquities Authority (1918–2006): The Jerusalem Experience." In Galor and Avni, *Unearthing Jerusalem*, 125–46.

————. "The Archaeology of Jerusalem—Between Post-Modernism and Delegitimization." *Public Archaeology* 12, no. 3 (2013): 181–99.

Seligman, J., and G. Avni, "Jerusalem, Church of the Holy Sepulchre." *Hadashot Arkheologiyot* 111 (2000): 69*–70*.

————. "New Excavations at the Church of the Holy Sepulchre Compound." In *One Land—Many Cultures: Archaeological Studies in Honour of Stanislao Loffreda OFM*, edited by G. C., Bottini, L. Di Segni, and L. D. Chrupcala, 153–162. Jerusalem: Franciscan Printing Press, 2003.

Shanks, H. "Death Knell for Israel Archaeology." *Biblical Archaeology Review* 22, no. 5 (1996): 48–53.

————. "Assessing the Jehoash Inscription." *Biblical Archaeology Review* 29, no. 3 (2003): 26–28.

————. " 'Brother of Jesus' Inscription Is Authentic!" *Biblical Archaeology Review* 38, no. 4 (2012): 26–33, 62–65.

Shapira, R. "Ruins from Ancient Syrian Synagogue Put on Display in Israel after 63-Year Delay." *Ha'aretz.* July 17, 2011.

Shavit, Y. "Archaeology, Political-Culture, and Culture in Israel." In Silberman and Small, *The Archaeology of Israel*, 48–61.

Shay, T. "Israeli Archaeology—Ideology and Practice." *Antiquity* 63 (1989): 768–72.

Shiloh, Y. *Excavations at the City of David, I: 1978–1982, Interim Report of the First Five Seasons.* Qedem 19. Jerusalem: Institute of Archaeology, Hebrew University, 1984.

Silberman, N. A. "In Search of Solomon's Lost Treasures." *Biblical Archaeology Review* 6, no. 4 (1980).

————. *Digging for God and Country: Exploration, Archeology and the Secret Struggle for the Holy Land, 1799–1917.* New York: Knopf, 1982.

————. *Between Past and Present: Archaeology, Ideology, and Nationalism in the Modern Middle East.* New York: Holt, 1989.

————. "Power, Politics, and the Past: The Social Construction of Antiquity in the Holy Land." In *The Archaeology of Society in the Holy Land*, edited by T. E. Levy, 9–23. London: Leicester University Press, 1990.

Silberman, N. A., and D. Small, eds. *The Archaeology of Israel: Constructing the Past, Interpreting the Present.* Sheffield: Sheffield Academic Publisher, 1997.

Simmermacher, G. *The Holy Land Trek: A Pilgrim's Guide.* Cape Town: Southern Cross Books, 2012.

Simons, J. *Jerusalem in the Old Testament: Researches and Theories.* Leiden: Brill, 1952.

Sivan, R. "Le Musée d'Histoire, Jerusalem 5000 Years of History." *Les Dossiers d'Archéologie* 165 (1991): 132–37.

———. "The Presentation of Archaeological Sites." In *The Conservation of Archaeological Sites in the Mediterranean Region. An International Conference Organized by the Getty Conservation Institute and the J. Paul Getty Museum, 6–12 May 1995,* edited by M. de la Torre, 51–59. Los Angeles: The Getty Conservation Institute, 1997).

Slae, B., R. Kark, and N. Shoval. "Post-War Reconstruction and Conservation of the Historic Jewish Quarter in Jerusalem, 1967–1975." *Planning Perspectives* 27 (2012): 369–92.

Smardz, K., and S. J. Smith. *The Archaeology Education Handbook: Sharing the Past with Kids.* Walnut Creek, CA: Altamira, 2000.

Smith, L. *Archaeological Theory and the Politics of Cultural Heritage.* London: Routledge, 2004.

Snyder, J. S. *Renewed. The Israel Museum, Jerusalem Campus Renewal Project.* Jerusalem: The Israel Museum, 2011.

Spaer, M. *Ancient Glass in the Israel Museum. Beads and Other Small Objects.* Jerusalem: Israel Museum, 2001.

Steiner, M. L. "Redating the Terraces of Jerusalem." *Israel Exploration Journal* 44 (1994): 13–20.

———. *Excavations by Kathleen M. Kenyon in Jerusalem 1961–1967, Volume III: The Settlement in the Bronze and Iron Ages.* Sheffield: Sheffield Academic Press, 2001.

———. "The Evidence from Kenyon's Excavations in Jerusalem: A Response Essay." In Vaughn and Killebrew, *Jerusalem in Bible and Archaeology: The First Temple Period,* 347–63.

St. Laurent, B., and I. Awwad, "The Marwani Musalla in Jerusalem: New Findings." *Jerusalem Quarterly* 54 (2013): 7–30.

Stone, P., and R. MacKenzie, eds. *The Excluded Past: Archaeology in Education.* London: Unwin Hyman, 1990.

Stone, P. G., and B. L. Molyneaux, eds. *The Presented Past: Heritage, Museums and Education.* London: Routledge, 1999.

Sukenik, E. L., and L. A. Mayer, *The Third Wall of Jerusalem: An Account of Excavations.* Jerusalem: University Press, 1930.

———. "A New Section of the Third Wall, Jerusalem." *Palestine Exploration Quarterly* 76 (1944): 145–51.

Taylor-Guthartz, L., ed. *A Guide to the Collection.* 3rd rev. ed. Jerusalem: Bible Lands Museum Jerusalem, 2002.

Thomas, D. *Skull Wars.* New York: Basic Books, 2000.

Titchen, S. *On the Construction of Outstanding Universal Value: UNESCO's World Heritage Convention and the Identification and Assessment of Cultural Places for Inclusion in the World Heritage List.* PhD diss. Canberra: Australian National University, 1995.

Trimbur, D. "The École Biblique et Archéologique Française." In Galor and Avni, *Unearthing Jerusalem,* 95–108.

Tsafrir, Y. *Eretz Israel from the Destruction of the Second Temple to the Muslim Conquest.* Vol. 2 Jerusalem: Yad Ben-Zvi, 1984 [Hebrew].

———., ed. *Ancient Churches Revealed.* Jerusalem: Israel Exploration Society, 1993.

———. "Procopius and the Nea Church in Jerusalem." *Antiquité Tardive* 8 (2001): 149–64.

Tsimhoni, D. "Demographic Trends of the Christian Population in Jerusalem and the West Bank 1948–1978." *Middle East Journal* 37 (1983): 54–64.

Tushingham, A. D., and M. L. Steiner. *Excavations in Jerusalem, 1961–1967.* Vol. 4. Ontario: Royal Ontario Museum, 1985.

Ussishkin, D. "Solomon's Jerusalem: The Text and the Facts on the Ground." In Vaughn and Killebrew, *Jerusalem in Bible and Archaeology: The First Temple Period,* 103–15.

Uziel, J., and I. Shai. "Iron Age Jerusalem: Temple-Palace, Capital City." *Journal of the American Oriental Society* 127 (2007): 161–70.

Vaughn, A. G., and A. E. Killebrew, eds. *Jerusalem in Bible and Archaeology: The First Temple Period.* Society of Biblical Literature Symposium Series 18. Atlanta: Society of Biblical Literature, 2003.

Vieweger, D., and G. Förder-Hoff. *The Archaeological Park under the Church of the Redeemer in Jerusalem.* Jerusalem: German Protestant Institute of Archaeology, 2013.

Vincent, H. *Jérusalem sous terre: les récentes fouilles d'Ophel.* London: H. Cox, 1911.

———. "Les récentes fouilles d'Ophel" [1]. *Revue Biblique* 20 (1911): 219–65, 566–91.

———. "Les récentes fouilles d'Ophel" [2]. *Revue Biblique* 21 (1912): 86–111, 424–53, 544–74.

———. "Garden Tomb: histoire d'un mythe." *Revue Biblique* 34 (1925): 401–31.

Vincent, L.-H., and F.-M. Abel. *Jérusalem nouvelle: recherches de topographie, d'archéologie et d'histoire,* II, 1–4 Paris: J. Gabalda, 1914–26.

Vincent, L.-H., and M.-A. Steve. *Jérusalem de l'Ancien Testament: recherches d'archéologie et d'histoire,* I–III. Paris: J. Gabalda, 1954–56.

Vitelli, K., and C. Colwell-Chanthaphon. *Archaeological Ethics.* 2nd ed. (Walnut Creek, CA: Altamira, 2006).

Viviano, B. T., "Profiles of Archaeological Institutes: École Biblique et Archéologique Française de Jérusalem," *The Biblical Archaeologist* 54 (1991): 160–67.

de Vogüé, M. *Les églises de Terre Sainte: fragments d'un voyage en Orient.* Paris: Lib. De V. Didron, 1860.

Von Hagen, V. W. F. *Catherwood, Architect-Explorer of Two Worlds.* Barre, MA: Barre Publishers, 1968.

Warren, C. *Underground Jerusalem.* London: Palestine Exploration Fund, 1876.

Warren, C., and C. R. Conder. *The Survey of Western Palestine: Jerusalem.* London: Palestine Exploration Fund, 1884.

Watson, P., and C. Todeschini, *The Medici Conspiracy: The Illicit Journey of Looted Antiquities from Italy's Tomb Raiders to the World's Greatest Museums.* New York: PublicAffairs, 2007.

Waxman, S. *Loot: The Battle over the Stolen Treasures of the Ancient World.* New York: New York Times Books, 2008.

Weber, M. "Wissenschaft als Beruf." *Gesammelte Aufsätze zur Wissenschaftslehre* (Tübingen 1922): 524–55.

Webb, T. "Appropriating the Stones: The 'Elgin Marbles' an English National Taste." In Barkan and Bush, *Claiming the Stones, Naming the Bones,* 51–96.

Weill, R. *La cité de David: compte rendu des fouilles exécutées à Jérusalem, sur le site de la ville primitive, campagne de 1913–1914.* Paris: P. Geuthner, 1920.

———. *La cité de David: compte rendu des fouilles exécutées à Jérusalem, sur le site de la ville primitive, II, campagne de 1923–1924.* Paris: P. Geuthner, 1947.

Weiner, J. R. "The NGOs, Demolition of Illegal Building in Jerusalem, and International Law." *Jewish Political Studies Review* 17, nos.1–2, (2005): 47–62.

Weksler-Bdolah, S., A. Onn, B. Ouahnouna, and S. Isilevitz. "Jerusalem, The Western Wall Plaza Excavations, 2005–2009. Preliminary Report."*Hadashot Arkheologiyot* 121 (2009). [23/9/2009].

Williams, G. *The Holy City: Historical, Topographical, and Antiquarian Notices of Jerusalem.* 2 vols. Cambridge and London: J. W. Parker, 1849.

Wilson, C. W. *Ordnance Survey of Jerusalem.* Southampton: Ordinance Survey Office, 1865.

———. "The Masonry of the Haram Wall." *Palestine Exploration Quarterly* 12 (1880): 9–65.

———. *Golgotha and the Holy Sepulchre.* London: Palestine Exploration Fund, 1906.

Wilson, C. W., and C. Warren. *The Recovery of Jerusalem: A Narrative of Exploration and Discovery in the Holy Land.* London: R. Bentley, 1871.

Wright, J. R. "An Historical and Ecumenical Survey of the Church of the Holy Sepulchre in Jerusalem, with Notes on Its Significance for Anglicans." *Anglican and Episcopal History* 64 (1995): 482–504.

Wurst, L., and S. Novinger, "Hidden Boundaries. Archaeology, Education and Ideology in the United States." In *Ideologies in Archaeology,* edited by R. Bernbeck and R. H. McGuire, 254–69. Tuscon: University of Arizona Press, 2011.

Yadin, Y., ed. *Jerusalem Revealed: Archaeology in the Holy City 1968–1974.* Jerusalem: Israel Exploration Society, 1975.

Yahya, A., "Archaeology and Nationalism in the Holy Land." In *Archaeologies of the Middle East: Critical Perspectives,* edited by S. Pollock and R. Bernbeck, 66–77. Maiden: Blackwell, 2005.

———. "The Palestinian-Israeli Draft Agreement on Archaeological Heritage." *Present Pasts* 2, no. 1 (2010): 72–74.

Yas, J. "(Re)designing the City of David: Landscape, Narrative and Archaeology in Silwan." *Jerusalem Quarterly File* 7 (2000): 17–23.

Yagna, Y. "Haredi Group Fights Ashkelon Construction to Save Graves," *Ha'aretz,* December 25, 2012.

Yifa, Y. "Visitors' Center Planned for East Jerusalem Draws Criticism." *The Times of Israel,* January 3, 2014.

Younger, K. L., Jr. "The Shiloam Inscription." In *The Context of Scripture,* II: *Monumental Inscriptions from the Biblical World,* edited by W. W. Hallo and K. L. Younger, Jr., 145–46. Leiden: Brill, 2000.

Ziffer, B. "Herodium Turns into a Cultural Settlement." *Ha'aretz.* February 22, 2013.

Ingram Content Group UK Ltd.
Milton Keynes UK
UKHW022235120523
421677UK00011B/101